form•Z Modeling for Digital Effects and Animation

form•Z Modeling for Digital Effects and Animation

David Rindner

CHARLES RIVER MEDIA, INC.
Rockland, Massachusetts

Publisher: Jenifer L. Niles
Interior Design/Comp: Publishers' Design and Production Services, Inc.
Cover Design: Sherry Stinson
Printer: InterCity Press, Rockland, Ma

CHARLES RIVER MEDIA, Inc.
P.O. Box 417, 403 VFW Drive
Rockland, MA 02370
781-871-4184
781-871-4376(FAX)
chrivmedia@aol.com
http://www.charlesriver.com

This book is printed on acid-free paper

form•Z Modeling for Digital Effects and Animation
David Rindner
  ISBN 1-886801-97-5
  Printed in the United States of America

99 00 01 02 7 6 5 4 3 2 1

CHARLES RIVER MEDIA titles are available for site license or bulk
purchase by institutions, user groups, corporations, etc. For additional
information, please contact the Special Sales Department at
781-871-4184.

DEDICATION

To my mother Eugenia, my number one creative director.

I wish to thank Chris and Alexandra Yessios, David Kropp, and all the folks at Auto-des-sys for making this book possible. Without you guys it would never be.

I wish to thank Andrew Hardaway of Industrial Light & Magic. Thanks Andrew, I learned a lot from you, without you I would never have had the skill to write this book.

Contents

1

Digital Production Pipeline and 3D Modeling Process

IN THIS CHAPTER

- Digital Production Process Overview
- The 3D Modeling Process
- Judging Model Quality and Suitability
- Argument for Use of form•Z as a Front-end Modeler

Digital Production Process Overview

To understand fully the 3-dimensional (3D) modeling process we must first understand the context in which effects 3D modeling works; that context being the *digital production pipeline*, or simply, the *production pipeline*. The purpose of the pipeline is to convert screenwriters' and directors' ideas into completed footage. While different production companies and effects houses have their own production pipeline that has been honed through the years, there is a general pattern of steps or phases. The digital visual effects production pipeline can be broken down as follows:

- Preproduction, sketches, and storyboards
- Modeling and texturing of digital actors, digital miniatures, and environments
- Motion tests
- Animation setup and tweaking
- Rendering
- Compositing
- Editing and media output

PREPRODUCTION, SKETCHES, AND STORYBOARDS

Visual effects production usually begins with effects studios bidding on and getting a job. This process is complicated and I myself am not very familiar with it—besides, it is beyond the scope of this book. Regardless of how a studio gets a job, the process moves into a preproduction phase. During preproduction, sketches and storyboards are produced. The sketches are usually of digital characters, digital miniatures, and environments that will have to be built during the modeling process. Figures 1.1–1.3 show examples of characters and miniature sketches. Quite often, practical models or maquettes of digital models are constructed in order to ease the 3-dimensional modeling process. Conceptual artists develop and refine the look of characters and other objects that need to be modeled. Storyboards are scene sketches describing the actions of characters and objects in relation to their environment, and their interactions with it and with each other. Additionally, storyboards describe approximate camera positions by showing what the camera should see. This is very significant and useful information as it defines the required detail of the digital models in the scene. If all the storyboards show a particular digital model faraway from the camera, then that model does not have to be built in great detail. On the other hand, if the storyboard shows an object in the scene that is very close to the camera, then extra attention needs to be paid to that model so it renders realistically. Traditionally, storyboards are prepared by dedicated teams of storyboard artists using traditional art tools. Recently, digital storyboards, or *animatics*, have come into use. Animatics use low-resolution geometry that is rendered very simply to describe proportions and movements of scene elements. Often they are used when detailed visual description, that a hand-drawn storyboard provides, is not required, but detailed temporal information on movement and interaction is desired. Completed animatics approved by the film's director would be later used by animators in setup of the scenes.

MODELING AND TEXTURING

Character sketches, maquettes, and storyboards are then passed along to the effects artists responsible for creating the imagery. At this point the actual digital work begins with 3D modeling. Before proceeding I want to point out that concurrently with modeling, procedural elements of the scene are created. Most obvious are procedural shaders that are written by dedicated teams of software engineers. Animators may also start creating motion and conducting preliminary motion tests using simple geometry and using animatics as a starting point. Okay, back to the modeling. In real-world effects production there is more than just simple geometric modeling. Shader writers, and procedural modeling animators, create models of waterfalls, rain, snow, animated liquids, and other natural world phenomena. Modelers create geometric models of scene objects, and it is the creation of those geometric models on which this book concentrates. All models are created with some kind of source material. Within the context of effects production, source material can be sketches created by concept artists, physical maquette models, and photographs of real-world objects. While many concept artists have their own styles of creating sketches, there are basically two types; *perspective* and *orthogonal*. Perspective sketch shows the overall look, shape, and proportions of the character or object. Orthogonal sketches are drawings of the object showing one or more elevations of it. Orthogonal sketches are more precise in their execution and are usually drawn to scale. Perspective sketches are intended to convey the concept of the object, while orthogonal sketches are intended to provide dimensions. Figures 1.1–1.3 show the two types of sketches. In regards for form•Z, I consider orthogonal sketches to be more useful as they can be used as *Underlays*.

Maquettes are among the best type of source material from which to create digital models. Maquettes are physical models made of common modeling materials, such as foam, plaster, plastic, clay, and other materials used for sculpting. Because of time and cost associated with them, maquettes are usually created for projects that can bear the cost. For feature films, it is not uncommon for one design studio to create concepts, sketches, and maquettes, and

FIGURE   *Character sketches.*
1.1

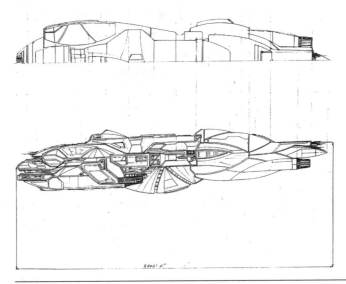

FIGURE   *Miniature sketches.*
1.2

then pass them along the studio that will be creating the shots. Maquettes are particularly useful to the modeling process as they can be digitized using a 3D digitizer such as Microscribe 3D, which is supported directly by form•Z. Alternatively, maquettes may be scanned at a digitizing bureau such as Viewpoint Datalabs, and polygonal mesh is refined in form•Z. Digitizing maquettes is most suitable for complex organic forms such as characters.

Photographs of real-world objects are very useful as far as source material goes. Photographs show detail and proportion that simply cannot be matched by the human hand. Photographs combined with an orthogonal elevation sketch are a must when building a real-world model. Photographs may also be used to supplant maquette or sketch source material, when details need to be added to the sketch. For example, a character sketch of a fish is provided. A modeler would model a digital fish according to the sketch and then use photographs of real fish to model details such as fin structures.

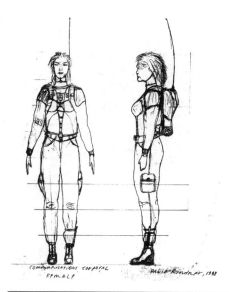

FIGURE *Character sketches.*
1.3

Just prior to beginning the modeling, art and technical directors, along with the modelers and animators, conduct tests and decide on what type of models are to be created and how they will be modeled: polygonal, patch, or NURBS surface geometry, or a combination of all three. This decision is based on needs of the project, type of animation, and capabilities of the animation package used. form•Z is primarily a polygonal application, although form•Z 3.0 has parametric surfaces, such as true NURBS and patches. Versions of form•Z beyond v.3 incorporate even more parametric surface modeling features. form•Z's polygonal nature makes it ideal as a front-end modeler to animation applications that are polygonal in nature, such as 3D Studio MAX, Lightwave 3D, Cinema 4D XL, and ElectricImage. With the source material assembled and modeling goals established, the modeling team gets down and dirty to generate the geometry. Geometry is generated through a 3D modeling process, which will be discussed in more detail later. After the geometry is complete it is then textured under the guidance of art and technical directors. Quite often the geometry is tweaked and reorganized to facilitate quick-and-easy texture mapping.

ANIMATION SETUP AND TWEAKING

After the geometry is modeled and textured it is passed along to the animation team, who light it and make it move. During the animation setup phase, the

geometry is tweaked, as animation may bring up shortcomings not apparent during modeling. The geometry may also be reorganized to facilitate easier animation. I wish to point out that the animation setup phase may begin at the start of or at any point during the primary modeling using incomplete geometry, or stand-in models. Just about any model can be effectively represented with a simpler version of itself to allow for faster animation workflow. In fact, in many studios it is standard procedure to animate with stand-in models and only replace the stand-ins with final geometry. A common procedure is to animate a low-resolution version, with the high-resolution "beauty shot" model set up as a child of the stand-in. During final rendering, the stand-in parent is hidden. This allows maximum use of time for creating and tweaking animation, materials, lighting, and geometry of the scene. Most professional animation packages have features that support this process; for example, Cinema 4D XL has Display Attributes that control whether an object is seen in editor and whether or not it is rendered.

RENDERING

Once the scene has been animated, it is rendered. Depending on the type of scene, software used, and studio procedures, shots are rendered in two basic ways: single pass, where the entire scene is rendered all at once, or in passes called *plates* that will be composited later on. I wish to point out that test renders are continually made during animation setup in order to tweak lights and materials. Final beauty shot renders typically include time-consuming effects such as volumetric lighting and volumetric particle effects. Rendering in passes allows animators to isolate rendered scene elements from each other so that effects and filters can be applied to them during compositing.

COMPOSITING

Once the scene is rendered, the plates are composited together, often with principal photography footage. Special effects such as glows, fire, and other effects are added to enhance the appearance or to stylize rendered imagery. Scene compositing is done on a variety of systems ranging from desktop software such as Adobe After Affects, 4D Vision Digital Fusion, Silicon Grail Chalice, and Chyron Concerto, to ultra high-end dedicated systems such as Quantel Henry, Avid Media Composer, and Flame/Flint/Inferno from Discreet. To seamlessly composite 3D imagery, artists using compositors rely heavily on alpha channels, depth channels, and other specialized channels to apply 2D effects to selected areas of the 3D image.

EDITING AND MEDIA OUTPUT

The completed shot is then delivered to the editor who edits the entire film. Sound and acoustic effects are added to the footage during editing. The editor, along with the film's director, generally carries out the editing process. The complete footage is then transferred to film to be reproduced and distributed.

The 3D Modeling Process

Now that we have an overview of the digital production process, I wish to expand upon 3D modeling as a process in itself. Within the digital production pipeline, 3D modeling plays a supporting role. As professional 3D modelers we are supporting a creative image-driven process. By "image-driven" I mean that, ultimately, the acceptance quality of the shot does not depend on what is in it but on how it looks to the viewer. This in no way diminishes the importance of digital content within the scene; it simply means that the quality of the rendered image is the criteria upon which the footage is judged. You can have the most intricate 3D models in a scene, but if their texture maps are lacking, the quality of the shot suffers. Likewise, a scene that is beautifully lit, realistically textured, and seamlessly composited, but where 3D geometry exhibits polygonal silhouettes and has shading errors, will ruin an otherwise perfect shot. As modelers we must understand how our models will be used, and create geometry that is compatible with the pipeline in the studio. Because the image quality is the most important criteria, the models that we build are judged on how they render, and how they behave inside an animation environment. When modeling for animation and special effects, beauty is only skin deep—we only care about the parts of the object that the digital camera sees.

This is akin to studios constructing real sets. When sets are constructed, they are built to appear real when shot with a camera. Entire buildings are not constructed on sets, only parts that the cameras will see. Likewise with digital models. When a digital model is built, its exterior is painstakingly detailed with geometry and with texture maps, but its interior is hollow. The exception, of course, is if the shot calls for a camera being located inside the model.

Although each production situation creates its own demands, typically 3D modeling is accomplished in the following three phases:

- Phase 1: Sketches and source material analysis
- Phase 2: Geometry generation
- Phase 3: Customizing geometry organization for animation and mapping

PHASE 1: SKETCH AND SOURCE MATERIAL ANALYSIS

In Phase 1 all source material is analyzed and a strategy is devised on how to approach the modeling. The type of animation that the model will undergo is also considered. Sketches and photos are converted to underlays. If possible, maquettes are digitized to provide a base 3D geometry. I wish to stress that digitizing in itself does not replace manual modeling: The digitized geometry still needs to be edited and details added that cannot be captured during digitizing. Digitizing can be a great timesaver as it provides the modeler with a very good base from which to start. What modeling tools and procedures will be used depends on the geometric shape of the desired model, type of animation it will undergo, and output requirements.

PHASE 2: GEOMETRY GENERATION

The geometry is created in Phase 2. This can be a time-consuming process, depending on the complexity of the model and skill of the modeler. During Phase 2 the work in progress is continually checked against source material, and is tested periodically within the target animation environment. During this phase, geometry is continually tweaked so it animates and renders without faults.

PHASE 3: CUSTOMIZING GEOMETRY ORGANIZATION FOR ANIMATION AND MAPPING

In Phase 3 the completed geometry is "cut up" and organized to facilitate efficient mapping and animation. Additional tweaks are continually made to the geometry during this phase.

I think that in real-world production there is really never a clear delineation of where one phase ends and another begins. To me it seems that they meld into each other, and the process is not linear. In the middle of Phase 2 you may be provided with better or updated source material and may need to rebuild some geometry. During animation it may be revealed that certain effects need to be restructured, thereby requiring a reorganization of geometry. There are an infinite number of possibilities. The whole process is a cycle of tweaks and changes until the shot is complete.

Judging Model Quality and Suitability

Before their use in animation, digital models should be evaluated as to their suitability for use in animation. What we need is a set of criteria that can be used to evaluate completed geometry with consistency. Over the course of my experience I have concluded that there are seven distinct criteria with which any model can be effectively evaluated. Notice that the criteria are for evaluating geometry only; quality of texture maps is a separate test.

- Geometric realism
- Lighting realism
- Mesh density.
- Polygonal topology
- Smoothing attributes and normals
- Texture mapping organization
- Animatable objects organization

GEOMETRIC REALISM

Geometric realism is the degree of realism, or resemblance, that the model has to its real-world counterpart. This includes the overall geometric shape of surfaces and the amount of realistic detail that is on the surface. For example, if the storyboard shows a close-up on a helicopter, the digital model of the helicopter should look like the real thing. Not only should the surfaces be shaped like those on the genuine article, but small details, such as antenna, rubber glass seals, and distinctive paneling, must all be there. If it is apparent that the interior of the helicopter will be seen, if only briefly, by the camera, then the necessary amount of cockpit and interior detail needs to be built.

LIGHTING REALISM

Lighting realism is the how realistic the surface looks when lit. It is important to understand that a surface that has a high amount of geometric realism will not automatically render realistically when lit. This is primarily caused by sharp edges. In the real world there is no such thing as a perfectly sharp edge. Usually, otherwise detailed models will not pass photorealistic scrutiny if they have un-beveled or unrounded edges. It is good practice to add bevel or round to every edge that will be seen by the camera. Adding bevels to edges is especially critical when modeling surfaces that are perfectly mated to each other. If two adjacent and mated objects, like panels, do not have their edges at the seam beveled, they will shade as a single surface, or at best there will a hairline seam. For the panels to render realistically, the edges at the seams should have a bevel. The two bevels, one on each edge, will form a V-groove that will catch a shadow at the bottom of the trough and the bevels will generate small subtle highlights. The combination of a bevel highlight and groove shadow creates a subtle yet realistic effect. Primarily this is due to the way we humans perceive the world around us. We have gotten very used to seeing things such as subtle shadows and highlights on the edges without realizing that they are there. When a layperson looks at a synthetic image in which bevels are missing, he knows something is amiss but is not sure what it is, and the shot comes off as not being real.

MESH DENSITY

Mesh density is the number of polygons per degree of curvature along each of the three axes. Desired mesh density is dependent upon the requirement of the shot. Some of the factors determining required mesh density are

- Closest proximity of the model to the camera
- Output resolution
- Deformation of the model

Polygonal silhouetting of the model in the rendered image is a sign of low mesh density. Mesh density is discussed in detail in Chapter 4 "Mesh Density and Topology."

POLYGONAL TOPOLOGY

Polygonal topology is the arrangement and shape of faces within the mesh. Polygons should be arranged along curves of force within the model. Polygonal shape refers to the shape and point count of polygons. Meshes with regular rectangular grid patterns comprised of four-point rectangular polygons result in the cleanest rendered images. A deficiency we should look for is the excessive aspect ratio of faces. In general it is best to avoid polygons with aspect ratios greater than 5:1. Very long rectangles and triangles, known as *slivers*, can cause shading anomalies. Incorrect mesh topology and slivered faces are a sign of sloppy modeling.

SMOOTHING ATTRIBUTES

Smoothing attributes and *normals* of mesh are vital to clean and smooth rendering of a mesh. Smoothing attributes are usually assigned during modeling but can also be assigned within the animation environment. An otherwise good model will render with visible face seams if it has no smoothing attributes. Incorrect smoothing attributes are at worst a minor inconvenience that is easily fixed, and should not be viewed as an obstacle. However, within a single model in which fine-tuning the smoothing attributes of subobjects can be time consuming, certain subobjects may render better with given smoothing attributes. A more serious problem lies with normals. There are two types of normals, *face* normal, and *vertex* normal. Face normals control the direction of the face, which determines whether or not a face will be shaded when is visible by the digital camera. A face with a flipped normal will appear as a hole in the surface where that face is supposed to be. Most professional 3D animation applications have utilities and features that can fix inverted normals. Vertex normals determine the smoothness, between faces that share that point, with which the seams are shaded. Vertex normals are adjusted via smoothing attributes. Problem vertex normals manifest themselves through various shading anomalies, especially random darkening or lightening of the surface. Quite often, vertex normals and shading anomalies occur when the renderer encounters a complex polygon and attempts to decompose it into either quadrangles or triangles. When modeling it is best to stay away from complex polygons, and manually decompose complex polygons into four- or three-point faces.

TEXTURE MAPPING ORGANIZATION

Texture mapping organization is the breakdown of a model's surfaces in order to facilitate quick and effective texture mapping. It is a measure of how effectively a model can be textured in a given animation package. For example, a fuselage of an aircraft is textured with either planar or cylindrical projections running along the length of the aircraft. Wings are best mapped with planar projections applied from the top. If the model has wings and fuselage joined into a single object, then effectively texture mapping it becomes a difficult if not impossible task. A model must be adapted to the animation environment in which it is going to be used.

ANIMATABLE OBJECTS ORGANIZATION

Animatable objects organization refers to the organization of geometry within separate animatable objects. Subobjects within the model may need to be animated separately, and should be separate objects. A model of a robot cannot be effectively walk animated if the legs are one single object. A decision on how effectively a model is structured for animation must be made within the context of a shot. A model may be suitable for one shot but not for another.

When we compare the model quality evaluation criteria against the features offered by form•Z, it becomes obvious that form•Z is a superior front-end modeling application and replacement modeler for just about every polygonal-based animation application. form•Z is especially effective when used as a modeler for 3D Studio MAX, Lightwave 3D, Cinema 4D XL, and Electric-Image Animation System.

Argument for Use of form•Z as a Front-end Modeler

Let me discuss why I hold this position. form•Z's extensive toolset and efficient workflow makes it possible to accurately create any shape that satisfies the *geometric realism* requirement. form•Z 3.0 expands this capability by adding parametric NURBZ and patch surfaces. In my experience, form•Z provides superior modeling capability to standard modeling features of 3DS MAX, Cinema 4D XL, and Lightwave 3D. Its feature set combined with bitmap underlay capability allows for the creation of geometrically realistic models. Of particular importance are the application's tools, such as C-Mesh and Smooth Mesh, for creating derivative surfaces. Round and Bevel tools combined with other tools allow for the creation of complex rounds and bevels, even on three-dimensionally curving surfaces, satisfying the *realistic lighting* requirement. Procedures and techniques for the creation of complex rounds and bevels are covered in this book. form•Z allows very detailed and precise control of mesh density through C-Mesh smoothing options, Mesh, Smooth Mesh, and Insert Point/Segment tools. With these tools and others you can refine the mesh density of a model until the *mesh density* requirement is satisfied. Many tools in form•Z, such as Triangulate, allow the user detailed control over face shapes and polygonal topology of the model. This aspect of modeling is especially controlled in many options of derivative surface tools. form•Z has specific tools to control the direction of face normals through the use of the Reverse Direction tool, and detailed control over smoothing attributes with the Smoothing Shading Attributes tool. Both face normals and smoothing attributes can be exported out of form•Z with the model, allowing control of both of these attributes during the modeling process. Finally, form•Z has one of the most flexible and powerful layering and geometry organization systems available for a desktop computer. The layering system combined with other form•Z tools allows the user to quickly and efficiently organize geometry for exportation to a particular animation system, making animation, texturing, and integration in general a reliable process. This book covers Version 3.0, 2.95, and is compatible with 3.1.

CHAPTER 2

Animatics and Volumetrics

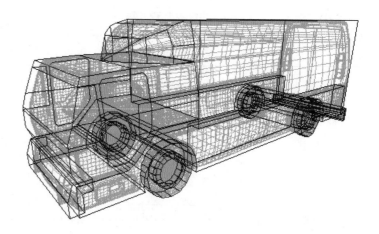

IN THIS CHAPTER

- Stand-In Models: Animatics and Volumetrics
- Truck Model and Its Animatic Equivalent
- Comparison Between Cab Model, Its Animatic and Volumetric
- Animatics
- Animatic Construction
- Animatics and Smooth Mesh and Patch Models
- Practical Real World Example of Animatic
- Animatics in ElectricImage
- Animatics in 3DS MAX

Stand-in Models: Animatics and Volumetrics

Animatics and volumetrics are very simple 3D models that are geometrically highly simplified versions of complex existing or planned 3D models. Animatics are used as temporary stand-ins for complex geometry inside the animation environment to speed up the animation work flow. Being very simple, and having only a fraction of the polygons of final models, animatics can be manipulated very quickly; very often the animation environment can manipulate animatic and volumetric models in real time, even with low-cost 3D acceleration hardware, or on systems using only software-based 3D acceleration. Both volumetric and animatic models are used in the same fashion, the only difference is that animatics have slightly more geometric detail than volumetrics. Ideally, both volumetrics and animatic geometry should have similar topological arrangements as the final shot models. That is, inside the animation environment, animatic and volumetric models have the same parent/child relationships, the same link/pivot points, and the same Inverse Kinematics constraints as the complex geometry they are standing in for. For some models containing many fine details, a single animatic object can describe a number of detail objects as long as these detail objects will be animated together. Figure 2.1 shows an example of a simple yet descriptive animatic model of a detailed delivery truck model.

Truck Model and Its Animatic Equivalent

In the high-resolution model, the cab is cut up into sections to facilitate planar texture mapping. The animatic of the cab is a single surface describing the general shape of all the cab surfaces. Door and windshield animatics were trimmed out of the cab animatic using the Trim/Split tool. There is only one animatic object describing the front bumper surface. In the shot model, the front bumper contains headlight surfaces, which are separate objects. However, because the bumper and headlights are going to be animated together, there is no need to model animatics for the headlights. All the surfaces in the truck model were cut up in order to be texture mapped using planar projections. The animatics were built to describe the volume and very general shape of the surfaces. The shot model has over 150,000 polygons—the animatic has only 200. Even on hardware with modest or software-only 3D acceleration, the animator can get real-time feedback animating the movement of the truck. Major animating components of the model should have their respective animatics. Notice that the doors have their own animatic geometry that was cut from the cab animatic. However, the door glass does not have an animatic as it would be animated with a door model—the door glass is sufficiently described by the door

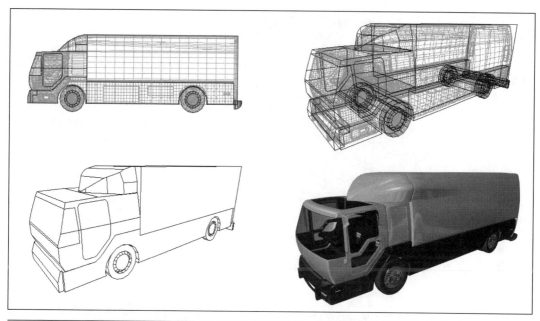

FIGURE   *Example of a simple yet descriptive animatic model.*
2.1

animatic alone. Each wheel and tire has its own animatic. Animatic and volumetric geometry is built to have nearly identical proportions and size as the final geometry. Practice minimalism when constructing animatics or volumetrics. If you know that object B is always going to be a child of object A, and that B volumetrically fits inside the extent of object A, then there is no need to build an animatic for B, only for A. Such is the case with the door surface. The shot might require the door to be opened, and as the glass will animate with the door and the door glass extent fits inside the extent of the door surface, there is only a need to build an animatic for the door. If there was an additional requirement for the door glass surface to roll down, be smashed, or animated in any way that would not affect the door surface (its parent), then having a separate animatic for the door glass would be prudent. As mentioned earlier, both volumetric and animatic geometry are used identically; the only difference is the amount of geometric detail. Animatics have more polygons and take a little longer to create than do volumetrics, but there are many cases in animation production in which having animatics versus volumetric stand-ins is invaluable. Figure 2.2 shows a volumetric and an animatic stand-in model for the cab geometry.

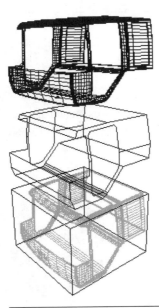

FIGURE *A volumetric and an animatic stand-in model for the cab geometry.*
2.2

Comparison of a Volumetric and Animatic Model for the Cab Geometry

What is a volumetric object? A volumetric model is a box describing the general space taken by a particular object. A volumetric model is identical in size to the bounding box, also called an "extent," of a complex object. If you are familiar with animation and modeling applications, you have seen volumetrics. Most 3D graphic software packages have a bounding box, or extent, display mode. Unfortunately, you cannot view the extents in their shaded mode, so an animator cannot see a shaded box moving behind another. Volumetric models are very easy to build, regardless of whether or not you have finished the final geometry or have not even started modeling it yet. It does take planning to build volumetrics. You have to know the overall dimensions of the model and its component objects, and the proportions of the objects to each other. The best way to build volumetrics is concurrently with the final geometry. You can build the volumetric first and then build the complex geometry to fit the volumetric, or vice versa. If you already have models prebuilt, then just build the volumetrics to be the same size as the extents of the models. If the modeling has not yet begun, it may be advantageous in certain cases to build the volumetric boxes inside the animation environment itself. The animator, or technical director (assuming that you are neither) can built the volumetric boxes, name them appropriately, and export them into form•Z for you to model or adjust the geometry to fit the volumetrics. If you are receiving or building the volumetrics inside the animation environment, set up the pivot points as well. Build simple geometric markers, such as a small box or sphere within a larger object volumetric, the center of which represents the location of the pivot. The box length should be oriented along the axis of the pivot. Two intersecting boxes should represent a two-axis rotational pivot. A sphere should represent a three-axis pivot. In all cases, as you build geometry you can use those markers to align geometry around the pivot to the pivot. A great example of this is an articulated robotic arm. Make a simple sketch of a robotic arm that has three objects: an upper arm, a forearm, and a wrist; don't worry about the fingers. Develop the volumetric for the upper arm, the forearm, and a wrist. You can create the volumetric boxes in form•Z and then import them into your animation program, or create them right in the animation environment directly. Apply and define pivot points, and IK limits. Perform a simple animation test to make sure that the pivot locations, axis definitions, and IK limits are what you want. Now create pivot point markers. For two-axis pivots create two very thin single polygon planes that intersect each other to form a "+" figure. The center of the cross should be located as precisely as possible at the 3D position of the pivot. For three-axis pivots create a small sphere, the center of which is located as precisely as possible at pivot locations. Export the volumetrics with pivot markers and bring them into form•Z. Build the robotic arms to the degree of desired detail. The geometry that represents the actuators for limb articulation should be built in a way as to be centered on the pivot markers.

Export the geometry, but not the volumetrics, and bring it into your animation application. Link the finished geometry to its volumetric, or copy/paste link, pivot, and IK information form the volumetric to the geometry. A dummy object that can be created in any application can serve as a volumetric, but it suffers from the same shortcomings as extents in that they cannot be viewed in shaded view, nor can the edges describing them be exported. You can, of course, create dummy objects that have same dimensions, pivot locations, and IK limits as volumetrics, so you can have the best of each. I would recommend keeping the volumetrics so you can see movement in shaded views at real-time or near real-time frame rates.

Spacecraft and vehicles are excellent candidates for use with volumetrics instead of animatics. Vehicles, aircraft, and spacecraft are seldom deformed; mostly they just move along paths, or they have relative movement to the camera. When there is only movement to judge, then volumetrics will suffice. For large and geometrically complex spacecraft, I recommend that you build two or three volumetrics describing the front, the middle, and the rear engine section of the ship. Aircraft are best described by three volumetrics: one for the fuselage, one for the wings, and one for the tail section.

Animatics

Animatics serve the same purpose and are used exactly the same way as volumetrics, except that animatics have major features of the final geometry. A volumetric of a head is just a box describing the extent box of that object. An animatic of it would have holes describing the positions of the eyes, mouth, and ears. Animatics take more time to build than volumetrics; as a matter of fact, animatics are actually volumetrics that have been further developed. An animatic model usually starts off as a volumetric. When to use animatics and when to use volumetrics? A number of factors go into that decision. The first is time: Always start with a volumetric box, and if you have the time, develop it into an animatic. Another is shot requirements: If a shot calls only for simple and general movements, you may be able to use volumetrics. If more complicated animation is required, such as the animation camera zooming in or flying into one of the eye sockets of the head, then the animator needs to see the position of the eye socket so he or she can adjust camera movement. Another example is a missile hitting a wall at a certain spot, such as a window. In both cases, simple geometry needs to be modeled into the volumetric to show the position and orientation of major features. How much detail to add to an animatic model depends on the amount of time available, the needs of the animator, and the real-time capability of the animation software/hardware you will be using to animate your model. As previously mentioned, one of the main purposes of an animatic model is to allow you or the animator to work in real time in shaded views. Therefore, you need to be aware of the real-time 3D performance limitations of your system. Keep close track of the number of polygons that you are building into your model. Build only the minimal detail needed to communicate only the information that needs to be communicated. If the scene calls for the camera to look straight into your character's eyes, there is no need to build the mouth hole or ear animatics. If time permits, delete all unnecessary polygons from the animatic to speed up the real-time performance. If the scene has lots of action involving dozens of models, then the need to watch animatic polygon counts becomes even more important.

Animatic Construction

The best way to build animatics is to start with a volumetric box and then use Booleans or trims to cut holes in it, or attach other volumetric boxes to represent appendages, limbs, and other major features. Use Insert Point to add discernible detail or markers. Here is an example of a very simple animatic, using a hypothetical head as an example. Start with a volumetric box of the head model. Using the Insert Point and Insert Segment tools with Midpoint snap option, split the front face of the box width-wise into two equal parts. Now split the upper of those two new faces. The front face of the box (representing the face on the head) should now split into three faces. The equal area right and left faces are where the eye sockets would be located. Split each one of the eye socket polygons into two triangles by inserting a segment diagonally, use the Point snap option. Set snapping to Midpoint and double-click on each of the diagonal segments. In the Wireframe options, activate Show Points. Set snapping to Point and connect the opposite points of each of the eye socket corners to that midpoint. Adjust the locations of the two eye socket midpoints to be centered on the eyeballs of the head model. Move those two points slightly inside the animatic to create depressions that are clearly discernible in shaded views. Use this technique to create depressions for the mouth and ears if necessary. Export the animatic and bring it into your animation environment. Link the head model as a child to the animatic. Be sure to set the head geometry to inherit all animation channels from its animatic parent. You can now hide the head geometry and perform animation on the animatic.

Animatics and Smooth Mesh and Patch Models

In cases where your final models are derived via Smooth Mesh (discussed in Chapter 14) from rough cages, you can use those cages as animatics. As mentioned earlier, animatic models need to be minimally representative of the final geometry. For single-surface mesh characters, model a volumetric box for the torso area and then create volumetrics for the limbs. Boolean the torso volumetric with limb volumetrics. Use Insert Segment or the Split/Stitch technique to insert a single row of segments at joint areas. These inserted segments can serve as geometric markers during animation setup. If you build character using Mesh Smooth for inverse kinematics and bone deformations, cages make the best animatics of all. Not only do they simply and clearly describe the final geometry, they will also deform and animate in a fashion similar to that of final geometry. Depending on the polygonal detail of the cage animatic models, you can set up and experiment with bone ranges. Because the cage models are relatively lightly polygonized in relation to their Mesh Smooth derivatives, they are far better suited for placement and alignment of bones within the animation environment. Since you don't have to see the thousands of polygons, you can place and align the bone skeleton for the character faster and more precisely. Link the final smoothed mesh to the cage as a child and enable inheritance of deformations. All professional-level animation applications allow for inheritance of deformations. In 3DS MAX, apply LINKED X-FORMS to both the cage and the child smooth mesh. In 3DS MAX, you need to have Character Studio (Biped and Physique), or Bones Pro MAX from Digimation.

Character Studio is an outstanding professional-level bone deformation and muscle animation plug-in available from Kinetix. If you are a serious about doing character animation with 3D Studio MAX, it is recommended that you get this plug-in. Bones Pro MAX is a bone deformation plug-in that can work in conjunction with Character Studio. Studio MAX does not come with bone deformations in its basic package. Both ElectricImage and Cinema 4D XL come with complete and powerful bone deformation tools. ElectricImage 2.8+ allows INHERIT DEFORMATIONS in child object attributes. In Cinema 4D XL, SET BONES in OBJECT MANAGER and YES the INCLUDE CHILDREN option. Apply DISPLAY PROPERTY to both smooth mesh and the corresponding cage. Set DISPLAY of cage to HIDE IN RAYTRACER, and set DISPLAY of smooth mesh to HIDE IN EDITOR.

Figures 2.3–2.12 show development of an animatic model for an existing arbitrary mesh of a dragon's head. Remember that animatic modeling is a very quick and loose job. It is an iterative process that starts with a volumetric box, followed by successive refinements, when time is available.

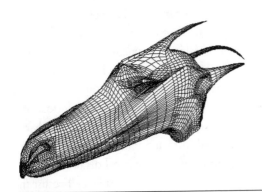

FIGURE **2.3** *An existing model.*

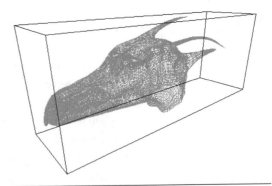

FIGURE **2.4** *A generated volumetric box.*

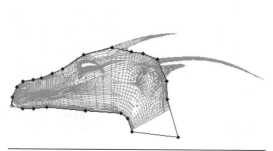

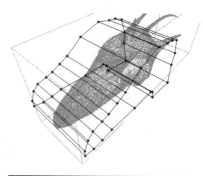

FIGURE **2.5** *A planar closed polyline is traced around the mesh from the side view.*

FIGURE **2.6** *That polyline is then used as a trim line in trimming and stitching the volumetric.*

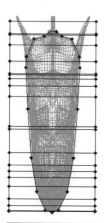

FIGURE **2.7** *A planar closed polyline is traced around the mesh from the top view.*

FIGURE **2.8** *That polyline is then used as a trim line in Trim/Split Stitch the volumetric.*

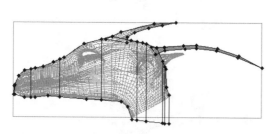

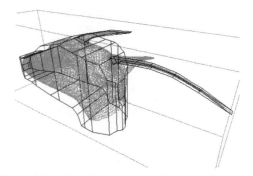

FIGURE **2.9** *Detail cross-sections are added; in this case, the horns. The cross-sections are extruded. The resulting solids are trimmed and stitched with lines to conform to the general shape. Then the detail solids are Booleaned with the main animatic solid.*

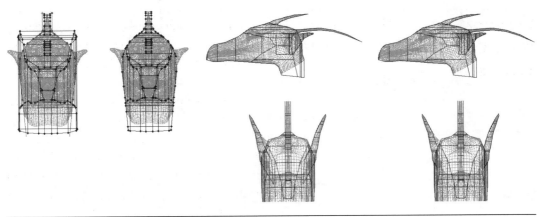

FIGURE **2.10** *More major details, like the earhorns, are added. The shape of the animatic is refined with either Booleans or trim/stitching.*

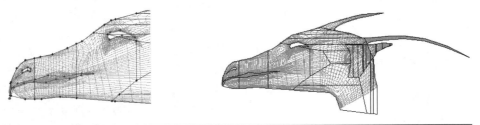

FIGURE **2.11** *The lines roughly tracing the eye sockets, mouth, and nostril are drawn. The lines are then used to Trim/Split Stitch the animatic solid to major key detail.*

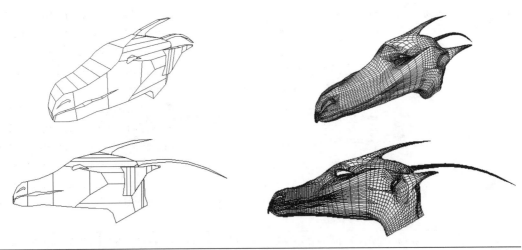

FIGURE **2.12** *Completed animatic model. Note how it simply but clearly defines the volumetricity of the shot mesh.*

Practical Real World Example of Animatic

The following example uses the truck animatic sample. The animatic geometry and final shot geometry are both brought into Cinema 4D XL. All animatic geometry is grouped together under a group name (a null object) of "TRUCK ANIM".

All animatic children are named appropriately; for example, the right wheel animatic is named "RIGHT WHEEL ANIM", and so on. You can use any naming convention that is clear to you. Both animatic and final geometry objects receive a DISPLAY PROPERTY. Each object, both animatic and final, receives a DISPLAY PROPERTY. Each shot geometry object is attached as a child to its corresponding animatic model. RIGHT WHEEL final geometry is attached as a child to RIGHT WHEEL ANIM (animatic) object.

DISPLAY PROPERTY of all animatic objects is set to HIDE IN RAY-TRACER, the DISPLAY PROPERTY of final shot geometry is set to HIDE IN EDITOR. You will see only the animatic objects in the Cinema 4D XL interface, but when you render the scene, only the final geometry will get rendered.

You can apply texture mapping coordinates and materials to the animatic objects. The final geometry child objects will inherit all properties from their parents unless the child objects have the same property, in which case it will be used. That is why DISPLAY PROPERTY must be assigned to both the animatic and final geometry. So if you apply mapping coordinates and materials to the parent animatic, don't apply DISPLAY PROPERTY to the children unless you want different settings for the children. If your animatic describes more than one final geometry object, then it should not be textured unless you want the same material applied to all the children using the same projection. Any children, which require different materials than the parent animatic, should not inherit the material. In Cinema 4D XL, if a child object does not have a MATERIAL TEXTURE property, it will inherit the material and its associated projection from the animatic parent.

Cinema 4D and Cinema 4D XL have the ability to "give" an animation channel or property from one object to another. This is accomplished by CONTROL/DRAG an animation channel, in the TIME LINE window, from one object to another. Properties are copied in the same fashion, but from the OBJECT MANAGER window. You can start by building the animatics first in form•Z to experiment with proportions, or build them in Cinema and export to form•Z.

Create animation channels and add any special effects that are needed When the shot geometry is imported into Cinema, just link it to the animatic.

There may be times when the Position/Direction/Scale of shot geometry does not match the PDS of the animatics. This can happen if you moved the animatic at frame zero and recorded, or incurred a positional error during modeling in form•Z. If this is the case, use the following procedure.

Import the shot geometry into Cinema. At this time DON'T link to the animatic. Note the position of the AXIS in the animatic. Optimally the axis should be center massed in the animatic. Move the shot model (en masse, linked to an empty object) to match as nearly as you can its position with the animatic. Don't worry about precision yet. Move the axis of the empty object to which the shot is linked to be in the same position as the axis of the animatic. Now "give" the position/scale/direction of the animatic to the empty object. This should precisely align the shot with the animatic. Link the shot model to the animatic. Now you can delete the PDS channels from the shot.

Animatics in ElectricImage

In ElectricImage, each final geometry object requires its own texture mapping and material definition. Versions 2.8 and higher allow COPY/PASTE for map projections, in addition to normal COPY/PASTE of colors and bitmap/shader files. Version 2.8 also allows referencing to a master material library in the project, and the saving of custom materials. Link the shot geometry as children to animatics. In the Group Links window, set the children to inherit all parent properties except VISIBILITY. For animation setup, turn all final geometry off, assuming that it has already been linked to the appropriate animatic parents. Animate the animatic geometry per project requirements. When the time comes to render, turn off all the animatic geometry and turn on all final shot geometry. Make sure that the final geometry does not inherit the VISIBILITY of its animatic parent.

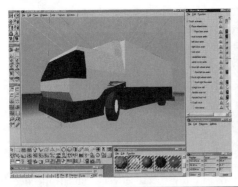 

FIGURE *Example of the truck scene as it appears in the Cinema 4D XL interface.*
2.13

Animatics in 3DS MAX

For 3DS MAX, the procedure is similar to ElectricImage. All final geometry should have its own mapping applied. You can apply a material and UV coordinated to the animatic parent first. Then when applying a UV modifier to the stack of final geometry objects, just ACQUIRE the mapping coordinates from the parent. For animation setup, hide all final geometry and apply any animation channels to the animatic parent. Prior to rendering, unhide all the final geometry and hide all the animatics.

Because of low polygon count in the animatic stand-in geometry, your interaction within the GUI will be very fast. Figure 2.13 is an example of the truck scene as it appears in the Cinema 4D XL interface.

CHAPTER
3

Layer Strategy and Animation Integration

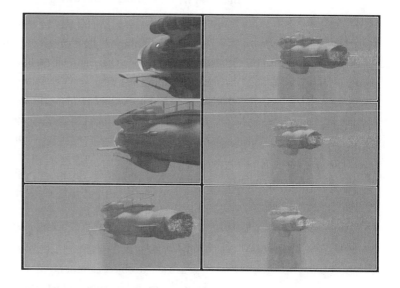

IN THIS CHAPTER

- Basic Project Considerations
- Repercussions of Not Having Geometry Management Procedures
- Types of Objects Organized By Its USP
- Layer Strategy
- form•Z/Animation Integration
- form•Z to Max Integration via Wavefront File Format
- form•Z and Cinema 4D XL
- form•Z and Lightwave 3D
- form•Z and ElectricImage Animation System
- Summary

Basic Project Considerations

As 3D modelers working in effects production, we are supporting a creative animation process. This goes beyond simply modeling the geometry so that it looks good when rendered in form•Z RenderZone. It must look good and be compatible with the features and workflow of the target animation package. Furthermore, we must be aware of how the model is going to be animated and textured. Both are important in deciding the organization of the model geometry once the model is brought into the animation environment. The basic goal is to create geometry in form•Z that behaves as though it was modeled in the internal modeler of the animation application. In order to properly accomplish that task, we must know the following:

- **The features and capabilities of the target animation environment.** Different applications have different features and capabilities. However, many applications have similar capabilities when it comes to animation and mapping features.
- **Established procedures and workflow of the effects team working on the shot.** Quite often an effects shop has established procedures for modeling, importing, mapping, and animating geometry. In a successful shop those procedures have been proven to work time and again.
- **The type of animation the model will undergo.** This is of prime consideration when the modeled geometry is organized prior to exportation. If you are modeling a robot that is not going to be animated, there is no need to spend time modeling the articulated assemblies. On the other hand, a model of a robot brought into 3DS MAX that has its arms and legs as a single object cannot be animated.
- **How the model is going to be textured.** This is also a prime consideration. Polygonal applications have no capability to create parametric mapping coordinates on an arbitrary imported mesh. That means that when mapping geometry imported from form•Z, we often have to rely on standard mapping projections: flat, cubic, spherical, and cylindrical. The geometry that we build must be shaped in such a way as to easily accept standard mapping projections. Usually that means "cutting up" what would otherwise be a single animatable object into multiple objects. In the animation program, these objects get grouped under a parent that is animated.

In the following paragraphs I present a modeling and geometry organization strategy that will give you maximum flexibility to deal with the preceding four considerations. This strategy is based on identifying the types of geometry that you work with inside form•Z and organizing this geometry within designated layers. This *layer strategy* allows for fast and flexible handling of geometry, allows a single modeling project to support multiple animation applications, and is easily adjustable to any animation workflow. Furthermore, this strategy, when used correctly, allows for efficient revision of the model as the project progresses.

Repercussions of Not Having Geometry Management Procedures

Digital models created for visual effects and animation can have dozens, hundreds, or even thousands of separate objects. The object count depends on how the model will be used and how it will be animated and textured. Both of these considerations are products of animation software capabilities and established workflows. The construction of individual objects may also involve the creation of other "source" geometry. In the end we have so much geometry that if all of it is visible, the model would be undecipherable and screen redraw would take so long that it would make the 3D modeling process very painful and frustrating. Because of the large amount of geometry, we need ways of efficiently managing what is and what is not visible on the screen. Additionally, modeling complex surfaces usually produces multiple objects, the desired surface, and a number of source and temporary objects. We need a way of managing complexity within our modeling projects. In form•Z, layers provide the means to efficiently manage even the most complex projects. Of the 3D modeling applications used to create models for animation and special effects, form•Z has the most powerful and flexible layering system. Building your models using layers is by far the most flexible method. Layers allow you to manage and organize geometry in ways that objects and groups can't. The key to successful layer use is to organize the layers according to the type of geometry they contain and properly place the geometry on correct layers.

Types of Objects Organized By Its USP

To properly organize geometry we must first understand the types of geometry that we will deal with. I am not referring to the topological state of the object, whether it is an open surface, closed surface, a point, or a solid. By *type* I am referring to the *intended* use of this geometry. In my experience I have concluded that there are 10 major types of geometry.

- **Source objects**, that can be open surfaces, closed surfaces, or even solids. Source objects are used as base shapes for the creation of other shapes. A cross-section for an extruded object is a source object. The extruded solid of a surface is a derivative.

- **Derivatives**. A derivative object is any object that is created using existing geometry. A vector line that is created by snapping its points to the edge points of an existing surface is a derivative. A boundary edge curve of an existing mesh is a derivative.
- **Trim objects**. Trim shapes are source objects that are used as cutting objects. Open surfaces (lines and curves), closed surfaces, meshed surfaces, and solids can all be trim objects.
- **Locators**. Locators are usually vector lines but can be any object, the points of which are used to precisely define a location in 3D space.
- **Temporary objects**. These objects are created to assist in the creation of other objects. They can be copies of existing geometry and are usually expendable. The most frequent use of temporary objects is to test the result of trimming or Booleans prior to accepting the object and continuing the modeling process.
- **Working objects**. Incomplete geometry, work in progress.
- **Symmetrical half** objects. Symmetrical objects are a type of working object for surfaces that are symmetrical across one or more axes. These objects are first built as a half. To get the entire surface, the symmetrical half is mirror copied across the axis of symmetry and the two halves are stitched to form a complete surface.
- **Virgin objects**. Virgin objects are direct derivatives that will be edited later. C-MESH surfaces, extrusions, sweeps, and a Boolean operand are examples of virgin objects. Virgin objects can be referred to as *direct derivatives*. The two terms can be used interchangeably.
- **Backup objects**. Backups are made of geometry prior to performing any editing operation on the object.
- **Export geometry**. This is the geometry, completed and arranged, ready to be exported to the animation application. The arrangement of the export geometry depends on the target animation package, intended type of animation, and texture mapping strategy.

Layer Strategy

The basic layer organizational strategy that I want to promote is that for each type of geometry there is an associated layer type. When modeling, place geometry into the appropriate layer type. There is no specific provision for layer type in form•Z. The layer type is defined by the name we give to that layer. Layers that contain trim shapes are named "Object X Trim Curves," virgin layers are named "Object X Virgin," and so on. When the time comes to trim Object X, copies of it and its associated trim curves are copied and pasted into a working Object X layer. Prior to performing the trim operation, all layers except Object X are either hidden or ghosted. Object X is then trimmed with Status Of Objects set to Delete. Let's assume that Object X is a fuselage of a helicopter. The fuselage itself was derived by lofting a number of cross-sectional curves. The cross-sections themselves are placed in a source layer named "Fuselage Cross-Sections." The lofted fuselage is derived with the C-Mesh tool with Status Of Objects set to Keep, and is placed in a virgin layer named "Fuselage Virgin." A copy of the fuselage virgin is pasted into a symmetrical half layer named "Fuselage 1/2." There it is trimmed with a straight line that is drawn along the axis of symmetry. The virgin and source layers are hidden. Trim shapes are created in a trim layer named "Fuselage Trim Curves." Major trim objects for the door and windows are created in this layer. Prior to trimming, copies of the trim curves and the symmetrical fuselage half are pasted into a working "Fuselage 1/2 Temp," and previous "Fuselage 1/2" is renamed "Fuselage 1/2 BACKUP." Prior to the trimming or splitting of the fuselage, all layers except "Fuselage 1/2 Temp" are hidden. The fuselage half is then trimmed or split with the trim curves in the "Fuselage 1/2 Temp" layer, with Status Of Objects set to Delete. The temporary status given to this layer is itself temporary. After the trims and splits are complete, the resulting surfaces are evaluated as to their suitability for further modeling. If they are accepted, the "Temp" part of the name is removed and this layer becomes a normal working layer. The Status Of Objects state plays an important role because it prevents excessive buildup of geometry. In the workflow that I use, the Ghost option is hardly ever used. My standard procedure is to Copy/Paste copies of the object to be trimmed and all trim shapes into a working or temporary layer, hide the layers containing the original objects, and then perform the trim. By retaining the source cross-sections, the virgin C-Mesh, untrimmed fuselage half, and fuselage trim curves in their own layers, we have a direct revision pipeline that is easily manageable. Prior to performing additional modeling operations on the fuselage or the surfaces split from it, copies of them are pasted into a backup layer named "Fuselage 1/2 BACKUP 2." The revision pipeline is linear in nature; that is, a change in a step requires that all the steps subsequent to it are redone, but it allows for that modeling to proceed at a faster pace. For example, the technical director decides that for a particular shot he will need a different version of the helicopter, perhaps one without any passenger windows. To create this version you would create a new layer, named "Fuselage 1/2 No Windows," and paste copies of the untrimmed fuselage half and appropriate trim curves, and create a new version of the fuselage. There is no need to re-loft a fuselage, you are using an untrimmed backup of the fuselage half. Obviously, the farther back you go in the revision pipeline, the more work you have to do. To alleviate this problem (you can never get rid of it) create multiple backup layers, perhaps one for every five operations. Don't overdo and create backup geometry after each editing operation as the large amount of geometry will consume your hardware resources. Getting the feel for when to create backups is a result of experience.

After the fuselage half is complete, a copy of it is pasted into a new working layer named "Fuselage." Note that "1/2" has been dropped from the name of this layer. The fuselage half is reflected across the axis of symmetry using Mirror coupled with Cont-Copy (form•Z 3.0) C-Copy (form•Z 2.9.5) modifier, and the two halves are stitched together to form a complete fuselage. The door, windows, and other details are likewise duplicated across the axis of symmetry. The objects in these layers will serve as base objects for "cutting" the geometry and placing it into appropriate export layers. The completed geometry now needs to be "cut up" to facilitate the texture mapping and animation process within the target animation environment.

The last step is the creation of exportation layers. As a standard procedure, I use the following system. An export layer in form•Z equals an object within the animation environment. This systems allows us to have an object with any amount of geometric surface detail, and provides a very tight and straightforward way of controlling how geometry is exported. As stated, geometry needs to be "cut up" to make texture mapping and animation articulation easy. All objects that will compromise a single animation or texture object should be placed in the same export layer. When exported, these multiple objects become a single object when imported into animation application. Prior to exportation, hide all except export layers. In export settings turn OFF, Include Hierarchy, and turn ON Export Visible Layers Only.

Let's assume that the helicopter fuselage needs to be textured in the following way, the roof and bottom will get their own materials applied via flat mapping. Fuselage sides will be flat mapped from the side projection. The doors will each receive the same flat mapping and will be animated to open and close. The following export layers are created:

"Fuselage Side Left," "Fuselage Side Right," "Fuselage Top," "Fuselage Bottom," "Right Door," "Left Door," "Right Door Glass," "Left Door Glass," and "Cockpit Glass." Copies of door and glass surfaces are pasted into appropriate export layers. A copy of the entire fuselage is pasted into the "Fuselage Side Left" layer. There it is "cut up" by detaching selected faces with the Separate tool and transferring the resulting surfaces into their appropriate layers. In this case, the faces of the fuselage roof and bottom are detached, forming four surfaces: the top, bottom, and two sides.

All layers except the export layers are hidden and the geometry is exported to the supported format. The export format that is chosen depends on the animation application with which form•Z is used. The following paragraphs discuss integration of form•Z with selected applications. The applications covered are by no means the only 3D animation environments with which form•Z can be integrated. The applications chosen represent the most common animation applications with which form•Z is used.

form•Z/ Animation Integration	When using form•Z as front-end modeler to an animation application in a visual effects or animation production setting, we must consider the issue of integration, not just of simply importing geometry from form•Z into MAX or any other animation environment. Exportation/importation are simply the most identified actions of integration. Integration begins with modeling and ends when imported models can be directly used in a target animation package. By *modeling* I am referring to the arrangement of exportable geometry in export layers within your form•Z project. Once again I must emphasize that you must understand the capabilities and established workflows of your target animation package and create exportable geometry for the application. As a modeler you are supporting the animation production process. In cases where multiple animation packages are supported, strive to arrange the geometry to be compatible with all of them. There may be cases where you will need to create multiple export versions of the completed model to be compatible with all the packages you are supporting. This is not as complex or intimidating as it seems. In models exported from form•Z, we deal almost exclusively with polygons; in general, major applications dealing with polygonal data (3D Studio MAX, Cinema 4 DXL, ElectricImage Animation System, and Lightwave 3D) all have similar capabilities and procedures in terms of texture mapping. All have similar ability to apply maps using common projection methods. There are differences in the amount of detailed control that each application gives in applying maps. 3DS MAX, for example, has to apply a material to a single polygon or a selection of polygons. This ability precludes the need to "cut up" the meshes prior to exportation. EI and Cinema 4D XL apply material on a per-object basis. In ElectricImage, a single object is referred to as a *group* (as in a group of polygons). Cinema 4D XL can apply any number of materials, each with its own projection, while EI can apply a single material but with an unlimited number of bitmaps and shaders, each having its own projection. All the

applications named in this section have the ability to "fit" a material or map projection onto the constraints of the surface. This is very fast and accurate way of mapping. For this reason, the geometry should be "cut up" in a way as to easily use projection fit features of these applications.

Object articulation is an important consideration, as it deals directly with how the model will be animated. A digital model typically contains many parts, or subobjects, that are themselves animated. In the case of the helicopter, the rotor blades are subobjects that have their own rotation animation, in addition to inheriting movement from the fuselage parent object.

FORM•Z AND DISCREET 3D STUDIO MAX

Kinetix 3D Studio MAX is a very popular and very powerful animation application, which was in version 2.5 when this book was being written. The application runs only in Intel architecture-based Windows NT 4.0/ Windows 98 systems. 3D Studio MAX's widespread use in the visual effects animation industry and a large array of third-party plug-in support makes it a must-have application in any professional 3D toolset. In visual effects, MAX is often used in the creation of digital miniature shots, such as spacecraft, aircraft, and so forth. For character animation Character Studio is available from Discreet as an add-on to 3DS MAX. Character Studio is composed of two modules: Biped for creating and editing bipedal character movement; and Physique, for applying realistic effects, such as muscle bulging, to the character mesh. Character Studio can use imported meshes from form•Z, such as those created with the Smooth Mesh tool. The integration procedures described later in this section apply to all versions of 3DS MAX v1.2 and above.

First and foremost, MAX is primarily a polygonal application; that is, it uses polygons to represent 3D geometry. Although MAX has full capability for surface modeling using NURBS surfaces and patches, all geometry in MAX is rendered as polygons. The conversion can take place before rendering, or surfaces are tesselated (polygonized) on the fly. Additionally, MAX utilizes triangles instead of quadrangles. In any case, geometry imported into MAX from form•Z is always of a polygonal nature. Therefore, geometry that is destined for MAX must get triangulated prior to exportation or as an option during the export.

In my experience there are three file formats that can be used to successfully transfer geometry between form•Z and 3DS MAX. These formats are, in order of desirability: 3DS, Wavefront OBJ, and DXF. The primary format of exchange between form•Z and MAX is the venerable 3DS format. This format has the advantage of being the most stable and reliable. When using 3DS format try to keep names of the export layer to eight characters or less. The reason is that this is an old DOS format that uses the DOS 8.3 naming convention. When object names inside this format have more than eight characters, the extra characters are chopped off. For example, if the object or group is named "Right Door" when saved in 3DS format, it will be renamed "Right-Doo." It gets worse as names get longer, Right Rear Door is renamed "Right Re," and so on.

There are a number of limitations and features of 3DS format that we must keep in mind. The first and most important limitation is the 65,535 triangle limit on any single object. The 3DS file also has an object limit of 65,535 objects. Therefore, the theoretical polygon limit of a 3DS file is 16.8 million triangles (65,535 squared). While the number of individual objects seems large, no single object within the file may contain more than 65,535 polygons. This limitation may present itself when exporting complex high-resolution single mesh characters, especially those modeled with the Smooth Mesh tool, and Patch tools. I have experienced three outcomes of exporting a mesh with more then 65K triangles. First and most likely, an error will be issued by form•Z. The second possibility is that form•Z may crash during export. The third is that the model may come in with the mesh split into two or more objects. The split does not occur along regular lines, every second polygon is detached and joined with other second triangles. The result is that while the two surfaces together look like a complete mesh, individually each object renders with holes in it. When the two meshes are rendered together, the surface renders as if it has no smoothing, as no two triangles share a co-edge. There is a rather time consuming-way to remedy this situation within MAX if reorganization and reexport of geometry is not feasible.

1. The second mesh is attached to the first using the Attach command found under EDIT MESH.
2. All vertices of the resulting single mesh are selected and welded. Depending on the total number of points, and host CPU, this can be a very time-consuming operation, possibly lasting for hours.
3. After welding the points, all faces are picked and Smoothing attributes are assigned.

When form•Z exports to 3DS format it saves all predefined views as 3D Studio R4 cameras, and saves 3D Studio R4 approximated lights. There is no way to turn off view and light export in form•Z 3DS export. I recommend that all predefined views and lights be deleted from the project prior to 3DS export. Otherwise, you have to manually delete the lights and cameras within MAX. The upside of this is that you can preset views and lights within form•Z and simply tweak them inside MAX. 3DS is the only general-purpose model export format within form•Z that exports set views and lights.

How form•Z organizes geometry within 3DS format depends on the 3DS export options. The first type of setting is

Grouping Method: Single Group
Texture Map Export: OFF
Export Visible Layers Only
Fix Smooth Shading; Angle: 40
Export Transformation: Leave at Default

With this setting, only objects within visible layers are exported, and each form•Z object becomes a 3D Studio object. Obviously, this can create many more objects than are necessary, and will slow down texturing and animation setup. If you choose to export to 3DS with this setting, first Join all objects within each export layer. Be sure not to accidentally Join objects in different export layers. The Join is a very loose type of organization and joined objects can be easily decomposed with the Separate tool set to the **Separate: Volumes** option. Of the grouping methods, Single Group is the only one that creates a single 3DS file with multiple objects in it. All other 3DS export grouping methods create multiple 3DS files. In subsequent 3DS export options I will concentrate only on grouping method options. Leave all other options as described earlier. Single Group method is the recommended way of exporting geometry via 3DS format. It produces a single, easily manageable 3DS file. The only caveat is that you must Join objects within individual export layers prior to exportation.

GROUPING METHOD: OBJECT

This grouping method produces the same organization as Single Group; however, each object is saved in its own 3DS file. With many objects this can be time consuming to import into MAX as there is no batch import capability within MAX. However, MAX has an open architecture and a plug-in can be written that will batch import multiple 3DS files. Contact Kinetix for information on how to obtain a 3D Studio MAX SDK.

GROUPING METHOD: COLOR

This grouping method works the same as Object except that all objects or faces of the same color are reorganized into a single object. Like **Object**, multiple 3DS files are created. The **Color** grouping method is intended primarily for architectural visualization and I do not recommend it for effects production.

However Color, can be a useful grouping method under some circumstances. It can be used to ease the problem of the 65K triangle limit. Let's assume that we need to export a mesh containing about 96,000 triangles and bring it into MAX.

1. Within form•Z, first triangulate the mesh using the Triangulate tool.
2. Bring the mesh into Texture Map. Create a new texture group and select about half the triangles. Try to create a clearly identifiable delineating line between selected and unselected triangles.
3. Apply a material of different color than the material applied to the object. The result is that now the mesh has half of its triangles one color and half some other color.
4. Export this mesh only with the Color grouping method. The resulting export creates two 3DS files: The first contains only triangles of the first color, and the second contains only triangles of the second color.
5. Import both meshes into MAX.
6. Attach the second to the first using the Attach command in Edit Mesh.
7. Select and Weld the points along the delineation line.

This method can be used to export a single mesh of any polygon count. You simply need to create texture groups in which the amount of triangles within each texture group does not exceed the 65,535 triangle limit. Be forewarned that with very high count meshes, its preparation in form•Z and reconstruction within MAX can be time consuming.

GROUPING METHOD: LAYER

As with the Object and Color methods, multiple 3DS files are created. Each layer becomes a separate 3DS file. Objects within layers are not joined into a single object. This method is useful if you wish to retain objects within export layers as separate entities within MAX.

GROUPING METHOD: GROUP

Group is the same as Object, but works with predefined object groups.

---

form•Z to MAX Integration via Wavefront File Format

Although any of the methods will successfully bring form•Z geometry into 3DS MAX, the Single Group method is your best bet for 3DS format. It offers you the most control over construction of individual MAX objects and it's placed within a single file. Earlier I mentioned that regardless of the grouping method, lights and preset views are saved within each 3DS file. In cases where multiple 3DS files are created for a single model, the lights and views are saved into each file. This creates a time burden as those lights and cameras must be deleted as each 3DS file is imported.

3DS format is not the only format that can be used to successfully transfer geometry from form•Z to 3DS MAX. Wavefront OBJ is an excellent format that has no polygon limit; however, it just has OBJ2MAX and MAX2OBJ file format plug-ins. Those plug-ins are free and can be found at the Kinetix Website (www.ktx.com) or at any of the many 3DS MAX user sites. form•Z has an excellent built-in Wavefront OBJ export/import capability. Because OBJ has no 65K polygon limit it is also an excellent format for bringing 3DS MAX geometry into form•Z. I have determined from experience that the following are optimal OBJ export settings:

Grouping Method: By Layer
Separate Files: OFF
Export Method For Solids/Surfaces: Object
Export Materials: ON
Preserve C-MESH & C-CURVE controls: OFF
Preserve Face Colors: optional
Subdivide Concave Faces: ON
Triangulate Faces: ON
Triangulation Options: Triangulate All Faces
Triangulation Method: Third.
Include Normals: ON
Fix Smooth Shading: ON   Angle: 40
Use Absolute Indices: optional
Export Transformation : Default.

form•Z does not save either lights or views within an OBJ file. The geometry is contained within a single file, and with Grouping Method set to By Layer, all objects within an individual export layer come in as single objects into MAX. I have experienced erratic memory, performance slowdown, and crashes when MAX imports large OBJ files. If you are experiencing problems during OBJ import within MAX, turn Separate Files ON, and bring in the geometry individually.

Now let's briefly discuss Export Transformation options as they apply to all geometric export formats. The primary purpose of Export Transformation is to modify the local space of the exported geometry in order to make it more compatible with the target animation package or with a preexisting project within that package. Export Transformation is especially useful when importing geometry into an existing project with models from other modelers. At times you end up with imported geometry that is very small in scale or in an incorrect orientation. The scale problem is due to the fact that there is not a set standard of measurement of what defines a unit across different applications. One inch inside form•Z may be interpreted as one millimeter inside another package, resulting in a model that is very small. You can fix the size by simply scaling the geometry inside the animation package, but you will also have to appropriately scale all subsequent alterations to the model as they are imported into the animation environment. Furthermore, you need to apply the exact scale amount and use the same base of scale or the replacement geometry will be out of modeled position. Export Transformation to the rescue. Export Transformation will automatically rescale and reorient the model to have a better initial fit. The downside is that you must first experiment with different settings in order to get the desired result. Once you obtain the proper settings, *always* use them when exporting replacement and updated geometry into the animation project. Recording the Export Transformation settings is important as they may differ from project to project, even when using the same animation package. Most of the time you can leave Export Transformation at its default settings; engineers at auto•des•sys have done a good job of setting it to work well with 3D Studio MAX, ElectricImage, and Cinema 4D XL.

form•Z and Cinema 4D XL

Cinema 4D XL is a new high end-effects and 3D animation package from MAXON Computer GMBH of Germany. It is a very popular application, especially in Europe, and a fairly recent entry into the North American 3D animation market. Cinema 4D is available in three versions: entry-level GO, general-purpose SE, and high-end XL. Since the XL version is the one that is most likely to be used in the effects production environment, I will concentrate on it. The differences between versions of Cinema 4D are in included features; otherwise, all three work in the same fashion. Cinema 4D XL is available for Intel- and Alpha-based Windows NT/98, PowerPC Mac OS, and soon will be available for BeOS and other operating systems. Contact MAXON Computer (www.maxon-computer.com) to find out more about this incredible package. A demo of Cinema 4D XL is included on the accompanying CD-ROM or can be downloaded from the MAXON's Website. Cinema 4D's main strength as a 3D animation package lies in its pseudo-procedural workflow and its incredible adaptive raytracer that combines blazing speed and special effects with motion picture quality rendering. In particular, Cinema 4D XL has a very powerful particle system that allows the creation of varied effects, from blowing steam to jet exhaust. To aid in the creation of realistic characters, Cinema 4D

XL has a free hair-generation plug-in called CineHair that can be used to grow geometric hair-like fibers from any model, including those originating in form•Z. Very sophisticated effects are possible when digital models from form•Z are combined with amazing special effects features of Cinema 4D XL.

Integrating geometry from form•Z with Cinema 4D XL is easily accomplished via the following formats: 3DS, 3DMF, FACT, and OBJ.

3DMF FILE FORMAT

In my experience 3DMF format is the most reliable for integrating form•Z with Cinema 4D XL. There is no polygon or object limit, file size is relatively compact, and export options allow for flexible geometry organization. Additionally, 3DMF has the advantage of being multiplatform as the import and export functionality exists on Mac OS and Windows versions of form•Z and Cinema 4D XL. As I proposed earlier in the chapter, organizing geometry so that a form•Z export layer becomes an object within Cinema 4D XL is fully supported by 3DMF file format with a couple of modifications. Because of the structure of 3DMF format, the names of layers are not written out. All visible objects within export layers are written out as separate objects with 3DMF files and are imported into Cinema. For example, if you have two visible export layers with 5 objects in each, the imported model in Cinema will have 10 separate objects. For this reason, Join all objects within each export layer into a single object. You should have one export object per export layer. As new geometry becomes available it is joined with existing geometry in the export layers. If exportable geometry needs to be deleted, the object is broken into its elements using the Separate tool with the Volumes option. You do not need to name the objects. This is due to the format of a 3DMF file. When originally conceived, 3DMF was intended as a viewing format for 3D geometry; hence, internally all objects are named Object1, Object2, and so on. When 3DMF geometry is brought into Cinema, all objects are renamed in this style, and should be renamed. This creates a time burden if the object count is high.

The optimal 3DMF settings, for export by layer, are as follows;

> 3DMF Export Options:
> File Type: Binary;m;m(*see below*)
> Grouping Method: By Object;m;mSeparate File: Optional (*see below*)
> Export Method For Solids/Surfaces: Object (Mesh)
> Preserve C-Mesh & C-Curve Controls: OFF
> Preserve face Colors: optional
> Export Visible Layers Only: ON

Subdivide Concave Faces: ON
Triangulate Faces: Optional (*see below*)
Include Normals: ON
Fix Smooth Shading: 40 (*see below*)
Export Transformation:
Scale: Project Dependent (*see below*)
Current Transformations: FACT (*see below*)

File Type: Can be ASCII, but will be significantly larger in size. **New-lines** should indicate the platform on which Cinema 4D XL is running on, but in practice has proven to have no negative or positive effect.

Separate File: Use this option only if the exported model size is too big to fit on a transport device such as a ZIP disk, or if the model is so large as to cause memory problems during import. This may be the case with a multimillion polygon model with thousands of objects on low-memory (128MB and below) Mac OS and Windows 95/98 systems. The Separate Files: option is invaluable as a debugging tool if you experience crashes in form•Z during export or in Cinema 4D XL during import. The crash is most likely being caused by a corrupt piece of geometry, and using the Separate Files: option helps to determine which layer this geometry is on.

Preserve Face Color: Cinema 4D XL 3DMF import does not support individually colored faces, so this option is ignored. This is due to how Cinema 4D XL handles materials applications. Internally Cinema 4D XL does not allow application of materials on a per-face basis. Instead, it allows an infinite amount of materials to be applied to an individual object, each material having its own projection. Future versions of Cinema 4D XL may address this issue; contact MAXON Computer for the latest information.

Triangulate Faces: Use this if you are experiencing shading anomalies with quad meshes in the imported models. However, it is recommended that in this case, exportable geometry should be triangulated manually inside form•Z prior to exportation.

Fix Smooth Shading: This option saves you the trouble of applying Smoothing Property to the model in Cinema 4D XL's Object Manager. When applied, the smoothing angle is always interpreted by Cinema as 89.5 degrees.

Export Transformation Scale: The amount of scaling is project dependent. If you are going to import the model into a new empty

XL project, export with Scale set to 1. The form•Z default is 5, but I noticed that models come into Cinema excessively large.

Current Transformations: The form•Z default for Current Transformations is 3DMF; however, the models are flipped about the Y-axis in Cinema. In Cinema the Y-axis is the vertical up/down axis. Setting Current Transformations: to FACT prevents this from happening.

3DS FILE FORMAT

3DS format is seamlessly read by Cinema 4D XL, including lights and cameras. Cinema 4D XL is able to read and write 3DS format on both Mac OS and Windows NT/98 platforms. In form•Z 3DS export/import capability is available only in the Windows version. Because of Cinema 4D XL's seamless ability to read and write 3DS files, all guidelines for 3DS export for 3D Studio MAX apply to Cinema 4D XL. 3DS is a good exchange format to use if you are on the Windows platform—do not have objects exceeding the 65K triangle count, and object names need to be eight characters or less.

FACT FILE FORMAT

FACT is a native model format developed by ElectricImage for the ElectricImage Animation System. It is a Mac OS native format. This is an excellent file format as it automatically organizes objects on a layer basis when the grouping method is set to **By Layer.** To use FACT files with Cinema 4D XL you must download the FACT plug-in for Cinema from MAXON Computer. This is a third-party plug-in written by John Deutch, and is available free of charge from MAXON Computer. FACT format is slated to be included as a core feature (versus plug-in), in Cinema 4D XL v5.5. Contact MAXON Computer for the latest information on FACT import/export.

Overall, integrating form•Z with Cinema via FACT format is identical to integrating it with the ElectricImage Animation System, described later. There are, however, a couple of things you should be aware of. The FACT plug-in is a shareware third-party plug-in, and difficulties have been experienced.

The first problem that some individuals may encounter with moderate to large FACT files is the random freezing of Cinema during import, or excessive import times. Both problems may be alleviated by increasing the buffer size of the FACT import to 32,000 and above. The buffer size is found in FACT Preferences under Cinema's Preferences. By default it is set to 3000 which is woefully inadequate.

The second problem is missing faces in imported geometry. This problem can be alleviated by manually triangulating all exportable geometry prior to export.

The main advantage of using FACT versus 3DMF or 3DS is that FACT is read on both MAC and Windows versions of Cinema 4D, and there is no need to Join or Group exportable objects prior to export. When the grouping method is set to By Layer, and Include Hierarchy is OFF, all objects with a single export layer become a single object. Modifications to exported geometry are easily done by transferring geometry to and from export layers. Within Cinema, imported objects carry full names of the export layers. On large models this an important timesaver.

In practice, FACT import in Cinema seems to work best on meshed surfaces. I have experienced incorrect vertex, segment interpretations when importing solids with holes. Solids with holes formed with Insert Hole modifier are especially susceptible. Remember that at the time of writing this book, Cinema's FACT plug-in was still in Beta, so you may or may not experience the described problems. The following is a short list of actions you can take to reduce the chance of problem occurrence.

- Decompose all exportable objects into meshed surfaces.
- Triangulate exportable geometry. Specifically avoid exporting complex polygons. A complex polygon is one with five or more points.
- Verify that surface normals are pointing in the correct direction, and none of the objects are Surface Solids (double-sized normals).
- Create holes in geometry using standard Booleans or Trim tools. Avoid using the Insert Hole modifier.

The optimal form•Z FACT export settings are

FACT Export Options;
Grouping Method: By Layer;m;mSeparate Files: optional (*see below*)
Include Hierarchy: OFF (*see below*)
Include Face Decomposition: OFF (*see below*)
Fix Smooth Shading: ON;m;m;mAngle: 40
Export Visible Layers Only: ON
Include Group Centroids: ON
Extended Coordinate Precision: ON
Include Normals: ON
Texture Map Export: OFF
Export Transformations: Default
Separate Files: Use this option to save the model in multiple files, thereby

reducing the size of individual FACT files. This is useful if the model is very large in both polygon and object count, which causes either hangs or excessive import times. This option should only be used if the FACT Import buffer size in Cinema is set to the maximum allowable and it's still not enough. In my experience, 99 percent of hangs in Cinema during FACT import are caused by insufficient buffer size. The remaining 1 percent is caused by randomly occurring corrupt geometry, which is also solved by saving geometry in multiple files and seeing which one causes the hang.

Include Hierarchy: This option does not form the separate objects within an export layer into a single object. Rather, the layer name is saved as an empty null object, and objects with that layer come in as children of the null object. This is a useful option if you wish to retain minute control over the texture mapping process. For example, an export layer contains geometry of the baffle plate of a spacecraft. Geometry consists of the main baffle plate object and a number of detail objects called *nurnees*. When exported with this option and imported into Cinema, the layer name is a parent object but contains no polygons. The actual geometry of the baffle plate are children of the null parent. In Cinema a child will automatically inherit the materials of the parent along with their projections, unless a child is assigned its own material properties. You can therefore apply one material to the null parent, causing all children to inherit it, and modify selected children by applying different materials to them. Accurate mapping is very fast and easy in Cinema 4D XL as not only materials but their projections can be transferred from object to object and from material to material. Consult the Cinema 4D XL manual for detailed explanation of the texture mapping.

Include Face Decomposition: This option should be kept off, as you should be manually triangulating export geometry prior to export. However, if you choose not to manually triangulate, set this option to **As Quadrangles**. If the imported geometry exhibits shading anomalies or incorrect importation, change to **As Triangles**.

OBJ FILE FORMAT

While OBJ is an excellent format for integrating form•Z with 3D Studio MAX, it should be considered a secondary format when integrating form•Z with Cinema 4D XL. The primary shortcoming of Cinema's OBJ import is its lack of ability to read multiple objects within an OBJ file. Whereas form•Z OBJ files come in as separate objects within 3D Studio MAX, Cinema groups all objects within an OBJ file as a single object. When exporting OBJ files for use with Cinema 4D XL, you must use **Separate Files:** and **Texture Map Export:** options, and import each file individually. The primary reason to use the OBJ format is importing parametric C-MESHES with Parametric or UV coordinates assigned to them in form•Z RenderZone with the Texture Map tool. When parametric surfaces are imported into Cinema via OBJ they retain the parametric mapping coordinates as UV map properties. If the UV mapped surfaces are going to be deformed, assign a UVW property to the object in addition to the UV property. Such objects can also be imported into 3D paint applications with OBJ import capabilities. In my experience with 3DS MAX, Cinema, and ElectricImage, only Cinema 4D XL could import parametric UV coordinates from form•Z, and only via an OBJ file. Aside from the **Separate Files:** option, use the guidelines for exporting OBJ files into 3D Studio MAX. As in the FACT format, objects within OBJ format retain their form•Z assigned names.

form•Z and Lightwave 3D

Lightwave 3D is a very popular 3D application available for a multitude of operating systems, including Mac OS, SUN Solaris, and SGI IRIX. It is published by Newtek Inc. of Topeka, Kansas. LW3D is a powerful 3D animation environment that has an illustrious history of being the tool of choice for many studios, and has been used to create effects for a myriad TV weekly episodes and in a number of feature films. 3D imagery created with Lightwave 3D can be seen in *Babylon 5*, *Star Trek: Voyager*, and other popular television series.

Lightwave 3D is composed of two applications, Layout and Modeler. Layout is where animation, texturing, and lighting take place. Modeler is where model importation and general modeling take place. The native geometric formats of Lightwave 3D are LWO and LWB. LWO, or LightWaveObject, is the newer of the two. Currently, form•Z does not support export or import of either of the two. However, Lightwave Modeler has the ability to import 3D Studio 3DS files. 3DS format is an effective means of transporting form•Z geometry into Lightwave 3D.

form•Z and ElectricImage Animation System

ElectricImage Animation System (EIAS) is a high-end 3D animation environment for the Mac OS from the ElectricImage Division of Play Inc., makers of popular Snappy low-end video capture digital cameras and the high-end Trinity video production and editing system. As of the writing of this book, ElectricImage is in version 2.8R and comes in two flavors: BROADCAST version, aimed at video designers working in television, video, and print markets; and FILM version aimed at special effects artists working in film and HDTV production. The two versions are identical, with FILM version being able to render up to 32K × 32K resolution and having Biovision motion capture as a standard feature. BROADCAST version is limited to NTSC/PAL rendering resolutions for animation, and 32K × 32K resolution for still images. Motion blur is not supported for still rendering in BROADCAST version for images with higher than NTSC/PAL resolution. ElectricImage has been called the granddaddy of MAC 3D animation programs, and was the first professional-level 3D animation application available for the Mac OS system. Effects created with EIAS FILM have appeared in major feature films, among them, *Terminator 2: Judgement Day, Mission: Impossible, Courage Under Fire, Star Trek: First Contact,* and others. ElectricImage's claim to fame is its ultra-fast scanline Phong renderer, and unsurpassed quality of its unique Motion Vector motion blur. Currently it is available only on the Mac OS, but ElectricImage has announced future availability of the application under the Windows/NT environment.

Like 3D Studio MAX and Cinema 4D XL, EIAS is a polygonal application. Unlike 3D Studio MAX, EI can effectively use quadrilateral or triangular meshes. Superior results are achieved with quad meshes. form•Z and Electric-Image have grown up and matured together. Both were originally developed and available only for the Mac OS, and both became available at about the same time. For years, until the arrival of Cinema 4D XL and Lightwave 3D on the MAC, ElectricImage and form•Z were considered the only high-end tools for professional 3D content creation on the Mac OS. In the ElectricImage community, form•Z is considered a de-facto standard front-end modeling system for ElectricImage, as EI does not have an internal modeler, and must have for anyone creating 3D graphics on the Mac OS.

Integration of form•Z with ElectricImage is very easy and painless through the use of the FACT file format as FACT is native to ElectricImage. EI has the ability to read DXF, OBJ, 3DMF, and 3DS formats, but FACT works best and takes advantage of EI's capability to deal with complex polygons. Because form•Z and ElectricImage have been used so long in production, an established procedure for integrating form•Z geometry with ElectricImage has been developed. The procedure is simple: Save in FACT file format using the settings given here:

FACT Export Options:
Grouping Method: By Layer;m;mSeparate Files: optional *(see below)*
Include Hierarchy: OFF *(see below)*

Include Face Decomposition: OFF;m;m(*see below*)

Fix Smooth Shading: ON;m;m;mAngle: 40

Export Visible Layers Only: ON

Include Group Centroids: ON

Extended Coordinate Precision: ON

Include Normals: ON

Texture Map Export: OFF;m;m(*see below*)

Export Transformations: Default

Separate Files: Use this option only if you need to transport the model using floppy or ZIP disks and the whole model cannot fit on a single floppy or ZIP disk. This is also useful if you need to send a large model across the Internet. In normal course where EI and form•Z are on the same machine or on the same network, there is no need to break the model into multiple files.

Include Hierarchy: This option does not form the separate objects within an export layer into a single object. Rather, the layer name is saved as an empty null object, and objects within that layer come in as children of the null object. This is a useful option if you wish to retain minute control over the texture mapping process. Unlike Cinema 4D XL, children objects do not inherit the texture mapping of the parents. You would have to copy/paste the parent's material onto its children or set up a master material. Refer to the ElectricImage 2.8 manual for details on texture mapping. I do not recommend using this option; rather, arrange geometry in as many export layers as needed.

Face Decomposition: This option has little effect, one way or the other, on the rendering quality of exported geometry. If the geometry renders clean within RenderZone, it is virtually guaranteed to render clean in ElectricImage. The reason is a little known mini-application called "Transporter" that hides inside ElectricImage. Every time a model is imported into ElectricImage, it is first internally processed through the Transporter, which cleans up the model and prepares it for use within ElectricImage. To achieve best results when using form•Z and Electric-Image, always *import, not add* the model to ElectricImage. The only time you can add a model to EI is if the FACT was written out of the same version of ElectricImage. If you experience shading anomalies with imported geometry, reimport the model, but this time use the FORCE CORRECT NORMALS option in the EI Model Import options. This option basically forces all normals to face outward. By default the option is set to Assume Correct Normals. With Assume

Correct Normals, ElectricImage assumes that normals, as they are in the model, are correct.

Texture Map Export: This option should be set to OFF. For one reason or another, textures written out by form•Z into FACT have never been able to be properly read by ElectricImage. It is not known whether the fault lies with ElectricImage or form•Z.

EXPORTING PARAMETRIC SURFACES

The export procedures outlined in the previous section all deal with meshed geometry. form•Z 3.0, in development at the time of this book's writing, has true parametric NURBS and patch surfaces. form•Z's NURBS (called NURBZ in form•Z 3.0) can be exported in parametric fashion via IGES file format. However, there are a number of difficulties involved in getting true parametric geometry from form•Z into the traget animation environment. The target application must have the IGES import plug-in capable of reading the flavor of IGES that form•Z 3.0 writes out. The second difficulty deals with how form•Z 3.0 deals with NURBS. form•Z 3.0 does not support trimmed NURBS surfaces. When a NURBZ surface is trimmed it is converted into a polygonal meshed surface, based on its Wires & Facets attributes. Parametric surfaces are exported only if they are not trimmed. So, while simple surfaces like revolutions and NURBZ lofted surfaces can be exported as true NURBS, these cases are relatively rare, as most complex surfaces that we model have been trimmed. This is also the case with patch surfaces. form•Z 3.0 offers an extensive set of patch modeling tools. Unfortunately there is no way to export patches as parametric patch surfaces, only as polygonal meshes. Remember that form•Z's main strength is its detailed control over the creation of polygonal models.

Summary

The information provided in this chapter gives you enough to successfully integrate form•Z with major 3D animation applications on Mac OS and Windows. However, each project has its own requirements, and it is not possible to cover them all. Consider this chapter as a general guide to integration of form•Z with the animation environment. I urge you to experiment with various export settings. The layer organization strategy that I presented in this chapter gives ability and flexibility to approach almost any modeling challenge, but there is no guarantee that it will work for all of your projects. It is up to you to adjust the layer strategy, and any other concepts offered, to suit your particular modeling style, experience level, and project requirements.

4 Mesh Density and Topology

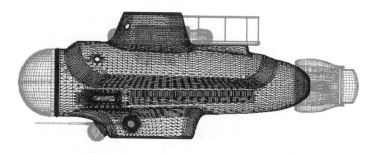

IN THIS CHAPTER

In this chapter we will discuss the process of determining the optimal mesh density and topology for a model given a set of project parameters. This step in the modeling process takes place prior to the creation of shot geometry, and can have serious consequences on the results or time consumed if not properly evaluated. Correctly planning the density and topology of the object mesh has direct bearing on how well the model renders, textures, and animates. For example, a model that is too lightly meshed will exhibit polygonal silhouettes during the rendering process, and may give away the model as being "digital." A model that has too many polygons for the task will render well, but may take much longer. In a situation where many of the models are overmeshed, the render times may put the project over schedule and budget. Depending on the degree of overmeshing, additional time spent in modeling and animation phases may be substantial. Doubling the number of polygons may quadruple modeling time. Heavily meshed models also place strain on the animation process, because they take longer to animate and may cause problems with animation software. Both cases are undesirable, one produces bad results, the other costs time and money and impacts artistic creativity. In addition to mesh density, mesh topology must be correctly planned. While mesh density determines the number of polygons in a model, topology describes the orientation and location of the mesh elements (faces, edges, and vertices) in the mesh. Topology is every bit as important as mesh density. Mesh topology is a direct result of the modeling operations, and must be planned so as to be compatible with the type of animation that the object will undergo, with respect to the animation application used.

Parameters of Mesh Density/ Topology Determination Process

There are basically three prime parameters that drive the mesh density/topology determination process: output requirements, project considerations, and animation system capabilities. It is not really possible to state which one is the most important. Failure to satisfy any of the three may result in failure. However, when planning or adjusting the model, output requirements should be the first parameter considered, as it is the easiest to deal with. Output requirements are simply the color depth, image resolution, and rendering style, the most important of these being image resolution. The higher the output resolution, the higher the mesh density should be. Assuming of course that the desired rendering level is photorealistic Phong or Raytracing. For other rendering styles the mesh density may need to be lower. If the rendering level is going to be cartoon cell shaded, then it is a good idea to lower the polygon count. Cell shaders may produce irregular outlines and may not generate interior outlines as desired on heavily meshed models. A model that it meshed optimally for Phong shading or Raytracing may be useful for cell shading. For wireframe or hidden line rendering levels, polygon counts should be lower still. Densely meshed models tend to produce noise, white pool areas, and other rendering artifacts when rendered in hidden line or wireframe mode. In deciding on mesh density, each of those factors must be considered. Regular test renders during the modeling process should show any deficiencies in the mesh density. In the next paragraph we will introduce a simple and effective technique for determining the mesh density based on desired output resolution.

Spherical Mesh Density Determination Technique

Spherical determination is a very simple but effective technique used to determine the average mesh density for a curvilinear model. In order to use this technique, the following parameters must be known:

- Output resolution
- Approximate motion of the model in question
- Approximate motion of the camera
- Approximate scale and size of the model in project units
- Planned rendering mode of the mode

Although not necessary, it may be helpful to know the following additional parameters:

- Planned light conditions in the scene
- Amount of desired motion blur

In a nutshell, the spherical determination method uses a visual evaluation of polygon primitive spheric objects to determine the average mesh density of a curvilinear object. Although this technique is best accomplished within the animation environment, it is possible to perform it inside form•Z, provided the closest relative position between the camera and the object can be duplicated. Two geometric primitives can be used, a revolved sphere or a Utah Teapot primitive. The first step is to create a new project with render settings set to the resolution and rendering level of the final output. Next, create and set up a digital camera with transformations similar or identical to those used in the final scene. Next, create a primitive sphere or a teapot for NTSC/PAL output resolutions starting with a 32 × 32 revolved sphere (for film, IMAX), or print start with a 64 × 64 sphere. If using teapot as test object, start with 14 patch points for NTSC/PAL resolutions, and 24 patch points for film and higher resolutions. Create a neutral lighting condition that clearly and realistically illuminates the model. Keyframe the animation of the camera and the test object similar to the planned motion in the scene. This is where storyboards and scene sketches are of tremendous value. If you are not the animator, communication is needed with the animator, technical and art directors involved with the shot. You don't need to be right on as far as test scene setup is concerned, but the closer the better. With the animation set up, scrub the timeline to the place where the test object and the camera are closest to each other. Now render a still image at the final output resolution. If the sphere exhibits polygon silhouettes, then a new sphere needs to be created at the same size, occupying the same position but having more polygons. Generally, increase the step amount by 1/3. Once you have a sphere that does not show polygonal silhouettes, don't assume that you have your target density. Reduce the step amount by 1/6 and rerender. Keep reducing the step amount until you just notice formation of silhouettes. Increase the step amount by couple of steps and rerender. If the sphere does not show polygonal silhouettes, then you have your target density. The next step is to render an animation and observe the polygonal density with motion applied. In some instances, you may decrease the target density, as motion, and especially motion blur, negates polygonal silhouetting. As a general rule, the faster the relative motion between the camera and object, the lower the mesh density can be. However, err on the side of caution. Export the sphere and bring it into form•Z. Inside form•Z use it as a general guide for judging mesh density of the actual objects. You may want to give yourself an extra margin of error by building your geometry slightly heavier than the sphere. Prior to doing the sample exercise, review the steps in Spherical Mesh Density Determination:

- Compile the relevant project information: output resolution, rendering style, lighting scheme, motion of camera, and motion of object.
- Set up a test project within the animation environment, using the above information.
- Create a sphere or a teapot primitive.
- Scale the primitive to be volumetrically similar to the proposed model.
- Position the camera and the object, and create animation paths similar to those that will be used in the scene.
- Go to the time when the object and the camera are closest to each other.
- Render the object at target resolution.
- Evaluate the rendering for polygonal silhouettes.
- Iteratively adjust the mesh density of the primitive until it is optimally meshed.
- Export the primitive and bring it into form•Z.
- Model the geometry to have similar mesh density.

In the following exercise we will use storyboard and project information to determine overall mesh density for a submersible vehicle. The script calls for the submersible to descend into a deep ocean canyon. The storyboards describe the camera pan as it follows the DSV. The general output requirements are photorealistic Raytraced output. The surface materials will generally be metallic with layered diffusion and specular maps. The final rendering will be rendered at film resolution, with 16:9 aspect ratio, and pixel size of 2100×1155. The scene will be rendered with a standard 35mm camera. The model will only undergo transformation-type animation, there will be no geometric deformation of geometry. The single frame from the storyboards, shown in Figure 4.1, shows the DSV at its closest proximity to the camera.

Begin by first setting up a test project in our animation environment and in form•Z. Because the relative motion between cameras is simple and the camera setup is straightforward, we can do the testing in either an animation environment or in form•Z.

1. In form•Z create a new project. Leave the default modeling window as is and create a new modeling window. For the second window, open the Image Options dialog. Set its pixel resolution to be same as the output resolution, 2100×1155, with the same aspect ratio.

2. Open the Underlay options and set the scanned storyboard image or a scene sketch as a 3D underlay. For this exercise the following view parameters were used:

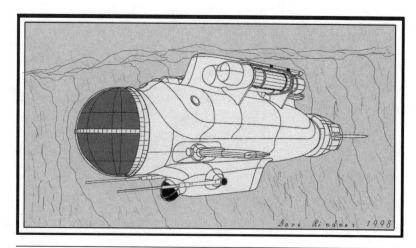

FIGURE *Storyboard showing closest distance of object from camera.*
4.1

View Type: Perspective
Orientation: –42.38 X: 28′–6″
Altitude Ang : –2.37 Y: –10′–11″
Distance: 34′–4″   Z: –0′–8″
Center Of Interest;
X: 3′–1″
Y: 12′–3″
Z: 8″
Spin: 0
Angle: 60

3. Using View Parameters and Set View controls, adjust the position and FOV of the camera perspective to match to underlay the image.

4. Open the RenderZone options and set the rendering quality to Raytrace and Background to display the storyboard image.

5. Now create a Revolved Sphere using the Spheric Object tool. Set the options to Revolved Sphere; Length Resolution: 32, Depth Resolution: 32. At this point, the radius is not important.

6. Working from both views, scale and position the sphere so it is roughly the size and aligned with the large bubble of the submersible.

Figure 4.2 shows the 32 by 32 sphere aligned with the bubble. In this case, the front glass bubble provides a convenient measure of curvature as it is large, spherically curving, and is the closest major part of the model to the camera. If the mesh density of the base primitive does not exhibit polygonal silhouettes in

Figure *32 by 32 sphere aligned.*
4.2

FIGURE *Hidden line rendering overlayed on top of sphere.*
4.3

this position, we can be relatively sure that all curvilinear geometry built with this mesh density will render without silhouetting. Unfortunately, the 32 by 32 sphere shows severe deficiency in mesh density. Polygonal silhouetting is clearly visible on the outline of the sphere, and polygons of the sphere are large in relation to the size of the image.

7. Since a 32 by 32 sphere is very deficient, we are going to leap all the way to a 128 by 128 sphere. Create a revolved sphere with Length and Depth Resolution set to 128. Use the existing 32 by 32 sphere as a guide for positioning and scaling of the 128 by 128 sphere.

Figure 4.3 shows the Hidden Line rendering of the new sphere overlayed on top of the image.

It is evident that if we constructed the model with similar mesh density, it would render beautifully. However, the geometry would also be unnecessarily heavy, and would take longer to render.

8. Evaluating the mesh of the 128 by 128 sphere, it is evident that the mesh is about twice as heavy as it needs to be. So now we need to create a sphere that is heavier than 32 and lighter than 128. A 64 by 64 sphere sounds about right. Using the steps described above create and position a 64 by 64 revolved sphere (see Figure 4.4).

As Figure 4.4 shows, a 64 by 64 sphere has optimal mesh density needed for this project.

Figure 4.4 *64 by 64 sphere has optimal mesh density needed for this project.*

Guidelines for Mesh Density Evaluation

As noted earlier, optimal mesh density is a judgment call. Furthermore, the mesh density often will not be uniform across the model. The base primitive only provides a general mesh density base to be used as a guide. Depending on the curvature of a particular model part, its mesh density may be increased or decreased as desired. Hidden Line rendering modes are invaluable for juding mesh quality as they let you simultaneously evaluate both geometric and topological quality and suitability of the mesh. When evaluating mesh density of transform-only animated curvilinear models, use the following guidelines.

- Render using Hidden Line rendering mode at final output resolution. Set the lines to be 1-pixel thick. For still images do not anti-alias the wireframe. Create camera and orthogonal renderings of the model and base primitive at output resolution.
- Look for polygonal silhouetting, especially along the outlines of the model. Visible angle breaks at vertices of curvilinear geometry is sign of lower than optimal mesh density. The tighter the curvature on a piece of geometry, the more potential exists for silhouetting. Look for polygonal silhouetting not only at outlines of the object but also in the interior mesh. This is the main reason why hidden line renderings should be used instead of Phong shading.
- Look for overly large polygons. In general, for static or transform-only curvilinear geometry, no single polygon should exceed 2 percent of the output image area. When modeling curving geometry, large polygons and polygonal silhouettes go hand in hand.

- For highest quality rendering, the mesh should be topologically clean. That is, the polygons should be arranged in an ordered quadrilateral grid. The mesh should not have slivered triangles or complex polygons. A complex polygon is a polygon that has more than four points. All renderers will break down the complex polygons into simpler quads or triangles. This breakdown may produce shading artifacts. To be on the safe side, manually break down complex polygons into quads, use triangles only when necessary.

Avoid overmeshing your geometry. Figure 4.3 shows mesh density that is higher than is needed for this shot. As stated earlier, mesh density is a judgment call: however, with experience you should be able to correctly judge whether the mesh density is too light or too heavy. Here are some ways you can prevent overmeshing.

- Examine the overall area of the rendering covered by the mesh. Compare the amount of empty or "white" space to the amount of wireframe pixels, "black" space. In the image viewer zoom out so you can see the entire rendering. You should still be able to clearly make out the white area between wireframe segments. If the amount of white space is small or the mesh appears to be very "black," then it is a clear indication that the mesh is heavy. Recall that the sphere only provides us with a general guide. Mesh density will vary across the model depending on the curvature of the geometry. Figure 4.5 shows the DSV mesh that is more or less optimally meshed for 2100 by 1155 output resolution. Notice that the main hull is meshed similarly to the base sphere. Other parts of the model have heavier mesh density depending on the curvature. In most cases it is not practical nor it is smart modeling to diligently adhere to the base sphere mesh density.

RAYTRACE/PHONG EVALUATION

Phong or Raytrace evaluation is intended to simply back up the results of the Hidden Line evaluation. Raytraced evaluation is usually performed after Hidden Line, and usually show no undesirable mesh qualities. Raytrace evaluation has two purposes. The first is to confirm findings of the Hidden Line evaluation, and the second is to locate any shading anomalies and mesh problems that Hidden Line failed to pick up. Although Hidden Line is very effective at evaluating quality of the mesh, there are some problems that cannot be detected by it. They are

- Flipped normals

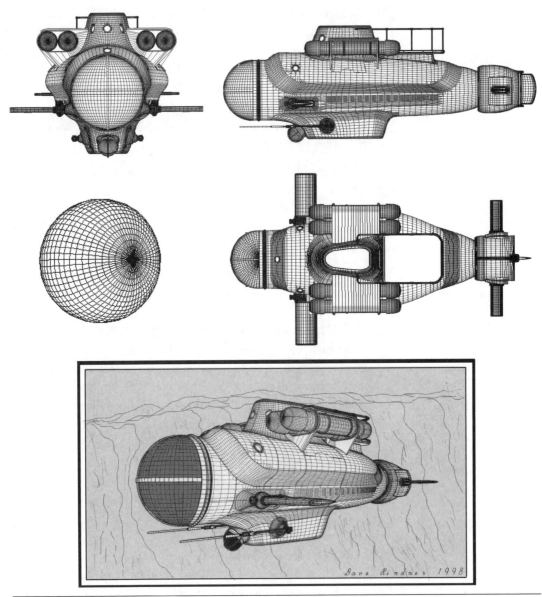

FIGURE *The DSV mesh that is more or less optimally meshed for 2100 by 1155 output resolution.*
4.5

- Individual missing polygons
- Unwelded vertices
- Smoothing errors
- Surface continuity and matching
- General shading anomalies

FIGURE *The DSV with neutral materials applied and lit under neutral lighting*
4.6 *conditions.*

Phong evaluation is best accomplished by applying neutral grey solid color material to opaque objects. No texture maps, procedural or bitmap, should be used as they can mask problems. Opaque materials should have plastic-like specularity. Transparent materials should have glass-like material applied, once again without any bitmaps except an environmental reflection map. Reflectivity for transparent objects should be kept low, about 10 percent. Lighting should be similar to the planned lighting of the final scene; however, there is a caveat to go along with that. It is not always possible to effectively evaluate the model given certain lighting conditions. In those cases, set up a neutral lighting condition as described in the following note. Figure 4.6 shows the DSV with neutral materials applied and lit under neutral lighting conditions. Although this lighting setup is not reflective of the underwater lighting condition of final rendering, it allows evaluation of geometry from all viewing angles. Notice that while the lighting is uneven, no part of the model is washed out or very dark. Shadows, while not necessary, add depth and character to the model. Additionally, shadows only slightly darken the shadowed geometry.

NOTE

Setting Up Neutral Lighting Conditions
The purpose of neutral lighting condition is to enable rendered or real-time shaded visual evaluation of mesh quality from all angles. Neutral lighting setup emulates natural lighting of an object suspended in space being illuminated by one or two indirect light sources, by placement of Phong light sources—usually one or two spotlights, and a number of low-intensity Omni/Radial light sources, with only one of the spotlights being a shadow casting light. The model is illuminated in a way that

allows evaluation of geometry from all angles without having any part of geometry not illuminated or being washed out by the light sources. Neutral lighting can be effectively set up in form•Z or in the animation environment. The most important condition of neutral lighting is that there is no dramatic effect that is created by the light placement. Dramatic lighting takes attention away from the model, and may obscure imperfections. While dramatic lighting plays an important role in image composition and storytelling, it interferes with the model evaluation process. Shadows pose a special problem, as they should be used to add depth and a sense of proportion. However, dark shadows can darken shadowed geometry to a point that problems in those areas would be obscured. Lights and shadows need to be defined in a way so that shadows do not darken the geometry by more than 50%. This accomplished through a clever placement of key shadow casting spotlight and non-shadow casting fill lights.

To create neutral lighting conditions within form•Z, follow the specs below. Delete all existing lights. form•Z does not allow deletion of SUN light. Nullify the SUN light by turning it off and set its Basic Intensity to 0%.

1. Create a Cone light and place it as shown in Figure 4.7 and set its properties as such.
   Name: Key Spot
   Type : Cone
   Basic Intensity: 60%
   Outer Angle: 38
   Inner Angle: 1
   Falloff: Square
   Shadow: Soft Mapped
   Quality: High
   Softness: 20
   Tolerance: 1
   Resolution: 2 or 3
2. In the Lights Menu Window, copy the KeySpot Cone light and rename it KeySpotFill. Change the following parameters:
   Basic Intensity: 40%
   Turn shadows OFF
3. Create a new Point light with following properties.
   Name: Fill1
   Type: Point
   Basic Intensity: 30%
   Falloff: Square

Radius: See Note below

The radius of Point light is dependent on the scale of the object. The DSV is 30′ in length. The radius of the Point light should be about 10 to 15 times the length of the model. In the DSV project the radius of the Point light was 400′. Notice that the fill Point lights are placed so that the distance between the light and the model is 1/2 radius.

4. Create three copies of the Fill Point light and place them as shown in Figure 4.7.

Take special note of the staggering of the Fill Point light position. Because of their distance from the model combined with the fall-off definition, the amount of light hitting the model from each light is substantially less than 30. But because there are four of them lighting the model from all directions, and they do not cast shadows, the four lights light the model more or less evenly. In effect, they fill the space that the model occupies with dim light. The main shading of the model comes from two key spotlights. Because we want to avoid having dark shadows we only have one of them casting shadows. To avoid washing the model out with light, the total strength of the two key spotlights is equal to 100%. Having a combined Key light strength larger than 100% will introduce extra illuminance into the scene. The 100% dark shadows cast by the shadow Casting spotlight will be lightened by the unshadowed light of the second nonshadow Casting Cone light, resulting in partially dark shadows. Since the shadow Casting light is set at 60% and the nonshadow Cone light is set to 40%, the cast shadow darkens the geometry by 60%. The shadowed areas are further lightened by the Point Fill light, resulting in shadows that are effectively only 30–40% in strength. The Fill lights also act as indirect diffuse light sources, lighting the geometry obscured from illumination by the Cone lights. This setup loosely emulates lighting conditions in a studio where physical models are created, and allows examination of the model from all angles. While this lighting setup is by no means radiosity, it loosely emulates effects of radiosity processing by cheating diffuse interreflections. Unfortunately, complex moderately meshed curvilinear models do not lend themselves well to radiosity processing as they have too many polygons for the radiosity to compute quickly. Yes it's true, even in this day and age of inexpensive radiosity engines, an animator still needs skill to manually light the scene using Phong lighting. The approach just described works well in form•Z, 3D Studio MAX, Cinema 4D XL, and ElectricImage. All of these packages use similar Phong-based shading models and all have similar light types. ElectricImage Animation System has specific control for shadow darkness in its Light Control dialog. In EI only

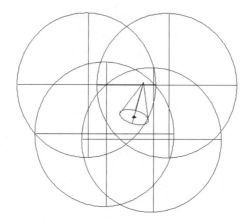

Front

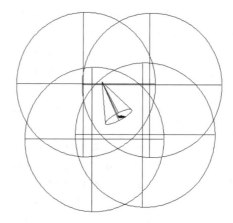

Right

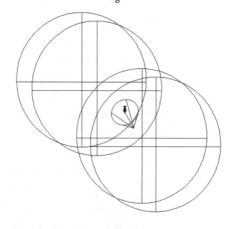

Top

FIGURE *Creating a cone light from 3 views.*
4.7

a single key spotlight needs to be created with its Shadow Darkness set to 50%. Point lights in ElectricImage are called "Radial lights." 3DS MAX creates shadows that are sharper than RenderZone shadows given the same Spotlight definition and placement, so to get shadows of similar softness in MAX, the Buffer size and Samples need to be reduced in MAX. 3D Studio MAX is a very powerful and popular package for animating digital miniatures (as opposed to characters). As a matter of fact, the neutral lighting procedure was worked out in MAX. In Cinema 4D XL set the shadow of the shadow casting KeySpotlight to be SOFT 768 by 768 with Bias set to .01%. For Point Fill Light placement use Figure 4.7 to approximate the fall-off distance. The circles represent the fall-off limit of the Point lights in form•Z.

Figure 4.4 shows the base 64 by 64 sphere, DSV model mesh by itself and overlayed on top of a storyboard image. Notice how the mesh density is fairly uniform across the hull of the submersible and is heavier only in certain areas. For the most part, its mesh density is similar or slightly heavier than that of the base sphere.

Project Considerations and System Capabilities

As mentioned, project considerations and animation system capabilities also a play a vital role in mesh density and topology determination. When dealing with output resolution, we only need to optimize the mesh density. However, for a model to animate, texture, and render, with high quality results, we need to optimize its mesh not only in its geometrical sense (mesh density) but also in its topological distribution. Project considerations consist of technical and artistic direction. Both drive how the model is going to be animated. The capabilities of tools within an animation environment impacts technical direction. As a modeler you need to have knowledge of how your model is going to be animated and manipulated by the animator. Of special importance is the kind of deformation that your model will undergo. When evaluating or planning topological constriction, you must know the answer to two prime questions:

- Where is the model going to be animated?
- How is the model going to be animated?

The where deals with which animation package and supporting plug-ins will be used, and specific requirements of the animation package and the plug-ins. form•Z is primarily a polygonal modeler. With few exceptions, all geometric export formats in form•Z are polygonal in nature. Internally, form•Z has powerful and sophisticated parametric modeling tools. Even so, in the majority of modeling, the resulting surfaces will be polygonal meshed surfaces. As such, form•Z is best employed as a front-end modeler to professional polygonal-based animation packages such as 3D Studio MAX, Cinema 4D XL, Lightwave 3D, and ElectricImage Animation System. Those animation packages, being primarily polygonal, all deal with imported polygonal geometry in a similar manner, with minor differences. Let's discuss some of them.

3DS Studio MAX Capability Consideration

form•Z makes an excellent replacement modeler for Kinetix 3D Studio MAX. Capabilities provided by form•Z can only be matched by augmenting 3DS MAX with numerous plug-ins. form•Z's superior modeling workflow and tool implementation, combined with unmatched layer control creates a modeling environment that allows faster creation of geometry with increased flexibility. For the most part, geometry modeled in form•Z can be directly exported into 3DS MAX without any modifications. However, there are certain times when user intervention is required, most of the occasions deal with the difference in how MAX and form•Z handle polygons. One of the main modeling strengths of form•Z is its ability to work with complex polygons. A complex polygon is one that is composed out of more than four vertices. 3D Studio MAX, on the other hand, is unable to deal with complex polygons, either imported or internally. Even geometry created within MAX is triangulated, although it may be drawn as quads. If you go to DISPLAY Tab inside MAX and turn off EDGES ONLY found under DISPLAY OPTIMIZATION you will notice that even rectangular polygons are each composed of two triangles. 3DS format, the main exchange format between 3D Studio MAX and form•Z supports only triangles. All exported polygons are triangulated by form•Z upon export via 3DS format. During 3DS export form•Z follows the same rules as it does using the Triangulate tool, only it will triangulate all faces, not just the nonplanar ones. Figure 4.8 shows a lofted surface as it appears in form•Z and the triangulated version that is exported via 3DS format. The triangulation of complex polygons may lead to shading anomalies within 3D Studio MAX. Depending on different Triangulation options, complex polygons will be triangulated to produce different topological structures. Figure 4.9 shows the effect of different triangulation options on a single complex polygon.

There are a number of tools and techniques within form•Z that generate complex and quadrilateral polygons and triangulation of those has several repercussions for us. First and most obvious is that a single complex polygon in form•Z translates to a multitude of triangles in 3DS file. Normally, this would not constitute a problem; however, a 3DS file has an internal limit of 65,535 triangles per object. So, while any 3DS file can have up to 65,535 objects in it,

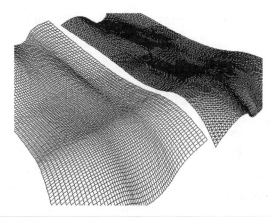

FIGURE 4.8 *A lofted surface as it appears in form•Z and the triangulated version that is exported via 3DS format.*

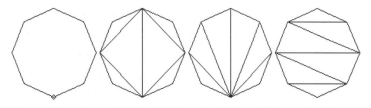

FIGURE 4.9 *The effect of different triangulation options on a single complex polygon.*

no single object may have more than 65,535 triangles in it. This limit can cause problems on complex single mesh models such as characters. If form•Z detects a mesh that exceeds this 65K limit it will break the mesh into two separate objects, requiring that the two objects be attached in 3D Studio MAX and their vertices welded. To prevent this happening, we recommend that all objects that are to be exported be manually triangulated prior to exportation. With manual triangulation you have direct control over how each and every object is triangulated, and you know its precise triangle count. While each surface may benefit more from one type of triangulation than from another, on the average it is the third triangulation method that normally yields the best results. Remember that a form•Z mesh can have a combination of complex and simple polygons. # OF Faces reported in Query will not tell you how many triangles the mesh will generate, although you can roughly estimate that the minimum number of triangles for a mesh containing no triangular will have 2X number of polygons. This is assuming a perfectly stitched mesh containing 100% four-point polygons. A good rule of thumb to use is to exercise caution, if the Query tool reports the number of faces to be more than 30,000. More detailed discussion on integration of form•Z and 3D Studio MAX takes place in Chapter 3.

Segment Bunching and Slivering

The second problem we have to deal with when triangulating meshes is segment bunching and triangular slivering. Result 2 in Figure 4.9 shows an example of segment bunching. Segment bunching occurs when four or more segments share a common point and the angle between the segments is small. In many cases, this bunching creates a smoothing problem for the 3DS MAX Scanline Renderer resulting in an ugly darkening of the area. On surfaces with slight curvature this, most likely, will not cause a problem, but if the point where segments meet is on a moderately curving area of the mesh, the darkening can be quite dramatic. Although it may be possible to alleviate the problem through modulation of smoothing attributes on affected triangles, it is best to avoid this type of mesh topology. Meshes triangulated with Methods 1 and 2 may also exhibit triangular slivering. A sliver is triangle whose width is less than 1/6 of its length. There are three primary reasons for avoiding slivered triangles:

- Possible shading anomalies caused by incorrect smooth shading of slivers.
- Slivered triangles prevent clean deformation of the mesh by causing shading anomalies during deformation, even though the mesh renders clean when it is not deforming.
- Slivered triangles can cause problems when special effects are applied to the mesh.

This very evident if the mesh undergoes a polygonal explosion effect. Most explosion effects in 3DS MAX and other 3D animation applications break the affected model into polygons or random groups of polygons—they do not break the triangles themselves. Bomb2 spacewarp in 3DS MAX breaks each quadrilateral polygon into its two element triangles. So, having slivered triangles in the exploding mesh creates debris that is out of proportion and does not look realistic.

Okay, now that we are aware of the triangulation problems we may encounter, what can we , as 3D modelers, do to prevent them from occurring. When modeling for 3D Studio MAX and other applications that require triangulated geometry, or if the exchange format requires triangulated meshes, follow these guidelines:

- First and foremost, create geometry that is arranged mostly out of quadrilateral polygons topologically arranged along regular rectangular grids.

The reason is that a single quad polygon will always be broken cleanly into two triangles. Rectangular polygons can only be triangulated one way: broken into two equal-size triangles. So regardless of the triangulation method, meshes with rectangular polygon grids will always triangulate and render clean. Figure 4.10 shows a close-up of the DSV hull before and after triangulation. The hull was triangulated using Method 3.

- When creating curvilinear surfaces, model so that the polygon grids follow along natural lines of force. Figure 4.11 shows the hull of the DSV as it was modeled inside form•Z. Notice that the blended surfaces comprising the hull have rectangular topology, and all the topological lines of force of the surfaces flow into each other. This topological arrangement results in a very clean rendering. It also allows the mesh to undergo geometric deformations, to a point, without losing its geometric integrity. So why would anyone ever deform the hull of a DSV? Well, if the shot call for the hull to buckle and eventually implode under water pressure,

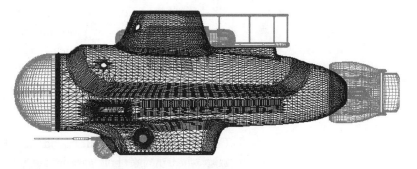

FIGURE *Closeup of DSV hull before and after triangulation.*
4.10

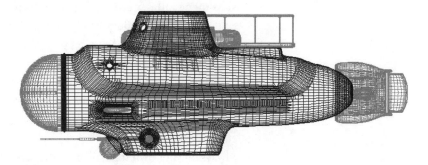

FIGURE *The hull of the DSV as it was modeled inside form•Z.*
4.11

the geometry of the hull would need to cleanly deform with deformation lattices applied.

- Avoid creating polygons that have their length more than 6X their width. This may not always be possible, and with smart modeling even long polygons and slivers can shade cleanly. On nondeforming flat surfaces, neither long quads or slivers are a concern. However, it is best to avoid them if possible.

- Manually break down complex or long polygons into quads and triangles using the Insert Point and Insert Segment tools. Quite frequently, during the modeling process, you may end up with a few complex polygons, even though the rest of the mesh has nice four-point rectangular polygons. You can prevent potential shading and triangulation problems from forming in the first place by manually breaking those complex polygons into quads and triangles. The areas that typically benefit from this treatment are stitched segments or trims in the mesh. In those areas, it is best to directly specify how the points are connected and not rely on the Triangulate tool. The tools to use for that are INSERT POINT/ SEGMENT in conjunction with various SNAP options. SNAP options that are usually used in this procedure are Snap To Point, Snap To Segment, Snap To Middle Of Segment, and Snap To Segment Part. Figure 4.12 shows the hull of the DSV (during the modeling process) before and after manual cleanup was done. Notice that complex polygons mostly occur along stitch edges, where the blend surface joins one of the main hull surfaces, and where the superstructure is blended into the hull. Complex polygons also occur around trim edges; in this case, a trim edge exists where the port hole was trimmed into the hull. The intent of the cleanup is to end up with as many four point-polygons as possible, with the rest being triangles. When breaking complex polygons down, try to keep the resulting quads and triangles as square as possible. This is a guideline, but you should avoid creating long polygons as much as possible. Manual cleanup of surfaces prior to triangulation and exportation can be a time-consuming chore depending on the complexity of the surface, its mesh density, and the number of surfaces to be cleaned up. This step should be performed as the last step prior to triangulation and export of the meshes. This can be usually put off until the final shot geometry is needed.

- Always do your own triangulation; that is, manually triangulate all objects to be exported using the Triangulate tool. Additionally, triangulate only copies of the objects—there is no Untriangulate tool. We recom-

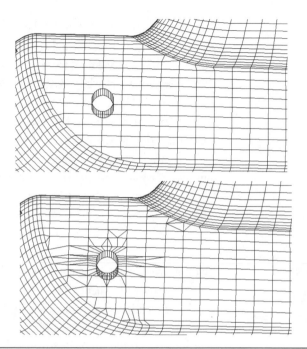

FIGURE   *The hull of the DSV (during the modeling process) before and after manual*
4.12   *cleanup was done.*

mend that you create specific export layers and Paste copies of exportable geometry into them. Triangulate those copies, test shade in RenderZone, and export them. Detailed discussion of integration of form•Z with various animation packages can be found in Chapter 3. Manually triangulating the exportable meshes allows you to catch any topological problems prior to exportation, helping you avoid surprises and wasted time.

The procedures and guidelines just described work very well when using form•Z in support animation done in 3D Studio MAX. Fortunately, these guidelines are all valid when using form•Z with just about any other polygonal animation package. Deformations, which are main considerations of mesh topology, work along similar lines in all applications that support polygonal deforms. However, there a few small details that we should take into consideration. Cinema 4D XL and ElectricImage Animation system do not need triangulated meshes, although both these packages fully support them. In both Cinema 4D XL and EIAS, meshes composed of primarily four-point polygons shade equal to or better than if they were triangulated. So, when exporting to Cinema 4D XL or ElectricImage, there is no need to triangulate the mesh. Still, you must manually break down the complex polygons along the stitch and trim edges as described. If you do not, the rendering engines in Cinema 4D XL and ElectricImage will do it for you. This may or may not cause problems. In our experience we have imported models with complex polygons from form•Z into Cinema 4D XL and ElectricImage. In some instances there were no noticeable shading errors; in other cases, a cleanup of geometry was required. Additionally, some rendering errors only crept up when the model was animated. We recommend that these potential problems be avoided by manually cleaning up all your complex polygons prior to exportation. Texture mapping considerations, model substitution, and other application and plug-in-specific details are discussed in Chapter 3.

Type of Animation Consideration

We now have a solid understanding of the factors affecting model construction given output requirements and target animation package. Earlier in the chapter, it was mentioned that animation type is one of the prime factors that needs to considered. Now we must consider it. The type of animation that the model will undergo greatly affects how the model is to be built. Regardless of the rendering method, any model can only be animated using four major types of animation:

- Standard keyframed transforms
- Deformations
- Bone deformations
- Special effects

It must be understood that a model built for one type of animation may not be suitable for other type. Specifically, a polygon count optimized model built for path animation may not be suitable for deformation animation or certain types of special effects. Conversely, a model built for heavy-duty deformation work is an overkill, in terms of polygon count, for animation involving the model moving from point A to point B along a path. It is of vital importance that you, the modeler, understand what kind of animation that the model may undergo. Close communication with technical directors, art directors, and animators is crucial. Your model may be used for more than one shot, it may be subjected to multiple types of animation in each one. Using the DSV as an example, in one shot the DSV moves across the camera field of view with the camera panning to follow its descent. In another shot it may be attacked by a deep sea creature that dents it, then drags it down into the ocean depths, where we witness it being crushed by the water pressure and imploding. Although this sounds kind of gruesome, it is indicative of the kind of actions that today's scripts call for. During the three shots the model undergoes three major animation types. It moves, keyframe transforms. It is dented and crushed, complex deforms. Finally it implodes, special effects animation. Unless you wish to build three models, each one optimized for a particular shot, the model needs to perform flawlessly under all three animation types.

Now let's discuss the animation types and the demands they put on geometry.

Keyframe Transforms

Keyframe transforms is the simplest type of animation and places the least demands on you as the modeler. The Spherical Mesh Density Determination technique described earlier in the chapter is intended to determine mesh density for curvilinear models that will undergo transform animation only. Keyframe Transform is an animation type where the model only undergoes geometric transforms. It is important to understand that transforms are relational; that is, if the model does not change its position, orientation, and scale, but the camera does, we still need to treat the model as if it is transforming. One of the basic principles of animation is that there should always be some kind of movement in the scene. Geometric transforms are

- Translation
- Rotation
- Uniform Scale

Translation is movement of the model from point A to point B in a scene or movement along a path. Translation of the model does not require that the model itself move.

For animation, translation of the model is referring to relative movement between it and the camera. If the model is static in scene, but it is the camera that is animated, there is movement of the model *in relation* to the camera. We define *camera* as either defined optical emulation with Field Of View, Aperture, and Focal Length, etc., or any point of view used to render the scene. The standard method of animating movement is by explicitly defining positional keyframes, or by designating a spline object as a path.

Like translation, *rotation* of the model should always be thought of in relation to the camera. Camera roll has the same effect as if the camera was kept still and the model rotated.

Uniform scale is best thought of as a change in the screen area taken up by the model. It can result from either geometric uniform scale of the model or change in relative proximity between the model and the camera.

Transform animation places the least strain on the model. The requirements are that the model render cleanly, and can be effectively texture mapped. Clean rendering is a combined product of optimal mesh density, mesh topology, and correctly assigned smoothing parameters. The Spherical Mesh Density Determination method is a very effective tool for creating curvilinear models for transform animation. Texture mapping preparation involves "cutting up" the model into pieces for effective texture mapping. Texture mapping preparation for various applications and smoothing parameters are discussed in detail in Chapter 3.

Deformation Animation

The broadest definition of *deformation* is any change in geometric shape, but not topology, of a model. For our situation we will modify this definition to mean any *animated* change in geometric shape but not topology of the mesh. Bend, Twist, Wave, Taper, Shear, Skew, Conform To Spline, and Bulge are all examples of standard geometric deformations found in most 3D animation applications. Nonuniform Scale is also a deformation, as it has the effect of stretching a model along specified axes. In some applications NU Scale is actually a Stretch tool. Deformation occurs in a model whenever a region of its topological entities is transforming at a different rate from others, and the result is that the elements change their relative positions to each other. Let me try to put this in perspective: Whenever a model is transformed (moved, rotated, uniformly scaled), all its topological elements (points, segments, and faces) all transform at a constant rate and retain their relative positions to each other. When a cube is translated (moved), all eight points are moved along the same vector with the same amount of positional displacement. The straight-line distance between any two points does not change. Likewise, in rotation, all points are rotated by the same angular amount about a same center of rotation. As in translation, the distance between any two points does not change. When the cube is uniformly scaled, only the distances between the points change, but not their angular relationship. Angular relationship between two points is the vector along which you must travel to go from one point to another. When a model is scaled 2X, the distance between any two points is doubled, but the angular relationship remains constant. In a polygonal mesh model, any two segments sharing a point have a particular *aspect* to each other. Aspect is the angle between the two segments. When a mesh is transformed, the aspect angle remains constant.

Deformation occurs whenever angular relationships between points and segment aspects change. These changes can apply to all topological elements of the model or to a selected region. In either case, the model is being deformed. Its geometric shape is changed. Although not usually associated with deformation, subobject transforms are also deformations. Many professional 3D animations packages allow animation to apply not only to objects but to their topological elements. Groups of faces, points, or segments can be selected and animated over time. Because even simple transformations of subobjects elements change the geometric shape of the model, their animation should be viewed as deformation of the model.

Depending on type, deformations affect the mesh in different ways. They do have some effects in common that we 3D modelers have to be aware of:

- **Increase the distances between points.** This causes segments to become longer and polygons to enlarge. Typically, this stretching occurs on the "outside" of the deformation.

- **Change the aspect angle between segments.** The aspect angle change is caused by different relative movement of points on the mesh. After a certain amount of deformation is reached, the mesh begins to exhibit polygonal silhouetting. Segment aspect change and differential vertex movement go hand in hand.

- **Decrease the distances between points.** A decrease in straightline distances between points causes decrease in segment length and reduction in polygon size. The problem occurs when the segment length is decreased by more than 100%. In those cases, polygons begin to intersect with each other, causing very severe shading anomalies. This effect occurs mostly with bend and bone deformation and on the "inside" of the deformation.

Figure 4.13 shows the "inside" and "outside" of a standard bend deformation.

Figure 4.14 shows an undeformed lofted mesh surface. The mesh density of the model is optimal if it were a transform animated only. Figure 4.15 shows the same surface undergoing animated bed deformations along its Y-axis (height). At a 45 degree bend, no problems are noticeable. At 90 degrees, the bend faces on the "outside" of the bend are stretched out in a radial fashion. At 90 degrees, polygonal silhouetting is just beginning to form and may not be noticeable when rendered due to "fuzzing" and blurring of the geometry by motion blur. At 180 degrees, the segments on the outside of the bend have been stretched to such an amount that polygonal silhouetting is clearly visible.

Although this example only shows bend deformation, it clearly presents a concept that, no matter what kind of deformation a mesh will undergo, a geometrical deficiency will only surface once deformation reaches a certain

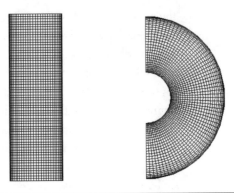

FIGURE *The "inside" and "outside" of a standard bend deformation.*
4.13

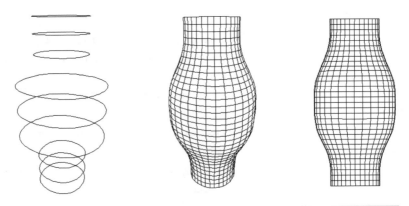

FIGURE *An undeformed lofted mesh surface.*
4.14

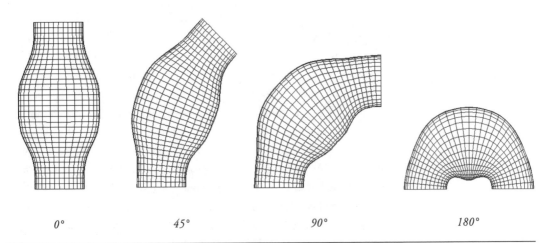

0°	45°	90°	180°

FIGURE *The same surface undergoing animated bed deformations along its Y-axis (height).*
4.15

amount. There is, of course, a "grace period", a grey area where the degree of deficiency is marginal. As modelers working in a production environment, it is vital for us to know what kind of deformation the model will undergo and to what amount. Unless the animation system that the model will be animated in has some kind of feature that would detect polygonal silhouetting and intelligently break up the model, the only to avoid polygonal silhouetting problems in deformable meshing is to increase their mesh density.

The Spherical Mesh Density Determination method, discussed earlier in the chapter, works well for determining by how much to increase the density. All of the method's rules apply; however we must add Deformation Type and amount to the list of project parameters:

- Approximate motion of the model in question
- Approximate motion of the camera
- Approximate scale and size of the model in project units
- Planned rendering mode of the mode
- Type of deformation
- Maximum deformation amount

Exercise

In the following exercise we will use the Spherical Determination method to create a lofted surface for animated bend deformation. We have the following information:

Output resolution: HDTV 1900 × 1080
Optimized revolved sphere: 72 segments

1. Create a new project and rename the default layer to "Crossections." From the top view create a 24″ by 24″ rectangle (Figure 4.16).
2. Create, place, and scale eight copies of the rectangle as shown in Figure 4.17. The middle three rectangles have dimensions of 36″ by 36″. Note the Z-axis (height) locations.
3. Convert the rectangles to 64-point 3rd Degree B-Spline C-CURVES using the C-CURVE tool, as shown in Figure 4.18.

Let's assume that the lofted surface will be animated using a bend deformation. The deformation will be synchronized to a sound file, and the maximum angle amount will be 180 degrees along the Y-axis (height). In many animation applications, Y is used as the height axis, and Z is the depth or length. By default, the Z-axis is height in form•Z. The base of deformation will be bottom center.

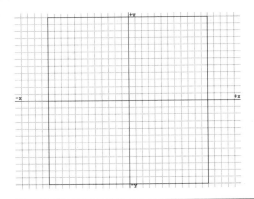

FIGURE **4.16** *Top view of 24" × 24" rectangle.*

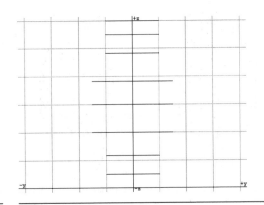

FIGURE **4.17** *Eight copies of the rectangle.*

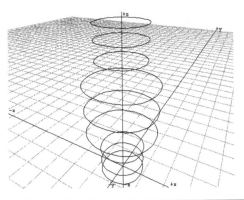

FIGURE **4.18** *Rectangle converted to 64-point 3rd degree B-spline C-curves.*

4. Now we will create a test by lofting the C-Curves with the C-Mesh tool. Open the C-Mesh tool and set it options as follows;

Construct Plain Mesh

Construct Directly

Length Of Net: Use Existing

Depth Of Net: Use Control Line Intervals

Mesh Length; # Of Segments: 64, Smooth

Mesh Depth; # Of Segments: 32, Smooth

Controlled Mesh Smoothing Options; Length: B-Spline, Depth: B-Spline

Adjust To New: Length and Depth. Both set to Degree: 3, # Of Points:32

Type Of Object: Surface

Status: Keep

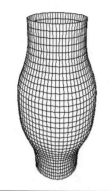
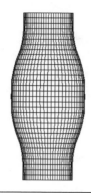
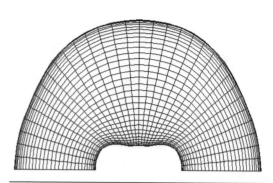

FIGURE **4.19** *A C-mesh lofted mesh.*

FIGURE **4.20** *Right side view with surface deformed at 180 degrees.*

Create a new layer, "Undeformed Surface," and make it the active layer. Prepick the cross-section C-CURVEs in sequential order, and create a C-MESH lofted mesh as shown in Figure 4.19.

5. Now we can test how well the surface with current mesh density deforms. Create a new layer, "Deformed Test Surface." Copy/Paste a copy of the lofted surface into this layer. Hide the previous two layers. Open the Deform tool dialog and set it as follows:

Deform Object: Radial Bend,

Base Reference Plane: XY

Initial Limits; Lower: 0, Upper: 100

Switch to Right Side view and deform the surface 180 degrees (Figure 4.20).

From visual evaluation, we can see that the lofted surface exhibits polygonal silhouetting when deformed the maximum amount (Figure 4.21). Examine the mesh density on the outside of the bend and compare it to the optimum mesh density of the 72 by 72 sphere. From rough estimation it looks like the outside mesh density of the lofted surface is 1/2 that of the reference sphere. Notice that the undeformed lifted surface is meshed optimally for the shot. It is vital that you, as the modeler, to test all the deformable surface as you are modeling them. Initially you can test the deformability of the surface inside form•Z using its Deformation tool. Eventually you will have to bring the uncompleted model into the animation environment and test it there using the same deformation tools that the animator will use.

• We have determined that in its maximum deformed state our surface has only 1/2 of the polygons it needs. Consequently, we must create a new

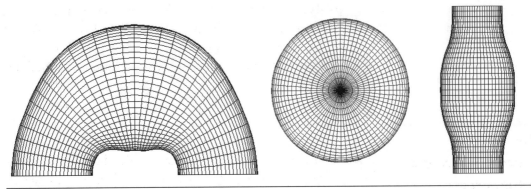

FIGURE **4.21** *Lofted surface exhibits polygonal silhouetting when deformed the maximum amount.*

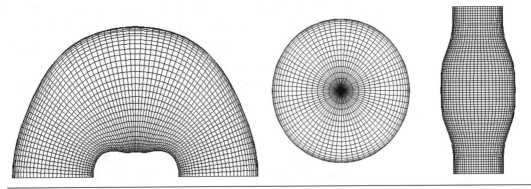

FIGURE **4.22** *Surface with new settings.*

one but we only need to double its polygonal density along the surface's height, which in C-Mesh is Depth of Surface. We can simply double the segment count along the Depth to 64. However, the Reference Sphere has 72, and that is a better segment count to use. Open the C-Mesh settings and make the following change: Mesh Depth; # Of Segments: 72, Smooth.

Delete the first test surface created and create a new one with new settings (Figure 4.22).

Evaluating a new surface we can see that the polygons on the outside of the bend are no longer exhibiting polygon silhouettes. The polygons on the outside of the bend , adjacent to the silhouette of the deformed surface, are nearly the same size as the polygons adjacent to the silhouette of the sphere. Notice that the underformed surface is quite a bit denser then the reference sphere. As you can see, surfaces to be deformed are naturally heavier than the underforming ones. When evaluating mesh density of the deformable surface, we evaluate it from the maximum deformation amount that the surface will be subjected to. In general, the larger the amount of deformation planned for a model, the heavier it should be.

Bones Deformation and Character Animation

One of the hottest topics in the CG industry, and a growing field, is character animation. Character animation is generally considered the hardest area of CG work, because it involves so many disciplines working synergetically. As modelers, we must be able to effectively and efficiently support the character animation process by building characters that are not only artistically pleasing, conforming to art direction, but be built in such a way as to make the technical aspect of the animation as easy and painless as possible. In order to do this successfully we must understand how polygonal-based characters are animated. Not too long ago, about four to five years, character animation on desktop (MAC & Windows) polygonal-based 3D animation systems was limited to simple deformations and simple Target Morphing. Today, Unimesh Bone Deformations are the predominant way of adding movement and gesture to polygon- and spline-based characters. Bones are field of influence deformers that act on vertices that fall within their radius of influence. This radius is user defined and forms a 3D cylindrical-shaped volume with hemispherical ends. Figure 4.23 shows a bone and the region it affects given a user-defined radius. Bones deform the polygonal mesh by capturing the vertices within the area of influence and imparting their transformations upon the vertices. To allow for more natural deformation, many 3D applications that use bones allow a user to define a fall-off region. Basically, this causes vertices on

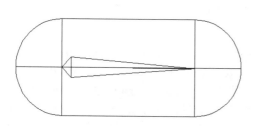
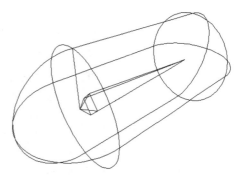

FIGURE *A bone and the region it affects given a user-defined radius.*
4.23

the fringes of the bone to accept less of a bone's transformation than the vertices closest to the bone. All applications that can deform meshes with bones include routines that correctly deform the mesh when regions of two or more bones overlap. Building characters for bones or skeletal deformations requires that we know the following:

- Skeletal arrangement
- Range of movement
- Output resolution
- Proximity of camera to the character

Output resolution of camera object proximity has already been discussed. All the guidelines for mesh density fully apply. In addition we must consider how the bones are going to deform the mesh. Let's assume that the characters we build have normal terrestrial-like body composition; in other words, they are not gelatinous. So, when they move, their flesh gets stretched, distorted, and deformed around the joints. Bone deformation tries to achieve this effect; hence, the need to define bone ranges and fall-offs. If all the bones in a character skeleton were to be defined without ranges, each bone would affect all the vertices in the character. When put in motion, the character would exhibit wobbly, gelatin-like movement. For a character to deform correctly with bones, the following parameters must be met:

- Bone skeleton and character mesh must have similar proportions.
- "Joint" areas of the character mesh must match the bone joints.
- Mesh density should be increased at joint areas.
- Mesh topology should be rectangular. The aspect ration of polygons at the joints should be as close to 1:1 as possible.
- The character should be built in "neutral" pose. The skeleton should also initially be set up in neutral pose.
- Mesh around joint areas should be built so as to compensate for stretching and compression caused by the bone joint.
- Bone ranges must be correctly defined.

Figure 4.24 shows a mesh of a human hand with matching skeleton. Notice that the mesh density varies across the model, it is heaviest around the knuckle areas. The mesh is heavy overall, it was built for high-resolution close-up rendering. Figure 4.25 shows a complete human character built specifically for bone deformation. Notice that it was built in "Spread Eagle" neutral pose. The mesh density of the character varies and is heaviest at and around joints, especially knees, shoulders, elbows, and knuckles. The topology is mostly rectan-

FIGURE **4.24** *Mesh of a human hand with matching skeleton.*

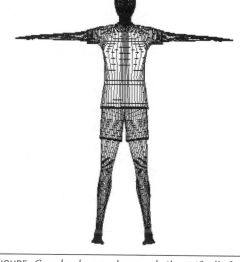

FIGURE **4.25** *Complete human character built specifically for bone deformation.*

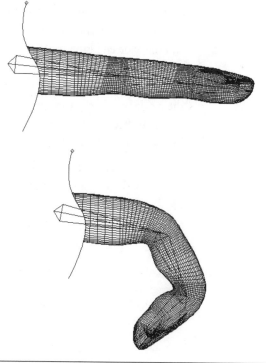

FIGURE **4.26** *A bone deformation of a finger mesh.*

gular, although there are some triangles. Character modeling is covered in detail in Chapters 14 and 15.

Bone deformations are similar to bend deformations in a way that both have "inside" and "outside" of the deformation. While bend generally affects the entire mesh, bone affects regions around the joints. That is, the bending of the mesh is a result of two or more bone ranges overlapping. Like in bend deforms, bones cause stretching of the polygon mesh on the outside of the bone joint and compression of the polygons on the inside. Figure 4.26 shows a bone deformation of a finger mesh. Some high-end bone deformation systems, such as Kinetix Character Studio, Digimation Bones Pro MAX, plug-ins for 3D Studio MAX, offer advanced controls for controlling not only the ranges of the bones but allow discreet assignment of vertices to individual bones. Additionally, Character Studio has controls for secondary deformation of the mesh, such as bulging around the center of the bone, allowing creation of advanced effects like bulging muscles, flesh compression, and fat wobbling, all being tied to the actions of the bone. In most cases, secondary deformation only introduces minor distortion of the mesh. For us, as modelers, it is the compression and stretching of the geometry at bone joints that concerns us the most. In order to compensate for stretching/compression, we recommend that mesh topology around joints be tapered so that the narrow end is on the outside of the joint, and the wide end is on the inside. When the mesh is bone deformed the precompressed polygons on the outside of the deformation will stretch, preserving mesh density and preventing formation of polygonal silhouettes. Conversely, the inside prestretched area of the mesh on the inside of the deformation will compress. Because the polygons are "stretched" they will compress, but will not intersect with each other.

5

Locators and Advanced Rounding

IN THIS CHAPTER

- Introductory Exercise
- Manually Constructing Round Surfaces
- Creating Rounds on Nonplanal Surface Edges
- Render Test and Conclusion

One of the more challenging aspects of modeling surface, as opposed to solids, in form•Z is creating rounded edges on surface objects. form•Z has an excellent beveling and rounding functionality within its Round tool. The Round tool has a limitation, however: it is only capable of rounding segments on a solid object. To round edges on meshed surfaces we would first have adjust it temporarily so it is a solid. This technique, while reliable, is feasible only on simple meshed surfaces. During production modeling, especially when modeling complex surfaces, you will encounter geometrically complex meshed surfaces that simply cannot be "capped" to convert them into a solid. A procedure for rounding edges on a simple meshed surface is as follows:

- The segments for capping faces are identified and selected. The segments should form a closed outline.
- A closed surface is derived using the Derivative Surface tool.
- The step is repeated for every open edge.
- Surfaces are stitched using the Stitch tool to form a solid.
- Segments are rounded using the Round tool.
- The capping faces are removed using topological face deletion.

Introductory Exercise

This simple exercise demonstrates the procedure. First we will create a simple swept surface to use as a starting point.

1. Create two vector lines as shown (Figure 5.1).
2. Convert the two polylines into 24-point 3rd degree B-Spline C-Curves (Figure 5.2).

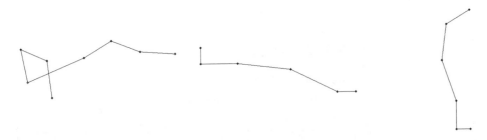

FIGURE *Two vector lines.*
5.1

FIGURE
5.2
Two polylines converted into 24-point, 3rd degree B-spline C-curves.

FIGURE
5.3
Sweep options.

3. Sweep the small curve (cross-section) using the large curve as the path. Use the following Sweep Options (Figure 5.3):

Axial Sweep

Keep Source Perpendicular to Reference Plane

Make Surface Object from Open Source Shapes

Cross-Section Alignment: First Point

We now have a surface that we wish to turn into a solid. The process begins with identifying the open segment chains that we will use to derive an edge curve. In this surface there are three segment chains: the two at the start and end of the surface, and a bottom segment chain. To get the third we first have to create the first two.

4. Create a new layer, *"Cap Faces,"* and make it active.

Select the segments at each end cap.

Derive edge curves using the Derivative Surfaces tool with Selected Segments option and Status of Objects set to Keep.

Close the two open-edge curves with the Edit Line Close/Connect option (Figure 5.4).

FIGURE **5.4** *Close-connect option.*

FIGURE **5.5** *Connect lines/close line sequence.*

FIGURE **5.6** *Point snap option for precise segment insertion.*

5. Derive two-edge curves from the bottom of the surface. Connect them into a single closed surface using the Edit Line **Connect Lines/Close Line Sequence** option (Figure 5.5).

6. Insert segments into the bottom face using the Vector Line tool Insert Segment modifier. In form•Z 3.0 Insert Segment is not a modifier, but a separate tool. Use the Point Snap option for precise segment insertion (Figure 5.6).

We now have a total of four surfaces, the original and three "capping" surfaces. The original surface is converted into a solid by stitching the four surfaces together. The stitching should be performed in a temporary layer, on copies of the four surfaces. Figure 5.7 shows an exploded view of the four surfaces.

7. Create a temporary layer, "*Test Solid 1,*" and make it active. Place copies of the four surfaces in this layer. Hide all other layers. Using the Trim & Split tool with **Stitch** option and **Status Of Object** set to **Delete**, stitch the four surfaces into a single solid object. In form•Z 3.0 Stitch is a separate tool but works identical to form•Z 2.9.5 (Figure 5.8).

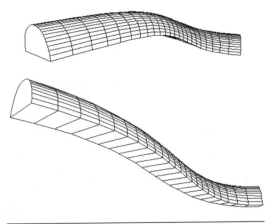

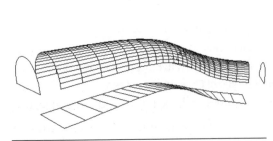

FIGURE **5.7** *Exploded view of the four surfaces.*

FIGURE **5.8** *Stitch the four surfaces into a single solid object.*

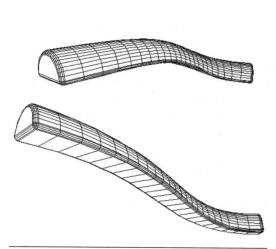

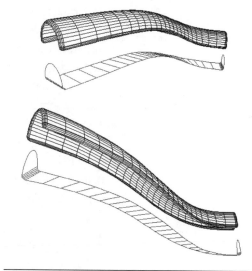

FIGURE
5.9
Round edges with the Round tool.

FIGURE
5.10
Surface with soft, rounded edge.

8. Select all edge segments and round them using the Round tool with the following options (Figure 5.9);

   Plain Rounding:
   Rounding Method: Use Radius: 1/2″
   # Of Rounding Points: 4
   Rounding Type: Edges & Points

9. Select the faces as shown and detach them from the solid using the Separate tool with At Boundary Of Selected Faces option. This results in two surfaces. The surface comprised of detached faces is then deleted. An alternate method is to individually delete each unneeded face using the Delete tool set to Topological Face deletion. The result is that the original surface with sharp edges now has soft rounded edges (Figure 5.10).

Manually Constructing Round Surfaces

The preceding technique is good for adding rounds to simple surfaces, where edges for "capping face" construction are easily identified. However , it is by no means a guarantee that you will only deal with such cases. You may have a meshed surface, the edges of which must be rounded, that has no solution for capping faces, and therefore cannot be rounded using the procedure just described. In such cases we must manually construct a round surface that has, at least, a visual C1 (tangent) continuity to the edge of a meshed surface. By *visual*

I am referring to the fact that surface smoothness in a polygonal mesh is a function of angle aspect between adjacent faces and the Smoothing Attributes of a meshed surface to which they belong. Tangency and other types of surface continuity are discussed in Chapter 7.

Manually constructing a round for an open edge of a meshed surface is by no means a simple or fast procedure, but it does give us freedom of creativity because it frees us from the limitations imposed by Round's requirement of a solid. Additionally, we have the freedom to create and shape the round surface as we see fit.

In its most basic form, rounding open edges on meshed surfaces by manually constructing the round surface has five steps:

1. Identifying the segments of the edge to be rounded.
2. Deriving an edge curve based on those segments using the Derivative Surfaces tool.
3. Creating two or more parallel curves to the edge curve, with identical point count. By *parallel* I am referring to the parallel *curvature* of the curves.
4. Creating a 2nd-degree lofted surface using the C-MESH tool with the curves as cross-sections.
5. Stitching the lofted surface with the main meshed surface.

The following simple example shows the basic procedure in rounding an open edge of a meshed surface.

1. Start by creating a 24″ by 12″ rectangle. Mesh it with the Mesh tool with X:, Y:, & Z: set to 1″. This will be our base surface. We wish to add a round to one of the length edges (Figure 5.11).

    We need to identify and select the segments of the edge we wish to round. The selected segments are then converted to an edge curve using Derivative Surfaces set to **Selected Segments** option, and **Status Of Objects** set to **Keep**. The derived edge curve, a derivative object and a cross-section, is placed into a cross-section layer appropriately named.
2. Create a new layer, "*Edge Round Cross-Sections,*" and make it active. Select the segments as shown, and derive an edge curve as described earlier (Figure 5.12).

The next step is to create two additional curves. We wish to have the round with a 1″ radius. This is easily accomplished by placing two duplicates of the edge curve 1″ apart in a step fashion. If the derived edge curve is the #1 cross-section, then the other two are the #2 and #3 cross-sections, respectively. The #2 cross-section is placed 1″ away from #1 along FORCE VEC-

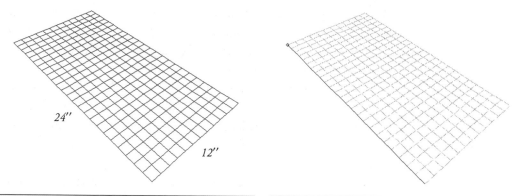

FIGURE *Add a round to one of the length edges.*
5.11

FIGURE *Derive an edge curve.*
5.12

TOR of the last two or three segments in a row perpendicular to the edge curve. The #3 curve is placed below the #2 curve such that a vector line connecting the first point of the #2 and #3 curves is perpendicular to the vector line connecting the first point of the #1 and #2 cross-sections. If a two-segment vector line was drawn connecting the first points of all three cross-sections, the two segments are perpendicular to each other. The placement of the cross-sections is critical to achieving C1 (tangent) continuity of the lofted round edge and the main surface.

3. Since our base surface is planar, the force vector is co-planar with the surface. Place the #2 cross-section, a copy of #1, 1″ away . Place the #3 cross-section, a copy of #2, 1″ down along the perpendicular. Figure 5.13 shows the placement of the three cross-sections and an imaginary vector line (in red) connecting the first points of the cross-sections.

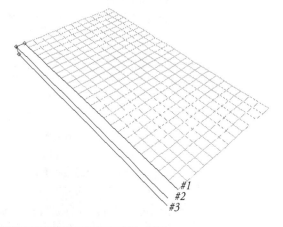

FIGURE *The placement of the three cross-sections and an imaginary vector line.*
5.13

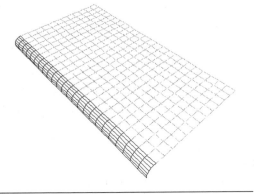

FIGURE **5.14** *Create the round lofted surface.*

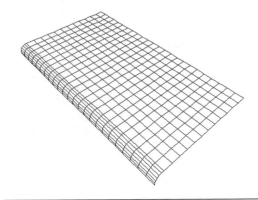

FIGURE **5.15** *New layer surface.*

4. Create the round lofted surface using C-Mesh with the following settings (Figure 5.14):

Controlled Mesh Options;
Construct Plain Mesh
Construct Directly
Length Of Net: Use Existing
Depth Of Net: Use Control Line Intervals
Mesh Length;
At Control Points
Mesh Depth;
Of Segments: 6 *
Per Segment: OFF *
Smooth : ON
Controlled Mesh Smoothing Options;
Length: NONE
Depth; B-Spline, Degree: 2 *, # Of Points: 128
Type Of Object: Open Ends (Surface)
Status Of Objects: Keep

5. Create a new layer, "Surface New." Copy/Paste copies of the base surface and the lofted round surface (Figure 5.15). Stitch the two surfaces together using Trim & Split with Stitch option. Stitch is a separate tool in form•Z 3.0. Set Status Of Objects to Delete to prevent buildup of extra geometry. After stitching the two surfaces, apply Smoothing Attributes to the resulting surface. If the base surface had texture coordinates applied to it in form•Z, the stitched surface will have two texture groups.

Usually it is a good idea to remove the texture group and have the surface textured using a single material.

OF SEGMENTS: X

The number of segments that goes in this field determines the mesh density of the round surface. The desired mesh density is a product of multiple considerations described in Chapter 2.

PER SEGMENT: OFF

This is optional but should be left OFF for C-Mesh loft assemblies containing three cross-sections. The mesh density generated with # Of Segments: 3 and Per Segment: ON is identical to the one generated with # Of Segments: 6 and Per Segment: OFF

DEGREE: X

For loft assemblies containing three cross-sections, this must be set to 2. Setting the degree to 1 will not create any kind of smoothness of the lofted surface. Since the object of the manual round is to create a "rolling ball" type of rounded edge, using three cross-sections the degree must be 2, as circles are perfect 2nd-degree curves. Additionally, when using B-Spline and NURBS smoothing interpolation, the degree must be smaller than the number of cross-sections in the assembly. Thus, the assembly containing three cross-sections can have 2 as its highest degree. For a B-Spline surface to have 3rd-degree B-Spline smoothing, it must have a minimum of four cross-sections. Use higher degree Depth Smoothing and more than four cross-sections only if you need a custom round that is not the "rolling ball" type.

A modification of the procedure that we just completed can be used to round the boundary of the surface, including the four corners. The four corners of the base surface will have to be rounded first. In this case, we are faced with an interesting challenge. We wish to create a rounded edge around the periphery of the surface without having any sharp corners. If we leave the four corners unrounded, we will end up with a result similar to rounding a solid with the Edges option and not Edges & Points. So, prior to generating the cross-sections for the round surface we must modify the boundary edge of the surface by getting rid of all the sharp points. Now we are faced with a limitation. We cannot use the Round tool as it only works on solids, and we cannot use the Edit Line / Fit Fillet tool because it works only on open and closed surfaces, not on meshed surfaces such as ours. Well, it turns out that we can use Edit Line / Fit Fillet if we do the following:

1. Temporarily detach the faces that contain the corner points from the base surface using the Separate tool with At Boundary Of Selected Faces option.
2. Round the corner points using Edit Line / Fit Fillet .
3. Stitch the faces with the base surface to reconstruct the base surface.
4. Create the round surface as described here.
   a. Start with the base surface (Figure 5.16).
   b. Select the four corner faces and separate them from the base surface, using the Separate tool with **Boundary Of Selected** faces option, and **Status Of Objects** set to **Delete** (Figure 5.17).
   c. Using Edit Line / Fit Fillet, round each of the corners using the following settings (Figure 5.18):
      Fit Fillet; # Of Edges: 5, Radius: 1″
   d. Reconstruct the base surface by stitching the five surfaces together using the Trim & Split tool with the **Stitch** option (v 2.9.5) or the Stitch tool (v 3.0) (Figure 5.19). Set **Status Of Objects** to **Delete**.

We now have a modified boundary edge ready for rounding. In the next phase we will add the round to the edge. This round is a called any "edge roll" or "edge lip," terms taken from the sheet metal industry. In cases such as this one, where we need a closed boundary edge, we do not have prepick segments; we can use Derivative Surfaces with **Boundary Of Surface Object** option, which is of a postpick type. When using this option, take care to click on one of the boundary segments.

5. Create a new layer, "*Edge Roll Cross-Sections*." Use Derivative Surfaces with **Boundary Of Surface Object** option to derive an edge curve. Set **Status Of Objects** to **Keep**. This is the #1 cross-section (Figure 5.20).

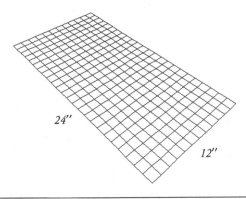

24″

12″

FIGURE *Base surface.*
5.16

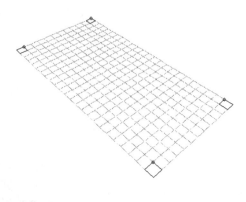

FIGURE *Four corner faces.*
5.17

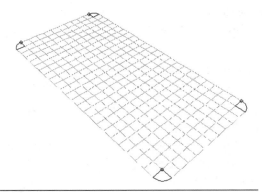

FIGURE *Rounding the corners.*
5.18

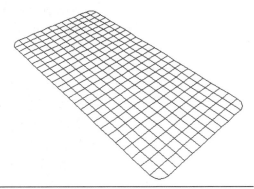

FIGURE *Stitching the five surfaces.*
5.19

In cases where the boundary edge curve is planar, it is always closed, so the #2 cross-section can be created using the Parallel tool. It is important to note that Parallel should only be used if the boundary curve is planar. Nonplanar boundary curves generate erratic shapes when paralleled. Prior to paralleling the boundary curve, it must be temporarily converted into an open surface. This is accomplished easily by topologically deleting any one of its segments. A parallel offset duplicate of the open surface is created using the Parallel Objects tool with **Single Parallel (Surface)** option and **Status Of Objects** set to **Keep**. The two cross-sections are converted back to closed surfaces by closing them with Edit Line / **Close Line**.

6. In the Delete tool, set **Segments** to **Topology (Edges)**. Delete the segment adjacent to the 1st point. Create a parallel duplicate of the curve using the Parallel Objects tool with the following settings (Figure 5.21):

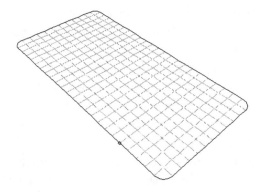

FIGURE *#1 cross-section.*
5.20

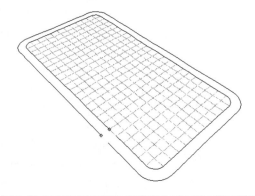

FIGURE *Parallel duplicate of the curve.*
5.21

Single Parallel (Surface): Out
Wall Offset: 1″
Slab Offset: 1″

7. Close the #1 and #2 cross-sections using the Edit Line tool with Close Line/Connect option.
8. Create the #3 cross-section by moving a copy of #2 perpendicular to the plane of the base surface down 1″ (Figure 5.22).
9. Create the loft round surface using C-Mesh with settings as per Figure 14. Stitch the round and base surface together (Figure 5.23).

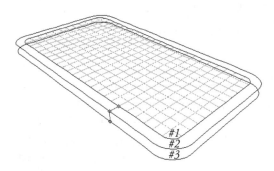

FIGURE #3 cross-section.
5.22

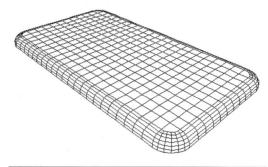

FIGURE Lofted round surface.
5.23

Creating Rounds on Nonplanar Surface Edges

The exercises and concepts presented so far in this chapter have introduced to you to the basics of manually creating edge rolls on open edges of meshed surfaces. Up to this point they have all dealt with simple cases where the edges to be rounded are planar. In most real-world situations, where surface modeling is involved, the edges will not be planar. In the following paragraphs and exercises I present methods and concepts by which an open edge of any arbitrary meshed surface can be rounded.

By far the most complex challenge when creating an edge roll surface for a nonplanar open edge is constructing the #2 and #3 cross-sections. Constructing the cross-sections precisely is the problem. With the three cross-sections constructed, lofting them and stitching the round surface to the base surface is simple. The #1 cross-section (edge curve) is derived using the Derivative Surfaces tool as described, but recall that the #2 and #3 cross-sections must have parallel curvature to the #1 curve. It is the parallel curvature of the #2 and #3 cross-sections that can be difficult to construct. When we start with a planar #1 cross-section, we can easily derive #2 and #3 by simply using the Parallel Objects tool to derive #2, and C-COPY Move to create #3. The problem with nonplanar edge curves is that Parallel Objects does not work correctly with them. Recall that prior to creating a parallel offset duplicate of a closed edge curve, it must be opened by topologically deleting one of the segments, resulting in an open surface object. This open surface is then paralleled and the two open surfaces are converted back into closed surfaces by closing them with Edit Line / **Close Line**. The problem is that the Parallel Objects tool is not capable of correctly paralleling nonplanar open surfaces. The resulting #2 curve is jaggy and has incorrect point placement, rendering it useless. Figure 5.24 shows an example of the #1 cross-section (edge curve), derived from an arbitrary nonplanar meshed surface, and the paralleled #2 cross-section. Note the corrupted geometry of #2. The problem that we need to solve is how to accurately create the #2 and #3 cross-sections. More specifically, we need a reliable method of placing the points of the #2 and #3 cross-sections accurately in 3D space, such that when the three cross-sections are lofted, the radius of the round surface will be consistent regardless of the attitude of the base surface at a given point. Such a method exists by the use of temporary objects called *locators*.

In general terms, a *locator* is a geometric vertex that is defined for the purpose of accurately fixing a location in 3D space. In form•Z any object can be used as a locator, or more precisely its points are. You may not have realized it, but you use a locator any time you use geometric snap options. In effect, when you snap to a point, or a midpoint, or any other geometric snap, you are asking form•Z to accurately locate and define a location in 3D space. However, while it is possible to use any piece of geometry as a locator, it is not wise to do so. It is a good idea to keep locator objects as separate entities from working geometry, and keep the locators in dedicated locator layers. The issue here is clarity.

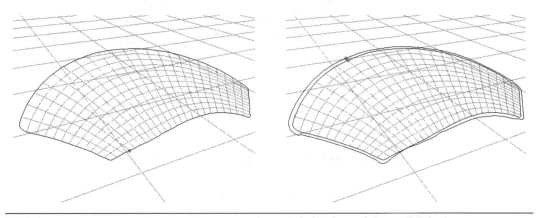

FIGURE   *#1 cross-section derived from an arbitrary non-planar meshed surface and the parallelled #2 cross-section.*
5.24

For example, if you use a surface that curves in all three axes, it is very hard to keep track of a point or a segment chain on the surface as you switch from view to view. It is possible but it takes more effort than is necessary. Likewise, I do not recommend using meshed surfaces or solids as locator objects. In my experience, I have determined that a vector line and point object make the best and most flexible type of locator. A point object was introduced in form•Z 3.0 specifically to serve as a locator. Recall that earlier in the chapter I mentioned that when the first points of the three cross-sections are connected with a three-point (two-segment) vector line, the two segments are perpendicular to each other. This is also true for any three points on each of the cross-sections provided that the three points are similar in terms of their sequence. That is, if a 10th point on each of the cross-sections is connected with a vector line, the segments of that vector line should be perpendicular to each other. This ensures that the depth curvature of the lofted surface is circular when lofted with Depth smoothing set to 2nd-degree B-Spline. The degree to which the segments of the vector are not perpendicular to each other determines the inaccuracy of the curvature of the round surface. We can use the concept of a two-segment vector to accurately construct the #2 and #3 cross-sections. The central idea here is to partially reverse the process as follows:

1. Derive the edge curve (#1 cross-section).
2. Create a two-segment vector line with segments perpendicular to each other and having identical length. The length of each segment is the desired radius of the edge roll.
3. Place and align copies of the locator at each point along the edge curve. The first point of the locator line is snapped to a point on the edge curve (#1 cross-section). Each locator is rotated, using snapped endpoints as a base, so that it is consistent with the force vector of the base surface at the snap point. The force vector is a product of the average of the last two or three segments running along the depth and length of the base surface.
4. Create the #2 and #3 cross-sections using the Vector Line tool with Point Snap option. The points of the #2 cross-section are snapped to the second point on the locator; the points of the #3 cross-section are snapped to the last point on the locator.
5. Loft the edge roll surface with C-Mesh and stitch it with the base surface.

The following example, using the base surface from Figure 5.24, illustrates the process of creating an edge roll surface with a 1″ radius. Note that the corners of the base surface have already been rounded. This is not an exercise.

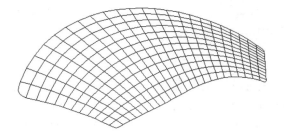

FIGURE
5.25
Base surface curved at all 3 axes.

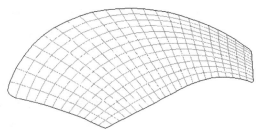

FIGURE
5.26
Edge curve in separate cross-section.

- The base surface is derived by deforming a copy of a surface from Figure 5.19 using the Deform tool so it curves in all three axes (Figure 5.25).
- The edge curve (#1 cross-section) is derived using the Derivative Surfaces tool with **Boundary Of Surface** option. The edge curve is placed in a separate *cross-section* layer (Figure 5.26).
- A two-segment vector line with perpendicular segments, each being 1″ in length, is created. Copies of the vector line are placed on the #1 cross-section and aligned to the force vectors of the surface. The vector lines now serve as locators for the creation of the #2 and #3 curves (Figure 5.27).
- The #2 and #3 cross-sections are created using Vector Line with **Point Snap** option. The points of the #2 cross-section are snapped to the second points of the locators, and the points of the #3 cross-section are snapped to the last points of the locator lines (Figure 5.28).
- The surface is lofted with C-Mesh and is stitched with the base surface (Figure 5.29).

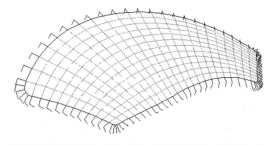

FIGURE
5.27
Vector lines.

FIGURE
5.28
#2 and #3 cross-section creation.

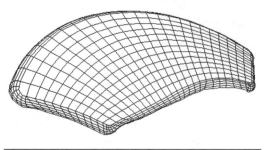

FIGURE *Surface lofted with C-mesh and stitched with the*
5.29 *base surface.*

In the following exercise we will construct a base surface with a nonplanar edge that we will manually round.

1. Create five 5-point polylines as shown. Each small grid square is 1″ (Figure 5.30).

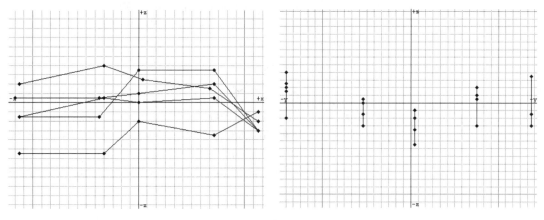

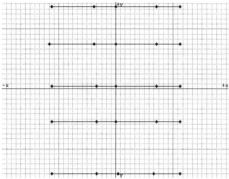

FIGURE *The 5-point polylines.*
5.30

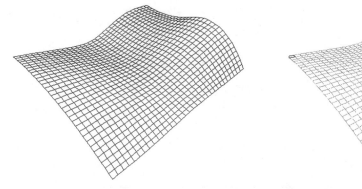

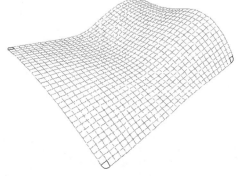

FIGURE **5.31**   *C-mesh surface using the polylines as cross-sections.*

FIGURE **5.32**   *Round the four sharp corners of the surface.*

2. Create a C-Mesh surface using the polylines as cross-sections (Figure 5.31). Use the following C-Mesh Smoothing options:

   Mesh Length; # Of Segments: 32
   Mesh Depth; # Of Segments: 32
   Controlled Mesh Smoothing Options;
   Length: B-Spline, Degree: 3, # Of Points: 128
   Depth: B-Spline, Degree: 3, # Of Points: 128

3. Round the four sharp corners of the surface (Figure 5.32). *Recall the described procedure.*
   a. Detach the faces with the Separate tool.
   b. Round the corner points using Edit Line / Fit Fillet.
   c. Reconstruct the base surface by stitching the faces with the base surface.

   In this case use the following Fit Fillet settings;

   # Of Edges: 4, Radius: 3/4″

4. This step is optional. Connect the point on the corner round with the closest interior point as shown, using the Vector Line tool with Insert Segment modifier (v. 2.9.5) or the Insert Segment tool (v. 3.0) (Figure 5.33). In both versions, use the Point Snap option for precision. The inserted segments will make it easier to align locators at the corners.

5. Derive a boundary edge curve using the Derivative Surfaces tool. Place the #1 cross-section into the "*Edge Roll Cross-Sections*" layer (Figure 5.34).

6. Create a new layer, "*Edge Roll Locators,*" and make it active.
   The edge roll will have a 3/4″ radius; therefore, we need a locator vector line with 3/4″-long segments. Construct the locator line using the Vector

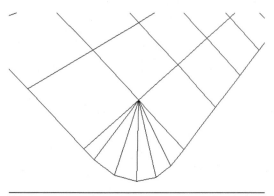

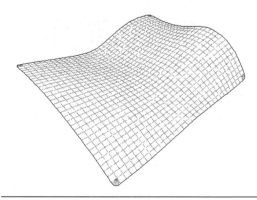

FIGURE **5.33** *Connect the point on the corner round with the closest interior point.*

FIGURE **5.34** *Place the #1 cross-section into the "Edge Roll Cross-Sections" layer.*

Line tool and place using the Point Snap option such that its first point is snapped to the first point of the #1 cross-section.

Align the locator by rotating it about its first point such that it is aligned to the force vector of the surface at the snap point (Figure 5.35). This alignment is visual, form•Z has no tool for automatic alignment. From experience, I have learned that visual alignment yields satisfactory results. As with other things, accuracy of visual alignment is a combination of meticulousness and practice.

7. Place and align copies of the locator at every point on the #1 cross-section (Figure 5.36). This is the most time-consuming portion and its success is critical to the successful completion of the edge roll.

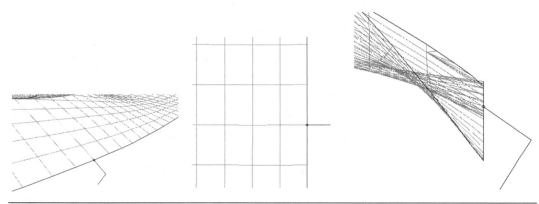

FIGURE **5.35** *Aligning the locator.*

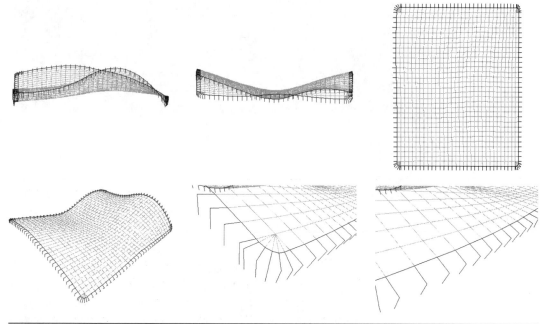

FIGURE
5.36
Align copies of the locator at every point on the #1 cross-section.

8. Create the #2 and #3 cross-sections by snapping their points to the second and third points, respectively, on the locators (Figure 5.37). After completion, verify the following parameters:
   - Matched point count on all cross-sections
   - Matched direction
   - Matched first point
9. Create the edge roll surface using the C-Mesh tool (Figure 5.38).

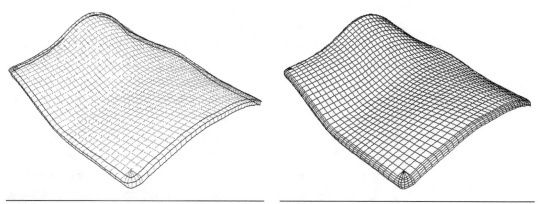

FIGURE *Snap points to second and third points.*
5.37

FIGURE *Edge roll surface.*
5.38

FIGURE *Base surface before and after rounding.*
5.39

Render Test and Conclusion

Figure 5.39 shows the base surface before and after rounding, brought into Cinema 4D XL for render tests. Notice how synthetic the unrounded surface looks, while the rounded surface looks like it has mass and closely resembles a man-made object. Highlight playing along the edge adds a great deal of realism. Remember that real-world objects almost never have perfectly sharp edges. Objects made out of sheet metal usually have edge rolls added to them with metal breaks, for safety. The manual rounding procedure is particularly useful when modeling photorealistic metal objects such as automotive surfaces. As a matter of fact, this procedure is heavily used toward the end of the book, where we model an entire automobile. Because of the time consideration and effort that goes into manually rounding an open edge, we must consider whether or not it should be done in a given case. As a general rule, geometry created for television and film special effects should not have sharp edges that will be seen by the camera. In practical terms, it is not realistic to guess which edges will or will not be seen. The model may be used in a different way for a different shot. It is a good idea to add some rounding or beveling to every open edge to avoid modeling them later. If your model is also destined for low-resolution use, such as multimedia, then an unrounded version of the surfaces should be retained.

There is an important difference between manually rounded meshed surfaces, and solids rounded with the Round tool. The manual method *extends* the surface in the direction of the round. When a well-formed solid, such as a box, is rounded with the Round/Bevel tool, its dimensions and extent box do not change. When a round surface is constructed with the manual method, its dimension and extents change by the amount of the round radius. Figure 5.39 shows an example of this. The rounded surface appears larger than the unrounded one, and it is not because of camera proximity or perspective. When using the manual method, we must consider this and adjust the surfaces accordingly. One way to compensate is, prior to performing the procedure, nonuniformly scale the surface using Nonuniform Scale coupled with Distance Snap set to the intended radius amount.

CHAPTER

6

Profile Lofting Emulation

IN THIS CHAPTER

- Concepts of Profile Lofting
- Types of Cross-Section
- Cross-Section Derivation
- Cross-Section Point Density
- Intermediate Cross-Section Derivation
- Exercises
- Evaluation of Profile Loft Geometry
- Optional Exercise
- Undercuts in Profile Lofting
- Conclusion and Summary

Concepts of Profile Lofting

Profile Lofting is a relatively simple but powerful technique for deriving complex single-object solids or surface mesh objects. Profile Lofting works best for objects whose silhouettes, when viewed from orthogonal views, do not self intersect. The basic concept of Profile Lofting is that the shape of any curvilinear solid or surface can be broken down into four basic construction components: two profiles (one side profile and one top profile), any number of cross-sections, and a general loft trajectory. The side/top profiles are closed curves of any shape, with the only restriction being that they cannot self intersect along the loft trajectory. The Profile Loft object can have any number of cross-sections of any shape with only one hard restriction: All cross-sections must be either closed or open. The cross-sections are placed perpendicular to the length axis and top profile of the intended object and are scaled nonuniformly such that their height conforms to the height of the side profile at a cross-section position when viewed from the side view. The width of the cross-section must conform to the width of the top profile at a cross-section position when viewed from the top view. The cross-sections are derived from the intended shape by visual determination or other means, modeled, and then placed at key locations along the loft trajectory, usually at positions of highest curvature of the profiles and the loft trajectory. Loft trajectory is a curve, which can be closed, but for the majority of Profile Lofting cases the loft trajectory is a straight line, a vector. Loft trajectory is not part of the geometry; it describes a single major flow curve of the object, something akin to a spine of the desired surface. Additionally, loft trajectory defines the rotational value of a given cross-section. For optimal results, cross-sections are not only scaled to match the respective height and width of the profiles, but are also rotated as to be perpendicular to the tangent of the loft trajectory curve.

When all components of the profile loft are put together ready for lofting using the C-Mesh tool, it is called "Profile Loft Assembly." A simple example of a 3D object suitable for modeling with Profile Lofting is an egg. The side and top profiles of the egg are irregular biased ellipsoids, and it has a single circular cross-section. The loft trajectory of an egg is a straight line starting at the top pole of the egg and terminating at the bottom pole.

An excellent case for using the Profile Lofting technique is building a lifting body design aircraft. The very gradual smooth blend of the airfoil surfaces blending into the fuselage can be modeled very effectively, easily, and quickly using Profile Lofting. The majority of the lifting body aircraft is the fuselage, and you can derive the 3D form rather quickly. The trick and the most time-consuming task is cross-section derivation and placement, a subject that will be covered later on.

PROFILE DERIVATION

A profile of the object is the closed curve describing its silhouette when looking at the object from the orthogonal side and orthogonal top view. There are a number of ways to derive profile curve. The best and easiest way is to use scanned plan drawings of the target object as underlays. The plans should contain side and top elevations. Simply sketch a polyline around the desired shape and convert to C-Curve. Use C-Curve controls to match as closely as possible the curvature of the C-Curve to the curvature of the elevation drawing. Be sure to include enough control points in the source polyline to handle the curvature changes. If you find you are unable to match the curvature because you lack necessary control points, ESC or cancel the C-Curve editing, UNDO if necessary to revert back to the original polyline, then use insert points as necessary.

For elevations that have a complex mix of curves and straight line segments, it is a good idea to create a C-Curve for each region and then use EDIT LINE/JOIN/CLOSE to join the separate curves and lines into one complete closed line. That way, you can keep individual C-Curves relatively simple and can zoom in on one area at a time. Once you are satisfied with the shape of the individual C-Curves, join them together and close the resulting 2D shape. Fine-tune the shape by zooming in and working at the vertex level, by either inserting or deleting vertices. The profile curves will only be used as visual guides, so don't spare the vertices on curving areas. You should be able to zoom fairly tightly on the curving region of the profile without seeing polygonal silhouettes. Conversely, it is a good idea to delete any unnecessary vertices on the straight regions of the curve. If your underlay is line art, you can use a raster-to-vector application such as Adobe Streamline to convert the lines on the drawing into Illustrator format, and then import that file into form•Z. You will still have to clean the vector by joining lines and deleting extraneous segments and points. If your source is a physical model, try to outline the profiles on the sheet of paper, if the shape permits it. A quick-and-dirty way to get rough profiles is with a dark room, a heavy-duty flashlight or lamp, a table, and suspension wire. Make sure there is at least one unobstructed wall in the room. Place the table close to the wall. Place the object on the edge of the table closest to the wall. If you can, suspend the object about 6″ away from the wall. Tape a large sheet of paper on the wall directly behind the object. Place the flashlight or the lamp very close to the object so the center of the light beam is perpendicular to the wall and bisects the object. Turn off all the lights and illuminate the object with the flashlight or lamp. Adjust the position of this light source so that it casts the sharpest possible shadow. With a pencil, carefully outline the shadow cast by the object on the taped paper. The outline should roughly approximate the silhouette of the object. If you have a very bright direct source, placed very close, the shadow should be very close to the desired shape of the profile. Repeat this process to get the other profile. Now simply scan them in and use the scans as underlays to generate your profiles. If you can, get an expendable clay molding of your object and then just slice the molding in half and trace. The last method, and the least reliable one, is visual inspection. Hold the object up to the light at eye level, close one eye and look at the silhouetted shape. Unless you are very good at judging form, you should refrain from this method as it is the least reliable. However, if nothing else is available and you have the luxury of playing fast and loose with the shape, then the visual inspection can work in many cases. Undoubtedly, there may be other methods of deriving profiles, feel free to pursue and experiment with them. For my money though, the best, most reliable, and least prone to error method is to use bitmap underlays. When using properly prepared underlays, you have the most control over the shape and topology of the profiles. Additionally, form•Z has excellent control over the position and scale of its underlays, so you can set up the underlay to match the real-world unit dimensions of your desired model. Regardless of how the profile shapes are derived, all initial profile construction should be done in its own layer, which is appropriately named. I recommend naming that layer "TRACED PROFILES." If you generated the profile curves from underlays, you should not change either the underlay settings or the position and orientation of the virgin profiles.

Select the top and side profile curves and copy them. Be sure that in your layer preferences you have PASTE ON ACTIVE LAYER checked off. Create a new layer (PROFILES) and paste the profile curves into that layer. Rotate the profile individually so that you can see the side profile from the left or right side (whichever is appropriate) and you can view the top profile from the top or bottom view. In all cases, the side profile is perpendicular to the top profile. The top profile is oriented so that its length is parallel to the loft trajectory, and it is lying on the XY plane. In many cases, the top profile has perfect bilateral symmetry. When the top profile is symmetrical it should be centered on the axis, and its frontmost vertex (or center of the edge) should lie at world center (0,0,0). I always recommend that when modeling, in general, don't place geometry on the negative quadrants unless the entire model is circular or is quadrilaterally symmetrical.

If you are modeling an aircraft, for example, the fuselage is best constructed using the Profile Lofting, then you should plan on locating the nosetip at 0,0,0.

LOFT TRAJECTORY

Loft Trajectory is best described as an imaginary curve (usually open) that follows a natural line of force of the desired object. In many cases, the Loft Trajectory is a straight-line vector bisecting the top profile in two equal halves. Loft Trajectory starts at the extreme front of the model and ends at the extreme rear. As I mentioned, the Loft Trajectory can be a curve, as the target 3D form may be curving and/or twisting on all three axes. Furthermore, it does not have to be a planar curve. If the Loft Trajectory is a curve, you have the option of bend deforming the profiles to match the curvature of the trajectory curve. Certain high-end modeling systems, with highly advanced lofting tools, call the Loft Trajectory curve a "Spine." If the curvature of the Loft Trajectory curve is very pronounced, it is to your advantage to deform the profile shapes to roughly match the curvature in all axes of the Loft Trajectory curve. Having contouring profiles will assist you in placing and orienting the cross-sections to fit the profiles and be perpendicularly aligned to the Loft Trajectory curve. The best way to derive a Loft Trajectory is by visual examination of the physical object, if available, or to "guess" based on plans and sketches provided to you. Begin by assuming that Loft Trajectory is a straight line starting at the front extreme of the model and ending at the extreme rear. If necessary, refine the curvature of the Loft Trajectory, first from the top view then from the side view.

The next step following derivation of profiles is generating and placing the cross-sections to complete the Profile Loft Assembly.

Types of Cross-Section

There are three basic types of cross-sections over which you have direct control. The fourth type is an interpolated and is generated by form•Z during C-Mesh computation. The first type of cross-section is the *Maximal Key*. The Maximal Key cross-section is basically a front profile projection of the desired model. Typically a Profile Loft Assembly has one Maximal cross-section, and it is the largest cross-section in the assembly. With certain 3D forms, especially the ones exhibiting periodic wave function, the Maximal cross-section may be repeated, but these kind of cases are not common. The second type is a *Standard Key* cross-section. A Key cross-section is a user-defined 2D shape, usually a planar closed curve that defines the shape of the 3D form at the location along the Loft Trajectory where it is placed. A Key cross-section is placed along the Loft Trajectory and is aligned to both profile shapes. With respect to profile shapes, a Key cross-section is placed at apex points of maximal curvature for each of the profiles. The position at which a Key cross-section is placed is called an "apex maximal," and it is a point on a curve where the degree of curvature is the greatest. The simplest example of an apex maximal point is the widest distance of the egg side profile when looking at it from the side. Using a lifting body aircraft design as an example, there is a point at which the blended airfoil surfaces begin. That point is the apex maximal and that is where a Key cross-section is placed. The cross-section is then scaled using Nonuniform Scale so that its height matches the height of the side profile at the cross-section's position, and its width matches the width of the top profile at the cross-section's position. Typically, the height fixing of the cross-section is performed from a side projection orthogonal view, and width fixing is done from the top/bottom orthogonal projection view. Each profile curve can have any number of apex maximal points, and their quantity depends on the complexity of the profile and the desired geometric integrity and resolution of the target 3D form. Determination of quantity and position of apex maximals are very subjective, and subject to later revision, as you refine the Profile Loft Assembly. During the refinement of the assembly you will find yourself generating additional cross-sections, slightly reshaping existing ones, and repositioning selected cross-sections, so that the curvature of the final C-Mesh 3D form conforms as closely as possible to the curvature of both profiles. The cross-sections that are created for the purpose of refining and fine-tuning the curvature of the 3D form are called *intermediate cross-sections*. Many times, intermediate cross-sections are simply duplicates of Key cross-sections that are transformed as to also be aligned to the profiles and trajectory curve. Intermediate cross-sections can also be generated from two adjoining Key cross-sections in the Profile Loft Assembly. The latter method is very effective for generating multiple intermediate cross-sections at one time. Generation of intermediate cross-sections from Key cross-sections will be discussed later on.

Cross-Section Derivation

There are a number of ways to derive Key cross-sections for the Profile Loft Assembly. If you are designing a model and you have a good idea of the desired shape, then just use form•Z 2D line tools and C-Curve to create the cross-sections. The Profile Loft Assembly has a minimum of one cross-section, but there is no limit on the maximum. If you were to look at your shape from the front orthogonal view, its silhouette is the shape's maximum cross-section. If you have a plan underlay, and use the drawing front elevation to trace the key maximal cross-section. Draw all base cross-sections on their own layer aligned to the underlay, use only copies pasted to the separate layer as actual C-Mesh construction elements. It's likely that you can derive the shape of nonmaximum Key cross-sections from the underlay by noticing the curvatures as drawn on the plans. If your source material is a physical model, determine the places of apex maximals and, using a pencil, trace the outline of the cross-section at the apex maximal. Then, as closely as possible, model a planar 2D shape in form•Z to match that shape. With practice you can evaluate the shape of the Key cross-sections on physical objects without the pencil trace step. With time and experience you will be able to see the shape of the 2D cross-section and its position/orientation in the Profile Loft Assembly. If the Profile Loft Assembly is set up correctly, you should be able to "see" the 3D form before performing the loft. As you are building the cross-section shapes, try to adhere to the following rules of thumb: Keep the point count the same across all cross-sections. If possible, build the most complex cross-section first, the one that you think will have the most points in it. Then build subsequent Key cross-sections with matching point counts. That way, form•Z will not have to insert any additional points to make up for the shortage. By keeping the matching point count, you can control the position of individual vertices. When form•Z generates a C-Mesh, it will not generate any extra polygons. By controlling the position of the vertices, you have direct control over the topological arrangement in the generated C-Mesh. This control will yield the cleanest possible meshes, with quadrilateral polygons arranged cleanly along a grid. This kind of mesh will greatly reduce chances of accuracy problems when performing Boolean or Trim/Stitch operations. A mesh composed of quad polygons arranged in a normal grid pattern will ensure the cleanest possible rendering and deformation free of shading anomalies in the target animation application. The second rule of thumb is keep first points consistent and aligned with respect to each other across all cross-sections. When all cross-sections are complete and properly placed, you should be able to draw a line or curve that is the same general shape as the loft trajectory by connecting all the first points together. The last rule is to keep the directions consistent across all cross-sections. This may seem trivial, but when you have a completed complex Profile Loft Assembly with 60 cross-sections, it takes time to pick all of them and generate a C-Mesh. Then you learn that there is a twist in the resulting mesh, so now you have to find the offending cross-section, reverse its direction, and then repeat the picking and C-Mesh generation. Better to align the directions and first point of individual cross-sections as you are building them.

Cross-Section Point Density

During creation of your first Key cross-section, you need to decide on the density of points on the shape. This density will define the polygon density of the derivative C-Mesh. Use a moving sphere test to determine a polygon density of the mesh, and from that determine how many points should be on the cross-sections. Give yourself some room for error by building some additional points to smooth out very heavily curving regions of the cross-section. It is better to overbuild the mesh, instead of finding out later that your derivative mesh exhibits polygonal silhouettes, forcing you to either accept the result as is, or rebuild the key and intermediate cross-sections, which can be time consuming. I also recommend that prior to constructing any more cross-sections, extrude (Status Of Objects set to Keep) these cross-sections. Perform render tests, both static and animated, using the extruded solid. Be sure to set up the render tests to approximate (as closely as time permits the output) motion and lighting conditions of the animation project. If possible, perform these tests inside the target animation application.

INTERMEDIATE CROSS-SECTIONS

The purpose of the intermediate cross-sections is to ensure that the curvature of the derived C-Mesh conforms to the curvature of the profiles, has the necessary polygonal mesh density to ensure that the model is free of polygonal silhouettes, and has sufficient mesh density for clean deformation in the target animation application. They are generated and inserted as necessary in selected areas between existing Key cross-sections or between existing intermediate cross-sections. You can generate a Key cross-section using the intermediate cross-section derivation method. For example, if you already have two Key cross-sections, and you need a third one between the first two, but your source material is vague on the shape, you can generate that third Key cross-section from the existing two. Yet another important function of the intermediate cross-section is to smooth the C-Mesh transition between two Key cross-sections of radically different shapes. Without the intermediate cross-section to smooth out the interpolation, there would be a jump in curvature, possible violating the geometric integrity of the 3D form.

Intermediate Cross-Section Derivation

There are two ways to generate intermediary cross-sections. The first and the simplest is to duplicate an existing, and already positioned key cross-section. Position the duplicate at the intermediate apex point on the profile, then adjust its scale like a key cross-section. The second and recommended way is to C-Mesh two adjoining key cross-sections to form an expendable 3D lofted ruled surface. In the front view create a rectangle that encompasses the surface as viewed from the front. From the side or top view move the rectangle along the loft trajectory and position at the point where an intermediate cross-section

is needed. Derive Line Of Intersection (LOI) between the temporary loft surface and the rectangle. Delete the loft surface (you should still have the original
Key cross-sections) and the rectangle. Fix the scaling of the intermediate cross-
section and, if necessary, adjust the first point and direction of this shape. If you
need to generate multiple intermediate cross-sections between two key cross-
sections, make the temporary loft surface as described (**Status Of Objects** set to
Keep), and make and position the rectangle as we discussed earlier. Make multiple copies of the rectangle and position the rectangle copies at points where
intermediate cross-sections are needed. Select all the rectangles and JOIN them
into a single object (**Status Of Objects** set to **Delete**). Derive LOI between the
rectangle object and lofted surface (**Status Of Objects** set to **Delete**). The result
will be multiple intermediate cross-sections. You will still need to adjust their
scaling, first point, and direction. Save yourself some time by ensuring that the
direction of the rectangles is the same as the direction of the Key cross-section.
The intermediate cross-sections will have the same directions and 1st-point
alignment as Key cross-sections, thereby saving you a step. The LOI method is
the preferred technique if the two cross-sections have different geometric
shapes. The LOI derived-intermediate cross-sections will have proportionally
compound shapes; that is, the shape of each intermediate cross-section will be
a hybrid of the two Key cross-sections. The degree of biasing one Key cross-section to another is automatically handled by placement of the rectangle. As you
are placing the intermediate cross-sections, you should be refining their position. An excellent way to test whether or not you have the correct number of
intermediate cross-sections and their placement is correct is to create a test C-
Mesh of a region of cross-sections. **B-Spline** interpolation should be used along
the mesh **Depth** smoothing, but you should not judge the curvature of the
mesh at the beginning and ending of the test region as this curvature is not
complete. Always set **Status Of Objects** to **Keep** when performing C-Mesh
tests. Once you have a good number of cross-sections generated and placed, C-
Mesh and test render the 3D form; even though it is incomplete, you can still
judge the geometric quality of the mesh for which you have cross-sections.

C-MESH SETTINGS FOR PROFILE LOFTING

Lofting is where you actually generate the 3D form from the assembly. The
profile generation, cross-section modeling and placement is all done so that the
C-Mesh tool will take the cross-sections and loft them into a single complex
curvilinear 3D form. Notice that although the technique is called "Profile Loft
Emulation," it is not actually a Profile Loft. In an actual Profile Loft tool, the
software would analyze the profiles, the shape of the cross-sections, and their

positions in relation to other cross-sections and to profiles, and then generate the 3D form. Currently, form•Z does not have this tool, so it is up to you, the user, to correctly place and scale the cross-sections. It is very important that the scaling of the cross-sections be correct. Ninety percent of the time the height and width of the cross-sections match those of the profile curves, but since B-Spline smoothing is interpolating, you may need to compensate for curvature interpolation by scaling the cross-sections slightly larger than the width or height of the profile at that cross-section's position. That is why you should constantly be performing C-Mesh tests with a group of adjoining cross-sections to make sure that the local curvature matches that of the profiles. Select five or six adjoining cross-sections, with the cross-section that you are modifying located in roughly the center of the selection. C-Mesh them with settings that you are going to use for the final C-Mesh, and observe the curvature of the test C-Mesh at the location of the cross-sections of interest. If the curvature of test C-Mesh at that cross-section is outside the bounds of the profile, you need to scale down the cross-section, and vice versa. This procedure is done for both the top and bottom of the interest cross-section, for side profile curvature matching, and for the left and right sides of the interest cross-section for top profile curvature matching.

All scaling is nonuniform; for side profile curvature matching, the base of nonuniform scale is the topmost or bottommost point of the interest cross-section, unless the side profile is bilaterally symmetrical. If it is, then the base of nonuniform scale is the line of symmetry of the profile. Top profiles are usually bilaterally symmetrical, so the base of nonuniform scale lies on the line of symmetry. If the profile is not symmetrical, you need to individually correct the scale of the cross-section to each side of the profile, using opposite sides of the cross-sections as bases for nonuniform scaling.

For Profile Loft, the Length setting should be set to At Control Points without any kind of smoothing. You are manually controlling the length smoothing by controlling the shape and point count of the cross-sections. This is the reason why you should keep the point counts the same across all the cross-sections in the Profile Loft Assembly. It is the Depth settings that will affect how the C-Mesh interpolates the curvature of the derivative mesh during generation. The cross-section quantity, relative cross-section position, and Depth smooth setting will affect the depth curvature of the resulting mesh. You need to control, refine, and adjust all these factors to mold the C-Mesh to conform to the curvature of both the side and top profiles.

For high-resolution results, set the # Of Segments to be between 3 to 5 with Per Segment turned on. This tells form•Z to insert the specified number of interpolated cross-sections between each two user-defined cross-sections, resulting in a final 3D form that very closely matches the curvature of the profiles. For animatic or low-resolution models, experiment with using a fixed number of segments. Depth Smoothing should be set to Nurbs, B-Spline, or Bezier. In my experience, B-Spline or Nurbs Depth smoothing yields the best results. If you want to relax the curvature of the final 3D form, set the Depth Smoothing to Bezier. The final form will now precisely match the profile curves, but the shape will be more fluid in appearance. I recommend that you stick to B-Spline Depth smoothing and make appropriate adjustments to the cross-section's position, scale, and quantity. Avoid using Broken Bezier as it can create very tight curvature changes resulting in harsh, nonflowing 3D form—then again that may be something you want. Create the Profile Loft Assembly on its own layer and name it accordingly; for example, "Fuselage Profile Loft Assembly." When creating the final C-Mesh set Construct Plain Mesh and Construct Directly to ON. Refrain from using the Edit option for C-Mesh creation, as the form•Z interface is not well suited for it, and besides, usually there are way too many control points to edit. Do all editing on the cross-sections directly, and if the curvature is not right, delete it, change the C-Mesh settings and create a new mesh. Set Status Of Operand Objects to Keep.

Exercises

MODELING A SINGLE SOLID OBJECT. LIFTING BODY FUSELAGE

1. Create profiles and loft trajectory vector.
2. Align the top profile so that the nosetip vertex lies at 0,0,0.
3. Align the side profile to the top profile.
4. Create a Key Maximal cross-section, and major Key cross-sections.
5. Insert, align, and scale the Key cross-sections. Place the Key cross-sections at Apex Maximals along the Loft Trajectory vector.
6. Generate, place, and align initial intermediary cross-sections.
7. Perform a C-Mesh test.
8. Refine the position, scaling, and quantity of intermediary cross-sections and Key cross-sections.
9. Perform a C-Mesh test to test curvature matching to the profiles.
10. Repeat steps 8 and 9 until the curvature of the C-Mesh matches both profiles.

MAKING A FUTURISTIC FLYING VEHICLE

1. Set up your construction grid settings to be 1'major with 12 minor sub-divisions. Set your snapping distance to 1".

2. Start with making a top profile closed line. For symmetrical closed profiles, start by making an open polyline, the endpoints of which lie on length Y-axis. Refer to Figures 6.1 and 6.2.

3. Create this polyline on its own layer ("Polylines"). Prior to using the C-Curve tool, have a backup of the original polyline. Copy/Paste the polyline on a separate layer ("Top Profile C-Lines"). Hide the "Polylines" layer and convert the pasted polyline into a C-Curve using Quick Curves: Cubic set to 3/4". Figure 6.3 shows the shape of the C-Curve.

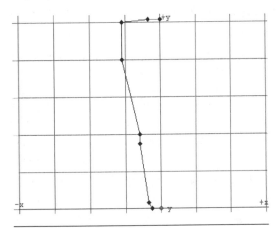

FIGURE **6.1** *Open polyline.*

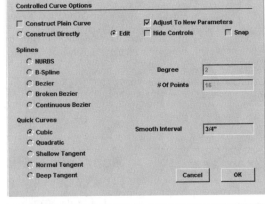

FIGURE **6.2** *Open polyline.*

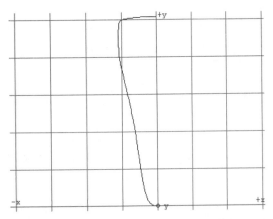

FIGURE **6.3** *C-curve shape.*

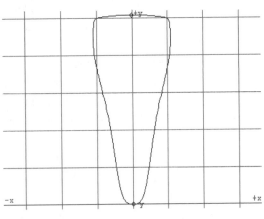

FIGURE **6.4** *Zoom in view of the two join points.*

4. Create a reflected duplicate of the C-Curve by reflecting, with COPY mode, the C-Curve using the Y-axis as the axis of reflection. Select both C-Curves and Copy/Paste then into a new layer ("Top Profile"). Hide the "Top Profile" Curves layer. Open the Edit Line dialog box and set options to CONNECT LINES with CLOSE LINE SEQUENCE turned ON. Set STATUS to DELETE.

5. Using the Edit Line tool, connect the C-LINES into a single closed line. The connection/closure will destroy the C-Curve settings parameters, decomposing both C-Curves. Always have a "virgin" copy of your controlled objects on another layer that you can go back to. You can now see the shape of the top profile of our flying car. We need to now clean up the join points by deleting the duplicate vertices there. Zoom in to each of the two join points, with TOPOLOGY set to POINT, delete the duplicate points (Figure 6.4).

With the top profile finished, the next step is to model the side profile of out flying car.

6. Make the "Polylines" layer active and hide all other layers. Draw a very rough polyline outline of the side profile. Initially create the side profile polyline on the XY plane, then rotate it 90 degrees to lie on the YZ plane. Starting the drawing of the polyline on the same plane as the top profile, we can easily align major side features to the major top features of the desired shape. Adjust the length of the side profile polyline to equal to the length of the top profile. Figure 6.5 shows the closed polyline for the side profile, already rotated and aligned.

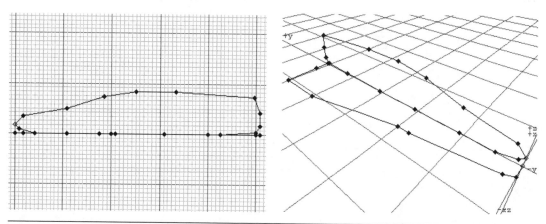

FIGURE *The closed polyline for the side profile, already rotated and aligned.*
6.5

7. Copy/Paste the side profile polyline into its own layer, "Side Profile," and hide the "Polylines" layer.

8. Convert the polyline into a closed C-Curve using the same C-Curve settings. In practice the C-Curve settings are determined by your desired shape; there is no requirement or preference of one type of C-Curve interpolation over any other. Feel free to experiment with various interpolation types. Each one will give a slightly different shape. It is up to you to decide which type of curvature best suits your needs. I decided on Cubic curves because I like the Bezier-type handles on the C-Curve curve, as they allow me to match curvatures with more precision. Convert the polyline to the C-Curve curve. After the initial conversion, refine the shape of the side profile so that it is the same length as the top profile. This is easily accomplished by stitching to the Axonometric top view, and Nonuniform Scale the side profile so that it matches the length of the top profile. Refer to Figure 6.6 for position of the handles. Figure 6.7 shows the profile's shape arrangement.

9. Copy/Paste both side and top profiles into their own layer, "Profiles".

Now that we have the profiles completed, the next step is the construction and placement of cross-sections.

The first cross-section that we will make is our Key Maximal, the number of points this cross-section has determines how many points all other cross-sections will have. It is imperative that the Key Maximal have an optimized number of points, not so few that the final 3D form will have clearly defined polygonal silhouettes, and not so many that the 3D form winds up with too many polygons. The Key Maximal location along the loft vector occurs at the widest part of the

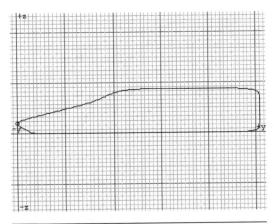

FIGURE *Position of the handles.*
6.6

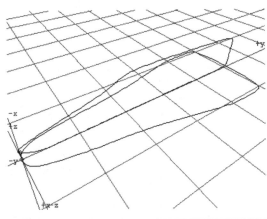

FIGURE *Profile's shape arrangement.*
6.7

wing when looking from the top view. Our intent is to construct a lifting body aerodynamic design with blended contoured wings. Initially, each unique Key cross-section will be created on the XY plane (from the top view).

10. Create the polyline for the cross-section as shown in Figure 6.8. Since the polyline is symmetrical, create one half of the cross-section of the polyline.

Depending on the desired cross-sectional shape of the 3D form, we can either convert the polyline into a C-Curve or perform point rounding on it, if we want generally straight sides with rounded corners. In either case, the operations will be performed on the copy of 1/2 polyline in a separate layer. For ease we use C-Curves set to Nurbs with shown settings.

11. Copy/Paste the polyline to a new layer (Cross-Section Curves). Refer to Figures 6.8, 6.9, and 6.10 for C-Curve settings, polyline shape, and shape of C-Curves.

12. Copy/Paste the resulting C-Curve into a new layer (Cross-Sections). Mirror and then join and close the two C-Curves into a single closed line, set Status Of Objects to Delete. If you wish to change the shape of the cross-section, you still have the original polylines and C-Curve to work from.

13. Clean up the cross-section by deleting the duplicate vertices at join points. Set the first point to be the topmost center point of the cross-section. The resulting shape should have 94 points and look like the shape shown in Figure 6.11.

This is our Key Maximal cross-section, all the cross-sections in this Profile Loft Assembly will have 94 points and have their first point be in alignment

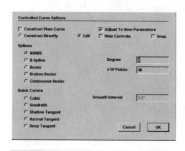

FIGURE
6.8 *Create the polyline for the cross-section.*

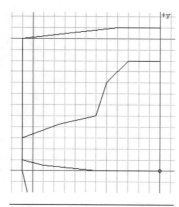

FIGURE
6.9 *Polyline shape.*

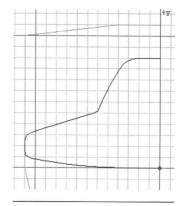

FIGURE
6.10 *C-Curve shape.*

with the first point of the Key Maximal cross-section. When reshaping the Key cross-sections, you may use C-Curve or any transformation tool available, but the cross-section must have 94 points, have the first point be the topmost center, and have its direction in alignment with Key Maximal. For very clean meshes in the 3D form, try to keep the point density consistent with the point density of the Key Maximal. In practice, you can deviate from this rule without any problem, but it does make the mesh easier to look at and gives it a more orderly appearance.

To assure that you have enough points in your Key Maximal, extrude a copy of it on a separate layer that will be deleted later on. Usually I name my temporary working layers "Temp1," "Temp2," and so on.

14. Copy/Paste the Key Maximal cross-section to a new layer, "Temp1."
15. From the Axonometric (30,60) view, switch the active plane to be YZ, and rotate the cross-section 90 degrees, using the bottom center point as the base of rotation. Use point snap to define the base and numeric input for rotation amount.
16. Set Extrude/Convergence options to **Perpendicular To Surface** with **Status Of Objects** set to **Delete**. Extrude the cross-section 24" and delete the capping faces with topological deletion.

You can now evaluate the surface quality by viewing it in OpenGL/QD3D or by rendering it at the resolution of your animation project. For test rendering purposes, I define the material to be very shiny with high specular value, and a reflection/environmental map. Any surface flaws, such as polygonal silhouettes, will stand out more prominently on highly specular surfaces. Figure 6.12 shows the test surface in OpenGL view.

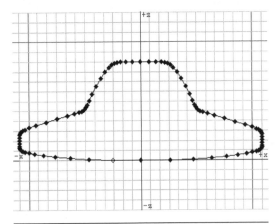

FIGURE **6.11** *Shape with 94 points.*

FIGURE **6.12** *The test surface in OpenGL view.*

If the test surface is shading without problems and you are happy with the polygonal density, then you can delete the test surface and the "Temp1" layer. In a production situation, you would adjust the cross-section, possibly even re-modeling the cross-section, then test extrude until you are satisfied with the results. Err on the positive side, slightly overpolygonized mesh will not harm the project or impact rendering times by any appreciable amount. An overly poly-gonized mesh will increase rendering times, but it is preferable to a light mesh that exhibits polygonal silhouetting during rendering. Practice building meshes that have polygonal density that is "just right." You need to consider that the 3D form that you derive from the Profile Lofting will be edited and undergo other modeling operations such as Booleans or trim/stitching. A very heavy mesh will take longer to process and is more prone to acquiring errors during those operations.

Before making subsequent Key cross-sections, let's place the Key Maximal into its position in the Profile Loft Assembly.

17. Switch to the Axonometric view (30,60). Set the active plane to be YZ. Rotate the Key Maximal 90 degrees using the bottommost center point as the base of rotation.

18. Switch to the top view, and move the cross-section along the Y-axis until it is positioned at the widest part of the top profile.

19. Switch to the right side view. Nonuniform Scale the cross-section along the height (Z-axis) using the bottommost point as the base (located on Z value of 0) of nonuniform scale, until the cross-section is the same height as the side profile at the cross-section position.

20. Switch back to top view and Nonuniform Scale the cross-section, using the Y-axis as the base of scale, until the cross-section is the same width as the top profile at the cross-section position.

Use Figure 6.13 as a guide for placement of the Key Maximal cross-section. There is no need to be perfect in scaling of the cross-sections. The profile curves serve only as visual guides, they are not used in the C-Mesh computation. However, the base of scale for the width needs to be consistent, as the cross-section needs to be perfectly symmetrical about the Y-axis.

The next Key cross-section that we will construct is the key cross where the wing begins to blend into the fuselage. This cross-section will be symmetrical about the Z-axis, with 94 points, with the topmost and bottommost points lying on the Z-axis, in alignment with corresponding points on the Key Maximal. The topmost center point will the first point and direction of this key cross will be the same as the Key Maximal.

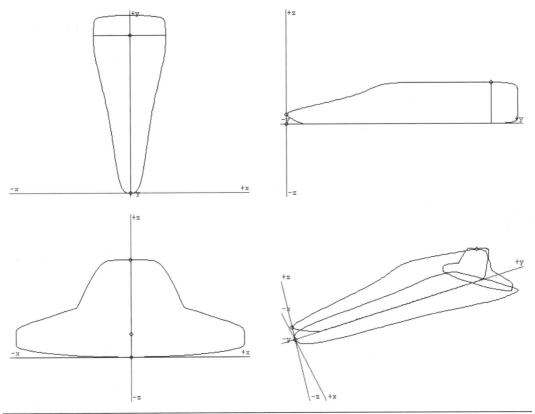

FIGURE
6.13 *Guide for placement of the Key Maximal cross-section.*

An excellent way to start modeling the Key cross-section is to use a copy of a 1/2 polyline from the Key Maximal as a starting shape and then reposition the point. Figure 6.14 shows the shape of the 1/2 polyline of the Key cross-section, and the Nurbs C-Curve with weight settings. The C-Curve is the same as the one used earlier for the Key Maximal 1/2 cross-section.

21. Make a copy of the C-Curve. Reflect and join the two halves. Clean it up, and set the direction and the first point. Query this cross-section to make sure that it has 94 points.

Now let's position it along the loft trajectory where the wing blend starts.

22. Switch to the top view and set Grid Snap Module to 1". Move this Key cross-section along the Y-axis until it is at a position where its width is more or less the same as the width of the top profile. Make fine corrections to this cross-section by Nonuniform Scale to match the width of the profile as precisely as possible. Don't scale it to fix the height right now. Move it and the Key Maximal cross-section to a layer "Cross-

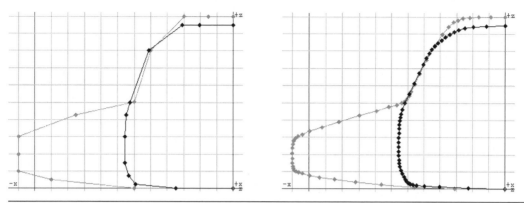

FIGURE
6.14
Shape of the 1/2 polyline of the Key cross-section.

Sections." This will be the layer where all finished cross-sections of the assembly will reside.

Figures 6.15 and 6.16 show the position of the cross-sections and state of the Loft Profile Assembly at this time.

23. Create two duplicates of the Key Maximal. Place one 4" in front of the Maximal along the loft trajectory and the other one 3" behind. Nonuniform Scale the two duplicates as to fix to the profiles. The two wing Key cross-sections and the Key Maximal form the major straight part of the wing. Refer to Figure 6.17 for guidance.

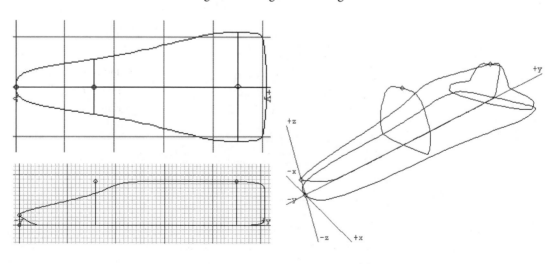

FIGURE
6.15

FIGURE
6.16

The position of the cross-sections and state of the Loft Profile Assembly at this time.

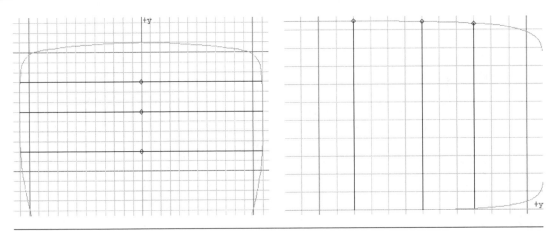

FIGURE
6.17 *Two duplicates of Key Maximal.*

From this point on, I will refer to cross-sections by their number in order of their placement along the loft trajectory. We need to create some intermediate Key cross-sections between the first and second cross-sections. Leave the active layer to be "Cross-Sections," and set **Status OF Objects** to **Keep**. Set the C-Mesh dialog as shown in Figure 6.18.

These settings should only be used when lofting between two cross-sections. It creates a plain mesh ruled surface that is used to generate intermediate Key cross-sections when LOI is performed between it and cutting plane polygons.

24. Create the surface between the fuselage and wing cross-sections as shown in Figure 6.19. Set the **Status OF Objects** to **Keep**, as this surface will be deleted later on.

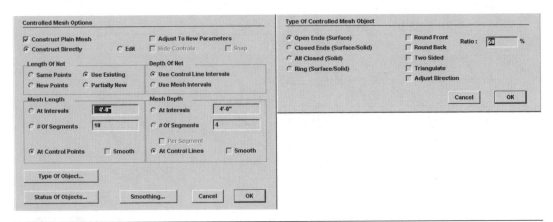

FIGURE
6.18 *C-Mesh dialog settings.*

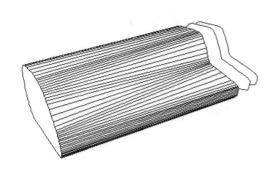

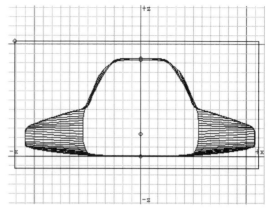

FIGURE *Surface between fuselage and wing cross-sections.*
6.19

FIGURE *Front view.*
6.20

25. Switch to the front view and create a rectangle that encompasses the ruled surface (Figure 6.20).

26. Switch to the front view. Set GRID SNAP to 1". Make four duplicates of the rectangle and place them to intersect the surface as shown in Figure 6.21. Select the rectangles and JOIN them into a single object, set **Status Of Objects** to **Delete** prior to joining.

27. Derive the Line Of Intersection between the ruled surface and the rectangles. Figure 6.22 shows the shape of the derived intermediate Key cross-sections. There are a couple of things you should notice. One is that the shape of each successive cross-section is automatically properly interpolated. Also, the direction and first points of the derived cross-sections are aligned automatically to the cross-sections that generated the

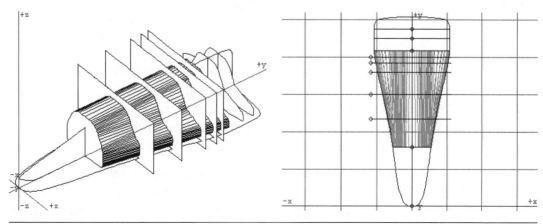

FIGURE *Four duplicates with intersecting surfaces.*
6.21

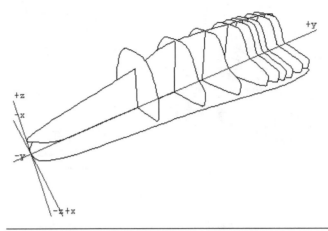

FIGURE *Shape of the derived intermediate Key cross-section.*
6.22

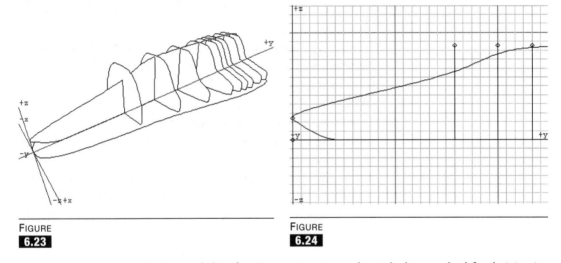

FIGURE
6.23

FIGURE
6.24

ruled surface. In my experience, this is the best method for deriving intermediate cross-sections.

28. Switch to the side view. We need to insert an additional intermediary cross-section between the first and second cross-sections. Remember that cross-sections are numbered from front to back of the assembly. Use the technique described earlier to derive a single intermediary cross-section between the first and second.

We now have a bunch of cross-sections. Now they all need to be fixed to the profiles. Nonuniform Scale each one individually to match the width and height of the profiles at the cross-sections' position. I recommend that you fix all the cross-sections from the side view first, then fix all of them from the top view. Point-perfect precision is not required, but be as precise as you can. After

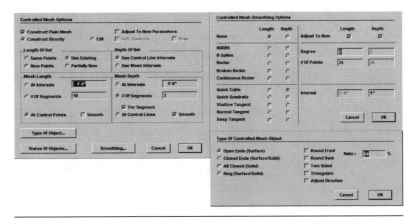

FIGURE   *Open the C-Mesh dialog and set the options.*
6.25

this initial fixing is complete, we can create our first test surface using the cross-sections we have placed so far.

29. Open the C-Mesh dialog and set the options as shown in Figure 6.25.
30. Set **Status Of Objects** to **Keep**. After the surface is fixed, transfer it into a "Test Surfaces" layer.
31. Make the "Cross-Sections" the active layer, and ghost the "Test Surfaces" layer. Figure 6.26 shows the shape of the test surface and it also shows a deficiency in the curvature of the surface at the top front sloping part of the side profile. The shape of the test surface conforms nearly perfectly to the top profile. Figure 6.26 shows the curvature deficiency occurring between cross-sections #1 and #2, and #2 and #3.

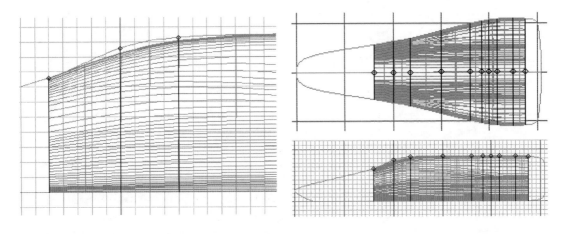

FIGURE   *The shape of the test surface.*
6.26

The curvature is easily fixed by inserting a single derived intermediary cross-section between #1 and #2, and a single intermediary cross-section between #2 and #3. Use the technique described earlier to insert and fix the cross-sections. Remember to set Status to Keep and turn Off all smoothing in C-Mesh when generating a ruled surface. Set Status OF Objects to Delete when deriving the Line Of Intersection. Insert the intermediary cross-section centered between the adjoining cross-sections. It is perfectly legal to generate intermediary cross-sections by copying a major Key cross-section and then fixing it to the profiles. In some cases it is okay, but in many situations it leads to an abrupt change in curvature in the Length direction of the 3D form, ruining the smoothness of the shape. In general, try to avoid using direct duplicates of Key cross-sections as intermediaries. Figure 6.27 shows the position of the inserted intermediary cross-sections. Create a new test surface using the settings in Figure 6.25. Figure 6.28 shows the new shape of the 3D form. Notice how much better the surface adheres to the curvature both of the profiles. Remember to create all test surfaces on the "Test Surfaces" layer and set Status Of Objects to Keep.

Now we need to add two major Key cross-sections and intermediaries to complete the nose sections of our model. The first major Key will describe the cross-sectional shape at the nosetip, and the other one will describe the cross-sectional shape at approximately the location of the front landing strut. This cross-section will be positioned approximately halfway between our current first cross-section and the nosetip of the side profile. Figure 6.29 shows the shape and construction progression of this major Key cross-section. Like the

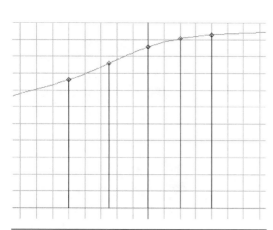

FIGURE
6.27 *The position of the inserted intermediary cross-sections.*

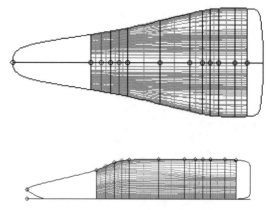

FIGURE
6.28 *The new shape of the 3D forms.*

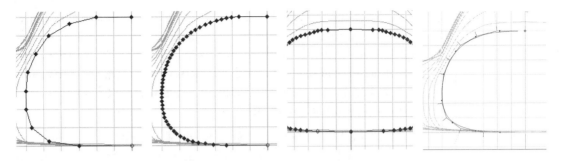

FIGURE *Shape and construction progression of this major Key cross-section.*
6.29

others, it has 94 points, is perfectly symmetrical about the Z-axis, and has the first point and direction in alignment with already existing cross-sections. Once again I will use the original polyline that I made for the Key Maximal cross-section and reshape it. Use Figure 6.29 as a guide. After completing this cross-section, move it into the "Cross-Sections" layer, if it is not already in there.

32. Move this cross-section to its position in the assembly, and fix it to the profiles. Along the Y-axis its position is 1′–0″.

33. To create the nosetip cross-section, start with 1/2 line that you saved from making the front strut position cross-section. Shape it as shown in Figure 6.30. Reflect/join it into a single closed line. As always, save a copy of the C-Curve before the reflection/join step. Move this cross-section to be about 1/4″ away from the nosetip, but DON'T fix its scale yet. Figure 6.30 shows the shape of the 1/2 curve and the completed nosetip cross-section prior to scale fixing.

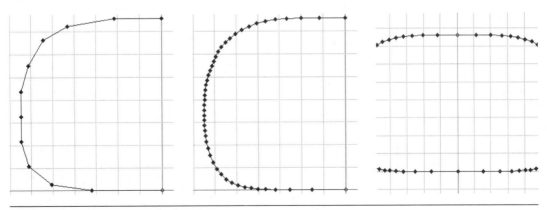

FIGURE *Reflect/join it into a single closed line.*
6.30

The nosetip and rear of the loft assemblies always pose a special challenge. All the other rules apply, but extra care needs to be taken to prevent meshes that do not shade correctly. Nosetips and the rear of the Profile Loft Assembly generally have the highest concentration of cross-sections. The cross-section density is directly proportional to the severity of curvature as both ends of the loft assembly are defined by profiles.

34. Scale the nosetip cross-section along the Z-axis and then the X-axis to be about the same height and width as the strut cross-section. Create a ruled surface between the #1 and #2 cross-sections (remember the numbering scheme, and that ruled surfaces have no smoothing).
35. Create and arrange the cutting planes as shown in Figure 6.31.
36. Derive the intermediary cross-sections, and fix them and the nosetip Key cross-section to the profiles.

The nosetip needs to be completed. Zoom in on the area as shown in Figure 6.32.

37. Make duplicates of the first cross-section and position and fix the duplicate cross-sections as shown.
38. Create a test surface using all of the cross-sections. Use the settings shown in Figure 6.25, except make the following changes: Change Type Of Object to be generated to be a solid, and change Depth Smoothing interpolation type to Nurbs.

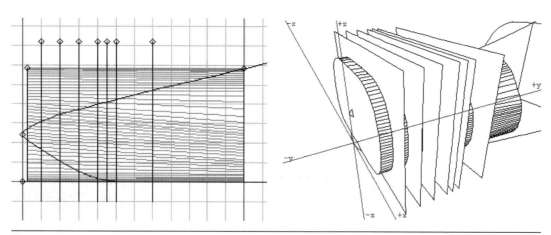

FIGURE *Cutting planes.*
6.31

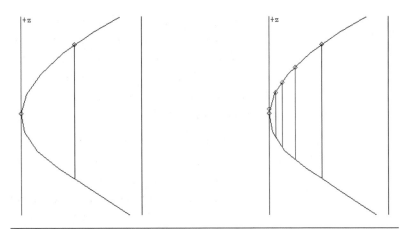

FIGURE *Zoom view of nosetip.*
6.32

NOTE

On computers with a large amount of physical memory, changing the INTER-POLATION from CUBIC to NURBS may not be necessary. On many machines running Windows 95 or Windows NT, and most of the Mac OS systems, the C-Mesh will issue the message "NOT ENOUGH MEMORY TO COMPLETE OPERATION" or "INTERNAL LIMIT EXCEEDED" when DEPTH smoothing is set to one of the QUICK types. Switching to NURBS with the ADJUST TO NEW DEPTH parameter set to DEGREE 2 will generate nearly the same mesh and will not issue the error messages.

Figure 6.33 shows the Profile Loft Assembly at its current state and the derived mesh.

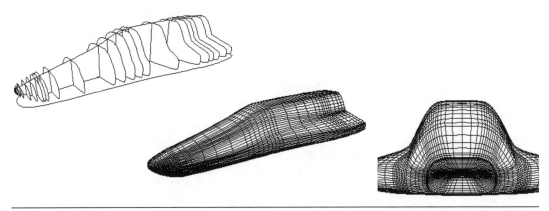

FIGURE *Profile Loft Assembly at its current state and the derived mesh.*
6.33

Evaluation of Profile Loft Geometry

Before we proceed to the completion of our Profile Loft Assembly, let's examine our test surface. When examining geometry for quality, examine both geometry (the shape) and topology. When examining topology, look for regular quadrilateral grid arrangement of quad polygons. Make sure there are no excessively long polygons. If the model is symmetrical, then the mesh must also have its polygons arranged in a symmetrical order. A deficiency in any one of those two conditions might spell trouble when the model is animated; specifically, if it is deformed. When evaluating shape there are three main things to judge. The most important, of course, is how close the geometric shape of the model is to the desired result based on art direction. The second item to watch for is polygonal silhouettes, which are formed on curved areas where there are not enough polygons. The silhouetting is of course subjective, depending on the rendering resolution of the project and how the model will be animated. The best way to validate mesh density is to render the model at the resolution of the animation with the camera positioned the closest it would be during animation. If time permits, create a simple fly-by animation of the mesh. The third item is the breakdown of the mesh with respect to texture mapping. The way the model is going to be textured should be planned prior to "cutting" the mesh. Preferably, you should have a fairly good idea of how you are going to texture the model, so a "cut up" strategy should more or less be complete in your mind. Many applications, when dealing with arbitrary mesh surfaces (meshes not directly derived from parameterized surfaces, such as NURBS), apply materials or align map projections based on a selection of polygons—3D Studio MAX and ElectricImage are prime examples. Having a regular symmetrical grid will make it relatively easy to do intricate, layered, multi-material application to the model.

To complete the assembly we now have to create the remaining cross-sections, both Key and intermediary, at the rear of the loft assembly. However, we have to keep in mind that later on during the modeling process we will need to build realistic engines and exhaust nozzles for our flying car. We will need to create a smoothly curving recess that goes inside the fuselage a small amount, where the engines will fit later on.

39. Initially make four duplicates of the last cross-section in the assembly, and position and fix them per Figure 6.34.

These cross-sections do not yet complete the assembly. The top profile shows a bulge at the rear. The side profile shows a straight line at the rear extreme. The 3D solution is to take a duplicate of the current last cross-section, align it to the side profile, and then BEND it from the top view to conform to

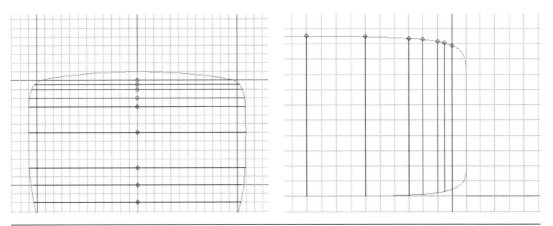

FIGURE *Four duplicates of the last cross-section in the assembly.*
6.34

the curvature at the end of the top profile. That bend cross-section will then be used as a template for other cross-sections to model the engine recess.

40. From the side view make a duplicate of the last cross-section and move it 1" so it aligns with the extreme rear of the side profile. Nonuniform Scale this cross-section along the Z-axis until it is the same height as the straight portion of the rear of the side profile, as shown in Figure 6.35.

41. Switch to the Axonometric view and open the Deform tool options. Set the options as shown in Figure 6.36.

Set view so you can clearly see the last cross-section. Bend the cross-section 10 degrees, switch to the top view and bend again until the curvature of the cross-section, as seen from the top view, matches the curvature at the rear of the top profile.

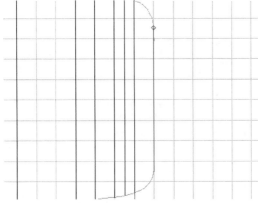

FIGURE *Straight portion of the rear of the side profile.*
6.35

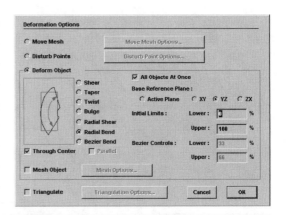

FIGURE *Axonometric view with Deform tool options.*
6.36

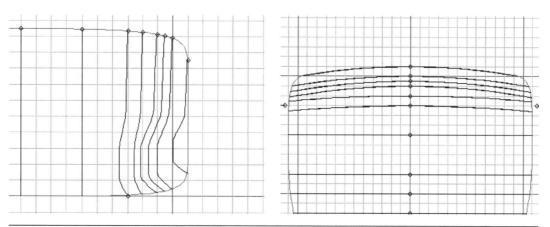

FIGURE *Shape and position of the engine section cross-sections.*
6.37

Select the adjoining four cross-sections. Bend them, at the same time, 15 degrees, using the same Deform settings. Fix those four cross-sections.

Counting from the rear, select the sixth cross-section and bend it 10 degrees. Fix the scaling of this cross-section. Figure 6.37 shows the shape and position of the engine section cross-sections.

42. Perform a test lofting using only the last eight cross-sections in our assembly. Figure 6.38 shows the shape of the test surface. The test surface exhibits serious curvature deficiency between the last and the next-to-last cross-section, which needs to be fixed.

43. Switch to top view. Make a duplicate of the next-to-last cross-section and move it midway between the two cross-sections. Fix the scaling of this derived cross-section.

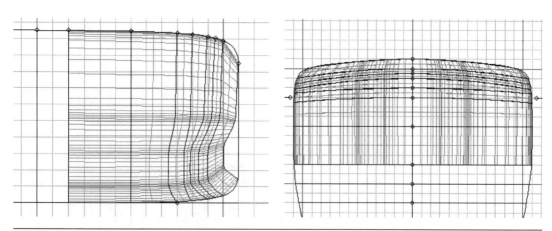

FIGURE *Shape of the test surface.*
6.38

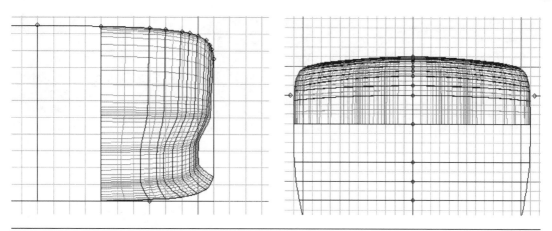

FIGURE
6.39 *Position of the engine section cross-sections and a test surface.*

44. Now make a duplicate of this cross-section and move it halfway between it and the last cross-section. Fix the scaling of that cross-section.
45. Repeat the last step to add one intermediary cross-section, and that should do it.

Figure 6.39 shows the position of the engine section cross-sections and a test surface. Notice that the curvature deficiency has disappeared, and the polygonal topology, though curved somewhat, still retains its rectangular grid arrangement assuring a clean render quality.

46. Create a new test surface, this time using all the constructed cross-sections. Generate it as a solid on its own layer, "Fuselage."
47. Either render it in RenderZone using Full Z Buffer or Full Raytrace, or export the fuselage into your animation application and render there. Set the material to be reflective metal with environmental reflection map. Don't overdo on the specular highlight settings.
48. Apply a subtle grayscale specular map. Set up a natural but neutral light scheme that fully, but realistically, illuminates the model with shadows. This is a recommended way of evaluating the geometric quality of your meshes. The reflective, metallic shading will bring up the majority of shading anomalies in the mesh. When rendered, the model should look like it is made out of shiny, polished, but slightly tarnished pewter. Figures 6.40 and 6.41 show the test Raytraced rendering of the fuselage with metallic material applied. Figures 6.42 and 6.43 show the completed Profile Loft Assembly and resulting SOLID mesh without the optional engine recess cross-sections, construction of which will be described later.

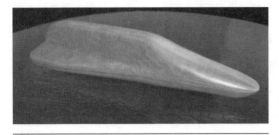

FIGURE
6.40

FIGURE
6.41

Test Raytraced rendering of the fuselage with metallic materials applied.

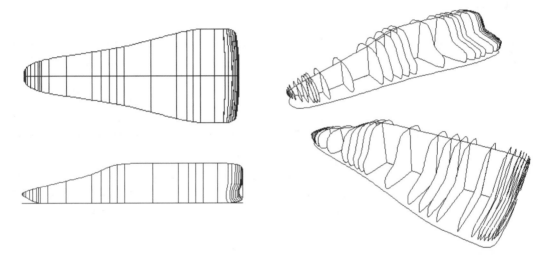

FIGURE
6.42

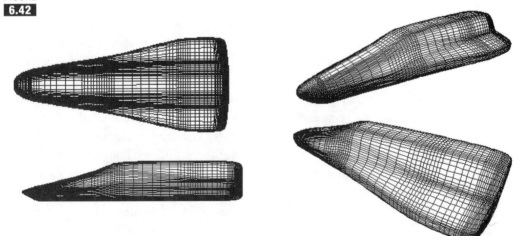

FIGURE *Completed profile loft assembly and resulting solid mesh without optimal engine recess cross-sections.*
6.43

Optional Exercise

From this point, the rest of the exercise is optional. The basic shape of the flying car is complete. The Loft Profile Assembly is complete. For the optional portion I want to describe how to add more complex effects and go into using the profile lofted mesh for further modeling. The real utility of the Profile Loft technique is that it uses the C-Mesh tool to generate the mesh. There is no limit on how many cross-sections your assembly has, how those cross-sections are arranged, and in what order they are picked. C-Mesh will generate a 3D form based on inputs.

Undercuts in Profile Lofting

Dedicated Profile Lofting modeling tools such as those found in 3DS MAX FIT DEFORMATIONS and ElectricImage Modeler PROFILE SKINNING do not allow curved cross-sections and, most importantly, they specifically do not allow undercuts in the profiles and in loft trajectories. What is an undercut? Let's first examine the shape and topology of a profile curve.

Imagine the loft trajectory curve, draw a straight line perpendicular to the TANGENT of the loft trajectory curve that intersects the profile curve. In the majority of cases, this line will intersect the profile at only two points. An undercut is present in a profile if any line that is perpendicular to the tangent of the loft trajectory intersects the profile at more than two points. Figure 6.44 shows an example of a legal profile (right) and a profile curve with undercuts (left).

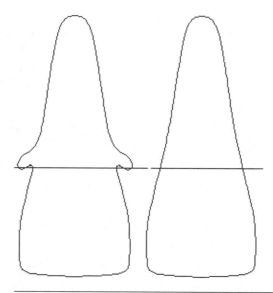

FIGURE *Example of a legal profile (right) and a profile curve with undercuts (left).*
6.44

Notice that on the profile with undercuts, the line crosses that profile at four points. A dedicated Profile Lofting tool, such as FIT DEFORMATION LOFT in 3DS MAX, would issue an error message stating that it detected an undercut in the profile. Profile Skinning in ElectricImage Modeler would attempt to correct the profile, but the results are unpredictable, usually resulting in strange geometry of a generated surface. Why is an undercut so bad? Well, in a basic sense, the loft trajectory curve is derived from the profiles, and in another sense the loft trajectory defines the shape of the profiles. There is a two-way relationship between the profile curves and the loft trajectory curve. An undercut in one of the profiles creates a loop in the trajectory, or it creates a U-TURN shape in the trajectory. In dedicated Profile Lofting systems, both cases are illegal; the software cannot solve the surface. However, with C-Mesh we are *emulating* the technique, so we are not bounded by its traditional constraints. By fixing the scaling of the cross-sections and by carefully placing them inside the trajectory, we are solving the position/scale problem for the system manually. In dedicated Profile Lofting tools, the software would do the exact position and scale fixing of the cross-sections, as in intermediary cross-section generation. With all this automation, a user does have to deal with constraints. Since, in form•Z, we are providing the cross-sections, and C-Mesh does not even know that profile curves exist, we do not have to deal with the constraints and limitations just described. Specifically, we can build Profile Loft Assemblies where loft trajectories contain loops and U-TURNS. The C-Mesh will build the 3D form per our setup, and it is definitely the case of "garbage in, garbage out." However, being able to place cross-sections along intricate loft trajectories, while still maintaining the assembly to be visually conforming to the profiles, gives us an enormous amount of flexibility and amount of 3D form variations that we can derive from the same Profile Loft Assembly. A recessed engine housing that we are going to build is a great example that would not be possible to build using a single assembly in dedicated systems. Basically, we will take the last cross-section in the assembly, duplicate it a number of times, and position/scale the duplicates to create a recess. The final 3D form will be a single lofted solid with the recess smoothly and realistically curving INSIDE the fuselage.

1. Begin by deleting the fuselage mesh that was created earlier. Hide all layers except "Cross-Sections" and "Profiles." "Cross-Sections" should be the Active layer and "Profiles" should be locked and Not Snappable.

2. Select the very last cross-section in the assembly and Copy/Paste a copy of it into a temporary layer, "Temp." For now, Ghost the "Cross-

Sections" layer and make it nonsnappable. The "Temp" layer should be the only visible layer and it should be active.

3. Switch to the front view and open the Projection tool dialog and set its options per Figure 6.45. Set Status Of Objects to Keep.

4. Flatten the cross-section by projecting it from the front view.

5. Break the projected cross-section curve as shown in Figure 6.47. Be precise where you click on the cross-section, it has direct bearing on where the cross-section will be broken. Set the Edit Line dialog and set options to break the line, per Figure 6.46.

6. Open the PARALLEL dialog and set the options per Figure 6.48. Set Status Of Objects to Delete.

7. Create an offset parallel open curve of the flattened cross-section.

8. Create an offset parallel curve from this new curve, but this time use 1/16" as the parallel amount. Set Status Of Objects to Keep so we end up with two offset parallel open curves derived from our last cross-section in the assembly.

9. Use the Edit Line tool with options set to Close Line/Connect to close the offset curves.

10. Delete the two extra points (around the original break point) to bring the number of points of those new cross-sections to 94. You will need to realign the first points and directions on the paralleled curves as to align them to the existing cross-sections in the assembly. Figure 6.49 shows the shape of the two parallel curves with the original last cross-section ghosted. The added amount of both parallel operations is equal to the

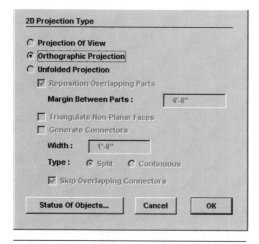

FIGURE *Status Of Objects to Keep.*
6.45

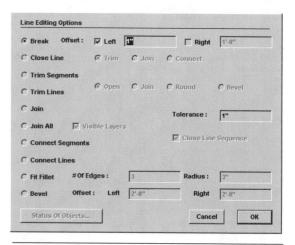

FIGURE *Edit Line dialog and options to break the line.*
6.46

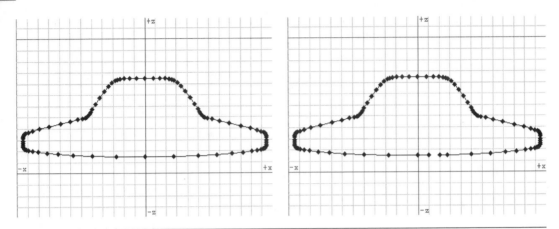

FIGURE *Break the projected cross-section curves.*
6.47

"thickness" of the engine recess wall. Move both cross-sections at the same time to position them at the extreme rear of the assembly aligned to the straight segment at the rear of the end of the side profile.

11. Open the Deform dialog box and set its options as shown in Figure 6.36.

12. Bend these new cross-sections as to align their curvature to the rear of the top profile and to the curvature of the cross-section from which they were derived. The bend amount should be approximately 18.5 degrees. Figure 6.50 shows the placement and curvature of those cross-sections. Notice that we did not have to fix the scaling of these cross-sections; the scaling was automatically computed by the offset parallel.

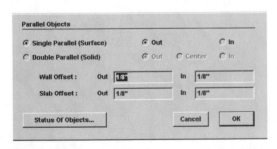

FIGURE *Status Of Objects to Delete.*
6.48

FIGURE *Shape of the two parallel curves with the original*
6.49 *last cross-section ghosted.*

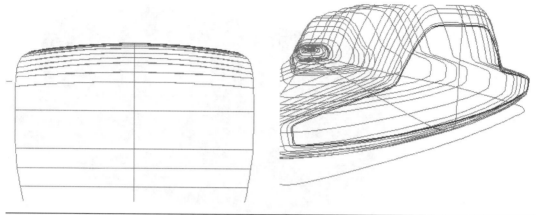

FIGURE
6.50 *Placement and curvature of cross-sections.*

13. Select the last innermost cross-section. Move a copy of it 1/8″ along the Y-axis inside the assembly.

14. Switch to the front view. Select the copy you just made. Project it from the front view, set **Status Of Objects** to **Keep.**

15. Select the next projected cross-section so it is 1 1/2″ away from the rearmost extremity of the side profile. Its location along the Y-axis should be 4′–11 1/2″.

16. Make a duplicate of this cross-section and move it along the Y-axis so its position along the Y-axis is 4′–9″. This cross-section will define the inner wall of the engine recess, and really is the last cross-section in the assembly. Figure 6.51 shows the position of the engine recess cross-sections.

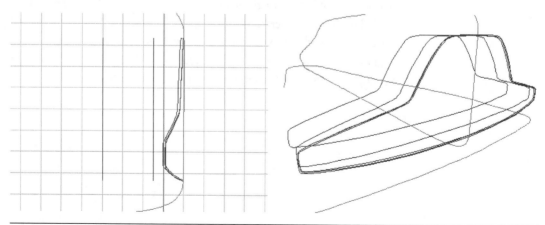

FIGURE
6.51 *Position of the engine recess cross-sections.*

FIGURE *Resulting engine recess.*
6.52

17. Select all the cross-sections, one by one sequentially. Start with a nosetip cross-section and end with the interior wall of the engine recess. Use the same C-Mesh settings that were used to create the first complete fuselage. The resulting engine recess should look like the one shown in Figure 6.52.

Conclusion and Summary

The basic shape of the fuselage is complete. Save the project in form•Z format. Later on, we will come back to it and will continue modeling the space car using various tools. The fuselage shape is complete, the model is not. Creating the solid shape is only the first phase in modeling with Profile Lofts. The goal of Profile Lofting is to generate a base complex 3D form that can be cut up and edited to derive other geometry from it in order to complete the model. The windows, and door surfaces, for example, would be created by trimming/stitching the surface with other curves or through Boolean operations.

7

Surface Trimming and Stitching

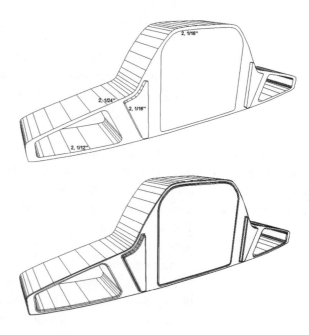

IN THIS CHAPTER

- Cutting and Slicing
- Trimming, Splitting, and Stitching Exercise
- Trimming Out Door Surfaces
- Modeling Engine Exhaust Nozzles

I n this section we will continue modeling the space car that we started in Profile Lofting. The Profile Lofting Emulation technique gave us a solid, geometrically complex shape describing the fuselage of the space car; however, it has no doors, no windows, and no detail to speak of. What we got from Profile Lofting is a single solid shape that we will use as a block to "carve" other surfaces from. Using the surface of the fuselage as a starting base we will derive other surfaces and solids to finish the model and add detail to the model. The goal is to add enough detail, both major and subtle, in order to bring its geometric complexity on par with the physical miniatures built by modelers at special effects studios. Although it's tempting to always build the digital version to be "better" (i.e., more detailed than the physical miniature), in certain cases the digital miniature needs to look identical to the physical one. More often than not, in those cases, you will be modeling your digital model to conform to the look of an already built physical miniature. If the digital model is built correctly, and textured from photographs of the physical miniature, there should be very little difference between how the two look on the screen. This assumes that the motion and, more importantly, the lighting of the physical and the digital sets match.

Cutting and Slicing

It is useful to think of the solid generated from Profile Lofting as a piece of hard polystyrene foamcore that you will cut and slice with an XACTO knife—the Trim/Stitch and Boolean operations acting as your XACTO blade. The paths that your virtual knives take are described by the geometry of the "dye" shapes. The "dyes" can either be planar 2D lines (open or closed) or 3d surfaces and solids.

In general, 2D shapes are used to trim or split the surfaces by projecting through them. Using a 2D planar shape is useful if you want to cut completely through the object orthogonally. Trimming, using projections, is useful when you want to maintain bilateral symmetry of the object you are modeling. This is extremely valuable when working with bilaterally symmetrical objects. Using a solid or a 3D (nonplanar) surface is useful if you need to trim an object without the imposition of symmetry, inherent in using projection trimming with lines. The "path" that the virtual knife will take is described by a Line Of Intersection between the surface to be cut and the "dye" object. You can visually see this "knife path" by either putting deriving Line Of Intersection, or putting the view into OpenGL/QD3D view. If you wish to stay only with solids, then you would have to use the Trim/Split options for 2D projection trimming and splitting. For 3D knives, Boolean operations replace the Trim tools. For 3D animation, I recommend that you use the Trim/Split tools, and keep your objects as meshed surfaces. There are a couple of reasons for that. The first is that in form•Z, the Trim/Split tools are faster than Boolean operations. The second reason is that the Trim/Stitch tools are more reliable than Booleans and tend to work in cases where Booleans will fail (although in form•Z, both Trim/Split and Booleans work reliably). In cases where objects are simple derived solids, use Booleans. A simple derived solid is a solid object derived from Extrude, Revolve, or a C-Mesh solid using two cross-sections. In situations where complex curved surfaces are involved, Trim/Split is a better tool to use. The central difference between Trim/Split and Booleans is that the intended result of the Boolean operation is a solid. In Trim/Split, with the exception of Trim and Stitch With Line, the output will always be a meshed surface. In many of those cases, your objects are very polygonally heavy. It is also easier on you, as it frees you from worrying about keeping your objects solid. There are times when you need to keep your working objects as solids, the most important one is when rounding and beveling. form•Z, unfortunately, cannot create rounds and bevels on nonsolid meshes. In this case, you will need to perform Trim and Stitch and Booleans to keep your objects solid, so their edges can be rounded. However, once all the edges that need to be rounded are rounded, you can perform normal trims that would result in meshed surface. The most important reason to sticking to meshed surfaces versus solids is texture mapping within your animation environment. Texture mapping limitations and surface parameterization is one of the challenges that you as a modeler must deal with. In the majority of today's professional-level animation packages, texture mapping works best if the materials are applied to a surface and not a solid. That is not saying that they cannot apply materials and shaders correctly to solids, they can; it is just easier to deal with map projection limitations when you have only surfaces.

Trimming, Splitting, and Stitching Exercise

Load the space car project. If you did not do it before, do the engine recess modeling part in the Profile Loft exercise. We will be starting with this shape.

First we need to slice our fuselage into sections, for the engine, the hood and the nose section area. The best way is to slice the solid with lines.

1. Create a new layer, and call it "Fuselage Dyes." In this layer create three straight lines as shown in Figure 7.1, from the right side view. Note the positions of the lines along the Y-axis. They are placed as not to intersect any vertical segment chains and they are placed more or less in between the vertical segments. The faces of the resulting solids, after the Trim/

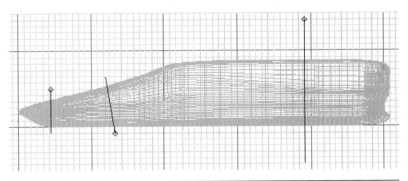

FIGURE *"Fuselage dyes."*
7.1

Stitch operations, will round easily and without errors. The topology of the resulting mesh will be arranged as to ensure very clean rendering.

2. Select the fuselage mesh and copy it into the form•Z clipboard. In the Layer Options make sure that Paste On Active Layer is ON.

3. Make a new layer, "Fuselage Virgin," and paste the virgin fuselage mesh into it. Now you can hide and lock this layer, also make it nonsnappable. For clarity, move the layer all the way to the top of the layer list. Prior to performing any Booleans or trims on your object, always make sure that you have a preparation version of it. Having it all within a single project makes it very fast and easy to roll back to prior versions. All you do is copy the virgin version of the object and paste it into a separate working layer.

4. Select all three lines and Copy/Paste them into the "Fuselage" layer. Hide the "Fuselage Dyes" layer. Like the virgin solids, you need to retain the original dyes should you need to change their shapes later. Keeping copies of unchanged originals in reference layers saves a lot of time and allows more flexibility to play with variations for conceptual modeling.

Now it's time to start slicing our solid fuselage into four solids. Instead of Trim we will Trim/Split, which will generate a solid. Open the Trim/Split dialog and set the options per Figure 7.2. Set Status Of Objects to Delete. Follow the instructions below carefully.

5. Select the fuselage and the first line only. Copy them into the form•Z clipboard.

6. Deselect.

7. Trim and Stitch the fuselage on the right side of the line by first clicking on any point on the fuselage left of the line. Remember, you are doing this all from the right side view. The result is a nose sensor tip that is topologically a solid. You can verify this by querying the result.

FIGURE *Set Status Of Objects to Delete.*
7.2

8. Paste the contents of the form•Z clipboard.

9. Trim and Stitch the fuselage on the left side of the line by first clicking on any point on the fuselage right of the line.

You should now have two solid objects generated from a single solid. If you are wondering why we simply did not use the Split option, it is because Split would have generated meshed surfaces instead of solids—initially, we want solids. The reason is beveling. Later on, we will bevel the flat wall faces generated by the Trim/Split to create V channels that when rendered will add a realistic effect of conformal sectioning of the fuselage. The geometry of the V channel will catch shadows and highlight realistically.

Repeat the above process to split the remaining fuselage into three additional solid sections. You should end with a total of four solid sections, as shown in Figure 7.3. Note the appropriate section names.

Now we will add subtle bevel to bring out the sectioning of the fuselage.

10. Open the Round dialog box and set options to Bevel with 1/64". Consult Figure 7.4 for settings.

11. Set Topology to Face and bevel the vertical face of the Nose section.

12. Ghost the Nose section, sequentially Unghost the individual sections, and bevel the vertical faces that were generated by Trim/Split. Figure 7. 5 shows a close-up of area where the sections meet. Ghost the "Fuselage" layer and turn Off its Snappability.

13. Make "Fuselage Dyes" the active layer. From the right view, draw two planar closed polylines. These two polylines represent the door

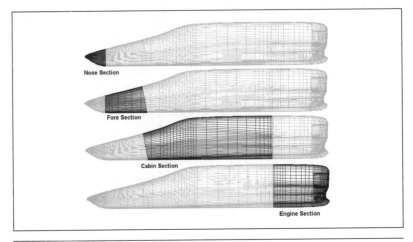

Figure
7.3   *Remaining fuselage split into three additional solid sections.*

Figure
7.4   *Round dialog box.*

projections. Use Figure 7.6 as guide. Note the scale and position of the door shapes.

14. Create a new layer, "Door Dyes." Copy/Paste the door projections into that layer. Don't delete the ones in the "Fuselage Dyes" layer. After Copy/Paste, hide the "Fuselage Dyes" layer.

15. Set Topology to Point. Using Edit Line, individually round the points as shown in Figure 7.7. The first number represents the number of points, followed by the round radius of the Fit Fillet option in Edit Line.

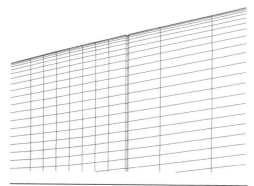

FIGURE
7.5
Close-up of area where the sections meet.

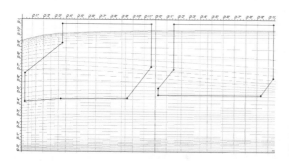

FIGURE
7.6
Two polylines representing door projections.

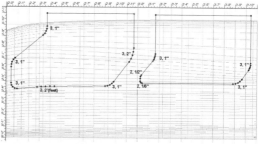

FIGURE
7.7
Rounding the points.

16. Extrude the door projection 8 1/2″. Set Status of Objects to Keep. Move the door dyes 1 1/2″ away from the Y-axis. Reflect the two door dyes about the Y-axis. Figure 7.8 shows the solid door dyes from the top and with the Cabin section of the fuselage.

17. Create a new layer, "Cabin Section," and Copy/Paste copies of solid door dyes and the Cabin section into that layer. Hide all other layers. Open the Trim/Split dialog and set (per Figure 7.9) Status Of Objects to Delete.

18. Split the Cabin section with the door dyes. Your result should be five meshed surfaces: the Cabin section surface and four door surfaces. Use Figure 7.10 to check your results. Your door surfaces should not be above the Cabin surface. In the illustration the door have been raised for clarity.

19. Create a new layer, "Door Surfaces," and transfer the door surfaces to that layer. For now, hide the "Door Surfaces" layer.

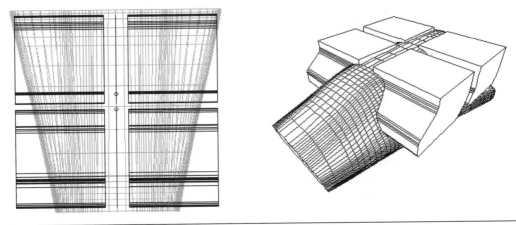

FIGURE **7.8** *Solid door dyes from the top and with the Cabin section of the fuselage.*

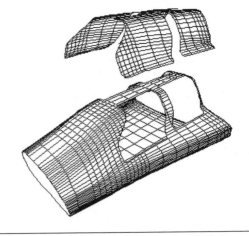

FIGURE **7.9** *Trim-split dialog.*

FIGURE **7.10** *Cabin section surface and four door surfaces.*

Using the same method that we used for creating the door surfaces, we will once again split the Cabin section surface to create the front windshield.

First we need to create a windshield projection line that is conformal to the curvature of the front door projection.

20. Create a temporary working layer, "Temp," and Copy/Paste a copy of the front door projection (the 2D shape) from the "Door Dyes" layer.
21. Use Edit Line to **Break** this line at the center of the top segment.
22. Delete all the vertices to get the line shape as shown in Figure 7.11.
23. Use the Parallel tool to offset the curve 1/2″ OUT, and delete the vertices as shown in Figure 7.12.

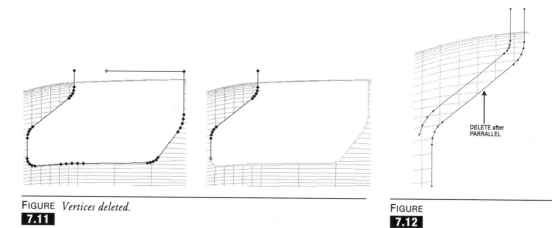

FIGURE
7.11 *Vertices deleted.*

FIGURE
7.12

24. Create an open polyline and convert to a C-Curve (NURBS 3rd-degree, 16 points).

25. Adjust the directions of the two lines and, using Edit Line, join the two together without Closing the result.

26. Parallel the projection 1/6″. Reverse the direction of one of the lines. Then join/close the two lines together. Set **Status Of Objects** to **Delete**. Refer to Figures 7.13 and 7.14.

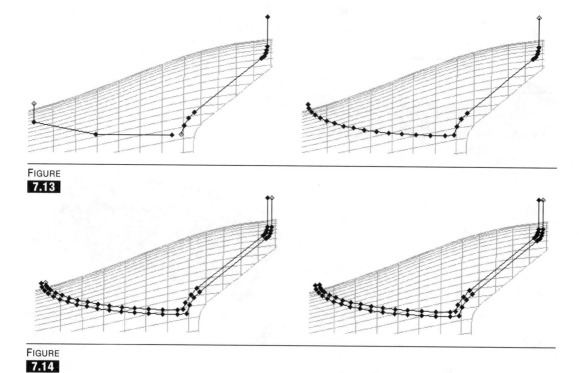

FIGURE
7.13

FIGURE
7.14

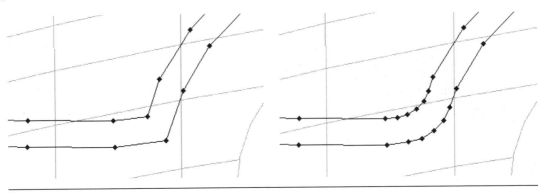

FIGURE
7.15

27. Individually round the two corner points on the trim line as shown in Figure 7.15.

28. Transfer the completed windshield trim line to the "Fuselage Dyes" layer and Copy/Paste a copy of it into the "Cabin Section" layer. You can now delete the "Temp" layer.

29. Make the "Cabin Section" layer the only visible layer, use the Trim/Split tool to Split With Line the cabin section surface with the trim line. Set Status Of Objects to Delete. The result should be three surfaces: the cabin section, the windshield, and the windshield seal. Figures 7.16 and 7.17 show the result of the split. Note that separate materials have been applied to the windshield seal and to the windshield surface.

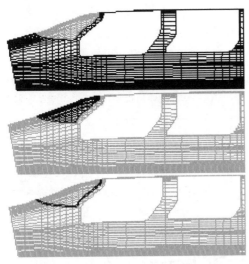

FIGURE
7.16

FIGURE
7.17

Results of the split.

FIGURE **7.18** *Current state of space car.*

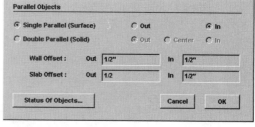

FIGURE **7.19** *Parallel tool options.*

30. Create the following new layers. "Nose Section," "Fore Section," "Engine Section," "Windshield," and "Windshield seal." Copy/Paste copies of the fuselage sections from the "Fuselage" layer into their respective layers. Transfer the (don't Copy/Paste) windshield and windshield seal surfaces to their respective layers. You can now hide the "Fuselage" layer; it will serve as a storage layer for the backup solid versions of the fuselage sections. Figure 7.18 shows the current state of the space car.

Trimming Out Door Surfaces

Now we will make the door windows. The process is the same as one described for the windshield. First the projections of the window shape will be modeled. Then they will be used to split the door surfaces into glass, seals, and door proper surfaces. Start by making the "Door Dyes" the only visible layer. Ghost or delete the solid door dyes (they are no longer needed, and can be easily regenerated from the door shape projections). Set the "Door Surfaces" layer to Ghosted and turn Off its snappability. Switch to the right side view.

31. Copy/Paste the door projection shape into a new layer, "Door Window Dyes," and ghost the "Door Dyes" layer. Turn off the Snappability of the "Door Dyes" layer.
32. Use the Line Edit tools line to break the lines. Break with both left and right offsets set to 1″. Click on the center of the top edge.
33. Set the Parallel tool options as shown in Figure 7.19. Depending on the direction of your lines you will need to set it to either In or Out. Set status to Keep.
34. Parallel the door projection shapes with 1/2″ distance. Close the door window projections using the Line Edit tools. Don't worry if some edges on the bottom are intersecting; they will be trimmed away later. Figure 7.20 shows the current shape of the door window projections. After paralleling you can delete the door shapes.

35. Create two open polylines. Use the Fit Fillet tool to round the middle segment as shown in Figure 7.21. Use the settings shown in Figure 7.21.

36. Trim the window projections with these lines. Then use Break with left and right offsets set to 1′.

37. Round the two corner vertices as shown in Figure 7.22 and Parallel the two lines using the distance of 1/7″. Set Status Of Objects to Keep. Reverse the direction of each parallel derivative line. Use Connect Lines (with Close Sequence option) on each pair to form the window trim shapes. Set Status Of Objects to Delete.

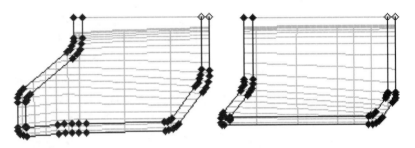

FIGURE *Shape of door window projections.*
7.20

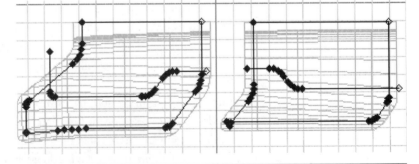

FIGURE *Rounding middle segments with Fit Fillet tool.*
7.21

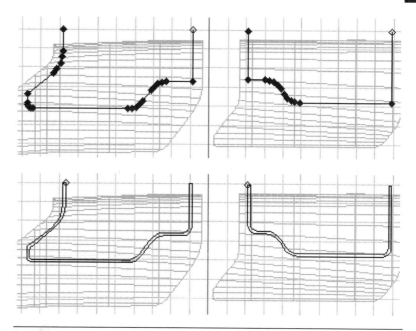

FIGURE *Rounding two corner vertices.*
7.22

38. Copy/Paste copies of the door window trim shapes into the "Fuselage Dyes" layer so you have a backup of them just in case.
39. Make "Door Surfaces" the active layer and Extrude each door projection by 12".
40. Create reflected duplicates of the solid window dyes. Use the Y-axis as the axis of reflection. Figure 7.23 shows the door surfaces and the dye solids prior to splitting.

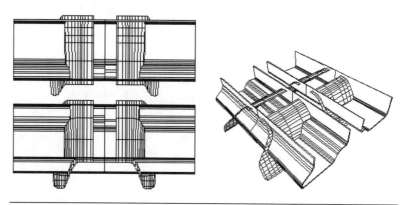

FIGURE *Door surfaces and the dye solids prior to splitting.*
7.23

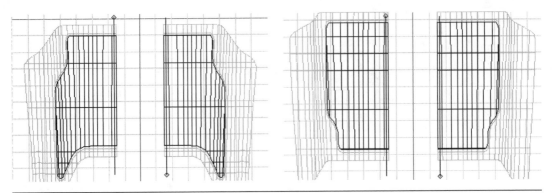

Figure
7.24 *Trim line for each window.*

41. Use the Trim/Split tool with Split First Object to split each door surface into three surfaces: the door surface proper, window glass surface, and seal surface.

42. We now need to perform an additional split to generate the seal surface on top of the window. Ghost all surfaces except the door glass surfaces. Switch to the top view.

43. Create a trim line for each window as shown in Figure 7.24. You may create a line for a right front and right rear window and then MIRROR COPY the two lines about the Y-axis.

44. Set the Trim/Split tool to Split With Line and make sure that Status Of Objects is set to Delete. From the top view, split the window surfaces. The thin strip that is split from the glass surface will be stitched to the seal surface.

45. Ghost the window glass surfaces, and Unghost the seal surfaces.

46. Stitch the adjoining seal surface and the thin strips together to form completed window seal surfaces. Figure 7.25 shows the completed glass seals.

47. Create a layer for each door, each glass surface, and each seal. The project will be exported by layer with each layer becoming an object in the animation environment. Name the layers accordingly. Use the following names:

    Front Right Door
    Rear Right Door
    Front Left Door
    Rear Left Door
    Front Right Glass
    Front Right Glass Seal

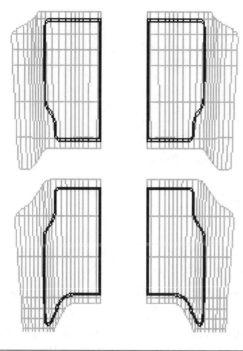

FIGURE
7.25 *Completed glass seals.*

FIGURE
7.26 *RenderZone view of the space car.*

Rear Right Glass

Rear Right Glass Seal

Use the same conventions for the left side.

48. After transferring the objects to their respective layers, delete the "Door Surfaces" layer.

Figure 7.26 shows the RenderZone view of the space car. If this were a production situation, you would now export it and bring it into the animation environment for render tests. It is not yet properly "cut up" for effective and easy materials applications and texture mapping. The cutting up of the surfaces for effective texture mapping is performed last, just before final exportation, but it is planned early on in the modeling phase. That is, as you are modeling your 3D forms, you should constantly be thinking of how you are going to texture map the surfaces and how you are going to "cut 'em up".

Modeling Engine Exhaust Nozzles

Continuing the modeling process, the part that we will model next is the engine exhaust. We will model the exhaust like a tight-fitting sleeve that slides tightly inside the engine recesses. By rounding the rearmost faces of the

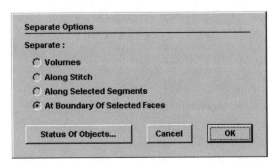

Separate Options

Separate :

- ○ **Volumes**
- ○ **Along Stitch**
- ○ **Along Selected Segments**
- ◉ **At Boundary Of Selected Faces**

[Status Of Objects...] [Cancel] [OK]

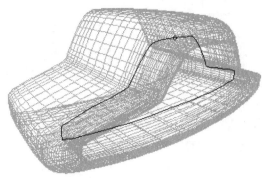

FIGURE *Separate dialog box.*
7.27

FIGURE *Derived cross-section of engine exhaust and*
7.28 *engine section solid.*

exhaust, we will add groove channels that will catch shadows and have specular highlights. Those grooves will add realistic fine-shadowed detail, a trick commonly used by physical model makers to enhance the "believability" of the model, and add depth to it.

49. Hide all layers except "Engine Section." Create a new layer, "Engine Exhaust Cross-Sections." Make it the active layer.

50. Select the inner face of the engine recess. Open the Separate dialog box and set per Figure 7.27. Set Status to Keep.

51. Separate the selected face. The face and the resulting mesh of the engine section will be deposited into the Engine Exhaust Cross-Sections layer, leaving the original solid intact. In the Engine Exhaust Cross-Sections layer delete the engine section mesh, leaving only the inner wall of the engine recess. The result should be that you have the cross-section of the engine exhaust, isolated in its own layer, and you still retain the original engine section as a solid. Figure 7.28 shows the derived cross-section of the engine exhaust and the engine section solid.

We need to create dyes for the exhaust nozzles. Switch to front view and set Wireframe options to show points. First we need to create a parallel offset line of the cross-section.

52. Break the cross-section.

53. Parallel to inside of the cross-section with a value of 1/5″. You may need to reverse the direction of the cross-section line. With this value, the Parallel tool will create intersection edges. Don't worry, we will fix this.

54. Using Line Editing tools, connect and close the lines, and delete the extra points created earlier by Break Line. Figure 7.29 shows the modeling of the parallel offset.

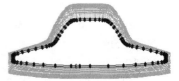

FIGURE *Modeling of the parallel offset.*
7.29

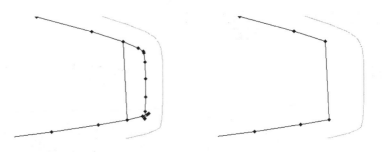

FIGURE *Inserting segment between the points shown.*
7.30

55. Now we need to get rid of intersecting edges. You may ghost the outer cross-section.

56. Use Insert Point and Insert Segment to insert a segment between the points shown. Then delete all the vertices as shown in Figure 7.30. Repeat this step for the opposite side.

NOTE

It was possible to use Trim With Line to accomplish the same effect; however, I wanted to demonstrate that you need not rely on only one way of accomplishing the task. In form•Z, by and large, there are at least two and sometimes four ways of getting the same geometry. The best 3D artists always develop at least three ways of accomplishing the same task.

NOTE

When deleting points on self-intersecting closed lines, form•Z sometimes will issue an error message as shown in Figure 7.31. This message will appear whenever the newly regenerated segment crosses another segment. The trick of getting around this is to delete points in a sequence that the regenerated segments will intersect each other.

57. Use Fit Fillet Bevel the four sharp corners of this line. Set options to Fit Fillet with # Of Edges set to 3, and Radius set to 1/6″. Use Figure 7.32 as a guide for this step.

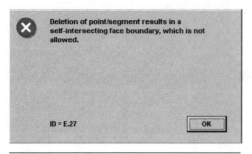

FIGURE *Potential error message.*
7.31

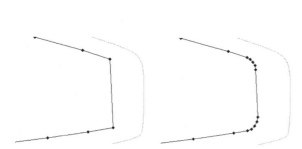

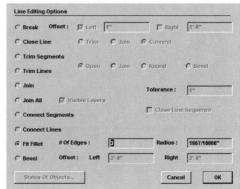

FIGURE *Fit Fillet Bevel.*
7.32

58. Unghost (if ghosted) the outer cross-sections.
59. Now we will create 2D shapes that will trim the inner cross-section to generate dye cross-sections. Set up the 2D shapes as shown in Figure 7.33.

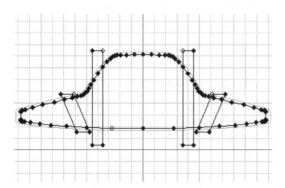

FIGURE *Setting up 2D shapes.*
7.33

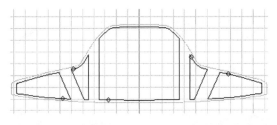

FIGURE   *Trimming the inner cross-section.*
7.34

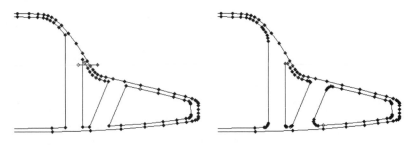

FIGURE   *Rounding the vertices of the dye cross-sections.*
7.35

60. Trim the inner cross-section. Use the Trim/Split tool with **Trim With Line** option. Compare your results to Figure 7.34.
61. Round the vertices of the dye cross-sections as shown in Figure 7.35. Use Fit Fillet/Bevel. As before, the first number is the **# OF Edges** followed by **Radius**.
62. Create a new layer, "Engine" and make it the active layer. Unghost the outer engine cross-sections and make the "Engine Section" layer ghosted.
63. Set **Status Of Objects** to **Keep**. Extrude the cross-sections as shown in Figure 7.36.
64. Copy and paste the engine solid and the dyes into a backup layer. Hide that backup layer and make "Engine" the only visible layer.
65. Perform the following Boolean operations. The engine solid is always object A. Set **Status Of Objects** to **Delete**.
    - Boolean Subtract Nozzle dyes from "Engine."
    - Boolean Union Separator Plate dyes with "Engine."
    - Boolean Split One Way "Engine" with Engine Housing dye. (Be sure to click on "Engine" first.)
    Compare your results to Figure 7.37.

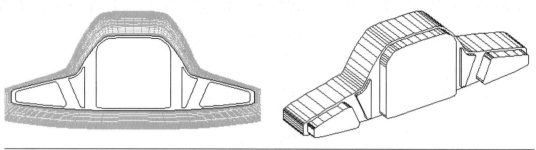

FIGURE *Extruding the cross-section.*
7.36

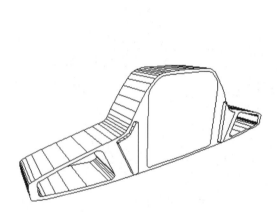

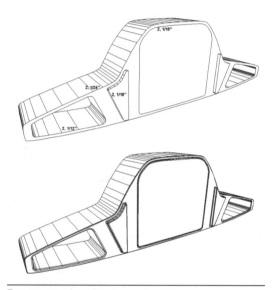

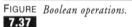

FIGURE *Boolean operations.*
7.37

FIGURE *Number of Radius and # Of Points to set in the*
7.38 *Round.*

Now we need to add rounds to the edges of the two solids. For this geometry it is best to use Outlines as the topological selection. You will need to ghost the "Engine" layer first. Round the Engine Housing, ghost Engine Housing, and then round the Engine.

Figure 7.38 shows the Number of Radius and **# Of Points** to set in the Round. Remember, you are rounding Outlines.

66. Make a new layer, "Engine Housing," and transfer the middle solid to that layer.
67. Save the project. We will continue adding details to this model later on.

Conformal Modeling Techniques

IN THIS CHAPTER

In this section we will further discuss advanced surface creation using conformal modeling techniques. We will continue building the space car. First let me define conformal modeling. *Conformal modeling* is a set of procedures ensuring the construction of 3D geometric entities that conform to the curvature of another 3D object or a group of objects in all three axes. Conformal modeling can also be thought of as a style of modeling where groups of objects are curved along the same lines of force. One of the simplest examples of conformal modeling is a case of two circles, with the circles having different radii and coresident centers. If you take an arc segment of both circles and examine the shape of the two arcs you will find that the larger arc is more shallow but is conformal to the smaller arc. In form•Z, conformal modeling is very easy when dealing with simple shapes. The tool that is most useful is Parallel Objects. With this tool you can create parallel offsets of both curves and surfaces. Conformal modeling is very useful to generate conformal plating on the spaceship or to generate surfaces that flow along other surfaces. Conformal modeling is a good habit to get into because when curvilinear models are built with their parts conformal to each other, the model looks more "tight" and the results look more professional. In many cases, adding a small number of conformal plates to a naked surface dramatically increases its perceived complexity, and dramatically increases its realism when rendered. In form•Z the Parallel Objects tool can be used on both curves/lines and surface meshes. Depending on how it is used will give you different results. Let's do a simple example to get acquainted with the tool.

Simple Paralleling Exercise

1. Create a line as shown in Figure 8.1. Draw the line from the front view. For scale reference, each small grid square is 1″. The Grid settings are set to 1′ with 12 subdivisions.

2. Convert the polyline into a C-Curve using the following settings. Figure 8.2 shows the smooth curve.
   Quick Curves: Quadratic
   Smooth Interval: 3/4″
   The result is planar curve.

3. To create a conformal curve to this curve, set the options in the Parallel Objects tool to Single Parallel (Surface) with 1″ offsets for both Wall and Slab. The IN or OUT options control the directions of the offset Dependent on the direction of the curve. In practice it does not really matter how the In/Out option is set. If the offset parallel results in a conformal curve on the wrong of the source curve, just Undo and change the

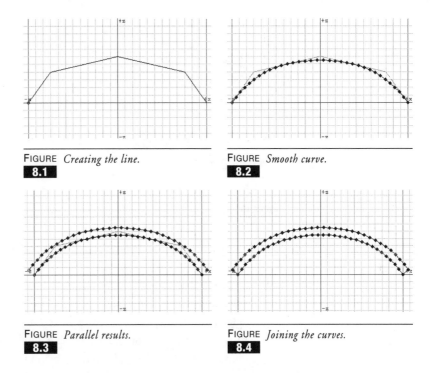

FIGURE **8.1** *Creating the line.*

FIGURE **8.2** *Smooth curve.*

FIGURE **8.3** *Parallel results.*

FIGURE **8.4** *Joining the curves.*

direction of the source curve or change the In/Out option. Prior to performing the parallel offset, set **Status Of Objects** to **Keep**. Perform the parallel. Figure 8.3 show the parallel result. Adjust the direction of your curve and In/Out option to match the result as shown. The blue curve is the parallel conformal curve.

4. Now join the two curves into a single closed surface using Connect Lines with the **Close Line Sequence** option. In form•Z 2.9.5 use the Edit Line tool with **Connect Lines & Close Line Sequence** options. Prior to performing the join, reverse the direction of one of the curves. Set **Status Of Objects** to **Delete** (Figure 8.4).

Alternate Conformal Modeling Methods

Using the simple technique just described, we made a single closed surface by paralleling a curve and then joining it with its parallel duplicate. As you progress through this chapter you will find paralleling lines to be an extremely simple, easy, and powerful technique in conformal modeling, especially when the source lines were themselves derived via Lines Of Intersection. Now we continue exploring more conformal modeling methods. Begin by Copy/Paste the closed surface into a separate layer. Leave the original closed surface that you just derived in the default layer. Hide that default layer.

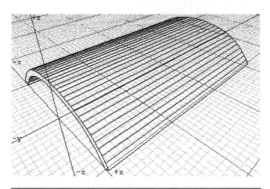

FIGURE *Surface extruded 3′.*
8.5

1. Using the Extrude tool, extrude the closed surface 3′. Set **Status Of Objects** to **Delete**. Right now all we want is a solid that is only curving along one axis (Figure 8.5).

2. We need to generate a Line Of Intersection. To do that, create a rectangle as shown in Figure 8.6. Move the rectangle 1′ along the Y axis. Figure 8.6 shows the position of the rectangle in relation to the extruded solid. Note that, when viewed from the top and front views, the rectangle encompasses the extruded solid. The rectangle is 2′–4″ wide and 6″ high. It is placed so that its lowest segment is at 2″ along the Z-axis (height). The grid is set up as follows. The XYZ Module is 1I with 12 subdivisions, so that each small grid square represents 1″.

3. In this step we will derive the Line Of Intersection between the extruded solid and the rectangle. We need to retain both the extruded solid and the rectangle, set **Status Of Objects** to **Keep**. Additionally, place the derived line of intersection on its own separate layer. Let's call this layer "LOI" for now. In form•Z 2.9.5, open the Trim/Split Options and set the option to Derive Line Of Intersection. Set **Status Of Objects** to **Keep**. Create a new layer and name it "LOI," and make it the active

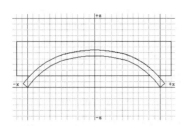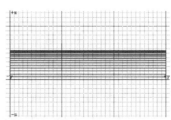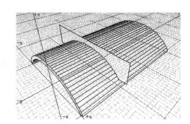

FIGURE *Creating rectangle and relationship to the extruded solid.*
8.6

FIGURE *Derived curves.*
8.7

layer. Perform the Line Of Intersection between the extruded solid and the rectangle. The derived curves should be generated in the LOI layer. Because of how the rectangle was intersecting the solid, two curves were derived. We only need the one on the top of the surface so delete the one on the bottom. Figure 8.7 shows the derived curves; the curve to be deleted is highlighted in grey color.

4. Now create a parallel offset curve using the derived LOI as a source curve. Set the Parallel Objects option to **Single Parallel (Surface)** with 1/2" offset, and offset direction to **OUT**. Set **Status Of Objects** to **Keep**. Create the parallel offset. The parallel offset curve needs to be created as shown in Figure 8.8, so you may need to adjust the direction of the curve using the Reverse Direction tool. In form•Z 2.9.5, use the **Topological Attributes** tool to reverse its direction. Figure 8.8 shows the result of this step.

5. Join and close the two lines using Connect Lines & Close Line Sequence. In form•Z 2.9.5, join the two lines together using the Edit Line tool with options set to **Connect Lines & Close Line Sequence**. Set **Status Of Objects** to **Delete**. Figure 8.9 shows the new planar closed surface. Notice that the closed surface lies perfectly on the solid, as viewed from the front view.

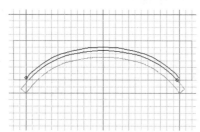
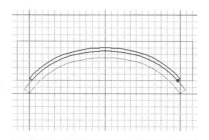

FIGURE *Topological attributes tool.*
8.8

FIGURE *New planar closed surface.*
8.9

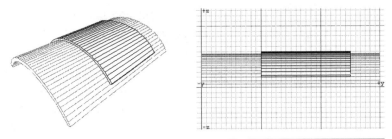

FIGURE *Surface extruded 1'–6'.*
8.10

6. Create a new layer called "Conformal Solid." Copy/paste the closed planar surface from above into this layer. Hide the LOI layer. Extrude the surface 1'–6" as shown in Figure 8.10. That is it, you have successfully modeled a perfectly conformal object that is conforming to another.

Summary of Basic Steps in Simple Conformal Modeling

The simple exercise introduced you to the basic steps of conformal modeling. Given an arbitrary solid or surface object;

- Generate LOIs
- Generate parallel offset lines from the derived LOIs.
- Join the above two lines into a single closed surface.
- Use the derived closed surfaces to generate conformal solids or meshed surfaces.

Multiaxis Conformal Modeling Exercise

In production modeling, you will often need to model conformal objects to solids or surfaces that are curved in all three axes. This is a more difficult case, but the basic procedure described earlier still applies. Let's do an example of creating a conformal C-Mesh surface to an existing C-Mesh surface. First we need to create our base surface.

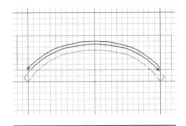

FIGURE
8.11

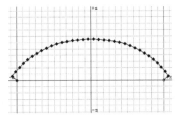

FIGURE
8.12A

FIGURE
8.12B

1. Go back to the closed surface in Figure 8. 4 and Copy/Paste a copy of it into a new layer, "Source Surface Cross-Sections." Hide all other layers.
2. In form•Z 3.0 use Topological Deletion. In form•Z 2.9.5 set Delete Options, set Segments, Outlines, & Faces to Topology (Edges), keep options for Points deletion as Geometry (Points). Delete two segments as shown in Figure 8.12A. This will create two separate line (open surface) objects. Delete the smaller red one. Figure 8.12B show the intended result, this will be our master cross-section for generating the master C-Mesh surface.
3. Make four duplicates of this line and arrange in 3D space as shown in Figure 8.13. Remember that each small grid is 1″. Each cross-section is placed 1′ from each other along the Y-axis.
4. Open the C-Mesh Options and set the options per Figure 8.14A. Set Status Of Objects to Keep. In production modeling, always keep a record of the C-Mesh settings and the source cross-sections so you can refer to them later on. When creating a C-Mesh surface, always set Status Of Objects to Keep and place the derivative surface in its own separate layer.
5. Select the cross-sections in order and create the C-Mesh surface. Place the surface into its own new layer, "Source Surface." Figure 8.14B shows the source surface. We will use this free-form surface as a base to create solids that are conformal to it.

OK, now we have the base surface. Now we need to generate some conformal plating that lies on this surface. The basic steps that we used when dealing with simple extruded surfaces also apply here, albeit with a few modifications. The general procedure for generating conformal surfaces for a C-Mesh surface is

- Generate LOIs at or very close to the source cross-sections of the base surface.
- Generate parallel offset curves from the derived LOIs.

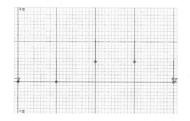
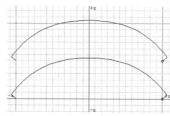
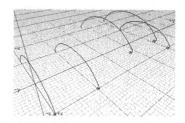

Figure *Four duplicates arranged in 3D space.*
8.13

FIGURE *C-Mesh options.*
8.14A

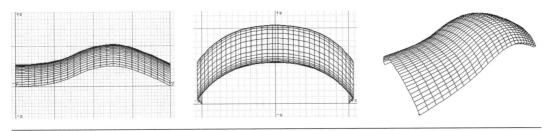

FIGURE *"Source Surface."*
8.14B

- Join the LOI with their parallel duplicates to create conformal cross-sections for the to be created conformal surface.
- Loft the cross-sections using the same C-Mesh settings as were used to create the base surface.

The fourth basic step is one of the reasons why you should always keep a record of the C-Mesh settings for each particular C-Mesh surface. In form•Z this is very easy by setting **Controlled Mesh Options** to **Edit**. The generated surface will retain its C-Mesh settings that can be viewed with the Query tool. As with source cross-sections, always retain a virgin copy of every C-Mesh surface. Place it in its own layer, or have one layer dedicated as a holding layer for all virgin C-Mesh surfaces. If you need to perform a Trim/Stitch or a Boolean operation on a C-Mesh object, perform the operation on a copy of it in a separate layer. In form•Z, layers are an enormously powerful way to isolate geometry to

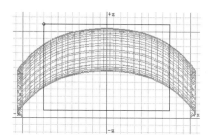

FIGURE *Front view.*
8.15

work on it without the display overhead of the rest of the project. Layer strategies and techniques are covered in Chapter 3.

Now let's generate a conformal solid plate to this surface.

6. From the front view draw a rectangle as shown in Figure 8.15. The polygon is 18″ wide and 12″ high. Its bottom segment is located at 1″ along the Z-axis (height).

It is a good habit to constantly save your work—every three steps is a good rule of thumb. You never can tell what may happen: crashes, a power outage, an accidental mistake, etc. We recommend that every 10 or so steps you save to a different file; example name "Conformal 1a.fmz," 10 steps later, "Conformal 1b.fmz," and so on.

7. Make four duplicates of the rectangle and arrange them as shown in Figure 8.16. Note that the rectangles are placed at the same Z-axis positions as the surface cross-sections. Additionally, the top segments of each of the rectangles are positioned to be above the surface. After positioning the rectangles, select them and use the Join Volumes tool to join the five rectangles into a single object. In the Join Volumes options, set the Status Of Operand objects to Delete.

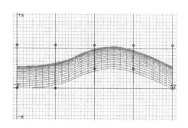 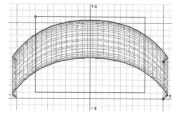 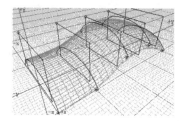

FIGURE *Four duplicates of rectangle.*
8.16

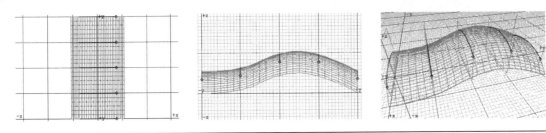

FIGURE *"Conformal Cross Sections" layers.*
8.17

8. Create a new layer and call it "Conformal Cross-Sections." Make it the active layer. Derive the Line Of Intersection between the surface and the rectangles. The derived lines should now be in the "Conformal Cross-Sections" layer. Figure 8.17 shows the derived LOIs. All the derived lines should have the same number of points and edges: 23 edges and 24 points. At this point, Ghost the rectangle objects or move them into another holding layer, and then make this layer invisible. As a matter of procedure, we always keep copies of all operands in special holding layers so we can refer to them when necessary. In form•Z 2.9.5 set the Trim/Split options dialog and set it to Derive Line Of Intersection, set Status Of Objects to Keep.

9. Open the Parallel Objects dialog and set it to Single Parallel (Surface) & Out.
Set Wall and Slab Offset to Out 1/2".
Set Status Of Objects to Keep.
Create parallel duplicates of each of the derived lines. Blue lines are the duplicates. In form•Z 2.9.5 use the Topological Attributes tool to reverse the direction of the paralleled duplicates. Figure 8.18 shows the results of the parallel.

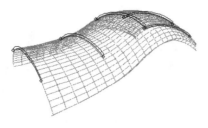

FIGURE *Results of the parallel.*
8.18

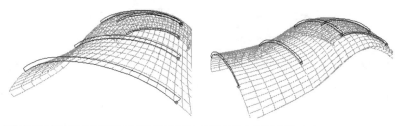

FIGURE *Results of lines and close line sequence.*
8.19

10. Using Connect Lines with the **Close Line Sequence** option, Join/Close each pair of LOIs and parallel duplicate into a single closed surface. In form•Z 2.9.5 open the Line Editing options dialog and set it to **Connect Lines & Close Line Sequence**. Set **Status Of Objects** to **Delete**. Figure 8.19 shows the result of this step. We have generated the cross-sections for our conformal plate. Notice how the cross-sections for the conformal plate flow along the base surface. The next step is to create a C-Mesh solid using the same C-Mesh settings as we used for generation of the first surface.

11. OK, now we need to adjust the height location of the intermediate cross-sections only. Make the base cross-sections layer visible but lock it. Move the conformal cross-sections up along the Z-axis so that they lie on top of the base cross-sections. Figure 8.20 shows the intended result.

12. Create a new layer and call it "Conformal Plate." Make it the active layer. Open the C-Mesh options dialog box and set to have identical smoothing options as were used to create the base surface. The options can also be found in Figure 8.14A. Change **Type Of Object** to **All Closed (Solid)**. Set **Status Of Objects** to **Keep**. Preselect the conformal cross-sections and create a C-Mesh solid. Hide the "Conformal Cross-Sections" layer. Figure 8.21 shows the conformal plate.

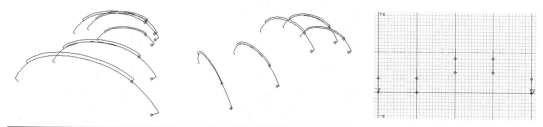

FIGURE *Moving conformal cross-sections up along the z-axis.*
8.20

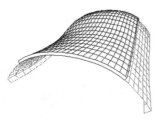
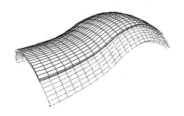
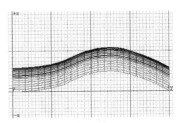

Figure
8.21 *Conformal plate.*

13. Now we Trim & Stitch the conformal solid plate to create a more interesting shape. Begin by drawing two polylines as shown in Figure 8.22. Convert these polylines into curves using the C-Curve tool. Set Quick Curves/Quadratic with Smooth Interval set to 1″. The C-Curve curves are shown in Figure 8.23. Before performing the Trim & Stitch Copy/Paste a duplicate of C-Curves into a holding layer.

14. Open the Trim/Split options dialog and set it to Trim/Split, Trim & Stitch, With Line. Set Status Of Objects to Delete. Prior to performing the Trim & Stitch Copy/Paste a duplicate of the conformal plate and place it in a hidden holding layer. Trim & Stitch the conformal plate with the two C-Curves by clicking first on any polygon of the conformal plate located between the two C-Curves, click on the C-Curve. Figure 8.24 shows the completed conformal plate.

The two previous examples dealt with relatively simple cases of conformal modeling. The procedures laid out earlier are by no means etched in stone as far as application and steps involved. form•Z is too flexible to only have one way of getting the same result. As we continue modeling the space car, we will

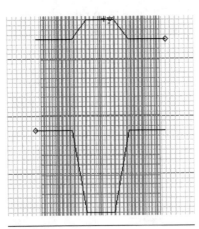

Figure
8.22 *Two polylines.*

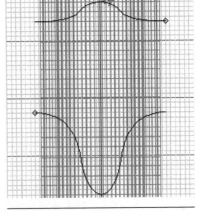

Figure
8.23 *C-curve curves.*

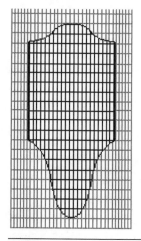

FIGURE Completed conformal plate.
8.24

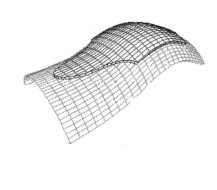

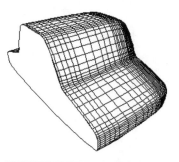

FIGURE Engine section layer.
8.25

see that the basic methodology of conformal modeling can be adapted to many situations. In one of the situations we will deal with modeling and blending of conformal surfaces, so they render as one surface while retaining their topological separation. Load the space car project that we left at the end of the last chapter. Prepare the project by making all layers invisible except the Engine Section layer (Figure 8.25).

Conformal Modeling in Ongoing Space Car Project

1. We are going to create some conformal plating that conforms to the top and to the sides of the engine section. As in previous examples, begin by creating a single rectangle from the front view. As before, our grid setup is 1' for XYZ modules with 12 subdivisions, so each small grid square is 1". Figure 8.26 shows the rectangle.

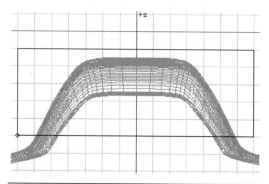

FIGURE Rectangle.
8.26

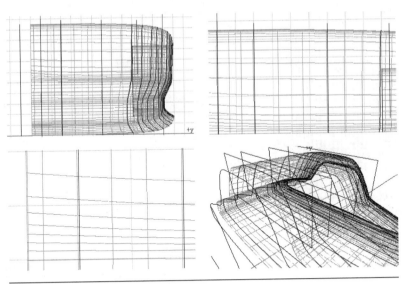

FIGURE *Three duplicates of rectangle.*

8.27

2. Make three duplicates of the rectangle and arrange the four rectangles as shown in Figure 8.27. The rectangles are blue, the fuselage cross-sections are black, and the engine section mesh is light grey. Take note of the placement of rectangles along the Y-axis (length) and Z-axis (height). Notice that along the length the rectangles are placed at Y location, nearly the same as the fuselage cross-sections. There is a small offset along the Y-axis, and the reasons for this are that we want the rectangles to neatly intersect the mesh and so all the derived cross-sections will have the same number of edges and points. Notice the careful alignment of the rectangles along the Z-axis (height). There is a slight curvature in the Z-axis topology and geometry in the engine section mesh of this area. We want to place the rectangles so their bottommost points are located midpoint along the height of the row of polygons. This placement will assist us in deriving the final conformal plate that is curving along all axes.

3. Select the rectangles. Use the Join Volumes tool to join the four rectangles into a single object. Set **Status Of Objects** to Delete.

4. Create a new layer, "Eng.Sec.Plate.Cross," and make it the active layer. Use the Trim, Split, & Stitch tools to derive the line of intersection between the engine section and the rectangles object. Set **Status Of Objects** to **Keep**. The result of this operation is shown in Figure 8.28. The derived lines should be automatically placed in the active layer, "Eng.

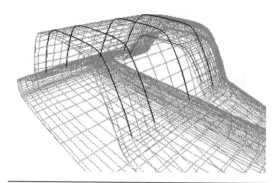

FIGURE
8.28
Results of operation.

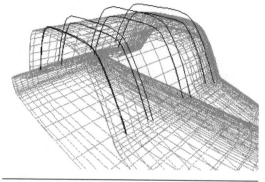

FIGURE
8.29
Parallel offset curves.

Sec.Plate.Cross," by form•Z. The last rectangle was intersecting with the engine section in a way that caused two lines to be derived. The extra line (shown in red) should be deleted as it is not needed.

5. Create parallel offset curves from the derived lines. Our intention is to create an aerodynamic but conform plate that is thin in the front, but gradually thickens towards the rear to create a more interesting 3D form than just a plain constant thickness plate. Set Status Of Objects to Keep and parallel Out. You may need to reverse the topological direction of the lines before paralleling. Figure 8.29 shows the result and parallel amount used.

6. Reverse the directions of the parallel offset curves only. Then use Join and close each pair of derived LOIs and its parallel offset companion line. Set Status Of Objects to Delete. Figure 8.30 shows the resulting cross-sections for the conformal solid. All the cross-sections should have

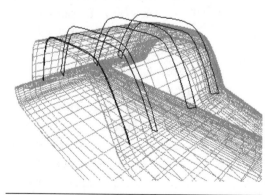

FIGURE
8.30
Resulting cross-sections for the conformal solid.

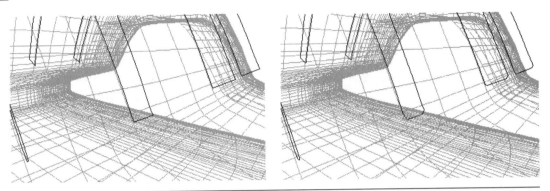

FIGURE
8.31
Offset amounts for beveling segments on individual cross-sections.

aligned first points and directions. Also, all cross-sections should have same number of edges (58) and points (58).

7. Before performing the C-Mesh to get the conformal solid, we should bevel the bottom segments of the cross-sections. Beveling the selected segments and points in cross-sections is easier and faster than beveling the C-Mesh solid. In general, beveling a sharp edge makes it look more realistic during rendering as the highlight will play on the edge faces.

   Use the Fit Fillet/Bevel tool to bevel the straight bottom segments *only*. In form•Z 2.9.5 use the Edit Line tool with options set to Bevel. Set the Topology to Segment. Figure 8.31 shows the result and the offset amounts that you should use for beveling the segments on individual cross-sections. The highlighted segments, shown in Figure 8.31, are the only ones to be beveled. Remember to bevel the shown segments on both sides. Align the first points of the cross-sections.

8. Create a new layer, "Eng.Sec.Plate," and make this layer active. Select the cross-sections in sequential order. Perform the C-Mesh using the same C-Mesh settings as were used to generate the fuselage. Set Status Of Objects to Keep, so we retain the cross-sections. After the C-Mesh solid is generated, hide the cross-sections layer. Figure 8.32 shows the generated conformal plate. Figure 8.33 shows the C-Mesh settings used to generate the plate.

9. Use the Round tool to bevel the rear face of the conformal using 1/20″ amount. Bevel the front face using 1/48″ as amount for beveling. For both set Rounding Options to Plain Rounding / Edges & Points / Bevel. Set Rounding Method to Radius using the distances specified. Figure 8.34 shows the result of the bevel.

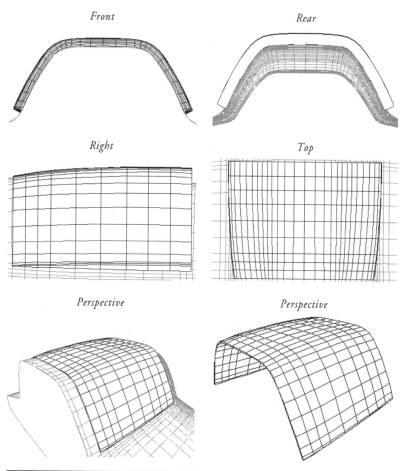

FIGURE *Generated conformal plate.*
8.32

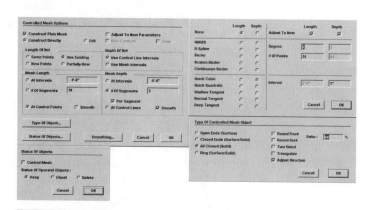

FIGURE *C-Mesh settings used to generate the plate.*
8.33

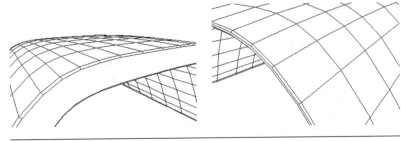

FIGURE *Results of the bevel.*
8.34

Creating Conformal and Blended Geometry

Conformal modeling can be used for more than just building conformal armor plates, we can also use the basic techniques to create geometry that is both blended and conformal to another object. Even though this is a space vehicle, it still needs to be able to maneuver in the atmosphere. What is needed is a vertical stabilizer. We are going to build a vertical stabilizer that extends from the conformal plate that we just completed. We are going to build the stabilizer root to be tangentially blended into the plate. In technical terms we are going to achieve tangent or C1 continuity between the vertical stabilizer root and the conformal plate. Surface-to-surface blending and surface continuity are covered in depth in Chapter 9.

1. Create a new layer, "Stabilizer Dye," and make it the active layer.
2. Draw a polyline as shown in Figure 8.35.
3. Convert the polyline into a curve using the C-Curve tool. For Controlled Curve Options use Construct Plain Curve / Edit, B-Spline / 3rd degree / 36 points (Figure 8.36).
4. Mirror the curve, and join the two halves together using the Connect Lines tool with Close Line Sequence option. In form•Z 2.9.5 use the Edit Line tool. Set Line Editing Options to Connect Lines & Close Line Sequence. Delete the duplicate points at each apex. The point count on the closed curve should be 70 (Figure 8.37).

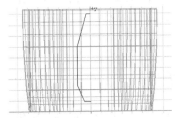

FIGURE *Polyline.*
8.35

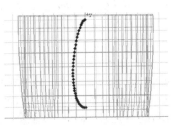

FIGURE *Convert polyline to a curve.*
8.36

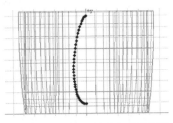

FIGURE *Duplicate points deleted at*
8.37 *each apex.*

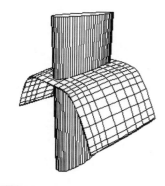

FIGURE **8.38** *Extruding the surface.*

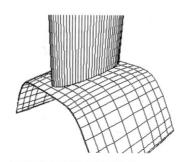

FIGURE **8.39** *Extruded "dye" solid up the Z-axis.*

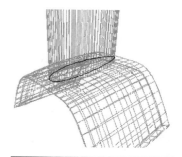

FIGURE **8.40** *Resulting closed line of intersection.*

5. Extrude the shape to any distance just as long as its "top" is above the conformal plate. Prior to performing the extrusion, set the Extrusion Options to Perpendicular to Surface. Set Status Of Objects to Ghost so we retain the original shape (Figure 8.38).

6. Before proceeding, we need to prepare the conformal surface to accept the vertical stabilizer surface. Move the extruded "dye" solid up along the Z-axis so it intersects the solid conformal along one line of intersection; that is, the dye solid does not go through the conformal. This is where OpenGL or QD3D is invaluable (Figure 8.39).

7. Create a new layer, "Stabilizer Cross-Sections," and make it the active layer. Derive Line Of Intersection between the conformal plate and the extrusion. In form•Z 2.9.5 set Trim/Split options to Derive Line Of Intersection. Set Status Of Objects to Keep. Query the resulting closed line of intersection (Figure 8.40). It should be a Closed Surface with
Of Faces: 1
Of Edges: 89
Of Points: 89

If your result is an Open Surface, then the dye solid is positioned too high. If you have two lines, then the extruded solid was too low. Just delete the bottom line of the intersection and proceed to the next step.

8. Create a new layer, "Trimmed Conformal Plate," and make it the active layer. Copy/Paste copies of the extruded solid and the conformal plate into this layer. Hide or ghost all other visible layers. Set Trim/Split options to Trim/Split,Trim,First Object. Set Status Of Objects to Delete.

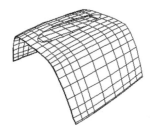

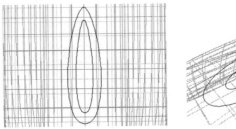

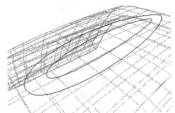

FIGURE **8.41** *Trimming the conformal plate.*

FIGURE **8.42** *Nonuniformly scaling the cross-sections.*

Trim the conformal plate with the solid extrusion by clicking first on the conformal and then on the extrusion (Figure 8.41).

9. Make the "Stabilizer Cross-sections" the only visible layer. Make the "Trimmed Conformal Plate" a ghosted layer and turn off its snappability. Switch to top view. With One Copy mode, Nonuniform Scale the first stabilizer cross-section, using the center of the surface as the base of scale. Use the following scale values .5, .8, 1.0. Switch to the right side view and set transformation mode to Self. Nonuniformly scale the second cross-section along the Z-axis only so its curvature matches that of the first stabilizer cross-section when viewed from the right side. Use the topmost point of the first cross-section as the base of scale (Figure 8.42).

10. Switch back to the top. Open the 2D Projection Type and set it to Orthographic Projection. Set Status Of Objects to Keep. Create a third stabilizer cross-section by orthographically projecting the second cross-section from the top view. Move the flattened third cross-section up a long the Z-axis to be at a height of 1′ (Figure 8.43).

11. Working from the top view, Nonuniform Scale the third cross-section, using its center as the base of scale. Use the following scale values: .45, .8, 1.0 (Figure 8.44).

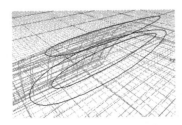

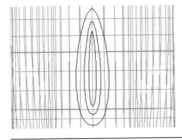

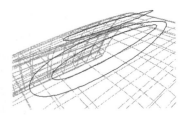

FIGURE **8.43** *Flattened third cross-section.*

FIGURE **8.44** *Nonuniform scale of third cross-section.*

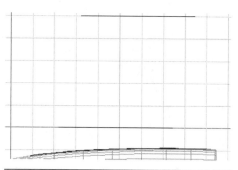

FIGURE 8.45   *Right side view with transformation mode at one copy.*

12. Switch to the right side view and set the transformation mode to One Copy. Move a copy of the third cross-section up along the Z-axis 5″ and 1″ along the Y-axis (Figure 8.45).

13. Nonuniformly scale the fourth cross-section individually along the X- and Y-axes. Set the transformation model back to Self and use the following scale values: Y .47, X .5. Use the rearmost point of the fourth cross-section as the base of scale (Figure 8.46).

14. Switch to the top view. Create the fifth cross-section by Nonuniform Scale the fourth cross-section, using the center of it as the base, and Transformation Mode set to Contin-Copy. In form•Z 2.9.5 set to C-Copy. Nonuniform Scale values are .5,.85,1.

15. Create the sixth cross-section by scaling a copy of the fifth cross-section using the same scale values (Figure 8.47).

16. Create a new layer, "Vertical Stabilizer," and make it the active layer. Open the C-Mesh options and set Type Of Object to All Closed (Solid). Set Smoothing as follows:

Construct Plain Mesh
Construct Directly
Adjust To New Parameters

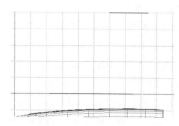
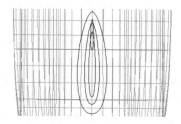
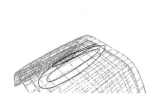

FIGURE 8.46   *Nonuniformly scaling the fourth cross-section.*

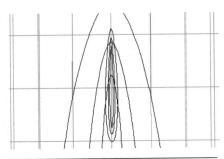

FIGURE *Creating sixth cross-section.*
8.47

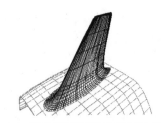  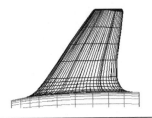

FIGURE *Creating a C-Mesh vertical stabilizer solid.*
8.48

Mesh Length: At Control Points (no smoothing)
Mesh Depth: # Of Segments - 4; Per Segment; Smooth
In Controlled Mesh Smoothing Options, set Length to None.
Set Depth to B-Spline. Adjust to New;Depth; Degree 3, #of points 25.
Set Status Of Objects to Keep.

Select the cross-sections in sequential order and create a C-Mesh vertical stabilizer solid. After the creation, hide all other layers. Topologically delete the bottommost base face on the vertical stabilizer. This will turn the solid into a meshed surface. In form•Z 2.9.5 set the Delete Options to Topology (Edges) for all entities except Points (Figure 8.48).

17. Query both the conformal plate object and the vertical stabilizer. Both are meshed surfaces. Make a new layer, "Aft Conformal," and make it the active layer. Set the Trim/Split option to Stitch, and set Status Of Objects to Keep. Stitch the vertical stabilizer surface and conformal plate together. Hide all other layers after the stitch is complete. Query the resulting object and notice that it is a solid (Figure 8.49).

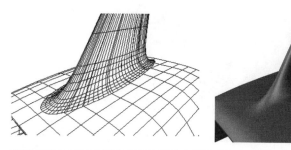

FIGURE *Resulting object.*
8.49

There is a little known feature in form•Z that is part of the Stitch tool. When form•Z stitches multiple meshed surfaces, if the result is topologically a solid, that result will be treated as a solid by form•Z and reported as such in the Query tool. This extremely powerful feature allows you migrate the object from solid to meshed surface and back again with relatively ease. One of the advantages of this topological migration is time saving. If you want to locally edit a heavily meshed solid object, just separate a region of faces. You would be left with two meshed surfaces. After completing the local modeling operations, the two meshed surfaces are stitched back to form the solid. In effect, we performed a similar operation with vertical stabilizer and the conformal plate. The extruded dye and the conformal solid were used to derive the first cross-section for our vertical stabilizer. We then used the extruded dye to trim the conformal plate. In the end we ended up with two meshed surfaces that share a common closed edge. When stitched together, the two meshed surfaces formed a solid.

18. The last step in stitching the conformal surface is to clean up the stitch edge (Figure 8.50). This is an optional step and the degree of the cleanup depends on a particular situation. If stitch edge renders "dirty" with shading artifacts, then cleanup work is required. The RenderZone rendering in Figure 8.49 renders clean, but the final decision has to be made while evaluating how the models renders in the target animation application. "Clean up" of stitch edges consists of using the Insert Segment tool to insert points and segments around the stitch edge to create only four-sided polygons or equilateral triangles.

19. The conformal and vertical stabilizer are one solid object, Aft Conformal. We want them to be two separate objects and, for now, solid objects. Draw a straight single vector line as shown Note that it is on a slight angle, and it is intersecting only the vertical segments. Select the

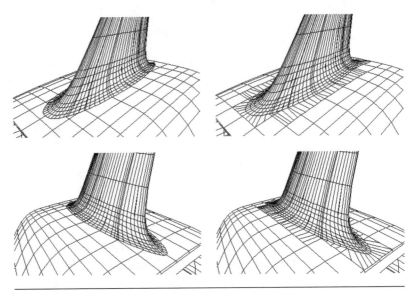

FIGURE *Stitching the edge.*
8.50

Aft Conformal and the line and Copy them into the form•Z Clipboard. Set the Trim/Split options to **Trim & Stitch With Line**. Set **Status Of Objects** to **Delete**. Create the new Aft Conformal object by clicking first on the old Aft Conformal object anywhere below the trim line, and then on line itself. Paste the contents of the Clipboard into the now empty "Vertical Stabilizer" layer. Create the new Vertical Stabilizer by clicking anywhere on the old Aft Conformal above the trim line and then click on the trim line. At the conclusion of this step, you should have two solids (Figure 8.51).

NOTE

The primary reason why we stitched the surfaces into a solid only to split them back apart is the texture mapping. The vertical stabilizer is most adept to be mapped using planar projection mapping. the new Aft Conformal can be texture mapped with either cubic or cylindrical texture projection. By leaving the old stitch edge in the Aft Conformal we are ensuring that the renderer will smooth the vertices at the stitch edge, insuring a "clean" seamless rendering. If we had not stitched the lofted stabilizer surface into the Trimmed Aft Conformal, there would not be any smoothing along those edges during rendering, resulting in a seam. It would clearly be visible that there are two surfaces present. By stitching and smoothing(render time) we are maintaining surface continuity at the stitch edges, the result being that the two surfaces, stitched into a solid, render as one complex seamless surface (Figures 8.49 and 8.52).

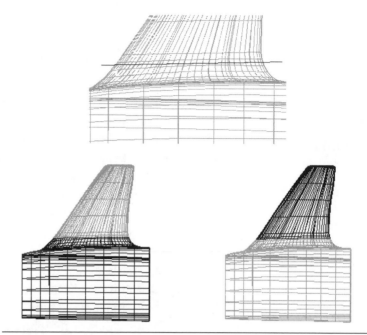

FIGURE   *Vertical stabilizer and resulting two solids.*
8.51

As mentioned earlier, conformal modeling is also a style of modeling where two or more objects conform to each other. Besides Lines Of Intersection, Trim/Split with Stitch option and Boolean operations can be used to create objects conformal to each other. In general, Trim & Stitch and Boolean approaches are used when we do not want the conformals to lie on top of each other but rather to look as if they started as one object. In this approach a master solid shape is first built and then "cut up" with either Boolean operations or Trim/Split with Stitch option. We recommend that you use Booleans or Trim & Stitch to cut up the master shape into conformal solids. In form•Z only the edges of solid objects can be rounded; hence the reason to use only Booleans or

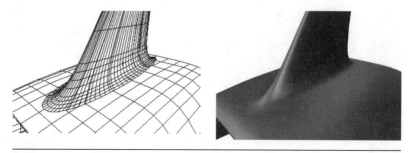

FIGURE   *Resulting object.*
8.52

Trim/Split with Stitch option. The following exercise introduces the Boolean and Trim/Split operations in conformal modeling. Start from the front view. The grid is set up with XYZ modules set to 1′ with 12 subdivisions, so a small grid square is 1″.

Conformal Modeling Exercise: "Trim/Split"

1. From the front view a sphere is created with its origin at 0,0,0 and 12″ radius. The sphere is created with a Spheric Tool set to Revolved Sphere with Length and Depth Resolution set to 38 (Figure 8.53).
2. Working from the right view, a rectangle is drawn (Figure 8.54).
3. Select the sphere and the rectangle and copy them into the form•Z clipboard.
4. The Trim/Split options are set to:
   Trim/Split
   Trim & Stitch With Line
   Status Of Objects is set to Keep.
   — The sphere is trimmed and stitched into a solid using the Trim/Split tool. The first click is on the sphere inside the rectangle, then on the rectangle.
   — The resulting solid is temporarily ghosted.
   — Contents of the Clipboard are pasted.
   — The second solid is created by the same method except that the first click on the sphere is outside of the rectangle. The results are two solid objects with the second solid composed of two volumes.
   — Leave the first solid created ghosted for now.
   — See Figure 8.55.

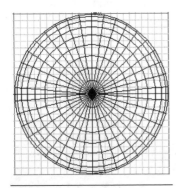

FIGURE
8.53

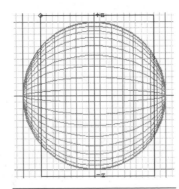

FIGURE
8.54

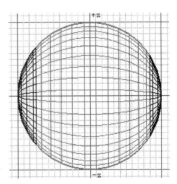

FIGURE
8.55

Conformal modeling "Trim/Split."

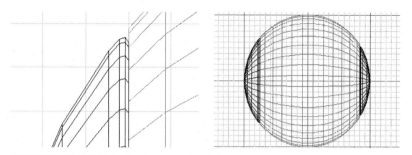

FIGURE *Radius 1/8″ and # of Rounding Points to 2.*
8.56

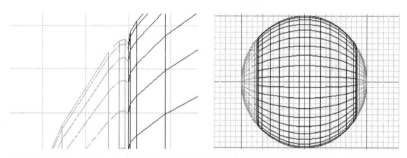

FIGURE *Radius set to 3/4″ and # of Rounding Points to 2.*
8.57

The Trim & Stitch operation creates solid well-formed objects. The flat faces are coresident and shaded as one complete sphere. The coresident flat faces are rounded to create a trough that will catch shadows and highlights, resulting in a more realistic rendering. When modeling conformals that have coresident faces or edges, round or bevel them to delineate the separation, unless you want the conformals to shade as single object with a subtle but visible seam.

5. Round the two planar faces of the second object using Rounding Method: Radius set to 1/8″ and # Of Rounding points set to 2 (Figure 8.56).

6. Round the two planar faces of the first object using the Rounding Method: Radius set to 3/4″ and # Of Rounding points set to 2 (Figure 8.57).

Conformal Modeling Exercise: "Booleans"

Now we will explore the Boolean approach to conformal modeling. Like the preceding example, it is simple and is an introduction.

1. A simple solid box is modeled. Starting in the right side view, a rectangle is draw and extruded. The box is then placed to intersect with the middle object (Figure 8.58).

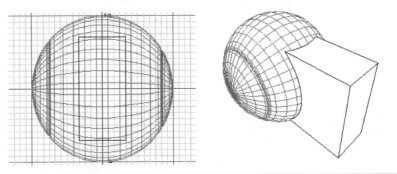

FIGURE *Modeling simple solid box.*
8.58

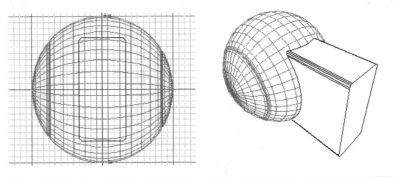

FIGURE *7/10″ Radius and # of Rounding Points set to 4.*
8.59

2. The four edges of the box are rounded using the Round tool with 7/10″ Radius and # Of Rounding Points set to 4 (Figure 8.59).

3. The two forms are then Booleaned together with the box acting as operand B using Boolean Split with **Split: One Way** option. The middle sphere object is operand A. **Status Of Objects** is set to **Delete** (Figure 8.60).

NOTE

The box "dye" was positioned so it intersected the sphere at a single LOI. In conformal modeling, use Booleans when symmetry is not desired. When perfect symmetry is needed, use the Trim & Stitch method and perform Trim & Stitch operations from a orthogonal view.

4. The coresident segments of the two resulting solids are rounded using the Round tool with **Radius** set 1/2″ and # Of Rounding Points set to 2. Segments are prepicked with topology set to Segment (Figure 8.61).

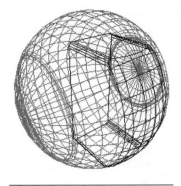

FIGURE *Booleaned together.*
8.60

FIGURE *Rounded segments.*
8.61

FIGURE *Trial RenderZone*
8.62 *rendering.*

NOTE

The last step prior to exportation to an animation application is to optimize the model. Faces that are not seen, such as those inside the sphere, are deleted. We recommend that polygon count optimization be done on copies of the models placed in separate layers. Only the objects in the "exportable" layers are exported. "Exportable Layers" and layer strategy inside form•Z are covered in depth in Chapter 3.

5. The final RenderZone rendering. Notice that the bottom of the troughs formed by rounded edges are shadowed and rounded edges are highlighted giving the what otherwise is a simple object a more complex and realistic appearance. This method of conformal modeling is well suited to modeling access panels (Figure 8.62).

Conformal Modeling: "Parallel Objects"

The last method of conformal modeling is to directly generate solids from meshed surfaces using the Parallel Objects tool. This method can generate triangular polygons and is less desirable than producing quadrilateral polygons as shown earlier. The main advantage of this method is its speed and directness. Its main disadvantage, as mentioned, is that it produces triangles from non-planar polygons. Those triangles may pose a problem later on in the modeling process. In particular, the Round tool may encounter difficulties when working with triangulated meshes. Being less desirable does not mean that it should never be used. In cases where time is a consideration, and the paralleled object will not be rounded, it is perfectly feasible to use this method. The following simple exercise demonstrates the pros and the cons of this method.

Begin by opening a new project and recreating the surface from Figure 8.14 and the two curves from Figure 8.23. If you saved the practice file, jut reload those three objects.

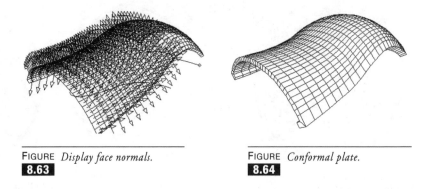

FIGURE *Display face normals.*
8.63

FIGURE *Conformal plate.*
8.64

1. Make sure that face normals are pointing Out of the surface—use the Reverse Direction tool if necessary. In form•Z 2.9.5 use Topological Attributes with the **Reverse Direction** tool to adjust the direction of the surface.

   Display Face Normals is found in **Wireframe Options** (Figure 8.63).

2. Set Parallel Objects to **Double Parallel (Solid)** & **Out**

   Wall Offset: Out 1″

   Slab Offset: Out 1″

   Set **Status Of Objects** to **Ghost**.

3. Create a conformal plate by paralleling the surface (Figure 8.64).

No triangles were produced by the Parallel tool because all the polygons in this mesh are planar. On meshes with nonplanar polygons, the paralleled polygons will be triangulated. Triangulated meshes can affect performance of Booleans and limit the maximum radius in rounding. A triangulated mesh can take up to twice as much memory as a nontriangulated one. Overall, it is best to avoid triangular meshes.

NOTE

4. The same base surface paralleled, but this one was slightly Deform Twisted first to create nonplanar faces. Notice that the paralleled solid is triangulated. It is not necessary to do this step. It is here to demonstrate a point (Figure 8.65).

5. Join and close the two trim lines using Connect Lines as described. **Status Of Objects** is set to **Delete**. Move the added segments 1″ along the X-axis as shown (Figure 8.66).

6. Working from the top view, Trim & Stitch the paralleled solid with the lines. **Status Of Objects** is set to **Delete**. The result is also a solid. After completing the operation, unghost the base surface (Figure 8.67).

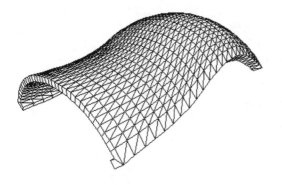

FIGURE
8.65
Triangulated paralleled solid.

FIGURE
8.66
Connecting lines.

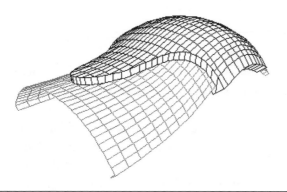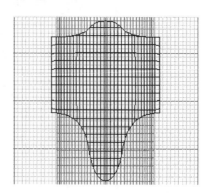

FIGURE
8.67
Unghost the base surface.

> *When the Double Paralleled (Solid) method is used, the entire meshed object is paralleled. The resulting solid might need more trimming or Booleans to adjust its shape. The Lines Of Intersection method almost always results in a geometrically and topologically superior form.*
>
> NOTE

Continuation of Space Car Project

We have covered four conformal modeling approaches. We will use these methods to continue building our space car. We will not cover the steps in the same amount of detail as before. By now you should be familiar with the various conformal techniques to follow along.

Using the Trim & Stitch technique, we will now build two access panels, one on each side of the Aft Conformal object. Close all projects except the space car, reload it if necessary.

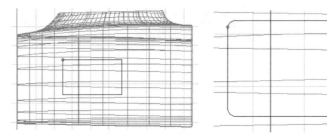

FIGURE *Right view rectangular shape.*
8.68

FIGURE *Rounded rectangle.*
8.69

1. A rectangular shape is drawn in the right view (Figure 8.68).
2. The rectangle is rounded with the Edit Line tool set to Fit fillet (Figure 8.69).
   # Of Edges: 2
   Radius: 1/8″
3. The Aft Conformal object is Trimmed & Stitched with the rectangle to produce three solid objects: the Aft Conformal and two access panels (Figure 8.70).
4. The coresident exterior edges of the resulting three solids are rounded. Segments of the edges are prepicked and then rounded with the Round tool set to Bevel Edges with 1/30″ Radius. One of the access panel solids was deleted prior to beveling. The beveled access panel solid was then reflected to create its symmetrical twin (Figure 8.71).

Next, a detachable auxiliary conformal thruster is constructed using the Lines Of Intersection technique.

5. Working from the front view a rectangle is drawn. It is duplicated seven times and the eight rectangles are positioned as shown (Figure 8.72).

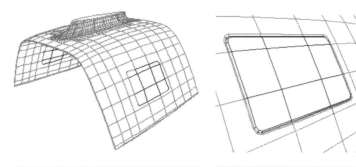

FIGURE *Aft conformal and two access*
8.70 *panels.*

FIGURE *Beveled access panel.*
8.71

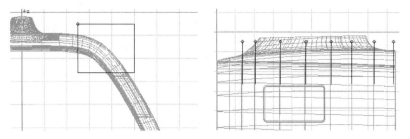

FIGURE *Front view duplicated seven times.*
8.72

6. Lines Of Intersection are derived between the Aft Conformal and the rectangles. The rectangles are then placed in a hidden holding layer. The extra derived lines "inside" of the conformal are deleted. Each of the remaining derived lines is an open surface with 6 edges and 7 points. Note the direction of the lines (Figure 8.73).

7. Parallel duplicates of the lines are created with the Parallel Objects tool set to **Single Parallel (Surface)** model and **Out** direction. Offset distances are as shown in Figure 8.74. The directions of paralleled duplicates are reversed.

8. Each pair of curves is joined and closed using Connect Lines into a single closed surface cross-section (Figure 8.75).

9. The four sharp corner points on each resulting cross-section are rounded with the Edit Line tool set to Fit fillet. The top two corner points of the last six cross-sections were rounded with Fit fillet set to **# Of Edges: 3 Radius: 1/4″**.

   — The second cross-section two top corner points. **# Of Edges: 3 Radius: 1/6″**

   — The first cross-section top two corner points. **# Of Edges: 3 Radius: 1/24″**.

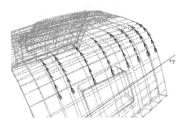

FIGURE *Derived lines with 6 edges*
8.73 *and 7 points.*

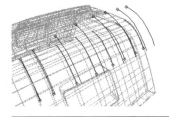

FIGURE *Offset distances*
8.74

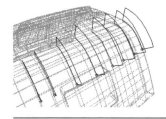

FIGURE *Joining curves.*
8.75

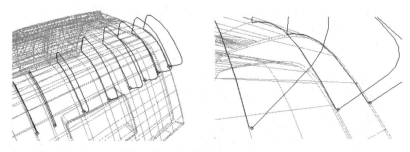

FIGURE *Closed surfaces.*
8.76

— The bottom corner points were beveled with the Edit Line tool set to Bevel with Offsets as below.
— The bevel offset amount for all cross-sections except the first one is 1/32″.
— The bevel offset amount for the two bottom corner points of the first cross-section is 1/128″.
— Each of the cross-sections has 24 edges and 24 points and is a closed surface (Figure 8.76).

10. To prevent polygonal silhouetting, the top three middle points on each cross-section are rounded with Fit fillet set to # Of Edges: 2, Radius: 2″. The first two cross-sections have radii of 1 1/2″ to compensate for their smaller size. Each cross-section has 30 edges and 30 points (Figure 8.77).

11. A C-Mesh solid is created in its own layer, "Aux. Thruster," with cross-sections retained but placed in their own layer. Smoothing is only for Depth with # Of Segments: 2, Per Segment. Smoothing Options are set to Length: None, Depth: B-Spline, Degree:2. The rearmost face is beveled with the Round tool with 1/48″ radius. A mirrored duplicate copy of the thruster is created with the Mirror tool (Figure 8.78).

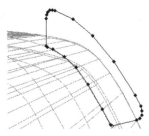

FIGURE *Cross sections.*
8.77

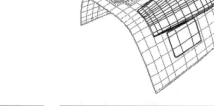

FIGURE *Mirrored duplicate.*
8.78

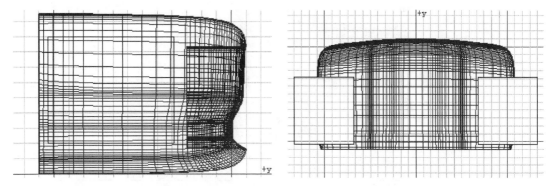

FIGURE *Rectangle drawn from right view and extruded.*
8.79

Next, a Boolean modeling approach is used to create a wing section conformal with the engine section.

12. A rectangle is drawn from the right view and extruded. The resulting box is then placed as shown and mirrored to create a symmetrical duplicate (Figure 8.79).

13. Working on copies of the two boxes and the engine section isolated in a new layer, the box on the right side is Boolean subtracted from the Engine Section. The Engine Section is then split into two solids using Boolean Split with **One Way** option with the box on the left side. Engine Section is the Operand A (Figure 8.80).

14. The coresident faces formed by the Boolean (shown in blue in Figure 8.80) are beveled with a radius of 1/48". The extra faces are deleted only from the wing section. The wing section is then mirrored with One Copy mode (Figure 8.81).

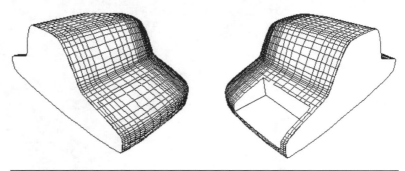

FIGURE *Engine section split into two solids.*
8.80

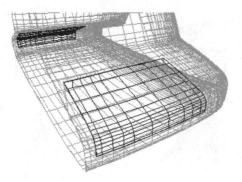

FIGURE *Mirrored wing section.*
8.81

Summary

Save the project; we will continue modeling the space car in the next chapter. This chapter introduced you to the concept of conformal modeling and presented you with possible ways to approach conformals. The information presented in this chapter is by no means absolute. form•Z is a very powerful and flexible application. Undoubtedly, other methods exists. Feel free to modify any of our techniques to suit a particular situation. We urge you to combine our approaches with your own techniques and make your own magic. Figure 8.82 shows the space car at this stage in its construction.

FIGURE *Space car.*
8.82

CHAPTER

9

Surface Blending and Matching

IN THIS CHAPTER

- Introduction to Concepts of Surface Blending
- Introductory Exercise
- Exercise
- Blending Surfaces Using C-Mesh
- Guidelines for Blending with C-Mesh
- Blending Surfaces Using Skin Method
- Blending Closed Loop Edges
- Contunuity Surface Matching
- Creating Blended Depressions and Elevations
- Summary

Introduction to Concepts of Surface Blending

In this chapter we will explore *surface blending* and how it applies to digital effects modeling within form•Z. Surface blending is the process of building a third surface to blend two separate surfaces. The third surface acts as a bridge blending the two surfaces together. Depending on the achieved continuity, the three surfaces will either shade with seams, or will shade as one continuous complex surface. The latter is usually the desired result and can be difficult to achieve, depending on the situation. As mentioned, the smoothness with which the surfaces shade is dependent on the achieved continuity between the two base surfaces and the blend surface. Specifically, it is the achieved continuity at blended edges that defines the smoothness of the rendered surface. In

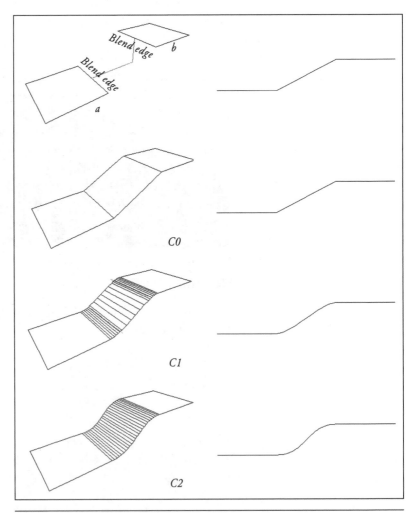

FIGURE   *Three kinds of blend surfaces.*
9.1

regards to surface modeling, there are three basic types of mathematical continuity: Positional (C0), Tangential (C1), and Curvature (C2). With C0 continuity, the blend surface has no curvature at the blend edge. Many times it is just a straight line ruled surface bridge between the two surfaces. It is called "positional continuity" because the blend edges of the blend surface are coresident with the blend edges of the two surfaces. C1 (tangential) continuity exists between two blended surfaces when the coresident blend edges have identical tangents. C1 blend surfaces have moderate "softness." The curvature of the C1 blend surfaces is most pronounced at the blend edges. The intermediate area has relatively shallow curvature. Think of this as curvature density. In Tangential blend surfaces, the curvature is "concentrated" mostly at or near the blend edges. The C2 continuous blend surface is the most desirable and most difficult to achieve of the three. It has the softest curvature that is evenly distributed across the blend surface. The 1/3 of the surface nearest a blend edge has the same curvature as the base surface at a, the last 1/3 of the surface at b has the same curvature as surface b at its blend edge. The intermediate 1/3 of the blend surface gradually transitions the curvature at a to curvature at b. Figure 9.1 shows the three kinds of blend surfaces, shown in blue, and the geometric difference between them. Even though the C2 blend surface has the "softest" curvature and is the prettiest of the three surfaces, it is very subjective. The kind of blend that is needed is dictated by the demands of the project. It is quite possible to mix the curvature types on the same blend surface for custom effects. It must be understood that in form•Z we are not deriving mathematically accurate continuities—at best we get surfaces that look right and render cleanly. Remember that we are modeling for animation—for us, beauty is only skin deep. We are not after mathematical perfection, and lack the specialized blending tools to do that. We want shading that looks as if it was generated with mathematical precision. An average person, at first glance, might think that it is simply not possible. Employing manual methods, a user cannot create surfaces that are mathematically precise. Understand that even dedicated mathematically precise modeling systems still approximate the blend surfaces by tessellating them into polygons for rendering. We can and will learn to use manual modeling methods to create smoothly flowing blends.

This chapter may be the most difficult one in this book. We will start with simple exercises and gradually advance to the more complex ones, including adding blended surfaces to our ongoing space car project. Even though this chapter presents basic rules you will need to create blend surfaces, we simply cannot predict every situation that might arise in real-world effects production. In those cases, we expect you to adjust the basic guidelines to suit your particular need.

In this chapter, we will be discussing the use of the Skin tool found in form•Z version and later. Skin, while not the easiest tool to use, is an extremely powerful one. It really shines when used to create blend surfaces. As you have seen by now, this book does not concentrate on explaining individual tools—form•Z manuals and tutorials are excellent sources for this information. Rather, we have decided to concentrate on advanced modeling topics and explain how to use selected tools for modeling within a particular topic.

Introductory Exercise

BASIC CONCEPTS OF SURFACE BLENDING

In this first exercise, we will introduce you to the most basic concepts of creating blends. We will create the three basic types of blend surfaces described earlier. Create a new project. As always, our Grid is set to 1′ XYZ modules with 12 subdivisions.

1. Working from the top view, create a 24″ by 24″ rectangle. Subdivide the rectangle using the Mesh tool. Mesh Options is set to Normal Alignment, X: 2″, Y: 2″, Z: 2″. Rename the default layer "Surfaces" (Figure 9.2).

2. Using the Copy Transfer Mode, move a duplicate of the mesh 12″ along the +Y-axis and up 6″ along the Z-axis (Figure 9.3).

3. Create a new layer, "Blend Edges," and make it active. Set Topology to Segment and select the highlighted segments shown in Figure 9.3. Set Derivative Surface Options to Selected Segments, and Status Of Objects to Keep. Create blend edges. Ghost the "Surfaces" layer. Notice that the "blend edges" lines have the same topological direction (Figure 9.4).

4. Create a new layer, "C0 Blend." Copy/Paste the blend edges into this layer. Hide the "Blend Edges" layer. Using the blend edges as source cross-sections, create a Positional (C0) blend surface using the C-Mesh tool (Figure 9.5).

   Set Controlled Mesh Options to:
   Construct Plain Mesh

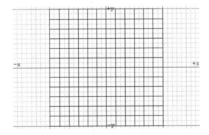

FIGURE *Default layer "Surfaces."*
9.2

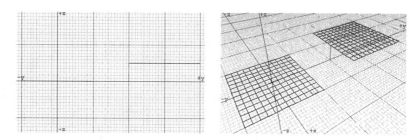

FIGURE *Duplicate of surface mesh—step 4.*
9.3

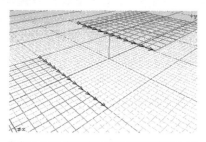

FIGURE *Surfaces layer—step 3*
9.4

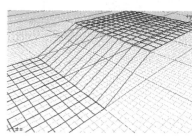

FIGURE *Positional blend surface.*
9.5

Construct Directly
Length Of Net: Use Existing, Depth Of Net:Use Control Line Intervals
Mesh Length: At Control Points, Mesh Depth: At Control Points
Controlled Mesh Smoothing Options : Length : None, Depth : None
Type Of Controlled Mesh Object: Open Ends (Surface)
Status Of Objects to Keep.

5. Now hide the "C0 Blend" layer. Create a new layer, "C1 Blend," make it the active layer, and paste copies of the blend edges into this layer. Set transformation mode to One Copy. Working from the top view, move a duplicate of each of the blend edges 3″ along the Y-axis (length) toward its opposite blend edge (Figure 9.6). In creating C1 and C2 blends, the immediate duplicate of the blend edge always lies on the same plane as the blend edge (Figure 9.6).

6. Now we are ready to create the C1 blend surface. Make the following changes to C-Mesh Options:

Mesh Depth: # Of Segments;6, Per Segment, Smooth
Controlled Mesh Smoothing Options; Depth; B-Spline, Adjust To new;
    Depth, Degree 3, # Of Points; 64
Set Status Of Objects to Ghost

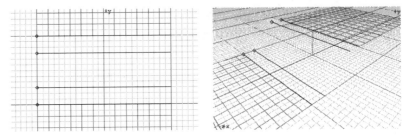

FIGURE   *C1 Blend new layer—step 5.*
9.6

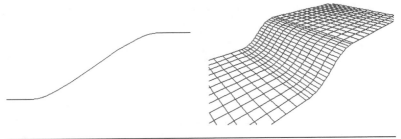

FIGURE   *Third degree B-Spline surface—step 6.*
9.7

The result is a third-degree blend B-Spline surface that has tangent continuity to the two surfaces at the blend edges. Notice the curvature and polygon density near the blend edges and shallow curvature in the middle of the blend surface (Figure 9.7).

7. The Curvature continuous (C2) blend surface is created in the same way as the C1, but with blend edge duplicates repositioned to be coresident along the Y-axis (length only). Both duplicates are located midway along the Y-axis between the blend edges. Figures 9.8 and 9.9 show the position of the duplicates and the resulting C2 blend surface.

Notice the "softer" curvature of this blend surface. The surface looks more natural and pleasing to the eye as the curvature is more or less evenly distributed along the length of the blend surface. As mentioned, C2 continuous surfaces are not just tangent at the blend edges to the base surfaces, they have the same curvature as the base surfaces that transitions along the length of the blend surface. It is perfectly all right to modulate the curvature of the blend surface by repositioning the blend edge duplicates. Where they are positioned to get the desired curvature is a matter of artistic creativity.

The preceding simple exercise introduced you to basic guidelines of creating blend surfaces with the C-Mesh tool. They are:

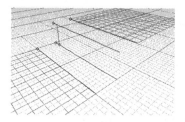

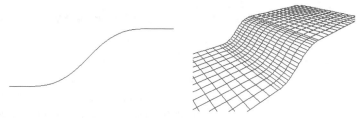

FIGURE *Position of the duplicates.*
9.8

FIGURE *Resulting C2 blend surface.*
9.9

- Identify and select segments defining the blend edges on two surfaces to be blended.
- Generate blend edges using the Derivative Surface tool.
- Generate and position blend edge duplicates per continuity desired. Closing the distance between the blend edges and the duplicates tightens the blend curvature.
- Generate the C-Mesh surface with third-degree B-Spline Depth Smoothing.
- Optionally stitch the two surfaces and the blend surface using the Stitch tool.

NOTE

It goes without saying that you should always retain copies of blend edges and blend edge duplicates in holding layers. If you need to stitch the surfaces with the blend surface, retain original copies of the surfaces. Stitching may not always be desirable; as always it is subject to production requirements.

NOTE

It is likely that, in the course of production, you will have two blend edges with different point counts. In this case, change Length Of Net, *under C-Mesh options, to use* New Points, *or* Partially New. *This will cause the C-Mesh tool to insert additional points as needed. While this is an effective, quick, and reliable technique, it may not always generate "clean" geometry. It is possible that the resulting blend surface will have excessively small or thin polygons, resulting in shading anomalies. If this happens, you need to manually insert new points into the lower count blend edge using the Insert Segment tool. As an alternative method, you may delete the points from the blend edge with the higher point count. If you do this, you must delete the corresponding points on the surface segments from which the blend edge was generated. In either case, the goal is for blend edges to have identical point counts. If time is available, we recommend, using the manual method, as it almost always results in cleaner meshes.*

Exercise

BLENDING BETWEEN TWO NONPLANAR SURFACES

The previous exercise dealt with surfaces whose blend edges, while not on the same plane, had the same vectors. Additionally, the surfaces themselves were planar. Very often, in production, this will not be the case. In the next exercise we will create a blend edge between two nonplanar surfaces that have different orientation in space. We will discuss two methods in creating the blend. The first method is the C-Mesh method, building on the knowledge from the previous example. The second, and more challenging, method will use the Skin tool. Start by creating a new project, save the one we just completed. Load or recreate the surface from Figure 8.14. Move it along the Y-axis so that its center is at world origin (0,0,0). Rename the default layer to "Surfaces."

1. Select 1/2 of the polygons on the surface, and separate from the surface using the Separate tool set to At Boundary Of Selected Faces. Set Status Of Objects to Delete. What we want are two base surfaces that we are going to blend. The two surfaces are shown in Surface1 and Surface2 (Figure 9.10).

2. Working from the right view, rotate the Surface 1 45 using 0,0,0 as the base. Then move it into position as shown in Figure 9.11. Now we proceed with modeling a blend surface to bridge these two surfaces.

3. Create a new layer, "Blend Edges," and make it active. Set Topology to Segment. Select the segment along the blend edges as shown in Figure 9.12. Convert the selected segment into blend edges using the Derivative Surface tool. Set Derivative Surface Options to Selected Segments. Set Status to Keep. After deriving the blend edges, Ghost the "Surfaces" layer. The blend edges will act as the first and last cross-sections for the C-Mesh operation.

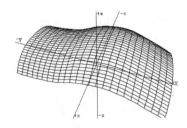

FIGURE **9.10** *Surface1 and Surface2.*

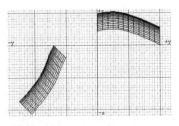

FIGURE **9.11** *Moving Surface1 into position.*

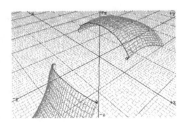

FIGURE **9.12** *Selected segment converted into blend edges.*

Blending Surfaces Using C-Mesh

To blend the surfaces using the C-Mesh method, we need to place the cross-section in such a way that we achieve desired blend surface continuity. The placement of the cross-section can be time consuming, as the only guide we have is the generated C-Mesh blend surface. If the curvature or continuity of the blend is off, we need to reposition the cross-sections and C-Mesh again. We do this until the rendered quality of the blend meets our criteria. Depending on the experience of the user, this can be a time-consuming process. One of the tasks of this book is to present you with time-saving procedures. We can save time by defining visual guides that we can use to place the cross-sections. In effect, we are visually defining a *curved space* in which the blend surface exists. Currently form•Z has no concept of *curved spaces* and surface continuities, the guides are only a visual reference. They can be used, as will be shown later, as source curves for Skin operations. In the C-Mesh method, these guides serve only as general visual references for positional adjustment of cross-sections.

1. Before we can create the curvature guide curves, we need to define custom construction planes on which the guide curves will lie. From the right side draw a 12″ by 12″ polygon as shown in Figure 9.13. Then, working from the Axonometric view, move the rectangle so one of its corners is point snapped to the endpoint on a blend edge as shown. Set topology to Face and use the Define Arbitrary Construction Plane tool to define a custom plane based on this rectangle. You may delete the rectangle after you save the plane (Figure 9.13).

NOTE

Be sure to save this custom plane using the Planes pallete. Some geometry will be created on this plane. When switching to Orthogonal view, form•Z turns off the custom plane and assigns the ortho view a default plane. You must manually override the default plane assignment by clicking on the custom plane in the Planes palette. A checkmark appears in the Planes palette denoting the currently active plane.

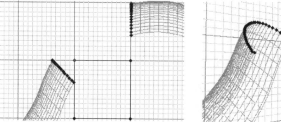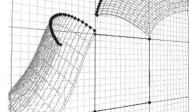

FIGURE *12″ by 12″ polygon—step 4.*
9.13

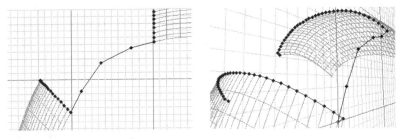

FIGURE *Polyline and average vectors—step 5.*
9.14

2. Switch to right side view and make sure that the custom plane is active. Draw a polyline as shown in Figure 9.14. Use point snapping to snap the polyline endpoints to the endpoints of the blend edges. Notice that the polyline has five points. A five-point polyline is the simplest polyline that will translate into a guide curve when converted into a third-degree B-Spline C-Curve. Additionally, note that the end segments of the polyline have the same vector as an average vector of the 2–3 lengthwise edges of the surfaces to be blended. It is vital to match vectors of the edges in order to achieve blend edge continuity. Average vectors are denoted by arrows in Figure 9.14. The middle point of the polyline is placed halfway between the blend edges.

3. Set Controlled Curve Options to Edit, Adjust To New Parameters, B-Spline, Degree: 3, # Of Points : 32. Convert the polyline to a C-Curve. Prior to conversion, paste a copy of the polyline in a hidden holding layer, just in case you make an unrecoverable mistake. After converting the polyline into a C-Curve, move a duplicate of it to align it to points on the other side of the blend edges. Use point snapping options (Figure 9.15).

4. We need to create a top center guide curve. Move a duplicate of the side guide curve and align it to touch the centermost points on the each of the blend edges. Use the C-Curve tool to sculpt the curve so it is contin-

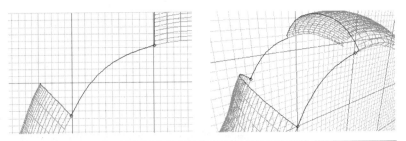

FIGURE *Converting polyline into a C-curve—step 6.*
9.15

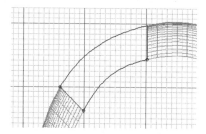 

FIGURE *Top center guide curve.*
9.16

uous with the curvature of both surfaces at and near the blend edges and touches the midpoints of the centermost segments of the blend edges (Figure 9.16).

Now we can create intermediate cross-sections for our blend surface and align them using the guide curves as a guide. Ultimately, the guide curves are visual guides to compare curvature of the blend surface. We would adjust the cross-sections so that the C-Mesh blend surface is aligned with the guide curves. As a rule of thumb, the number of cross-sections for the C-Mesh blend surface should equal the number of control points on the guide curves. The cross-sections should be placed at or near the locations of the control points along the length of the intended blend surface. Looking from the side, the angle vector of the cross-section should be perpendicular to the tangent of the guide curve at the control point location. We have five control points on our guide C-Curves, and we have two blend edges as first and last cross-sections. That leaves us to generate the three intermediate cross-sections.

5. First we will generate the middle cross-section. In this particular case, we can use a copy of one of the blend edges as an intermediate cross-section. However, in production, very often you will have blend edges of different shapes. You need to generate an intermediate cross-section that is a mix of the two. The following steps show how. To start, we need to generate a straight-ruled surface between the two blend edges. Set C-Mesh Options as were used for Fig. 9.1. Set **Status Of Objects** to **Keep**. Be sure that both blend edges have the same topological directions (Figure 9.17).

6. From the front view, create a rectangle that encompasses the ruled surface when viewed from the front. Switch to the right side view. Move the rectangle until it intersects the ruled surface at approximately the midpoint. Rotate the rectangle so that it is perpendicular to the tangent of the top middle guide curve. Adjust the position of the rectangle so it

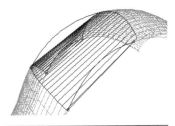

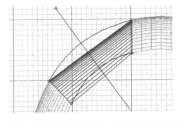

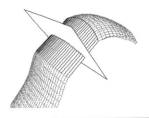

FIGURE **9.17** *Intermediate cross-section—step 8.*

FIGURE **9.18** *Right side view—step 9.*

passes through the position of the center control point of the top guide curve (Figure 9.18).

NOTE

The ruled surface is a C0 continuity blend surface.

7. Derive a line of intersection between the rectangle and the ruled surface. In form•Z 2.9.5 Line Of Intersection is found under Trim/Split Options. Set Status Of Objects to Delete as we no longer need the ruled surface and the rectangle. Adjust the direction of the derived cross-section to match the direction of the blend edges, if necessary (Figure 9.19).

Now we are ready to place the intermediate cross-section and to place blend edge duplicates. Our goal is to create a third-degree B-Spline C-Mesh surface that has the same curvature as the guide curves and point matches the base surfaces at the blend edges. Because of how B-Spline smoothing interpolates the surface across the cross-sections, we cannot simply align the our cross-sections to the guide curves. We need to place the intermediate blend cross-sections so their tops and bottoms are aligned to the positions of the control points on the C-Curve guides.

8. Copy and paste copies of the original polylines used for the C-Curve guides into the current working layer (Figure 9.20).

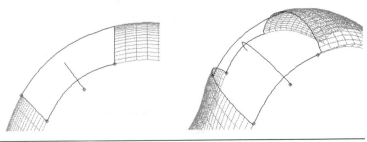

FIGURE **9.19** *Derived intermediate cross-section.*

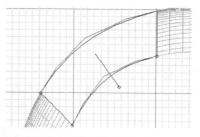

FIGURE
9.20
Original polylines pasted into working layer—step 11.

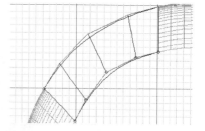

FIGURE
9.21
Positioning top and bottom polylines—step 12.

9. Working from the right side view, Move, Rotate, and Nonuniform Scale the middle cross-section so that its top is aligned to the middle point of the top guide polyline, and its bottom point is aligned to the middle point of the bottom guide polyline. Create a duplicate of each of the blend edges. Transform them in a similar manner but align them to the next to last points on the top and bottom polylines. Remember that this just orthogonal alignment, *do not* use any geometrical snaps. We recommend turning off Distance snapping and zooming in to refine the position (Figure 9.21).

10. Now we can create the blend surface. Create a new layer, "Blend C-Mesh Surface," and make it the active layer. Set the Controlled Mesh Options as shown for Figure 9.7. Set **Status Of Objects** to **Keep**. Preselect the cross-sections in sequential order and create the C-Mesh blend surface (Figure 9.22). Figure 9.23 shows the matching curvature of the blended C-Mesh surface to the guide curves.

11. The last and optional step is to stitch the base and blend surfaces into one meshed surface. The advantage of stitching is that form•Z will smooth across the blend edges, completely eliminating any visible seams. Figure 9.24 shows the rendering of the stitched surfaces.

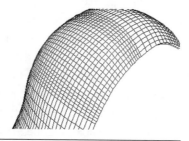

FIGURE
9.22
C-Mesh blend surface.

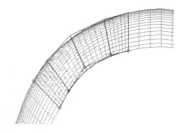

FIGURE
9.23
Matching curvature of blend surface to guide curves.

FIGURE *Rendering of stitched surfaces.*
9.24

Guidelines for Blending with C-Mesh

Let's now review the general guidelines for blend surface creation for surfaces that have different spatial orientation using the C-Mesh method.

- Identify segments and generate blend edges.
- Create top and bottom guide C-Curves.
- Generate an intermediate blend surface cross-section, and create blend edge duplicates.
- Align the cross-sections to the control points of the guide curves.
- Create the C-Mesh blend surface using the smoothing attributes of the guide C-Curves.
- Optionally stitch the surfaces with the blend surface.

Blending Surfaces Using Skin Method

In the previous two exercises, we dealt with creating a blend surface using the C-Mesh method. The C-Mesh method is a reliable, but slower way of modeling blend surfaces. A more efficient method of modeling blend surfaces makes use of *skinning*. The Skin tool is a powerful feature in form•Z, that when used properly is very fast, reliable, and controllable. It is one of the most powerful and flexible features found in form•Z. Unfortunately, it is not the easiest tool to use, but Skin has been improved and refined in form•Z 3.0. The implementation of the tool is excellent, and the difficulty lies in successfully satisfying the parameters for successful Skin tool employment. In the following exercise, we will learn about and satisfy parameters to successfully employ the Skin tool in surface blending. Before proceeding, I wish to clarify, that while I recommend the use of the Skin method over the C-Mesh method, this recommendation is not absolute—as a matter of fact, very few things in CGI are absolute. The method that you choose to employ depends on your particular situation, time available, and your modeling style. There are times when the C-Mesh method may even be superior to the Skin method.

To successfully employ the Skin tool, we must meet a few parameters. Basically, for the Skin tool to work you must supply a properly constructed network of curves and lines.

- Meet the minimum requirement for number of paths and source shapes.
- Meet the geometric snapping requirement of the Skin tool. Basically, the endpoints of source curves must be snapped to points of path curves, and vice versa.
- All source shapes must have the same topological direction.
- All path shapes must have the same topological direction.
- All curves must meet the point count parameters stated in Skin Options.
- The Skin Options must have proper settings.

Since we are using the Skin tool in the construction of the blend surfaces, we must satisfy the following additional parameters:

- The source shapes (blend edges) must be properly constructed to match base surfaces.
- The path shapes must have curvature that defines the intended curvature of the blend surface, and must have continuity to the base surfaces.
- The Skin Options must be defined and both source and path shapes must be constructed and positioned as to create topologically clean and geometrically continuous Skin surfaces.

We wish to explain the parameters a bit more closely and how they are affected by blend surface modeling considerations.

- **Meet the minimum requirement for the number of paths and source shapes.** The minimum number of source shapes allowed by the Skin tool is one, the minimum number of paths is three. However, since the blend almost always occurs between two surfaces, the minimum number of source shapes for blends modeling is two. Blend edges should always serve as source shapes. We do not recommend, and it is not wise, using blend edges as paths. The minimum number of paths allowed is three, a blend almost always occurs between edges of two surfaces. There are blends that blend three or more surfaces, called *compound blends*. More on compound blends later.
- **All endpoints of each of the source and path shapes must be snapped.** The two endpoints of the source shapes must be snapped to the endpoints of the path shapes. This is where many problems arise. The curve network will look right, but the Skin tool will still generate errors. This mostly happens when the paths are C-Curves. Because of the interpolating

algorithms used in evaluation of C-Curves, the geometric endpoints may not be coresident with the end control points of the C-Curves, and are not coresident with the endpoint of the path or source point that it is supposed to be snapped to. To make sure that everything is snapped in the Skin curve network, set Topology to Point and manually point snap each and every endpoint.

- **As stated, the minimum number of paths is three.** In regards to blend modeling, we will use path curves to define the geometric continuity of the blend surface and use them to topologically match the blend surface to the base surfaces. Even though it is not a hard requirement, all path curves should have identical point counts. By directly controlling the point count on path curves, we can modulate the polygonal resolution of the blend surface to optimize its polygon count.

- **All source shapes (our blend edges) must have the same topological direction.** The direction of the blend edge segments is defined by face normals of the base surfaces. Topology Attributes is used to change direction. In practice, it makes no difference which way the source shapes are going, as long it is in the same direction.

- **All path shapes must have the same topological direction.** The same rules apply as for source shapes.

- **Both source curves (blend edges) should have the same number of points.** The point count and point density of the source curves (blend edges) defines the mesh resolution of skin mesh. Ideally, both should have the same number of points, but this is not a hard requirement. If the point count is not the same, the Skin tool will insert new points to compensate, and the resulting blend surface might not have the same *topology* as the base surfaces. This can cause shading anomalies during rendering at the seams. By keeping the point count the same on both blend edges, we ensure that we have point matching of the blend edges of the blend surface and the blend edges of the base surfaces. Point matching combined with curvature continuity results in nearly perfect seamless rendering.

- **Keep the point count the same on path C-Curves.** This is a rule of thumb, and is not a hard requirement. It is good modeling practice. By keeping the point count the same on all path curves, we directly control the mesh resolution along the depth of the blend. Later on we will cover compound blends where both source and path curves are derived from blend edges. By matching the point counts on all path curves and all source curves, we ensure that the blend surfaces will match the base surfaces in continuity and in topology.

Using the base surfaces from the previous exercise, we will create a blend surface using the Skin method. Begin by hiding all layers except "Surfaces," make sure the two surfaces are the only objects in this layer.

1. The first step in the Skin method, as in the C-Mesh method, is to identify blend edge segments and create blend edges using the Derivative Surface tool. Create a new layer, "Skin blend curves," and make it active. Recall that we already have constructed the blend edges. Copy/Paste copies of blend edges into this layer. If you wish to practice, derive new blend edges using the procedure outlined earlier. Blend edges will serve as *source* shapes for the Skin tool (Figure 9.25).

2. The next step is to create path curves. The procedure for creating the path curves is identical to the one used to create guide curves for the C-Mesh method, with one difference. The endpoints of *path* curves must be snapped (with Point Snapping) to the points on the *source* curves. You may practice the procedure by creating new path curves or Copy/Paste them into the current layer. If you Copy/Paste, you need to fix the snapping of the middle curve. In the C-Mesh method, it was loosely positioned, as it was a visual guide. In the Skin method it must be precisely snapped to the points on the source curves, nearest the center. Always make sure that points are snapped properly. If in doubt, set Topology to Point and resnap the endpoints. Figure 9.26 shows the completed Skin curve network.

NOTE

To keep the procedure consistent, we will always treat blend edges as the source shapes in the Skin curve network. In form•Z terminology, the "width" of the surface is referred to as Length, and the "length" is referred to as Depth. The guide curves act as path curves. The use of blend edges is interchangeable with source curves, and guide curves are interchangeable with path curves.

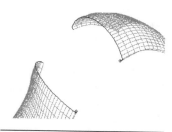

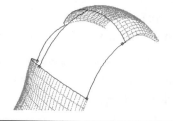

FIGURE **9.25** *Active skin blend curves layer—step 1.*

FIGURE **9.26** *Completed skin curve network.*

NOTE

The following are rules of thumb that will make working with the Skin tool easier. The Skin tool works best with plain curves (non C-Curves). After sculpting the shape of any C-Curve in Skin network, manually resnap individual endpoints— this has to do with the interpolation of the C-Curves from the polylines. Often the endpoints on C-Curves using Spline *interpolation will be slightly off the position of the polyline endpoints. Consequently, they will not be snapped, causing the Skin tool to generate an out of tolerance message error. You could get around this by setting* Use Tolerance *in Skin tool options. However, this is not recommended as it might create the blend surfaces with points that do not match the edge points on base surfaces. To compensate for the precision error, set Topology to Points and manually resnap the endpoints of the C-Curve. Paths should have equal or nearly equal source curve point spacing between them. If the source curves (blend edges) have 64 points, then each of the three path curves must have 32 points between them. If you need to use four paths, then the paths should be placed at every 16th points along the source curve. The Skin tool, when used properly, is very reliable and very fast. However, you may come across cases where you have met all the parameters, but the wrong surface is generated. It may have geometry that does not conform to the shape of the path or source curves. The most likely solution is to add more paths. The problem comes from the lack of information provided by the three paths. In a two source X 3 path Skin network, add two additional path curves, spaced equidistantly between the end path and the center path. Adjust the shape to match the curvature, and don't forget to resnap the endpoints. Adding additional paths solve 95% of Skin problems. If you are unable to solve the blend surface using the Skin method, fall back on the C-Mesh method.*

3. With the Skin curve network complete, we can now create the blend surface using the Skin tool. Create a new layer, "Skin Blend Surface," and make it active. Set the Skin Options as shown.

Skinning Along Paths, # Of Sources;2, # Of Paths;3
Boundary Based
Placement Type: By Current Position
Point Paring; Must Have Same # Of Points
Status Of Objects set to Keep.

Create the blend surface by first sequentially clicking on source curves and then on paths curves. Figure 9.27 shows the completed skinned blend surface.

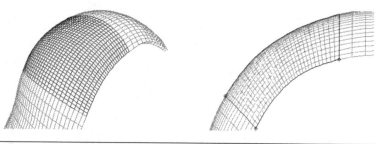

FIGURE *Completed skinned blend surface.*
9.27

Blending Closed Loop Edges

So far in this chapter we have dealt with creating continuous blends between surfaces whose blend edges are open; that is, the lines that were defined as blend edges are reported by the Query tool as open surfaces (open lines). This may not always be the case. About half the time you will be tasked with blending two surfaces whose blend edges are closed loops. A closed loop blend edge gets reported by the Query tool as a closed surface. Both C-Mesh and Skin blend construction methods may be employed. As with open blend edges, the Skin method is the recommended method. We will cover both but will concentrate on the Skin method, because it is superior in almost every case to C-Mesh. Figure 9.28 shows a simple case of blending two meshed surfaces with geometrically dissimilar closed loop blend edges. The figure shows the geometric and topological differences between a closed loop blend done via skinning and via C-Mesh methods. All the guidelines and rules of thumb used for open blend edges fully apply. The main difference between blending open and closed blend edges is the amount of preparation that the closed blend edge must undergo. Often the closed loop blend edge is a result of a Trim operation, resulting in a blend edge that is "dirty," that is, it has excessively small segments and an excessive number of points. Both can cause small polygons in blend surface mesh resulting in shading anomalies and unnecessary "heavy" meshes. Prior to generating the lines from blend edges, described earlier, you may wish to clean up the meshes of the surfaces to be blended. The cleaning up involves deleting extra points and segments, and inserting additional segments as necessary. The goal of the cleanup is to create blend edges that do not have points excessively close together, and if possible, for both blend edges to have the same number of points. Examine Figure 9.28 and compare the open blend edge guidelines to the blend, solved by skinning and by lofting. Recreating the surfaces in this figure is the subject of the next exercise.

1. Begin by creating a new project. Recall that our grid settings are set to XYZ modules 1′ with 12 subdivisions.

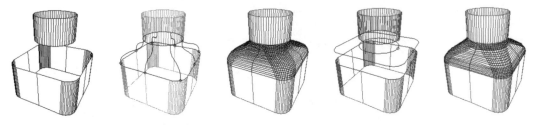

FIGURE *Blending two meshed with dissimilar closed loop blend edges.*
9.28

2. Rename the default layer to "Surfaces."

3. First we need to create our base surfaces. Working from the top view create a 64-point circle with 7" radius, and a 24" by 24" rectangle. The center of both 2D shapes is at world origin (0,0,0) (Figure 9.29).

4. Round the rectangle with the Fit fillet tool. In form•Z 2.9.5 use the Edit Line tool. Set options Fit Fillet; # Of Edges 14, Radius 4"

   Using Insert Point or Inset Segment (form•Z 2.9.5), insert four additional points as shown, one in the middle of each straight segment. The point count of rectangle should be 64 (Figure 9.30).

5. Extrude the circle 8" up along the Z-axis.

   — Extrude the rectangle –12" down the Z-axis.

   — Move the extruded cylinder 7" up along the Z-axis.

   — Topologically Delete the capping faces of the extruded solids, to convert them into meshed surfaces.

   — In form•Z 2.9.5 set the Delete tool to delete **Topology** for all entities except **Points**.

   These two objects will serve as our base surface which we will blend (Figure 9.31).

6. Create a new layer, "C-Mesh Blend cross-sections," and make it active. Next we identify and generate blend edges by selecting the blend edge segments and converting them into lines using the Derivative Surface

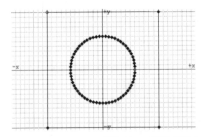

FIGURE *64-point circle with 7" radius.*
9.29

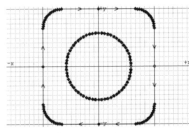

FIGURE *64-point count rectangle.*
9.30

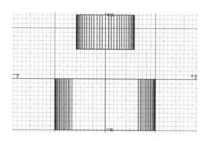
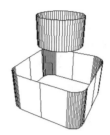

FIGURE *Base surfaces to blend.*
9.31

tool that is set to **Selected Segments**. Adjust the directions of the two lines and align their first points (Figure 9.32).

7. Working from the right view, create duplicates of the blend edges. Move each duplicate halfway between the two blend edges (Figure 9.33).

8. Set the C-Mesh options per the settings used to create the surface in Figure 9.7, but make the following change:

— Mesh Depth: # Of Segments;8, Per Segment, Smooth
— Set **Status** of **Objects** to **Keep**.
— Create a new layer, "C-Mesh Blend Surface", and make it active.
— Select the cross-sections in sequential order (Figure 9.33) and create the C-Mesh blend surface.

Figure 9.34 shows the completed C-Mesh blend.

Before proceeding to constructing a Skin blend surface, hide the "C-Mesh Blend Surface" and "C-Mesh Blend Cross-Sections" layers.

9. As before, the first step in constructing a Skin blend is to identify and derive two blend edges that will serve as source *curves*. You may derive new ones or Copy/Paste them from the "Blend Edges" layer into a new layer, "Skin Blend Curves." Align the directions and the first points of both blend edges using the Topological Attributes tool (Figure 9.35).

10. Begin constructing the *path* curves by drawing a straight two-point line

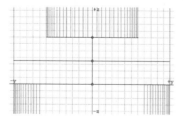

FIGURE *Right view of two blend*
9.32 *edges.*

FIGURE *C-Mesh blend surface.*
9.33

FIGURE *Completed C-Mesh blend.*
9.34

that is snapped to the first points of the two *source* curves. Turn Distance Snap Off and enable Point Snapping option, then draw the line (Figure 9.36).

11. Insert three points using the Insert Segment mode, and Midpoint Snapping options. First insert a single point in the middle of the segment, then one in the middle of each of the two segments (Figure 9.37).

12. Working from the front view, move two intermediate points as shown along the X-axis until the segments that they define have the same angle vector as the edge segments of the base surfaces. In this case, the segments are perfectly straight. This polyline will define a C1 continuous *path* curve. Moving the points along the Z-axis until they are at the same height, as the middle point will define a C2 continuity *path* curve. For this exercise we will deal with C1. Feel free to experiment with various *path* curvatures (Figure 9.38).

13. Set C-Curve options as per settings used to generate the *path* curve in Figure 9.15. Convert the polyline into a C-Curve, and do not modify any control points. Prior to conversion, Copy/Paste the polyline into a hidden holding layer. Notice the soft curvature of the C-Curve *path* that tangentially matches the curvature of the base surfaces at the ends. Remember to resnap the endpoints of the curve to the first points of the *source* shapes (Figure 9.39).

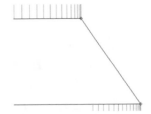

FIGURE *Blend edges that will serve*
9.35   *as source curves.*

FIGURE *Beginnings of path curve construction.*
9.36

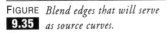

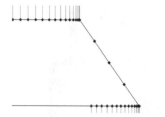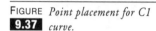

FIGURE
9.37 *Point placement for C1 curve.*

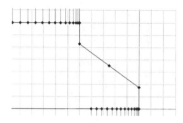

FIGURE
9.38 *C1 continuous path curve.*

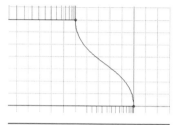

FIGURE
9.39 *C-curve path.*

To achieve more natural curvature, just move the two intermediate control points (don't move the middle point) up or down along the Z-axis until both are midway between the blend edges. Delete the middle point. Figure 9.40 shows the placement of the point for a C2 continuous *path* curve and Figure 9.41 shows the curve. Compare this curve to the one in Figure 9.39. You have total creative freedom to achieve any kind of curvature that you wish by simply repositioning the points on the polyline. This allows you to mix curvatures to get something in between C1 and C2 or between C0 & C1. In dedicated surface modeling applications you would not have this freedom—there is no one "right" curvature. The kind of curvature and continuity depends on the demands of the project, and your creativity.

14. Using the Cont-Copy (C-Copy in form•Z 2.9.5) transformation mode, create seven rotated duplicates of the *path* curve, using 0,0,0 as the base of rotation and an angle offset of 45 degrees for each duplicate.

    After the rotation the four curves should be precisely snapped to points, but the four points in the corners are not. Nonuniformly scale them using the Point Snap option. Verify that endpoints on all path curves are snapped properly. Recall the rule that paths must be snapped equidistantly (point count). Each path endpoint should be snapped to every eighth point on the *source* curve. End point snapping is crucial and is the cause of most Skin problems (Figure 9.42).

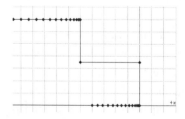

FIGURE
9.40 *Point placement for C2 curve.*

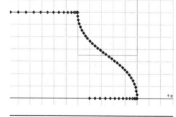

FIGURE
9.41 *C-curve path.*

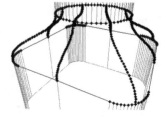

FIGURE
9.42 *Verification that endpoints on all path curves are snapped properly.*

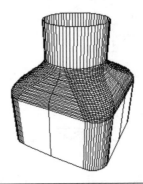

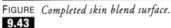

FIGURE **9.43** *Completed skin blend surface.*

FIGURE **9.44** *RenderZone rendering of final product.*

15. Set the Skin Options as follows:

    Skinning Along Paths:#Sources 2 ; #Paths 8 ; Boundary Based
    Placement Type: By Current Position, Use Tollerance is OFF
    Point Paring: Must Have Same # Of Points
    Status Of Objects: Keep.
    — Create a new layer, "Skin Blend Surface," and make it active.
    — Create the Skin blend surface. When prompted, select the source shapes first in sequential order, and then select path curves in sequential order. The sequential order is shown in Figure 9.42. The completed Skin blend surface is shown in Figure 9.43.

16. The last and optional step is to stitch the copies of the base surfaces and the Skin blend surface in a separate layer. Figure 9.44 shows the RenderZone rendering of the final product. Notice that we cannot discern where the individual surfaces end and begin.

Continuity Surface Matching

Blending does not always involve creation of a third surface to blend two existing surfaces. At times, you will need to construct a second surface that has continuity with a single existing surface along defined blend edges. "Edges" is plural because it is possible for two surfaces to be matched at more than one blend edge. The procedure is called "Surface Continuity Matching." For speed we will also call it "surface matching." We have seen an example of this in Chapter 5 where we constructed a vertical stabilizer to conform to and be tangentially matched to the Aft Plate. There is overlap between conformal modeling and surface blending as often you will need to build surfaces that are both conformal and continuous with preexisting surfaces. Fortunately, it is easier to match surfaces than to blend them as there is only one base surface to deal with. The majority of the rules used in blending are easily applied in matching.

A common use of continuity matching is building blended depressions or elevations into an existing surface. In the following exercise we will use the three surfaces that we created in the preceding exercise. The objective of this exercise is to create a curving trim on the surface with blended edges.

1. Begin by creating a new project. Copy/Paste the two bases and a blend surface in a default layer. Rename the default layer to "Base Surface." Set Status Of Object to Delete and Stitch the three surfaces into a single surface. In Query Object /Edit, assign it Smooth Shading attributes (Figure 9.45).

2. Now we create a trim curve that will delineate the orthographic projection of the trim. Working from the front view, create a closed polyline as shown. Convert the polyline into a 64-point third degree B-Spline C-Curve using the C-Curve tool. You may wish to place a copy of the polyline in a hidden holding layer first.

3. Extrude the closed curve 24″ (you may need to reverse the curve). Set Status Of Objects to Delete. Prior to extrusion, Copy/Paste a backup of the C-Curve into a holding layer (Figure 9.47).

4. Create a new layer, Blend Edge, and make it active. Derive LOI between the extruded solid and the base surface. After derivation of the LOI, make the "Base Surface" the active layer and hide or ghost the "Blend Edge" layer (Figure 9.48).

Prior to proceeding to the next step, Copy/Paste copies of the base surface and the extrusion in a hidden holding layer.

5. Trim the base surface with the extrusion. Set the Trim, Split, & Stitch Options to Trim/Split ; Trim ; First Object (Figure 9.49).

FIGURE   *Base surface figure.*
9.45

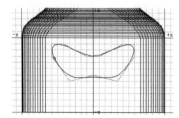

FIGURE   *Created trim curve.*
9.46

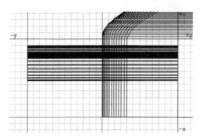
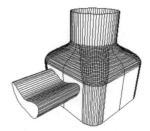

FIGURE *Closed curve extrusion.*
9.47

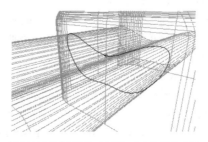
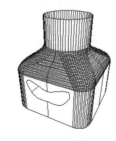

FIGURE *Blend edge layer.*
9.48

FIGURE *Trimmed base surface extrusion.*
9.49

6. Ghost the "Base Surface" layer and make the "Blend Edge" layer active. Working from the front view, create an inner offset duplicate using the Parallel tool.

— First topologically delete any segment. In form•Z 2.9.5 set **Segment Option** set to **Topology** in the Delete tool.
— Parallel the curve inside with 1/3" offset.
— Close both curves. In form•Z 2.9.5 use the Edit Line tool.

7. Select the paralleled duplicate and switch to the right side view. Set **Transformation Mode** to **Copy** and move it +1/3" along +Y-axis. The result should be three curves, equidistantly spaced with 1/3" separation (Figure 9.51).

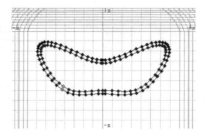

FIGURE *Inner offset duplicate.*
9.50

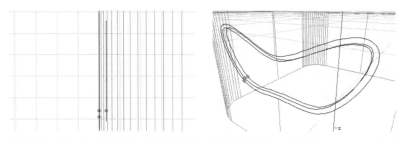

FIGURE *Three curve duplicate.*
9.51

8. Create a new layer, "Edge Blend." Set the Controlled Mesh Options per the settings used for the surface in Figure 9.7. Change Degree from 3 to 2, and change Mesh Depth: # Of Segments from 6 to 3. We cannot generate a third-degree surface with only three cross-sections. However, a second degree B-Spline surface will still be tangentially matched with only three cross-sections. We do not need six segments as it would create unnecessarily heavy mesh, three will more than suffice (Figure 9.52).

9. The last and optional step is to stitch the surfaces together and assign smoothing attributes to the result. Figure 9.53 shows the RenderZone rendering of the result.

The blended edge surface that we created is called an "edge roll." This simulates rolling or bending the edges on a surface. This is very common when dealing with simulating sheet metal surfaces. In real life, a metal break would be used to roll the edges. In CGI, rolled edges add a significant amount of realism to the model. The decision whether or not to stitch the edge roll surface with base surface depends on texture mapping and material applications considerations.

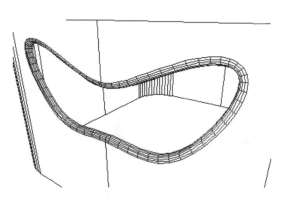

FIGURE *New "Edge Blend" layer.*
9.52

FIGURE *RenderZone rendering of the "edge roll."*
9.53

Creating Blended Depressions and Elevations

A slight modification of the technique used to create an edge roll in the previous exercise can be used to create a blended depression or an elevation on the base surface. In the next exercise we will create a depression on the base surface. For the base surface we will use the surface from the previous exercise. If you have not done so, stitch the base surface and an edge roll surface together. Create a new project and Copy/Paste the base surface into a default layer of the new project. Change the name of the default layer to "Base Surface."

1. Working from the right side view, create a 36-point circle with 4″ radius as shown in Figure 9.54.
2. Copy/Paste a copy of the circle into a hidden holding layer. Extrude the circle 24″ as shown in Figure 9.55, set Status Of Objects to Delete.
3. Derive the LOI between the base surface and the extrusion. Keep the operands. Place the LOI into a new layer, "Depression Cross-Sections." Keep the "Base Surface" as the active layer (Figure 9.56).
4. Ghost the "Depression Cross-Sections" layer. Use the Trim/ Split tool to trim the base surface with the cylindrical extrusion. Set the Status Of Object to Keep, but place copies of both operands into a holding layer (Figure 9.57).
5. Ghost the "Base Surface" layer and make "Depression Cross-Sections" the active layer. Working from the right view, with Copy transformation mode, Nonuniformly Scale the blend edge cross-section using the center of it as the base. Use the following scale values; 1, .75, .75. Notice that the blend edge and the first duplicate are coplanar (Figure 9.58).
6. Select the duplicate and switch to the front view. Create another duplicate and move it 1″ in the -X-axis. The 1″ is the depth of the depression (Figure 9.59).
7. Select the second duplicate and switch to the right side view. Create a smaller duplicate of this cross-section using the Nonuniform Scale tool

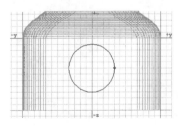

FIGURE 9.54 *36-point circle with 4″ radius.*

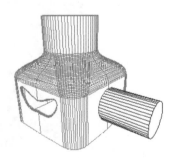

FIGURE 9.55 *24″ extruded circle.*

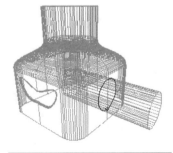

FIGURE 9.56 *"Depression cross-sections" layer.*

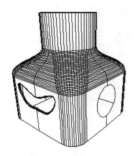

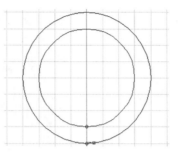

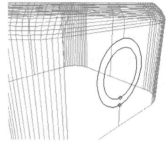

FIGURE *Trimmed base surface.*
9.57

FIGURE *"Depression Cross-sections" active layer.*
9.58

and using center of the cross-section as the base. Use scale values of 1, .75, .75. Notice that the last two cross-sections are coplanar (Figure 9.60).

8. Set C-Mesh options per those used to create the surface in Figure 9.7. Change **Mesh Depth: # Of Segments;** from 6 to 4. Create a new layer, "Depression Surface," and make it active. Select the cross-sections in sequential order, (shown in Figure. 9.60), and create a depression C-Mesh surface. Set **Status Of Objects** to **Keep.** Copy/Paste into this layer a copy of the #4 cross-section. Hide the "Depression Cross-sections" layer. Stitch the surface and the #4 cross-section together. Set **Status Of Objects** to **Delete** for the stitch only (Figure 9.61).

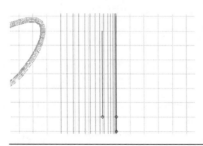

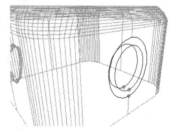

FIGURE *Front view of duplicate.*
9.59

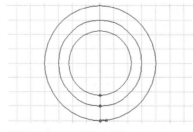

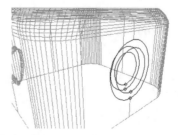

FIGURE *Right side view of second duplicate.*
9.60

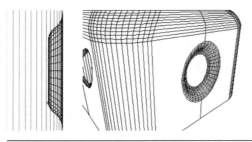

FIGURE
9.61
Completed surface depression.

FIGURE
9.62
RenderZone rendering of the surface depression.

9. The RenderZone rendering of the surface depression surface and base surface stitched and Smoothing Attributes applied (Figure 9.62).

To set up a Skin network, we go through the process of generating and positioning cross-sections (sources) but delete the two intermediate ones before generating paths. Since we already have the source curves, just Copy/Paste them into a new layer, "Skin Blend Curves." (Figure 9.63).

1. Create a 4-point polyline for generating a C2 continuous path curve as shown in Figures 9.40 and 9.41, adjusted for this surface (Figure 9.64).
2. Convert the polyline into 12-point third-degree B-Spline path C-Curve. Confirm that the geometric endpoints of the path are snapped to the first points of the source curves. Correct if necessary using Move with the point snapping option. Create two rotated duplicates of the path curve, each with a 120-degree offset. After rotation, confirm snapping of the endpoint. Use center of blend edge as the base for rotation (Figure 9.65).
3. Create a new layer, "Skin Depression Surface," and make it active. Create a skinned matched depression surface using the Skin Options settings from Figure 9.43 except that # Paths: should be changed to 3. As usual, Status Of Objects is set to Keep. Copy/Paste the smaller path into this

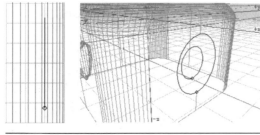

FIGURE
9.63
"Skin Blend Curves" layer.

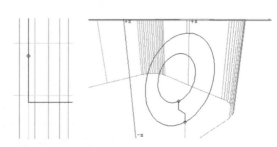

FIGURE
9.64
4-point polyline for C2 continuous curve.

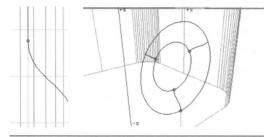
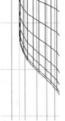

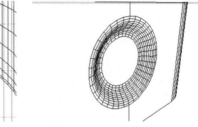

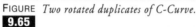

FIGURE *Two rotated duplicates of C-Curve.*
9.65

FIGURE *Completed "Skin Depression Surface."*
9.66

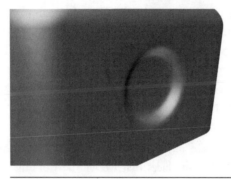

FIGURE *RenderZone rendering of base surface and*
9.67 *skinned depression.*

layer. Stitch the skinned surface with the path with **Status Of Objects** set to **Delete** (Figure 9.66).

4. RenderZone rendering of a base surface and skinned depression stitched and smoothing attributes assigned (Figure 9.67).

Summary

We have gained enough basic information to geometrically solve almost any blending or matching problem. Feel free to modify and adapt the ideas that we presented to suit your particular situation. From experience, we can tell you that all rules and guidelines do not work all the time. However, all of them work most of the time. Knowing when and how much to modify the techniques is a factor of experience and feel. Practice and experimentation is the key. Set up your own situations and apply the described techniques to them. If you do not get the desired results, review the techniques and simulate how to adapt them to the situation. We recommend that you start with situations similar to the exercises shown. While creating your own models, gradually increase the difficulty, recognizing that the same techniques will work with slight modification according to the situation. If you are having difficulty understanding the procedures and concepts, go back and do the exercises as many times as it takes for you to feel comfortable with the techniques. You should feel comfortable with your level of understanding before proceeding to the final exercise of this chapter. In the final exercise, we will use the learned blending and surface matching techniques to continue modeling our ongoing space car project. At this point we are assuming that you are comfortable with the procedures and concepts outlined in earlier exercises, so the descriptions will not be as detailed as they were in earlier exercises. Certain implied tasks, such as retaining originals, holding layers, Copy/Paste, will not always be specified. By now we expect you to be proficient in layer and geometry management. Also, we will refer to **Status Of Objects** as simply Status; for example, Status to Delete means that you should set **Status Of Objects** to **Delete**.

The objective of the following exercise is to add blended headlight surfaces to the Fore section. Load the project. Rename the current Fore Section layer to "Fore Section Virgin." Create a new layer, "Fore Section," and Copy/Paste the Fore Section geometry into it. Hide the virgin layer. Figure 9.68 shows the Fore Section ready for modeling.

1. To ease and speed up the modeling workflow, we should separate and isolate the faces that we will be working on. Select and separate the shown faces, Status to Delete. The capping faces (but not the bevels) were separated and ghosted. After separation, Ghost, but don't delete, the faces. They will be needed later (Figure 9.69).

2. Working from the top view, create a line as shown. Turn off Distance Snap and use the Face Center snap option. After creating the line, orthographically project it (Status to Delete) to flatten it. Create a mirror duplicate of it (Figure 9.70).

3. Join & Close the two lines into a single closed surface (Figure 9.71).

4. Using the Fit fillet, round the front and rear segments. Use the following Fit fillet values:

   Rear segment; # Of Edges: 8, Radius: 1″.
   Front segment; # Of Edges: 16, Radius: 3″.

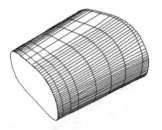

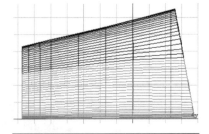

FIGURE *Fore Section ready for modeling.*
9.68

FIGURE *Isolated bevel faces.*
9.69

FIGURE
9.70
Mirror duplicate of "Fore Section."

FIGURE
9.71
Single closed surface.

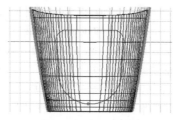

FIGURE
9.72
Top orthographic shape and blend edge boundary of headlight.

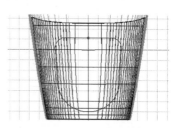

FIGURE
9.73
Split base surface with extrusion.

The resulting closed surface delineates the top orthographic shape of the headlight surface and the blend edge boundary (Figure 9.72).

5. Extrude (Perpendicular to Surface) the closed line 7″, Status to Delete. Derive LOI between the extrusion and the Fore Section base surface, Status to Keep. Then Split the base surface with the extrusion, Status To Delete (Figure 9.73).

NOTE

Don't forget to make backups of operands in holding layers.

Recall that there are times when cleaning of the blend edge is necessary. In the Wire Frame Options, turn on **Show Points**. Notice that at the trim edge there are clumps of points, and in certain places points are almost on top of each other. If left alone, those closely positioned points will translate into slivered polygons that can cause shading anomalies during rendering. As we know, extra polygons take more RAM and can cause modeling problems later. As mentioned, cleaning up the edges consists of carefully deleting selected points and segments, and inserting new segments. What makes this time consuming is that we have to equalize the point count on three objects (in this case): the Fore Section base surface, the inner trimmed surface, and the derived LOI. When complete, the number of edges and points of both surfaces and the LOI must be identical. When deciding which points to delete, the following guidelines may be of assistance:

- Avoid having points in close proximity to each other in relation to overall size of the surface. That is, avoid clumping of points. Points should be as equidistant from each other as possible.
- Avoid overly small polygons adjacent to the trim edges. Sometimes the trim will occur in such a way that very small polygons and triangles will result adjacent to the trim edges. If possible, the segments (except the segment on the trim edge) should be deleted.
- When deleting points that are shared by more than two segments, first delete the segments topologically. In form•Z 2.9.5, Delete tool options set to Segments: Topology (Edges). Delete enough segments so that the target points are shared by no more than two segments. Then delete the point. After point deletion, it may be necessary to reconnect adjacent points using Insert Segment.
- Geometric curvature integrity of trim edges takes priority over everything. If deleting a point causes polygonal silhouetting to appear in the trim edge, do not delete this point. This is very subjective, and is dependent on project requirements. If in doubt, don't delete the point.
- Points shared by more than two segments should not be deleted. This is by no means an absolute guideline. However, overall it is best to leave those points alone and delete only the (two segment shared) points that are in very close proximity to the multiple (more than two) segment shared points.
- Test shade in OpenGL/QD3D, and RenderZone often. Test shade often to see the progress you are making. It is possible that deleting certain points will inadvertently create serious shading anomalies. It would not do to delete 50 points and then find out that you created more problems than you solved.
- Work with the Show Points Wire Frame option ON. Seeing the points makes it a lot easier to work. We recommend that you map the option as a keyboard shortcut so you can toggle the display quickly.

1. Using Figures 9.74 and 9.75 as before/after guides, clean up the trim blend edge by deleting points and inserting new segments. Recall using Topology delete when deleting segments, deleting segments first, then points. Match as closely as you can your result to Figure. 9.75. Don't be too concerned if your result does not precisely match ours. The objective is to optimize the point count while keeping rendering clean. Your objective is to end up with blend edges consisting of 56 points and 56 edges. When deleting points (on the trim edge) zoom into it. Remember that for every point deleted, two coresident others must be deleted also.

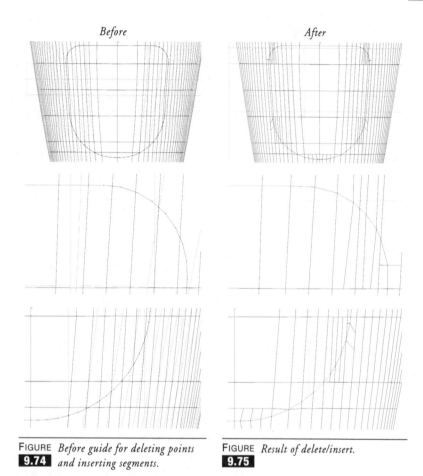

FIGURE **9.74** *Before guide for deleting points and inserting segments.*

FIGURE **9.75** *Result of delete/insert.*

The trim edge point count on both surfaces and the LOI *must* be identical, and the respective points must be positionally matched.

2. Create a new layer, "Blend Edges." Place a copy of the LOI into this layer, take care not to move it, then LOCK this layer. Afterwards, make "Fore Section" the active layer. Select the inner trim surface and the LOI. Working from the top view, Nonuniform Scale the two objects together using the center of the inner trim surface as the base of nonuniform scale. Use the following scale values; .5, .5, 1. Then, working from right and front views continue the Nonuniform Scale using the first point of the smaller blend edge as the base of scale. Match it as closely as possible to Figure 9.76. Notice that when viewed from the front view, both objects were nonuniformly scaled so as to be curvature conformal to the main Fore Section surface.

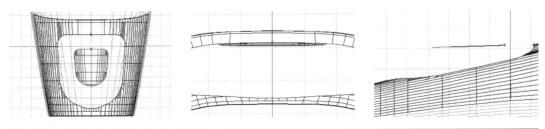

FIGURE
9.76
"Fore Section" active layer.

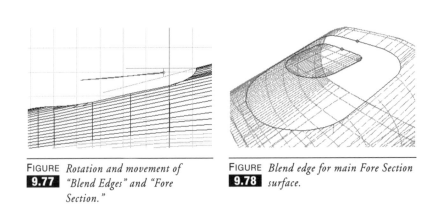

FIGURE
9.77
Rotation and movement of "Blend Edges" and "Fore Section."

FIGURE
9.78
Blend edge for main Fore Section surface.

3. Reselect the two objects from the previous step if deselected. Working from the right side view, Rotate and Move them as shown in Figure 9.77. Use the first point of the smaller blend edge as the base for rotation. Don't worry about precision, just get it as close as you can to the illustration. For vertical placement of the objects, imagine three straight lines. The first line passes through, has an angle vector that is an average of two lengthwise segments adjacent to the topmost point of the blend edge. The second line starts at the topmost point of the blend edge and has an orthogonal (Y-axis) vector. The third line is orthogonal (Z-axis), and passes though the first point of the smaller (inner) blend edge and terminates where it touches the two vectors. The inner surface and its blend edge are positioned so that the first point of the blend edge is located at midpoint of this line.

NOTE

By placing a copy of LOI in a separate locked layer and then scaling the original, we defined the two blend edges, one for each surface. By transforming the original LOI with the inner trimmed surface we ensure that we have positional matching of the inner surface and its blend edge. The copy of the blend edge is the blend edge for the main Fore Section surface (Figure 9.78).

By successfully splitting the base Fore Section surface, deriving LOI, and performing transformations, we have successfully modeled the two base surfaces and derived blend edges that we will use as our *source* curve for creating a skinned blend. Even though we could have derived the blend edges without the use of LOI, it would have taken us longer as we would have to select the trim edges of both base surfaces after completing the trim edge cleanup.

1. We start modeling the paths by first creating 4-point base polylines. Recall that we should place the polylines to equal the number of points between source shapes. Since we have 56-points we shoot for placement at every seventh point along the source shapes. The first polylines are placed at the front middle and rear middle points. Then additional polylines are placed at every seventh point. We can leave the Skin network as is, but the resulting skinned surface, while geometrically blending the two base surfaces, will not topologically match. Two additional polylines need to be placed in the side center points to keep the skin mesh topology consistent with the base surfaces. Even though we are deviating equidistant point placement guideline, this deviation is needed in this case. Notice that there are an equal number of points on each side of the two extra side paths, the deviation is localized, and will not create a problem for the Skin tool. Figure 9.79 shows the correct placement and geometric shape of the polylines. Notice the adherence to the vector angle matching guideline. The vector matching is consistent across all the axes.

2. Convert the polylines into third-degree 16-point B-Splines. Don't forget to save copies of the polylines in a holding layer. Confirm geometric endpoint snapping. Confirm consistent direction of both *source* shapes and *path* curves. Figure 9.80 shows the completed Skin network of 2 *sources* and 10 *paths*.

3. Set up the Skin Options as discussed earlier in the chapter, except that # Of Paths is 10. Skin the curve network and place the blend surface in the

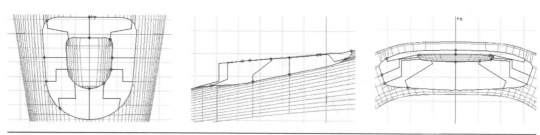

FIGURE *Correct placement and geometric shape of the polylines.*
9.79

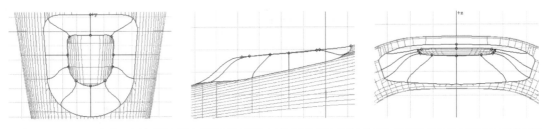

FIGURE *Completed skin network of 2 sources and 10 paths.*
9.80

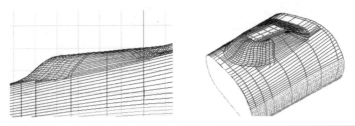

FIGURE
9.81

"Fore Sections" layer. Figure 9.81 shows the skin blend surface. In the Wire Frame options, activate Show Face Normals. Reverse the direction of the skinned blend surface if necessary. In general, prior to stitching surfaces you should align their normals. After deriving the skin surface, hide "Skin Blend Curves" layer.

4. Unghost the separated faces object and stitch all the surfaces back together. Topologically, the resulting object is reported as a **Solid** by a Query tool. Assign Smoothing Attributes of (135–140 degrees). Notice the high quality of the rendering without any visible seams (Figure 9.82).

To seamlessly render blended surfaces as one continuous surface, meet the following parameters:

- Positionally matched points, on blend edges of base and blend surfaces.

FIGURE *High quality rendering without visible seams.*
9.82

- Continuity match of segments and faces sharing and adjacent to the blend edge.
- Surfaces are stitched.
- Aligned face normals on all faces of the stitched surface.
- Smoothing attributes applied to the surface.

TIP

If the blend surface exhibits polygonal silhouetting in the path direction, reevaluate the path curves using a higher point count. 90% of the time, polygonal silhouetting can be visually evaluated by observing the path curves and source curves. While fixing polygonal silhouetting on path curves is easy, it can be time consuming to fix source shapes. Take care in creating the trim dyes that are sufficiently meshed, and always retain copies of the original objects.

The objective of the following exercise is to create recessed headlight glass and a continuity matched lip of the recess.

1. Create a new layer, "Lip Cross-Sections," and make it active. Ghost the "Fore Section" layer. Working from the front, with Face Center snapping only, create a polyline as shown in Figure 9.83. Orthographically project this line from the front view to flatten it (Figure 9.83).

2. Fit fillet the two corner points using the following values (Figure 9.84):

   Bottom Corner Point # Of Edges : 2, Radius : 1/40″
   Top Corner Point # Of Edges : 2, Radius : 1/10″

3. Create a parallel offset duplicate of this line, with the Parallel Objects tool. Set tool options to Single Parallel (Surface), IN, Offset: 1/64″. Status to Keep (Figure 9.85).

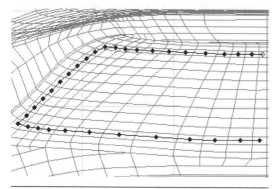

FIGURE *Active "Lip Cross-Sections" layer.*
9.83

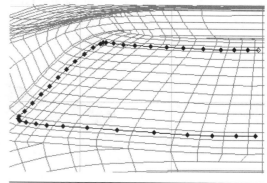

FIGURE *Fit fillet of 2 corner points.*
9.84

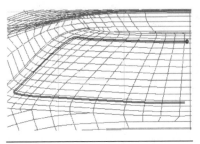

FIGURE **9.85** *Parallel offset duplicate.*

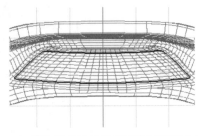

FIGURE **9.86** *Mirror copy of both lines.*

The Trim With Line *function in form•Z is an excellent tool, although it has a few limitations. One of the limitations is that it cannot compute the trim if the points of the trim line are projected onto the points or segments on the surface to be trimmed. For that reason, we used Face Center snapping in Figure 9.83 instead of Point Snapping.*

4. Mirror Copy both lines. Join and close each pair to form two closed coplanar surfaces. Set Status to Delete. Use the Boolean tool to subtract the smaller surface from the larger one. Set Status to Delete (Figure 9.86).

5. Extrude, **Perpendicular To Surface**, the closed surface from the last step. Set Status to Delete. Extrude it so that it intersects the "Fore Section" surface along a single line of intersection about 12″ (Figure 9.87).

6. Derive an LOI between the extrusion and the Fore Section surface. Retain both operands. The result of the LOI derivation should be two closed nonplanar surfaces with equal 140-point counts. Their first point may or may not be aligned, so you need to align it if necessary. After deriving the LOI, transfer the extrusion into the "Fore Section" layer and make this layer active. Ghost the "Lip Cross-Sections" layer (Figure 9.88).

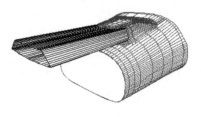
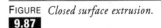

FIGURE **9.87** *Closed surface extrusion.*

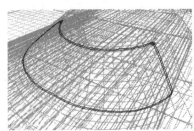

FIGURE **9.88** *Extrusion transfer into "Fore Section" layer.*

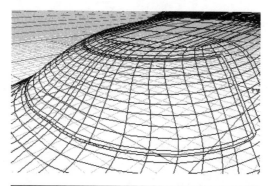

FIGURE **9.89** *"Fore Section" surface and "Headlight Glass" surface.*

7. Working in the "Fore Section" layer, and using the Trim/Split tool, Split the "Fore Section" Surface with the extrusion. Set Status to Delete. The result should be three surfaces. The main "Fore Section" surface, the "Headlight Glass" surface, and the thin strip border. Delete the border strip surface as we do not need it. Optionally, you may transfer it to a hidden holding layer (Figure 9.89).

8. Ghost the "Fore Section" layer and make "Lip Cross-Section" the active layer. Create a duplicate of the inner LOI and move it +1/24" along the Y-axis. Turn on the "Fore Section" layer and move the headlight glass surface the same amount (1/24"). The result is that we wind up with three lip cross-sections, and the headlight glass surface having coresident edges with the three lip cross-sections (Figure 9.90).

9. Create a second-degree B-Spline plain C-Mesh surface. Set the C-Mesh options per the settings used for the surface in Figure 9.7. Change **Degree** from 3 to 2, and change **Mesh Depth: # Of Segments** from 6 to 2. Set

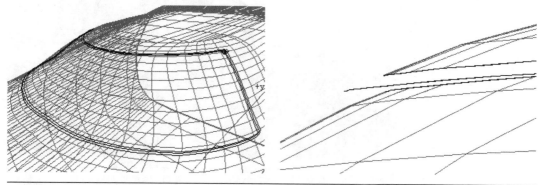

FIGURE **9.90** *Three lip cross-sections.*

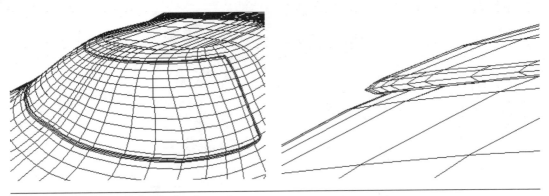

FIGURE *Completed "Headlight Glass" surface mesh.*
9.91

Status to Keep. After deriving the lip surface, hide the "Lip Cross-Sections" layer. Stitch the lip surface with the "Fore Section" surface. Create a new layer, "Headlight Glass," and transfer the headlight glass mesh into it (Figure 9.91).

10. Apply Smoothing Attributes to the newly stitched surface and the headlight glass. You may apply whatever surface styles you wish. Figure 9.92 show the RenderZone Raytraced closeup of the head enclosure surface.

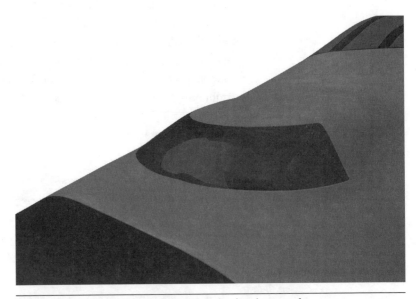

FIGURE *RenderZone Raytraced closeup of the head enclosure surface.*
9.92

CHAPTER 10

Terrain Modeling

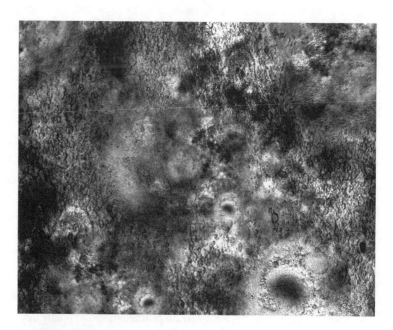

IN THIS CHAPTER

- Introduction to Digital Terrains
- Trees, Shrubbery and Rocks
- Creating Displacement Maps in Photoshop
- Modeling Amorphic Terrains with Displace Tool
- Arbitrary Displacement Maps
- Mesh Density of Displaced Terrains
- Terrain Modeling Using Terrain Model Tool
- Contour Heights
- Exercise

Introduction to Digital Terrains

The use of terrain in visual effects is nothing extraordinary. Physical terrain miniatures have been modeled for special effects since the early days of film-making. Today much of the terrain used in visual effects is often intricately constructed physical miniatures, shot with cameras mounted on elaborate motion control rigs. 3D digital terrain is an anachronism in visual effects. Digital terrain models are relatively easy to construct and manage, but can be difficult and time consuming to make photorealistic. However, there are situations that will require the use of 3D digital terrain. Normally, in digital visual effects, digital terrains are best utilized when the camera is moving high and fast relative to the digital terrain. In these cases, the motion blur cancels out most visible geometry and texture imperfections. The closer and the slower the digital camera is to the digital terrain, the more attention needs to be paid to the modeling and texturing of the terrain. There will not always be a need to create photorealistic terrains. Terrains for multimedia, real time, previsualization, and screen graphics, only need to be just right for the situation. The basic problem with creating digital terrains is that the real world has too many subtle details that are very hard to digitally reproduce. Examples are trees, shrubbery, rock formations, boulders on the ground, grass, and flowers. While it is possible to create digital data for each detail, it is not really practical, as it would create scenes of enormous polygonal count, take too long to create, and cause unreasonably long render times. For those cases, specialized nature modeling tools should be utilized. Many effects artists and studios have also developed proprietary techniques of seamless mixing real-world footage and digital terrain to complement each other.

Typically, digital terrain has the following characteristics:

- **Terrain geometry is polygonally heavy.** Usually, digital terrain models in digital effects work are polygonally heavy models. A powerful CPU combined with a large amount of RAM is a must for efficient terrain modeling work. The amount of polygons in the terrain model is dictated by the proximity of the digital camera at the closest point to the terrain. The closer the camera to the terrain, the heavier the terrain model must be. The slowest relative velocity between camera and terrain also affects the detail level of the terrain geometry.

- **Photorealism of terrain** is a combination of geometrical detail resolution, terrain topology (polygonal subdivision), texture mapping, and geographical correctness.

- **Detail resolution** determines how much detail the viewer can discern from the model. Can the viewer see individual rock formations, streams, the fractal nature of landscape, and growing things? Some detail can be inferred; that is, an illusion is created to show more detail than is actually there.
- **Terrain topology**, or its mesh subdivision, works alongside the geometrical resolution. Having optimized polygonal subdivision allows form•Z smoothing functions to properly smooth the mesh to prevent polygonal silhouettes.
- **Texture mapping** is a vital element of terrain modeling. Seldom will a terrain model be adequate for use in digital visual effects without the use of an appropriate texture map. For the map to be effective and complete the effect of terrain, it must be painted and applied correctly. The size, detail, and application of the texture depends on the closest proximity of the animation camera to the terrain map. Once applied, the map should be crisp (but not noisy) and not blurry. Even though it is acceptable, don't rely on motion blur to hide defects in the map.
- **Topographical Correctness** is the correct placement of topographical features on the terrain with respect to each other.

In this chapter we will discuss three possible techniques for modeling terrain. The first makes use of form•Z's excellent Displace tool that uses 2D grayscale bitmaps crated in any image editing application to create 3D terrain. The second technique uses the Terrain Model tool, an excellent tool that uses map-type contour lines to generate terrain. This technique uses the Terrain Model in concert with Smooth Mesh and Displace tools to generate detailed rolling terrain.

Before proceeding we need to discuss considerations in terrain modeling. The primary purpose of terrain modeling is to generate an irregular amorphic 3D mesh that best approximates the natural contours and irregularities of desired land form. The source of the desired shape can come from site maps, a photograph of a real-world geographical location, or simply an artist sketch. In visual effects, the terrain is often located in exotic places, such as a subterranean cave, an ocean bottom trench, or the surface of an alien planet. Quite often, combining various sources, you can create fictitious but still convincing looking terrain. At times, you will need to match your digital terrain with a physical miniature used for another shot. In this case, close communication with the physical effects crew is needed. Take as many photographs of the miniature as possible under neutral lighting conditions, from as many angles as possible. If possible, obtain footage of the terrain miniature so you can derive lighting and texturing conditions as well as placement of details.

One of the most important aspects of terrain modeling is the desired mesh density of the terrain. Terrain models that are too lightly meshed for the shot will appear jagged and unrealistic. Models that are too heavily meshed will unnecessarily eat up render time memory needlessly. Through experience and experimentation, you can develop a feel for the optimum meshing of the terrain model. Determination for mesh density is best accomplished by evaluating the terrain from the digital camera's point of view when the two are in the closest proximity to each other. In simpler words, if the terrain looks good when it and the camera are closest to each other, you can safely feel that the terrain will look good across the length of the shot. A simple rule of thumb is that you should not see any polygonal silhouettes, no polygon should be larger than 10% of the output screen area, and angles between segments should not visually exceed 5 degrees. All visual evaluations of the terrain mesh should be performed from the animation system camera view or perspective view in form•Z set up with similar values. As stated, place the digital camera (in form•Z) at the closest proximity to the terrain that the camera will be during animation. For non-photorealistic work, such as games, multimedia, and previsualization, use your best judgment to determine the needed mesh density.

In terrain modeling, texture mapping quality is as important as geometric integrity. Texture maps for the terrain need to be of necessary high resolution depending on the resolution of the terrain and the closest proximity of the camera. Terrain maps should look crisp with a low level of detail, depending on the desired look. In general, avoid using small maps that are stretched, and consequently blurred, over the terrain. Additionally, avoid over-tiling a small map. You can use tiling to increase the amount of the texture that the camera sees, but avoid tiling setups where the viewer can see the seams or mirrored tiles. For optimal results, the map should be very large in size, roughly two to four times the final output resolution, and have an aspect ratio equal to that of the terrain mesh. The map should be matched to the terrain, so that low areas of the terrain should be darker than the high areas. For best results, render the terrain from the orthogonal top view at the resolution of the texture map. When rendering the "base" image, render under neutral lighting conditions, with 30% ambient, no specular, and no shadows. In Photoshop or any other image editing application, paint right over the rendering. Apply the resulting texture map from the top view to be sure that the rotation is aligned. For painting, use satellite or high oblique photos of natural terrain to determine color mixing, or composite the photo imagery, with your own art.

Trees, Shrubbery and Rocks

There are various ways of modeling or simulating shrubbery, trees, and rocks. There are third-party applications such as TREE Professional, WORD CONSTRUCTION SET, World Builder, and Bryce 3D, that specialize in modeling natural scenes. We encourage you to use those programs appropriately, as they can be a great time saver. It is very possible to create those models in form•Z, and we will discuss them. Use photos and your own artistic sense to place the details on the terrain. Be careful not to overdo it as too much detail can lead to very heavy scenes, causing excessive memory usage and excessive render times.

The first terrain modeling technique that we will discuss is the Displace tool. Displace is an excellent terrain and irregular surface modeling tool within form•Z that uses grayscale images created in external image editing applications to create meshes based on the luminosity values of the pixels within an image. As in texture mapping, the Displace tool uses the PROJECTION of the grayscale map around the displaced object to determine the offset of individual points in 3D space. The displaced terrain mesh's geometric and topological quality is dependent on three prime parameters:

- Resolution and quality of the displacement image
- Geometry and topology of the original mesh
- Displacement tool settings, including displacement map projection

As stated, the Displace tool uses a grayscale image to displace an existing model. Most of the effort involved in using this approach is in creating the displacement map. To create the map, we must first decide on the topography of the terrain and the desired mesh density. Topography defines the topographical features of the terrain such as hills, valleys, ridges, draws, spurs, canyons, and bodies of water. Additionally, plan out the heights and locations of the planned topographical features. It may be useful to create a quick sketched topographical map using contour lines. The topographical map can be created by referencing available source material and drawing a sketch on mathematical grid paper. Alternatively, you can create a sketch directly inside form•Z using C-Curves to represent contour lines and a rectangle. If you have no experience in reading maps, consult books on cartography and civil engineering. In them you will learn how to draw major terrain features using contour lines.

Figure 10.1 shows a topographical contour map. Notice that the steeper the terrain, the closer the contour lines are to each other. Additionally, the stream bed is shown in blue contour lines. The ability to read a topographical map is a learned skill, and it improves with practice. An easy way to approach topographical map reading is to start at a body of water, which is usually the lowest

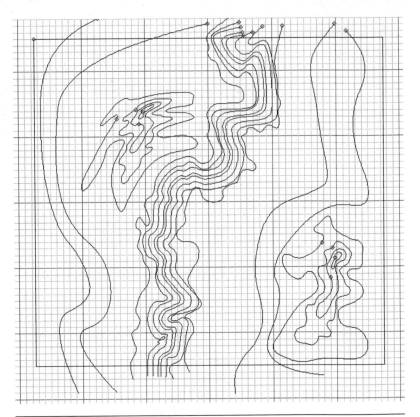

FIGURE   *Topographical contour map.*
10.1

in height, and read outwards. When one stream flows into another the junction location is "downstream" or lower than the source of the stream. The source of a stream or a linear body of water is said to be "upstream." Streams and rivers are always located in depressions or canyons. Include a "site" in your terrain sketch. A site is a closed polyline or rectangular boundary defining the outer limits of the your terrain. Open contour lines always "run" off the site.

The terrain map sketch serves as a plan for the terrain model. After completion of the sketch, scan (if drawn) or export as a bitmap out of form•Z and bring it into Adobe Photoshop or any compatible image editing application. Once there, paint a grayscale map using the sketch bitmap as a background. The displacement map is painted as to have the darkest pixels representing the lowest terrain elevation and the whitest pixels representing the highest elevations. The elevation differential between the lowest and highest displacement is defined in the Displace tool options. As an example, if the *min(d)* and *max(d)* elevations are defined as 0′ and 100′, respectively, the pure black pixels (0) will

Framework Cage   **Grafted Patch**

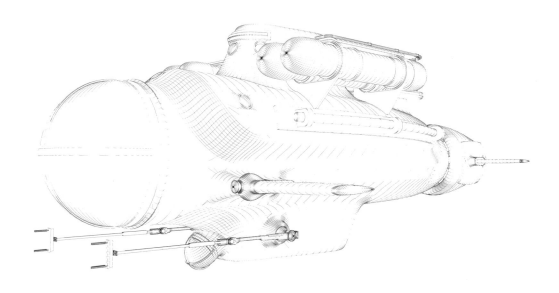

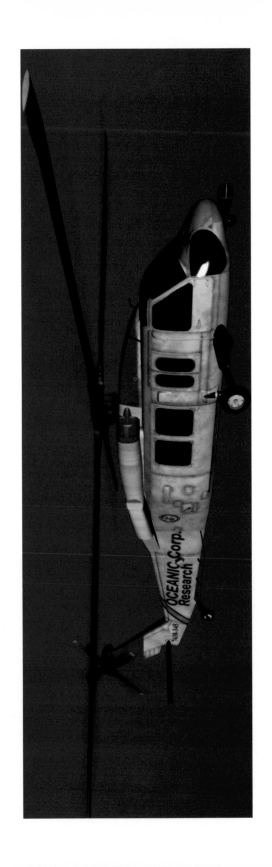

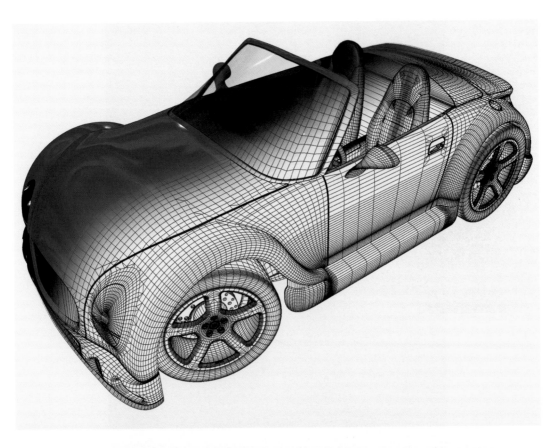

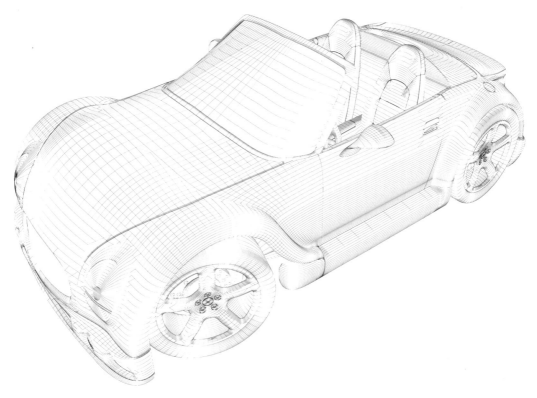

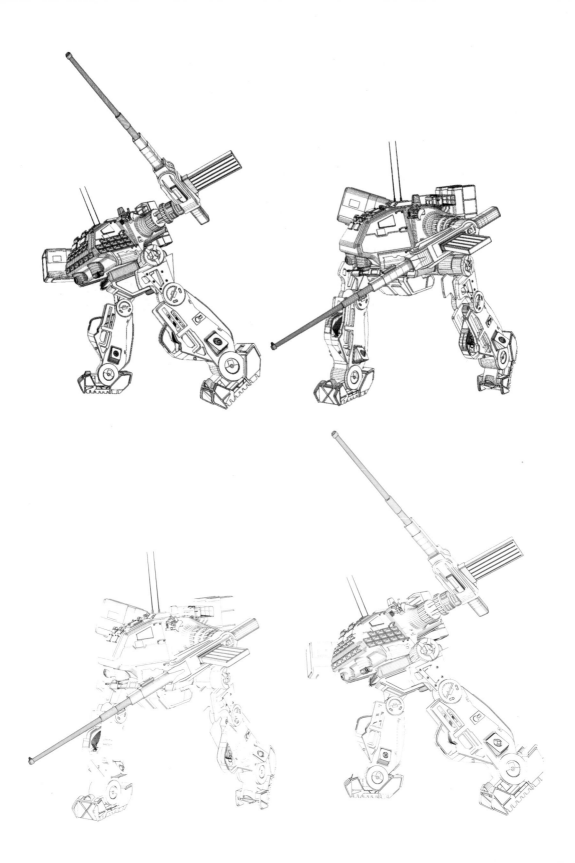

define no displacement, and the white (255) pixels will define a displacement offset of 100′. A gray pixel (128) defines a displacement of 50′, or half the offset between *min(d)* and *max(d)*. A simple math formula for determining a displacement amount of a particular pixel is to first determine a grayscale value of a pixel, v. Determine the percentage of displacement p, or p= v/255. Determine the displacement differential range r, or r = abs(min(d)) + max(d). Displacement amount d = r * p. So a complete formula for the displacement amount of a given pixel is

$$d = (abs(min(d)) + max(d)) * (v/255).$$

Creating Displacement Maps in Photoshop

For our first exercise, we will use form•Z to create the terrain elevation map, and Adobe Photoshop to create a displacement map based on the elevation map. Working within form•Z, reproduce the terrain map as shown in Figure 10.1. Use C-Curves to create the contour lines. After the elevation map is complete, export it as a bitmap image from an orthogonal top view. If you wish, scan the image to save time. Bring the image into Adobe Photoshop.

1. Using the site rectangle as a guide, crop the image as shown in Figure 10.2. The reason that we need to crop the image based on the site rectangle is so we have the displacement map being of the same aspect ratio as the terrain mesh that will be based on the site rectangle.

FIGURE   *Cropped image of site rectangle.*
10.2

2. Create a new Photoshop layer, "Base." Use the Color Fill tool to fill this layer with neutral medium gray (72, 72,72). The medium gray represents the "ground level." Examine the elevation map. Notice that there is a small river inside a canyon-like depression. On each side of the river canyon are small hills complete with draws and spurs. Both hills sit on slightly rolling terrain. That intermediate rolling terrain is represented by the medium gray. Since the medium gray is our base color, whenever we paint lower elevations we use darker grays, with black being the lowest elevation. Whenever we paint higher elevations we use lighter grays, with pure white being the highest elevation. To make it easy to paint over the background, we duplicate the terrain map (Background layer) and place it on top of the layer list. Set its transfer mode to DARKEN and leave the layer's transparency at 100%. Whenever we create new layers, we need to reposition the terrain map layer on top of the list.

3. Now we will paint the first of the canyon depression layers. Create a new Photoshop layer, "Canyon Outer," and set its transfer mode to DARKEN. Using the Airbrush, paint the first canyon layer as shown in Figure 10.3. Notice that it was painted with a very wide airbrush (set to Normal with 100%). Match the darkness as best you can; pixel-perfect precision is not required.

4. Finish painting the canyon using Figure 10.4 as a guide. Notice that the more inner the canyon region, the more depressed it is and the darker the color. The riverbed itself is pure black. If you desire even more accuracy and realism, make the upstream part of the riverbed slightly lighter than the downstream part. Be sure to paint each successive canyon layer on it own layer set to DARKEN. Experiment with transparency sliders and the following filters on individual layers: Brightness/Contrast, Levels,

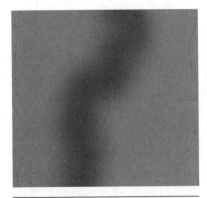

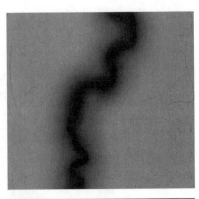

FIGURE **10.3** *Darkened "Canyon Outer."*

FIGURE **10.4** *Canyon paint layer.*

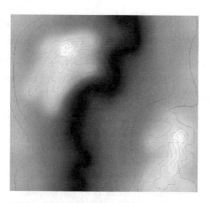

FIGURE
10.5
Hills painted on canyon layer guide.

and Curves. Additionally, the more inside you paint the canyon, the smaller the brush size. This is more of an artistic endeavor. The airbrush is usually the best tool to use when painting terrain displacement maps because the softness in the map translates to smooth transitions in the displaced mesh.

5. Using similar techniques we now paint the hills on each side of the canyon. The difference is that since the hills are elevated terrain, we use gradually lighter shades of gray, with pure white regions representing the highest elevations. On the elevation map the highest areas are represented with the smallest and innermost closed contours. Use Figure 10.5 as your general guide. Remember that each successive elevation should be painted on its own layer. For elevated terrain the Photoshop Transfer mode should be Screen or Lighten. The type of brush that is used depends on the desired transition rate from darker to lighter regions.

With the basic map completed we can export the initial version of it to a raster format that form•Z can read. We recommend the use of an LZW compressed TIFF file as it offers the smallest size and has no loss of quality. For best results, convert the image to Grayscale inside Photoshop or your image editing application prior to exporting. Additionally, it is good practice to save the layered version in a Photoshop native file, and the actual displacement map in a common raster format. The primary reason, of course, is so we retain the ability to adjust the displacement map later on. The best way is to first create a duplicate in Photoshop of the layered map, turn off the contours layer (we don't want it in the bitmap), and then flatten the image (discarding all hidden layers).

Creating the displacement map is also very much an artistic exercise. You should experiment with various layer transfer modes and layer transparency values. Recall that the Displace tool will use the grayscale value to determine the intermediate displacement amount given the specified minimum and maximum displacement limits. One feature of the image that will most strongly influence displacement is the relative contrast between the brightest and the darkest pixel in the image. Experiment with Brightness/Contrast sliders of the whole image. In the native Photoshop layered file add a Brightness/Contrast, Levels, or Curves Adjustment Layer and place it on the top of the layer list. With those Adjustment layers you can easily and quickly experiment with the lightness or darkness levels of the whole image. So, given constant min. and max. displacement values, the more contrast there is in the displacement map, the more contrast there will be in the generated terrain. You may also apply various Photoshop and third-party Photoshop filters to the selected layers. Noise followed by Gaussian Blur is a particularly effective technique for creating dimples in the terrain. By combining various layers with different transfer modes you can create some unique terrain features that still conform to the sketched elevation map but add subtle realistic detail that is so important in digital effects.

In the next phase of the exercise we will apply the grayscale displacement to a mesh to create our terrain. If necessary, Review the steps on the creation of the map. Export the displacement map as an LZW compressed TIFF file. Turn off the contour guided layer prior to flattening the image. Be sure to retain the original unflattened version of the map in Photoshop native format. If you are unfamiliar with how displacement works in general, forego filter experimentation until you are comfortable with the process.

1. Open the form•Z file where we created the terrain map and Copy/Paste a copy of the site rectangle into its own layer.
2. Use the Mesh tool to subdivide the site as shown in Figure 10.6. The distances that you use will depend on the scale of your site. In our example, the site rectangle was approximately 5000' by 5000' (1 sq. mile), and was meshed using 250' increments.

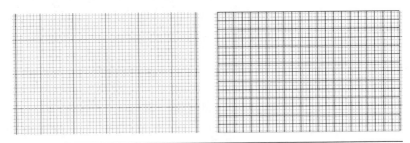

FIGURE *Subdivided site rectangle.*
10.6

Since we are creating a terrain from scratch and not displacing an already existing model, we need to create a suitable "substrate" surface. The lightly meshed version of the site rectangle will usually provide an acceptable substrate surface.

3. In form•Z, set the Displace tool options as follows:

Origin, X: 0, Y: 0, Z: 0 ; Rotation, X: 0, Y: 0, Z: 0
Mapping Type : Flat
Horizontal Tiling; Size: 5050′, Center, 1 Times
Vertical Tiling; Size 5050′, Center, 1 Times
Lock Size To : Current Proportions or None
Min: 0′, Max: 600′
Smoothness: 1 (Use range of 1–4)
Adaptive Meshing : On
Maximum # Of Subdivisions: 4
Maximum Segment Length: 30′
Threshold: 0

4. Load the displacement map.
5. Apply the displacement to the substrate surface. The result should appear as shown in Figure 10.7. Experiment with different Displace tool settings to get the feel of how it works. In this case, the lowest terrain elevation is 0′ and the highest is 600′. Be careful about using high numbers in Maximum # Of Subdivisions; the number of generated polygons and generation times rise exponentially.

FIGURE *Result of displacement to the substrate surface.*
10.7

The following list details the certain specific settings and their effects.

Origin, X: 0, Y: 0, Z: 0 ; Rotation, X: 0, Y: 0, Z: 0. These settings control the placement and orientation of the displacement map projection. The coordinates are world coordinates. Most of the time, the origin is placed at the same location as the center mass of the substrate surface. In certain cases, you may need to determine the centermost location of the surface and record it. form•Z will align the projection to the surface, but may be a little off, in which case you can manually define the origin of the projection. Like Origin, Rotation of the projection is defined in the World coordinate system. Unlike Origin, form•Z will not automatically align the projection to match the angles. This can cause a problem if the substrate mesh is oriented along an odd angle. You need to manually align the rotation of the projection to the substrate mesh.

Mapping Type: Flat. This controls the geometrical shape of the projection. form•Z offers three types: Flat, Cylindrical, and Spherical. In the modeling of terrains, Flat projection is used most often. Caverns and caves are best displaced with a cylindrical projection. For asteroids and planetoids, spherical projection usually yields the best results. A good rule of thumb is to use the projection type that most closely approximates the shape of the substrate. As in texture mapping, projection plays an important role in the final shape of the displaced terrain. The same displacement map applied via flat and spherical projections will yield vastly different results. Experiment with all three projection types, keeping all other settings constant.

Horizontal Tiling, Vertical Tiling, Size: Times. These settings control the actual size of the projection along the horizontal and vertical axes. Times controls the tiling and is a function of size of the substrate surface. On our substrate, 5000' by 5000' Times of 2 would have a projection size of 2500'. The units are in World coordinates. Ideally, a displacement map matched to the substrate should have the same size; however, there is a slight adjustment that is needed for proper application. A projection that has a size precisely equal to that of the substrate will not cover the vertices that are on the edges of the substrate mesh. The projection size needs to be slightly larger than the size of the mesh. That is why the size of the projection in this exercise was 5050' by 5050'. Extra length and width compensate for some minor internal errors in form•Z, and are very small, 1/10 of a percent larger than the substrate mesh.

Lock Size To : This setting is used to automatically align the size of the projection to the size of the substrate mesh. It is a very quick and useful feature, but you should not depend on it entirely, as you may encounter minor errors with the projection size not entirely covering the mesh. Additionally, it does not align the rotation of projection—that needs to be done manually. **Lock Size To:** is very effective in getting the projection very close, then manually increase the size of the projection per the instructions above. There are five options in this field, and each one is useful depending on the situation.

— When set to **None**, you manually set the horizontal and vertical independent of each other.

— When set to **Current Proportions**, changing the size of tiling in either axis will cause a change in the other axis. The new settings will have same aspect ratio.

— **Square Tile** works similar to Current Proportions but forces a 1:1 aspect ratio for sizes.

— **Displacement Map** settings force an aspect ratio of sizes to that of the map being used. A 4000 by 3000 pixel displacement map forces a 4:3 aspect ratio onto the projection sizes.

— **Object Extent** will force the projection sizes to conform to the extents of the substrate mesh.

Min: & Max: These are the prime parameters of the Displace tool that define the *amount* of displacement that occurs on the mesh. These numbers are offsets and are not absolute to the world. This means that the vertex that will is lowest on the displaced mesh will be offset by the absolute value of the Min: number. The highest vertex on the displaced mesh will be offset by the absolute value of Max:. The offsets will occur per projection type; on Flat projection, the offset occurs along the projection Z-axis. The total *On Axis Straight Line* distance between the lowest and highest vertices of the displaced mesh is *abs(min) + abs(max)*.

Smoothness: This is a smoothing function within the Displace tool that is used when dealing with low-resolution displaced meshes, or when the displacement map is very noisy. Its primary purpose is to prevent generation of errant vertices that jut out of the displaced mesh. Smoothness has an effect of lowering the displacement min and max amounts. When modeling terrain, keep this number low, about 1–4 range. If your displaced mesh is exhibiting artifacts, increase this number. Generally, it is not a good idea to use high numbers, as they will make the terrain mesh look very smooth and partially negate the effects of min/max, although for effects such as melted surfaces, it is perfectly feasible.

Adaptive Meshing: This is a very useful and powerful setting that allows you to simultaneously apply displacement and adaptive smoothing subdivisions to a very coarse substrate mesh. Without this feature, we would be forced to always apply displacement to highly meshed substrate surfaces. If you do not wish to increase the polygon count of the displaced mesh over the substrate, have this feature turned off.

Maximum Number Of Subdivisions: is the maximum number of iterations that the smoothing algorithm will use when evaluating the curvature of the displaced mesh. In general, it is also the number of smoothed polygons that each individual substrate mesh polygon will be subdivided into.

Maximum Segment Length: is an internal limiter. Often when displacing very coarse substrate meshes into high-resolution terrains, even having a high number of subdivisions may still result in relatively large polygons. Maximum Segment Length forces form•Z to keep subdividing an already subdivided polygon if its segments are longer than the maximum segment length.

Threshold is the sensitivity of smoothing to the angle deviation of the substrate mesh. The smoothing always follows the displacement, so the smoothing algorithm looks at the displaced substrate mesh and then decides where to smooth. The lower the number, the higher the sensitivity to curvature change.

Modeling Amorphic Terrains with Displace Tool

Displacement techniques are quite useful for creating amorphic objects such as rocks, boulders, and asteroids. The procedure is fairly simple and fast. First a fractal grayscale map is created and then applied to a spherical substrate mesh, such as a single-depth geodesic sphere. Afterwards, the displaced mesh is deformed using form•Z's Deform tool. The key is to create a crisp looking fractal displacement map, and correct projection alignment. The following exercise shows a generic procedure for amorphic object creation. In a production situation, a sketch or a storyboard would be used to determine the overall look of the rock, which drives the displacement map creation. We will bypass this step and just create a generic fractal displacement map. The displacement map creation takes place in Adobe Photoshop 4.01, the current standard in image editing. If you are using a different image editing application, the described steps will need to be adjusted to your application.

1. Create a new 1000′ by 1000′ file in Photoshop. Set its background color to medium gray, value 128. Duplicate the layer, and rename it "Layer1." Set the foreground and background colors to black (0) and white (255), respectively.

2. Apply the Render Clouds filter to "Layer 1."

3. Duplicate "Layer 1," rename the new layer "Layer 2."

4. Apply Difference Clouds filter to "Layer 2."

5. Set the transfer mode for "Layer 1" to *Multiply*, and *Screen* for "Layer 2." At this point, you should have an image that is similar to Figure 10.8.

6. Duplicate "Layer 1," rename the copy to "Layer 3," set its transfer mode to *Multiply* and move it to the top of the layer list.

7. Apply the Brightness/Contrast filter to "Layer 3," Brightness: 0, Contrast: +100.

8. Apply the Noise filter to "Layer 3." Set it to Amount 125, Gausian, Monochromatic.

9. Apply the Torn Edges filter to "Layer 3." Set it to Image Balance: 41, Smoothness: 3, Contrast: 13.

10. Change "Layer 3" opacity to 30%. Notice that the map is taking on a quasi 3D layered look, as in Figure 10.9.

11. Duplicate "Layer 3," rename it "Layer 4," and move it to the top of the layer list if it's not there already.

12. Apply the Noise filter. Amount: 48, Gausian, Monochromatic.

13. Apply the Trace Contour filter to "Layer 4." Amount: 128.

14. Apply the Gaussian Blur filter to "Layer 4." Amount: 2.

15. Apply the Noise filter as above.

16. Apply Gaussian Blur. Amount: 3.

   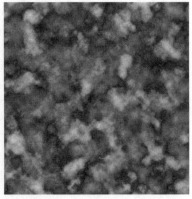

FIGURE **10.8** *Transfer mode for "Layer 1" and "Layer 2."*   FIGURE **10.9** *"Layer 3" opacity at 30%.*

17. Select "Layer 4" and Copy it into the Clipboard.

18. In Channels create #2 channel, and paste it into #4 channel.

19. Apply the Brightness/Contrast filter to #2 channel only. Brightness: 0, Contrast: +75.

20. Drag #2 channel into Make Selection and go back to the "Layer 4" color channel.

21. Press DELETE one time.

22. Set transfer mode of "Layer 4" to Color Burn with 15% Opacity.

23. Apply the Noise filter to "Layer 4" Amount 999.

24. Follow with the Gaussian Blur filter. Amount 1.5.

25. Duplicate "Layer 1," rename the copy to "Layer 5" and move it to the top of the layer list.

26. Apply the Reticulation filter to "Layer 5." Density: 0, Black Level: 40, White Level: 27.

27. Set "Layer 5" transfer mode to Lighten with 20% opacity.

28. Create a Brightness/Contrast Adjustment layer and set Contrast to +15.

29. Save the native Photoshop file. Duplicate it in Photoshop, and flatten it.

30. Apply the Distort/Polar Coordinates filter to the flattened map. Use the Polar to Rectangular option.

The displacement map is complete. Save it as an LZW compressed TIFF file. Compare your results with Figure 10.10. The Polar Coordinates filter was necessary since the map will be applied spherically. If you need to change the map, perform the changes in the original file and then flatten and distort that copy.

1. Create a new form•Z project. Sets its grid modules to 10′ with 10′ subdivisions.

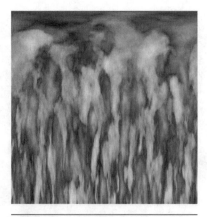

FIGURE *Completed displacement map.*
10.10

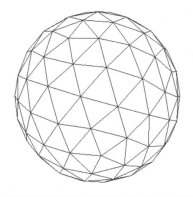

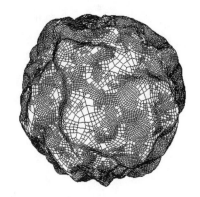

FIGURE *Two-level geodesic sphere.*
10.11

FIGURE *Geodesic sphere after*
10.12 *displacement.*

2. Create a two-level geodesic sphere with 10′ radius, as shown in Figure 10.11.

3. Select the Displace tool and click on the geodesic. Set the Displace options as follows (Figure 10.12):

Origin; X: 0, Y: 0, Z: 0

Rotation; X: 0, Y: 0, Z:0

Mapping Type: Spherical

Horizontal Tiling; Size: 360, Center, Times: 1

Vertical Tiling, Size: 180, Center, Times: 1

Lock Size To: Current Proportions

Min: 0, Max: 3′

Smoothness: 9

Adaptive Meshing: On

Maximum # Of Subdivisions: 4

Maximum Segment Length: 1″

Threshold: 2

The preceding exercise produced an amorphic mesh that would be very difficult and time consuming to model by any other means. Still, the displaced mesh is generally spherical in nature. To make it more interesting, it needs to be more irregular. As we have seen, displacement modeling is relatively easy, with most of the effort spent in refining the displacement map and Displace options. Recall that the final shape and topology of the displaced mesh is influenced by the geometry and topology of the substrate mesh. By altering the shape of the mesh prior to displacement you can achieve effects and prevent problems before they occur. In the following exercise, we will first create the same two-level geodesic. Prior to performing displacement we will perform some standard editing operations on it. We encourage you to experiment with your own shapes and Displace options. Experience and experimentation is the key to getting the "feel" for this technique.

1. Working from the right side view, Nonuniform Scale the geodesic. Use the following values, Base: 0,0,0 ; 1.0, 2.0, 1.0 (Figure 10.13).
2. Still working from the right side view, move the segments as shown in Figure 10.14. Don't worry about precision, just get it close to the figure.
3. Switch to the front view and move the segments as shown in Figure 10.15.
4. Continue working from various views and move points, segments, and faces. Match as closely as you can the shape shown in Figure 10.16.
5. The resulting substrate has very sharp angles and very large polygons in relation to the model. We can help the Displace tool by first making our substrate mesh a little more detailed. We do this by processing the mesh with the Smooth Mesh tool. Use the following Smooth Mesh settings and compare your results to Figure 10.17.

Smooth Meshing Options
Maximum # Of Subdivisions: 2
Maximum Segment Length: 1″
Smooth;
Maximum Face Angle: 1
Curvature: 80

6. With the substrate mesh ready, we now apply displacement to it. Use the earlier Displace options but change the following settings:

Origin: Object Center
Lock Size To: Current Proportions

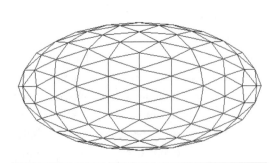

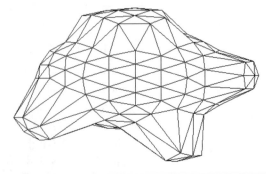

FIGURE **10.13**   *Right side view of the geodesic.*

FIGURE **10.14**   *Right side view of the geodesic after step 2.*

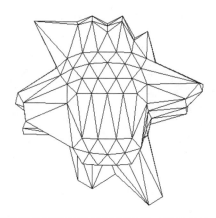

FIGURE *Front view of geodesic.*
10.15

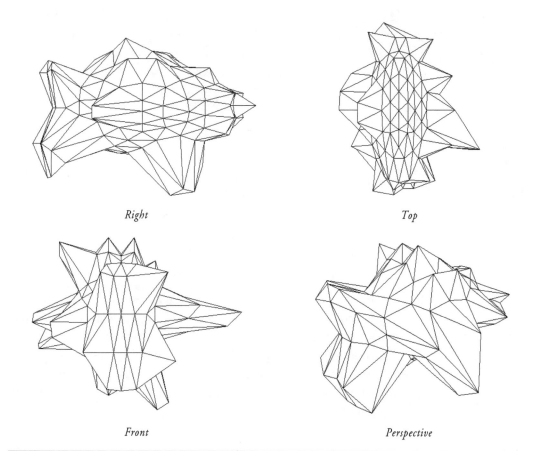

Right

Top

Front

Perspective

FIGURE *Various views of geodesic at step 4.*
10.16

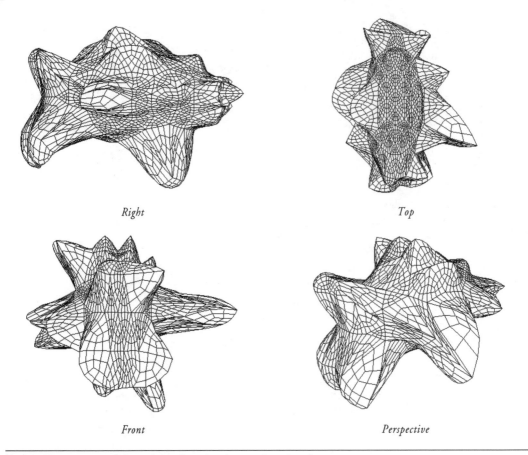

Right   *Top*

Front   *Perspective*

FIGURE   *Various views of the geodesic after using the smooth mesh tool.*
10.17

Min: 0′   Max: 10′
Smoothness: 20
Smooth Mesh: Checked

The reason for increasing the values is to compensate for the sharper angles on the substrate mesh. There is really no good rule of thumb that we can present you—experiment with settings until you are satisfied with the result. The larger Max is compensate for increased bounding volume of the substrate.

Figure 10.18 shows the front 3/4 perspective and rear 3/4 perspective views. Hard to imagine that we started with a geodesic sphere and ended with an asteroid.

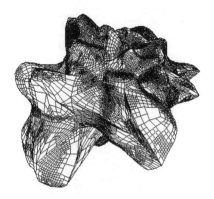
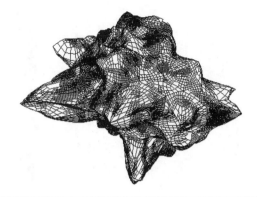

FIGURE   *Front and rear 3/4 view of the geodesic sphere.*
10.18

Arbitrary Displacement Maps

It is not always necessary to create a contour map and site prior to creation of the displacement map. Sometimes all you will be given is a generic idea. In those cases, you can just "shoot from the hip" and quickly make up a displacement map as the following example. The shot calls for a missile flying through a canyon of unspecified topography, so all we need is some kind of canyon. In effect, we are compressing the elevation map and displacement map creation into one step. For this to be effective, you have to develop a skill of looking at a grayscale map and visualizing the derived 3D terrain. This skill only comes with experience. This is really a quick solution, best used for experimentation or when topographically generic terrain can be used. The basic steps are as follows:

1. Based on artistic direction, create a grayscale displacement map.
2. In form•Z create a rectangle with the same aspect ratio as the displacement map.
3. Apply meshing to it.
4. Use the Displace tool to apply the displacement map to the flat mesh. Use Smooth Meshing features of the Displace tool to create a high-resolution terrain as needed.
5. In your image editing application, use the displacement map as the basis for creating the texture maps for the terrain.

Let's do a simple exercise.

1. To the best of your ability, recreate the map as shown in Figure 10.19.
2. Working from the top view create a rectangle that has the same aspect ratio as the map. The map has an aspect ratio of 1:10 (length is 10X of width).

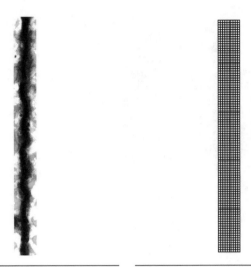

FIGURE *Displacement map.*
10.19

FIGURE *Final substrate mesh.*
10.20

3. We want the canyon to be 5000′ long, so we need to create a substrate rectangle that is 500′ wide and 5000′ long.

4. Using the Mesh tool, subdivide the rectangle using 50′ increments. The final substrate mesh is shown in Figure 10.20.

Notice that the displacement map is very thin as is the substrate mesh. Consequently, the resulting mesh will not have terrain data outside of the canyon. Because of the inherently heavy nature of the terrain meshes, care should be taken in their creation, with respect to terrain data provided. Ideally, create only what is necessary for the shot, and keep in mind what the camera see and does not see. In this particular case, the canyon terrain was custom created for a hypothetical shot of flying through the canyon, so the movement of the camera must be constrained so it never sees over the top of the canyon walls. If the shot calls for the camera to rise above the canyon, then additional terrain would need to be created. Terrains that are both highly meshed and cover large a geographical area can wreak havoc on your production times.

5. Displace the substrate using the displacement map and the following settings:

Origin: Object Center (X- 250′, Y- 2500′, Z- 0′), Rotation: X- 0, Y- 0, Z- 0
Mapping Type: Flat
Horizontal Tiling : Size: 505′, Center 1 Times.
Vertical Tiling: 5050′, Center, 1 Times

Lock Size To: Current Proportions
Min: 0′, **Max:** 100′ Smoothness: 10
Maximum # Of Subdivisions: 4
Maximum Segment Length: 1′–0″
Threshold: 1

Mesh Density of Displaced Terrains

A final note on the Displace tool. Notice that the generated canyon terrain does not have the depth of fractal detail that the displacement map does. The depth of detail that the terrain mesh has in relation to the displacement map is a product of Smoothing and Subdivisions settings. While it is possible to achieve very high mesh density to closely approximate the amount of fractal detail, it is not practical to do so given the time and hardware resources available. A displaced terrain mesh is always a trade-off between topographic and topological accuracy. A 100% topographically accurate displaced mesh would have so many polygons as to be unrenderable, and would incur generation times that can last many hours. The desired meshing of the terrain is based on following considerations:

- **Closest proximity of the digital camera to the mesh.** The closest distance during the shot that the camera comes to the terrain mesh. For high-resolution work (film and above), the largest polygon that is seen, through the camera view should not exceed 1% of the total area of the rendered image. If, on the other hand, the polygons closest to the camera are so small that it is hard to make out individual segments, then this is an indication that the terrain mesh may be more dense than is necessary. Exceptions to this rule are large flat polygons representing large flat areas of the terrain. The camera wireframe display in Figure 10.21 is a general guide for the polygonal density of the terrain used for film resolution rendering. Depending on the needs of your project, your terrain may need to be heavier or lighter. The final judgment on the mesh density is how it renders.

- **Desired topographical accuracy, and output resolution.** The topographical accuracy is a combination of geometry and topology of the mesh. Simply put, it defines how realistic and detailed the terrain mesh looks when rendered. Topographical accuracy is an artistic direction decision, and is based on the desired caliber of the shot. If the animation is destined to be simple previsualization or motion planning for a practical effect, then the topographical accuracy of the mesh can be relatively inaccurate; that is, its polygonal density is relatively light. However, if the

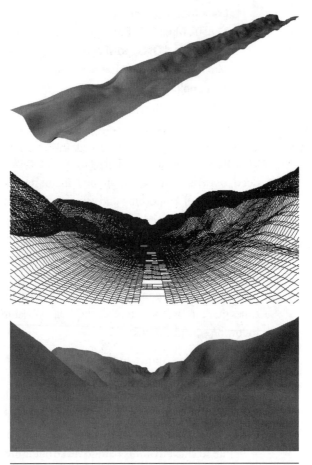

FIGURE *Camera wire frame display.*
10.21

terrain mesh is going to be used in a final shot, then it must be of the highest quality possible.

- **Slowest relative velocity between camera and the terrain.** Frequently, during animation, motion blur is used to simulate optical effects of real-world cinematography. One of the most helpful features of motion blurring a scene is suppression of geometric and texture errors. The higher the relative movement between the camera and the terrain, the longer the motion blur, and more imperfections are hidden. Very slow relative movement may not completely hide all the imperfections on the terrain mesh.

- **Lighting and atmospheric conditions of the digital set.** Like motion blur and camera distance, scene lighting and atmospheric settings can either hide or bring out geometric and textural problems of the terrain mesh.

Dark and/or very hazy scene setup may hide or render imperceptive the majority of geometric or textural problems. Brightly lit daylight scenes would require terrains that have both high geometric and textural quality.

Terrain Modeling Using Terrain Model Tool

As we have seen, displacement can be very effective in quickly generating rolling terrains. Another method of terrain generation is through the use of the Terrain Model tool in combination with the Smooth Mesh tool. The Terrain Model tool uses prebuilt and preselected *contour lines* and a *site* closed surface to generate a terrain mesh based on user settings. The Terrain Model approach has the following advantages over the Displace method:

- Better previsualization of terrain prior to generation.
- Faster generation of contour and site objects than painting the displacement map.
- The ability to create more geometrically and topologically complex terrain meshes.
- Easier and faster editing.

The Terrain Model approach is not a solution all the time and has the following disadvantages when compared to displacement:

- It is more difficult to use for beginners.
- It requires skill in reading and creating contour maps.
- Terrain Model has limitations that need to be considered.
  - For digital effects work, Terrain Model should be used in conjunction with the Mesh Smooth and possibly Displace tools, requiring understanding of how the three tools work together.
  - Terrain meshes from Terrain Model are smoother than displaced terrains and have very little or no fractal detail, which may require further modeling using the Displace tool to add detail.

As stated, the Terrain Model tool uses contour lines that are either open or closed lines, or C-Curves and a site, which is always a planar closed surface, and evaluates them based on user-defined settings. Based on those settings, a terrain mesh is then generated. There are two basic ways in which the Terrain Model tool evaluates contour lines, and both are used to determine the elevation of terrain at a point that lies on the contour line. The modes are selected in the Terrain Model Options. The first and most flexible way is Use Contour Heights. When this option is selected, form•Z will use the heights of the contour lines as the basis for determining terrain elevations. There are several advantages that Use Contour Heights has over the second way Height Interval:

- Contour lines do not have to be planar.
- Height interval between contour lines does not have to be equal; it is manually determined by Z-axis placement of contour lines.
- Contour lines do not have to be picked in any particular order, which leads to faster workflow.
- Easier 3D visualization of terrain prior to generation.

The second contour evaluation mode is **Adjust Heights At Intervals**. In topographical terms it is called "Height Interval" or "Contour Interval." When using this option, form•Z assumes that the height offset is constant between each contour line. Thus, with this mode the steepness of the terrain is controlled by projected proximity of contour lines to each other and a defined contour height interval. When viewed from a orthographic projection view, usually the top view, the distance between contour lines defines the steepness, or rate of elevation change, of the terrain. For example, if three contour lines are positioned to be 200 meters apart, when viewed from the top, with 10 meter contour intervals, then this particular region of terrain will gently rise 20 meters along its 400 meter length. The main rule to remember is, the closer the contour lines, the steeper the terrain. If the same three contour lines were moved to be only 1 meter apart with the same 10 meter contour intervals, then the terrain would rise 20 meters while only traversing 2 meters in the horizontal. It would be almost vertical! While the Contour Height mode is preferable to the Contour Elevation mode, the Contour Elevation mode is preferred when:

- Creating contour lines from a scanned elevation map underlay
- Constant elevation change between contours is desired

The disadvantages of using Contour Interval are:

- All contour lines should be coplanar. Their heights are ignored.
- Careful picking and topological organization of contour lines are required.

Contour line creation for both methods is very similar, except that in the Contour Heights method you need to position the contours along the Z-axis (height). Contour lines can be created by any method used to create other lines or C-Curves. There are several rules that are required for both methods:

- Open contour lines must intersect with the site surface at least 2 points, when projected onto the site.
- The site surface must be a planar closed surface.
- Contour lines cannot intersect each other, nor can they lie on top of each other. Overlaying or crossing contour lines signify perfectly vertical cliffs

or overhangs. Both conditions are not allowed under the current implementation of the Terrain Model.

For Contour Interval mode, additional rules are used:

- All Contour lines representing the same elevation should be grouped together using the Group tool.
- Contour lines must be prepicked in ascending order prior to activation of the Terrain Model tool. The first contour line group picked represents the lowest elevation. The last represents the highest elevation.

In the next exercise we will create a terrain using the Contour Interval mode.

1. Create an new project and recreate the elevation map from Figure 10.1.
2. Using the Group tool, group the contour lines as shown in Figure 10.22. When grouping contours, go from lowest to highest.

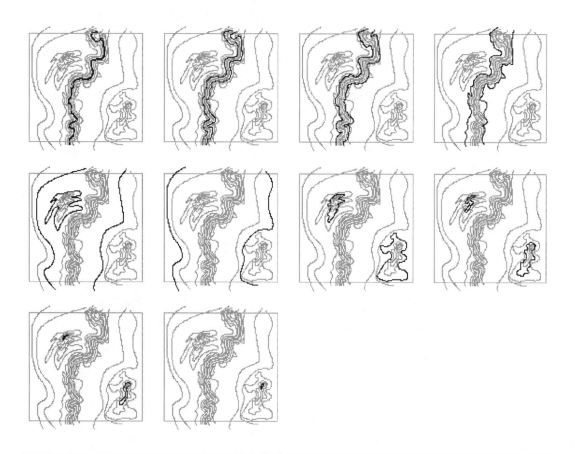

FIGURE *Grouping of contour lines go from lowest to highest.*
10.22

3. Set Terrain Model options as follows:

> Mesh Model;
> Interpolation: Fall Lines
> Mesh Options; Normal Alignment, X: 100′, Y: 100′, Z: 100′, All Directions, XYZ Lock
> Stepped Model : OFF
> Triangulated Contour Model: OFF
> Mesh Direction: From Picked Segment
> Site Starting Height: 1′
> Contour Heights: Adjust Heights At Intervals Of: 50′
> Smooth Contour Lines at Distance: OFF
> Precheck for Intersecting Contours: OFF
> Status Of Objects: Keep

4. Set the topological level to Group and preselect the contour lines in ascending order. Use the pick sequence as shown in Figure 10.22, starting with the stream bed contour lines and ending with a single contour line group on top of the hill located on the bottom-right map quadrant.

5. Create a new layer, "Terrain 1," and make it active. Click on the Terrain Model tool and then click on the site rectangle. Make sure that your active construction plane is the default XY plane. The resulting terrain is solid as shown in Figure 10.23.

The Terrain Model tool always creates solid models. This is usually not desirable so the extra faces need to be deleted with the Delete tool set to delete faces topologically.

NOTE

6. We need to delete the five large flat faces. Set the Delete tool to delete topology on all topological entities except points, and delete the faces as shown in Figure 10.24.

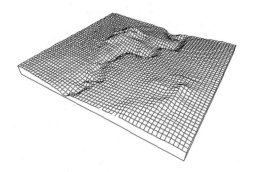

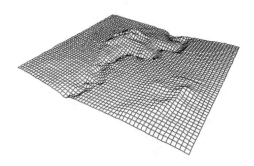

FIGURE **10.23** *Resulting terrain.*

FIGURE **10.24** *Terrain after deletion of faces.*

FIGURE   *High resolution terrain mesh after smooth mesh.*
10.25

7. Set the Smooth Mesh options as follows:

Maximum # Of Subdivisions: 2
Maximum Segment Length: 10′
Smooth: ON
Maximum Face Angle: 1
Curvature: 75
Triangulate Mesh: OFF

Smooth Mesh the low resolution terrain mesh into a high resolution (Figure 10.25).

NOTE

Notice that initially we generated a relatively light terrain model. The reason for that is the limitation of the Terrain Model tool itself. Although Terrain Model has the ability to generate highly meshed terrain mesh by using a small number in the Mesh Options portion of the dialog, its accuracy seems to deteriorate as the polygon count increases. This may result in terrains that have a stair-step appearance that look like rice paddies. To get around this shortcoming we generate low-resolution terrains and then Mesh Smooth to derive the high-resolution meshes. Mesh Smoothing a low-resolution terrain has an additional benefit of creating terrain meshes that are optimized in terms of their mesh density.

The Smooth Contour Lines at Distance *settings is set to OFF because our contour lines have already been smoothed with the C-Curve tool. It is possible to use unsmoothed polylines as contours, in which case* Smooth Contour Lines at Distance: *should be set with appropriate smoothing distance. For generating good initial (un-smoothed) terrain meshes, we have found that this settings works best when set to 1/2 of* Mesh Options *distance settings. However, this is a general guideline. As a matter of procedure you should convert the polyline contours into C-Curve.*

Contour Heights

The next exercise will use the Use Contour Heights option in the Terrain Model options. This option uses the heights of contour lines to generate the terrain. Additionally, the Use Contour Heights option allows us to use nonplanar contour lines. This is a very significant advantage over the Contour Interval method as it allows creation of more topographically complex terrain. In certain cases, we do not need to have as many contours as we would in the At Height Interval method. Prior to starting the next exercise, examine Figure 10.26. It shows the placed contours and the generated (but not smoothed) terrain. Notice that it is much easier to predict and edit the shape of the terrain then it is with Use Height Interval.

1. Copy/Paste the contour lines and sites from Figure 10.22 into a new layer. Individually move each group along the height (Z-axis) as shown in Figure 10.27. Precision is not a necessity in this case.
2. Set the Terrain Model options as follows:

   Mesh Model;
   Interpolation: Fall Lines
   Mesh Options; Normal Alignment, X: 50′, Y: 50′, Z: 50′, All Directions, XYZ Lock
   Stepped Model: OFF
   Triangulated Contour Model: OFF
   Mesh Direction: From Picked Segment
   Site Starting Height: 1′

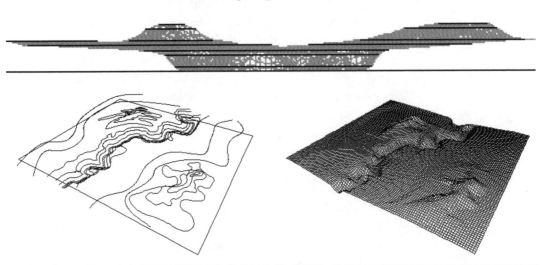

FIGURE *Placed contours and generated terrain.*
10.26

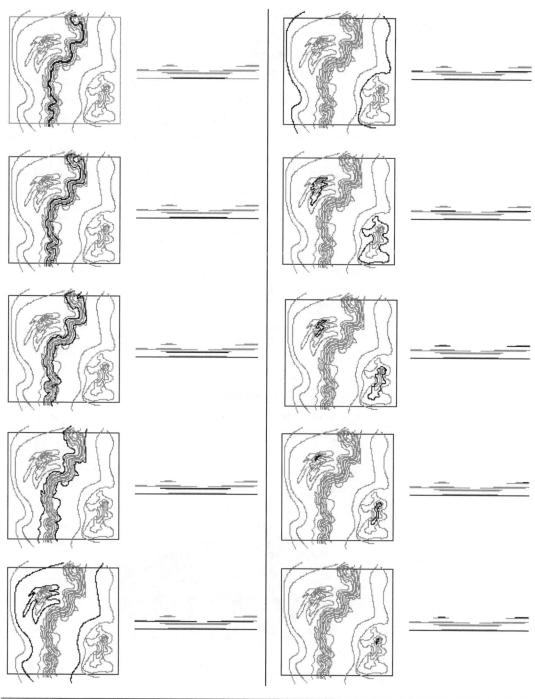

FIGURE   *Contour lines and sites from Figure 10.22 moved along the Z-axis.*
10.27

Contour Heights: Use Contour Heights
Smooth Contour Lines at Distance: OFF
Precheck for Intersecting Contours: OFF
Status Of Objects: Keep

3. Preselect the contour lines, order does not matter, and generate the terrain. Delete the extra faces to turn the terrain solid into a meshed surface. Figure 10.28 shows the resulting terrain mesh.

4. As it is, the terrain mesh has too few polygons to be used for close-up renderings. The finishing step is to use the Smooth Mesh tool to adaptively subdivide the terrain mesh (Figure 10.29).

   Use the following Smooth Mesh options:

Maximum # Of Subdivisions: 2
Maximum Segment Length: 10′
Smooth: ON
Maximum Face Angle: 1
Curvature: 75
Triangulate Mesh: OFF

Let's review the basic steps in modeling of terrain with Terrain Model tool.

- Plan out the terrain.
- Create contour lines and a site.
- Group same elevation contours together, for Adjust Intervals At Heights Of: option.
- Place the contour lines along the Z-axis to define heights, for Use Contour Heights option.
- Preselect the contour lines.

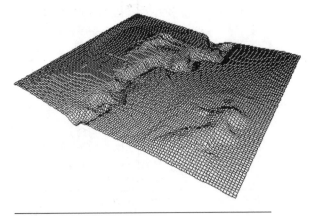

FIGURE *Resulting terrain mesh.*
10.28

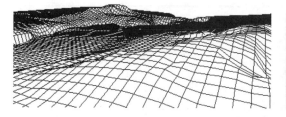
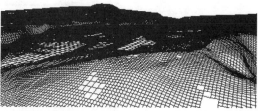

FIGURE *Subdivided terrain mesh using smooth mesh tool.*
10.29

- Generate the low- to medium-resolution terrain mesh.
- Topologically delete the large faces created by the Terrain tool, turning the terrain mesh into a meshed surface.
- Process the terrain mesh through a Smooth Mesh tool, settings dependent on desired mesh density.

Exercise

In the following exercise we use the Contour Heights method and use nonplanar contour lines to create more interesting terrain topography. As an example, the script calls for the heroes to fly over an ancient 1000′ diameter asteroid crater worn by eons of erosion. The crater texture map will be painted by a matte artist and the shot will be rendered using the camera projection method. What is needed is a 3D crater, initially rendered without textures. The matte artist will then use the rendering to paint a digital matte that will be projected onto the crater for the final beauty shot. The hills in the background will be location shots composited as a separate plate. The final rendering will have 16:9 aspect ratio with a pixel resolution of 2048 by 1152. You have artistic license as to the actual topography of the crater berms, but make it look similar to what the scene sketch shows. Figure 10.30 shows a simple sketch describing the scene.

The first phase is to determine the size of the site, create the site rectangle, and perspective match the view to the scene sketch or a storyboard.

1. We know that the crater has a 500′ radius, and is generally circular.

FIGURE *Simple sketch describing the scene.*
10.30

2. Working from a top view, draw a 128-point 500′ radius circle, the origin of the circle is at 0,0,0 (Figure 10.31).

3. In order to properly determine the size of the site rectangle we need to create a new modeling window that has the same aspect ratio and pixel resolution as the final rendering. Create a new modeling window with 2048 by 1152 pixel resolution.

4. Set up the scanned scene sketch as an underlay for that window. Then using form•Z's View Parameters and Edit Cone Of Vision, align the circle to the crater sketch (Figure 10.32).

   Note: View perspective matching is a learned skill that increases with experience. Ideally, the View Parameters inside form•Z should match the

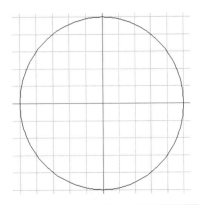

FIGURE *128-point 500′ radius circle.*
10.31

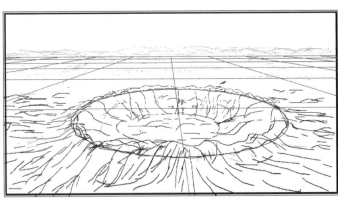

FIGURE *Circle alignment on crater sketch.*
10.32

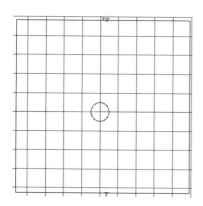 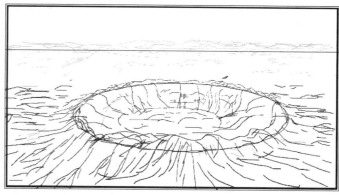

FIGURE   *Rectangle with far segments on the horizon line.*
33

digital camera settings inside the animation program. For this project the View Parameters are as follows:

Keep Vertical Lines Straight: OFF
View Point;
Orientation: –90.43
Altitude Ang: 15.09
Distance: 1109′–6″
X: –41′–6″
Y: –1073′–12″
Z: 314′–11″
Clip Hither/Yon: OFF
Center Of Interest; X: –33′–5″, Y: –2′–9″, Z: 26′–1″
Spin: 0
Angle: 75

5. Create a rectangle whose far segment lies on sketch horizon line, and side segments extend just a little beyond the view. Keep in mind that although the final scene is going to be rendered via matte projection, the animator is still able to pan the camera a little bit. To be on the safe side, extend the side segments so that the edges of the site will not be seen even with large camera pans. If possible, ascertain limits of the camera movement for the shot (Figure 10.33).

With site and view defined, in the second phase, contour lines are created and positioned.

6. Working from the top orthographic view, create the polyline contour lines as shown. Notice that the perspective matched view is used as a

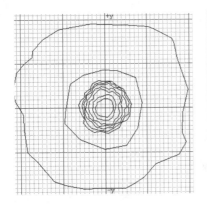
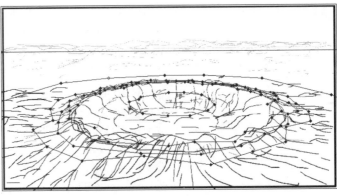

FIGURE *Contour lines and their perspective view.*
10.34

visual guide in creation of the contours. At this point, all contour lines are coplanar and look like they are floating above the crater when viewed from perspective view with the underlay ON (Figure 10.34).

7. Working from the matched perspective view and the PERPENDICU-LAR TO PLANE option enabled and XY plane being active, move the contour polylines along the Z-axis as shown in Figure 10.35. Periodically verify vertical placement of the contour polylines from the right side view to make sure that a contour that is supposed to be higher than the one next to it is not actually lower. Sometimes you will come across this optical illusion. Figure 10.35 shows side views with three levels of zoom. Precision is not vital, just get as close as you can to Figure 10.35. Note the ground level contour line, the height of it will the height of the site in Terrain Model Options.

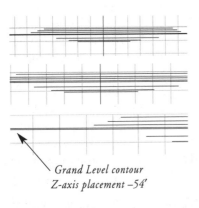

Grand Level contour
Z-axis placement –54'

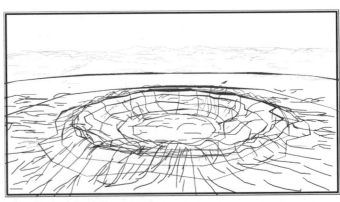

FIGURE *3 side views contour polylines moved along the Z-axis.*
10.35

8. Now that we have initial vertical placement of the contours, we should run a quick test of the contour heights. Simultaneously we will also start experimenting with Terrain Model options to get the feel of how they work in a particular situation. Set the Terrain Model Options as follows:

Mesh Model:

Interpolation: Fall Lines

Mesh Options: Normal Alignment, X: 50′, Y: 50′, Z: 50′, All Directions, XYZ Lock

Stepped Model: OFF

Triangulated Contour Model: OFF

Mesh Direction: From Picked Segment

Site Starting Height: –60′

Contour Heights: Use Contour Heights

Smooth Contour Lines at Distance: 50′

Precheck for Intersecting Contours: OFF

Status Of Objects: Keep

Notice that Site Starting Height: is set to –60′. Recall that the ground-level contour identified in Figure 10.35 has its Z-axis location at –54′. We should have the site height to be slightly lower, with respect to the overall height of the terrain, than the ground level contour. The Mesh Options and Smooth Contour Lines At Distance: are set to relatively high numbers, which will result in a coarse mesh. This is done to save time. Later on, contour polylines will be converted into C-Curves, so the Smooth Contour Lines At Distance option will not be used.

After generating the test terrain, be sure to remove the extra wall faces that the tool always generates.

Notice that while the mesh is low resolution, the parapet of the crater is already showing fractal irregularities found in nature. In the following steps we will amplify these irregularities and follow through with the Mesh Smooth and Displace tools to further randomize the terrain surface (Figure 10.36).

9. The next step is to "rough up" the contour polylines to delineate high and low areas. On the top contour, move points, as shown, up along the Z-axis. The goal is to have a nonplanar polyline. Which points to move, how much, and in which direction is an artistic decision. Set the Perpendicular Plane to ON and using Figure 10.37 as a general guide, try to follow the topographical features shown in the scene sketch. Move each point individually. After the vertical movement, move the points parallel

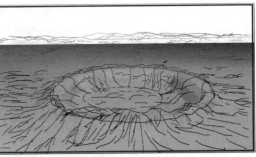

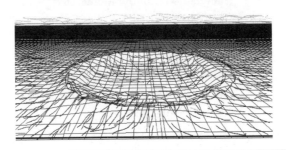

FIGURE **10.36** *Randomization of terrain service using mesa smooth and displace tools.*

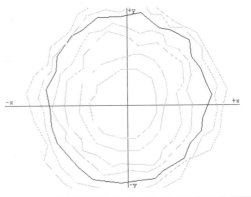

FIGURE **10.37** *"Roughed Up" contour polylines to deliniate topographical features.*

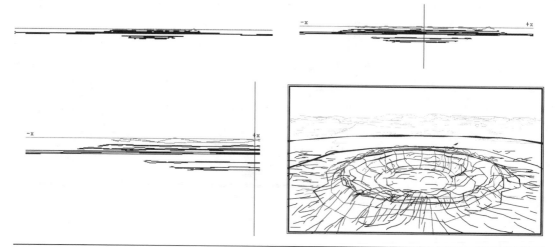

FIGURE *General guide for point position.*
10.38

to the plane to improve point alignment to the drawn edges of the crater parapet.

10. Slightly move the points on the remaining contour polylines to "rough" them up a bit. The general idea is to have the points be slightly out of plane. This will result in realistic geometric imperfections in the generated terrain, much like in real life. In effects production situations, the amount and shape of imperfections is a decision driven by artistic and technical direction, subject to artistic skill and time available. Use Figure 10.38 as a general guide for positioning of the points.

11. Convert the crater polylines into Quadratic curves with 25′ Smoothing Interval, using the C-Curve tool. The type of smoothing interpolation used and number of points generated is dictated by the needs of the project (Figure 10.39).

NOTE

Conversion of contour polylines is not a required step. In cases where you choose not to convert the polylines into C-curves prior to terrain generation, you will need to use the Smooth Contour Lines At Distance Of: *settings in the Terrain Model tool. Typically those settings would be the same as the* Smoothing Interval *settings in the C-Curve options.*

12. Now that we have the completed contour lines, we can generate the basic terrain mesh.

Set the Terrain Model options as follows, and then generate the mesh on its own layer, retain the contour lines, and site in a separate layer.

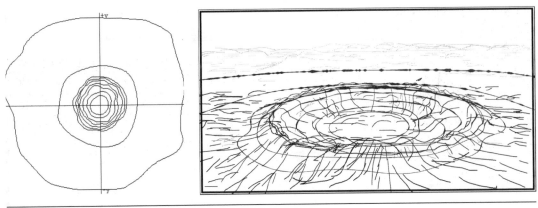

FIGURE **10.39** *Crater polylines converted into quadratic curves.*

Type Of Model:

Mesh Model: Interpolation: Fall Lines

Mesh Options: X: 40′, Y: 40′, Z: 40′, Normal Alignment, All Directions, XYZ Lock

Site (Starting) Height: –60′

Contour Heights: Use Contour Heights

Status Of Objects: Keep

After generation of the terrain, delete the extra faces, as previously discussed (Figure 10.40).

13. Now we use Smooth Mesh on the crater to smooth out the sharp peaks and increase polygonal density. We do not need to Smooth Mesh the entire terrain, only the crater portion. Working from the top view and using Lasso selection mode, select the faces bounded by the outermost

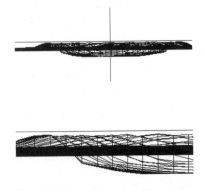

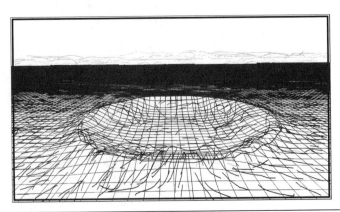

FIGURE **10.40** *Terrain after deletion of extra faces.*

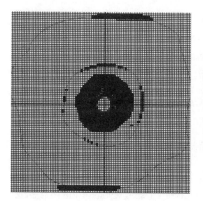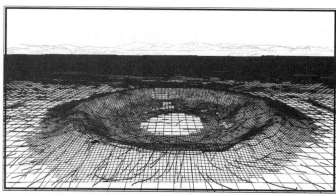

FIGURE *The smoothed crater.*
10.41

contour line. You may find it useful to set the contour lines layer to a Ghosted visibility setting. Use the following Smooth Mesh options:

Maximum # Of Subdivisions: 2
Maximum Segment Length: 10′
Smooth: ON
Maximum Face Angle: 1
Curvature: 75
Triangulate Mesh: OFF

Figure 10.41 shows the smoothed crater.

14. The next step is to slightly randomize the terrain mesh by applying a displacement map. For displacement we have two choices. The first is to apply displacement as a modeling operation within form•Z prior to export. The second is to apply displacement as a map within the animation application. If the displacement is applied as a modeling operation, then you cannot easily change the amount of displacement once the terrain model is brought into the animation environment. The decision of where and how to apply the displacement is a technical direction decision. In general, applying displacement as a map in the animation environment to be computed at render time gives you more flexibility, but may lead to increased render times and increased memory usage. However, you can apply displacement to the model within form•Z and still retain a certain amount of flexibility. Within form•Z displacement models are parametric and retain their displacement controls provided no destructive modeling, such as trimming, is performed on the displaced mesh. So, if it turns out that the displacement amount was too small or

too large, just change the options and reexport the model. When displacing within form•Z, you may experience faster rendering times and lower memory usage, within your animation application, as there is no need to apply displacement as a map.

For the purposes of this exercise we will apply displacement as a modeling operation. To create a matched displacement map, render the terrain from the top view first. Use Phong, or Preview Z-Buffer modes, without shadows. The terrain should have a material that is only slightly specular. The size of the rendered bitmap should be approximately two to four times the resolution of the final output. Since the rendered image will be used as a visual guide in the creation of the displacement map, it can be rendered at screen resolution (1280 by 1024) and then scaled in Photoshop. Figure 10.42 shows the terrain rendering ready for painting of the displacement map.

Use a neutral solid color material for rendering of the base images. Lighting should be as neutral as possible, without shadows. Specular highlighting should be kept to a minimum. Bring the rendering into Photoshop, and apply Desaturate, and Brightness/Contrast filters to the image. Figure 10.42 shows the rendering as it appeared in RenderZone and the grayscale image with filters applied. The actual displacement map should be painted on the grayscale version. The purpose of the displacement maps, discussed earlier in the chapter, was to add major topographical features to a mesh; the task of this displacement map is to add subtle variations to the terrain mesh. Therefore, high-contrast luminance variations should be avoided. Furthermore, the map will be applied with relatively small displacement min(d) and max(d). As stated earlier, the final displacement map should be about two to four times larger than the final output resolution. The X (width) pixel reso-

NOTE

FIGURE **10.42** *Terrain rendering ready for painting of the displacement map.*

lution of the final output for this shot is 2048. Since our terrain mesh has an aspect ratio of almost 1:1, the largest size we need is 8192 by 8192 pixels. However, the scene sketch shows the camera to be a good distance away from the terrain. We will settle for a minimum of 2X, or 4096 by 4096 pixels. The RenderZone rendering was rendered at 6" by 4" at 300dpi. Cropped to the size of the site rectangle (using image Alpha) the base map has the following size: Width: 4.52", Height: 4.287", Resolution: 300 dpi. Pixel resolution 1356 by 1286.

15. Within Photoshop, resize the image by 300% in both Width and Height. The resolution of the displacement map will be 4068 by 3858 pixels, just about the desired 4096 by 4096 resolution.

Painting a displacement map is an artistic endeavor. Use the general steps, described next for application of filters.

16. Create a new layer, "Crater." Set the foreground color to black and the background color to white. Apply the Render/Clouds filter to this layer.
17. Scale the entire layer so it covers only the crater area and is centered on it. This is best accomplished by first setting the layer's transparency to about 10%, then scaling and moving the layer (Figure 10.43).
18. With Lasso and Feather amount set to 100, select the area that is slightly larger than the crater. Inverse the selection and delete. Change the layer opacity to 20%. Figure 10.44 shows a blown-up view of the layer.
19. Create a new layer, "Ground1." Place it between the "Crater" and "Background" layers.
20. Apply the Render/Clouds filter to this layer. Set its Transfer mode to Overlay with 50% transparency.
21. Change Transfer of the "Crater" layer to Overlay with 50% transparency.

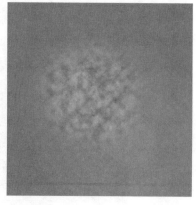

FIGURE **10.43** *"Crater" transparency at 10%.*

FIGURE **10.44** *Blown up view of "Crater" layer.*

22. Apply the Noise filter to the "Ground1" and "Crater layers." For Noise, use the following settings: Amount: 25, Distribution: Gaussian, Monochromatic: ON.

23. Apply the Gaussian Blur filter to "Ground1" and "Crater." Use a blur amount of 1.

24. Apply the Noise filter to the "Ground1" and "Crater" layers, using the same settings as above but with Amount being 15 (Figure 10.45).

25. Duplicate the "Ground1" layer ("Ground2"), place it between the "Ground1" and "Crater" layers.

26. Scale the layer by 1/2, and center it on the crater.

27. Make a circular selection, centered on the crater, with 100-pixel feather, and with a diameter of about 3/4 width of the "Ground2" layer.

28. Reverse the selection and delete.

29. Scale the "Crater1" layer so it slightly overlaps the crater's berms.

30. Set "Crater1" transparency to 80%.

31. Set "Ground2" transparency to 60%.

32. Set "Ground1" transparency to 50%.

33. Duplicate Background layer, ("Ground0"). Place it between the "Background" and "Ground1" layers.

34. Apply the Brightness/Contrast filter to the "Ground0" layer. Brightness: 0, Contrast: −100.

Figure 10.46 shows the completed displacement map. Notice how the fractal detail decreases in size as it approaches the center. Since part of the map that lies over the crater is closest to our POV, we want this area to have the highest detail. The amount of crispness decreases from the center of the map. In production, the actual detail displacement maps are painted with artistic and tech-

FIGURE **10.45** *Noise filter applied to "Ground1" and "Crater" layer.*

FIGURE **10.46** *Completed displacement map.*

nical direction in mind. As the map is being created, intermediate versions are applied to the terrain to check on the progress, and correct any mistakes.

35. Now we apply the displacement map to complete the modeling of the terrain. Set the Displacement Mapping options as follows:

Origin: Object Center (XYZ should be set automatically)
Rotation: X: 0, Y: 0, Z: 0
Mapping Type: Flat
Horizontal and Vertical Tiling: Center, 1 times.
Lock Size To: Object Extent
Min: 0′–0″, Max: 40′
Smoothness: 2
Adaptive Meshing: NOT USED

Figure 10.47 shows the completed terrain model ready for texturing.

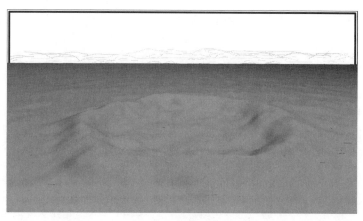

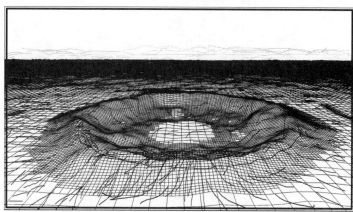

FIGURE *Completed terrain model ready for texturing.*
10.47

This chapter introduced two major approaches to modeling realistic, detailed terrain. The two approaches, Displacement and Terrain Model, are both equally valid—one is not always better than the other. Which approach to use depends on the particular situation. The decision, is a result of your particular modeling style, technical/artistic direction, and time available. All those are weighed and a decision is made. The last exercise showed how the two approaches can be used together to complement each other's strengths and negate the weaknesses. As with the other techniques described in this book, we encourage you to adapt them to your own situation and needs.

CHAPTER

11

Wheels and Tires

IN THIS CHAPTER

- Modeling Tires

I n the next three chapters we will model a realistic concept automobile. Of all the models that we build in this book, this is the most detailed, and is covered in detail. Building automotive surfaces is a very effective way to learn and practice complex surface creation and complex project management. I have broken the construction of our car into three chapters, with a complete exercise in each chapter. In this chapter we will construct the wheel and tire for our car. In the second exercise we will construct the exterior surfaces of the vehicle, and in the third exercise we will build interior surfaces that are mated to the exterior body panels.

Modeling automotive surfaces is really putting concepts that were discussed in the surface construction chapters to work. As you go through the exercises you will notice more complex, but realistic examples of concepts learned earlier in the book. Modeling automotive and other complex compound surfaces is very much an exercise in management. From an artistic point of view we manage curvatures, shapes, and proportions so the model adheres to our creative vision. From a technical execution point of view, automotive surfaces modeling is managing continuity relationships between a multitude of surfaces, while constraining the shape of the surfaces to the artistic vision. Furthermore, we need to manage topological relationships of surfaces, both in how the surfaces "flow" and the topological construction of the surfaces. This is important as we strive for our surfaces to render clean.

In the following exercise we will model an alloy, five-spoke performance rim.

1. Rename the default layer "Rim Edge." Create a 60-point 36″ diameter circle centered on world axis (0,0,0). Then create a 5-point polyline as shown. Grid Snap Module is set to 1″ (Figure 11.1).

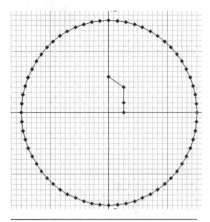

FIGURE   *60-point 36″ diameter circle*
11.1   *with 5-point polyline.*

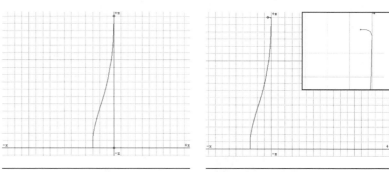

FIGURE *20-point Bezier curve.*
11.2

FIGURE *2-point line.*
11.3

2. Create a new layer, "Rim Cross-Section," and make it active. Transfer the polyline into this layer. Rotate the polyline 90 degrees about the Z-axis using 0,0,0 as the base of rotation. Then convert the polyline into a 20-point Bezier curve using the C-Curve tool (Figure 11.2).

3. Create a 2-point line as shown, adjust its direction if necessary, and join the two lines together. Delete the single extra point on the corner and round the corner point using the Fit Fillet/Bevel tool with the following settings (Figure 11.3):

Fit Fillet:
 # Of Edges: 2
Radius: 1/4″

4. Create a new layer, "Rim Virgin," and make it the active layer. Using the Revolve tool, lathe the rim cross-section 360 degrees with 60 steps. Having 60 steps is important as we will we see later. Our goal is to create a surface representing two halves of adjoining spokes. That surface will then be Rotated with Cont-Copy (C-Copy in form•Z 2.9.5) four times, and five surfaces will be stitched into a complete rim (Figure 11.4).

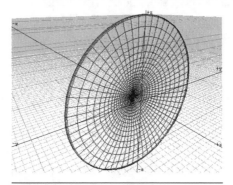

FIGURE *Five surfaces stitched into complete*
11.4 *rim.*

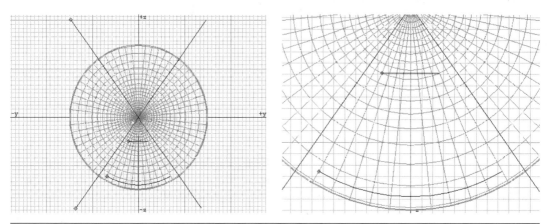

FIGURE *"Rim Dyes" layer.*
11.5

5. Ghost the "Rim Virgin" layer, create a new layer, "Rim Dyes," and make it active. Working from the right side view, draw a straight line along the Z-axis. Rotate the line 36 degrees, using 0,0,0 as the base of rotation, and Mirror duplicate it across the Z-axis. Create a bottom boundary of the rim trim, using the Midpoint Snap option. Create the top boundary of the rim trim curve using the Point Snap option. Flatten both trim boundary lines using the 2D Projection tool set to **Orthographic Projection**. Notice how the rotated lines lie precisely on the segments of the rim. This would not be possible if the revolution steps were less or more than 60 (Figure 11.5).

6. Using the Line Edit tool (v 2.9.5) or the Connect Lines tool (v. 3), connect the two twin edges. Then use the **Fit Fillet** option (v 2.9.5) or the Fit Fillet tool (v. 3) to round the four corners of the trim dye. For the top segment use **# Of Edges: 6, Radius: 4″**. For the bottom two corners use **Of Edges: 6, Radius: 1.5″**. Delete the two points that were created lying near the existing points. The resulting point count should be 35 (Figure 11.6).

7. Create a new layer, "Rim 1/5," and make it active. Copy/Paste copies of the revolved rim surface, the trim dye, and the two lines into this layer. Hide all other layers afterward. Trim the rim surface with the three shapes (Figure 11.7).

8. Clean up the trim edge using the guidelines presented in Chapter 5. Since the rim 1/5 surface is symmetrical, you can temporarily halve the surface, clean up the edge, and copy mirror/stitch (Figure 11.8).

9. Create a new layer, "Inner Spoke Curves," and make it active. Using the

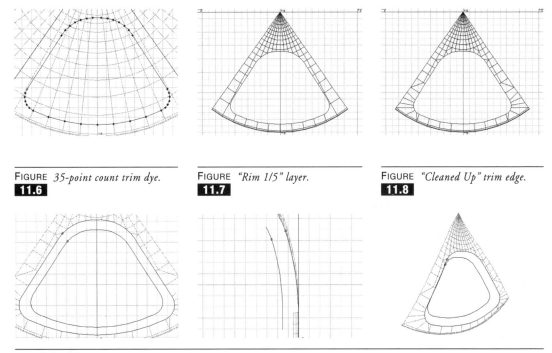

FIGURE *35-point count trim dye.*
11.6

FIGURE *"Rim 1/5" layer.*
11.7

FIGURE *"Cleaned Up" trim edge.*
11.8

FIGURE *Source curves for skinned surface.*
11.9

Detrivative Surfaces tool, set to **Boundary Of Surface Object** and **Status Of Objects** set to **Keep**, derive a closed line from the trim edge. Create a uniformly scaled duplicate of the edge curve with .85 scale value, and center of the edge curve as the base of scale. Move the duplicate –1 1/2″ long the X-axis. These two curves will serve as *source* curves for the skinned surface (Figure 11.9).

10. Using the Point Snap options, create vector lines at positions shown, snapped to points on source curves. Follow up by dividing the lines into three equally sized segments, using the Inser Segment (v. 2.9.5) or Insert Points tool (v. 3) with Segment Part and Midpoint Snapping options. These lines will be converted into *path* curves (Figure 11.10).

To divide a single segment into three equal segments, first insert a point using the Segment Part snap option set to 3 divisions. Then subdivide the larger segment by inserting a point using Midpoint snap options.

NOTE

11. Review the guidelines for creating path curves for tangency (C1) continuous matched surfaces. Place the points on the path lines as shown (Figure 11.11).

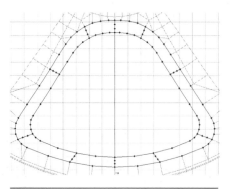

FIGURE
11.10
Lines to convert into path curves.

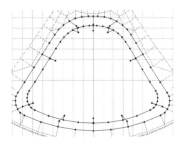
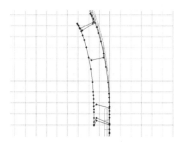
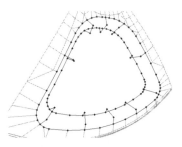

FIGURE
11.11
Path curves for C1 tangency.

12. Convert the path polylines into second-degree 12 point **B-Spline** curves using the C-Curve tool. Verify endpoint snapping, and verify the consistency of all the *path* curve directions, and of *source* curve directions. We are using second-degree source curves because we only need to match the surface along a single edge. Additionally, the second-degree **B-Spline** interpolation gives us path curves that are more semicircular versus third-degree, which results in a more elliptical shape. The number of points in path curves is a judgment call, and depends on the desired mesh density (Figure 11.12).

13. Make the "Rim 1/5" the active layer. Using the skin curve assembly, create a skin surface using the Skin tool with the following Skin Options;

Skinning Along Paths:
 # Sources: 2, # Paths: 10, Boundary Based
Placement Type: By Current Position
Point Pairing: Insert New Points As Needed
Status Of Objects: Keep.

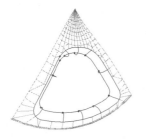

FIGURE
11.12 *Second degree path curves.*

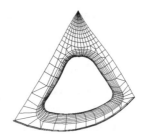

FIGURE
11.13 *Surfaces stitched together after skinning.*

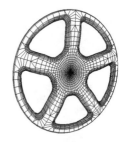

FIGURE
11.14 *"Rim" layer.*

After skinning, Stitch the two surfaces together into a single surface (Figure 11.13).

14. Create a new layer, "Rim." Copy/Paste the Rim 1/5 surface into it. Hide all other layers. Working from the right view, C-Copy Rotate the surface, using 0,0,0 as the base of rotation, and 72 degrees as the rotation offset. Stitch the five surfaces into a single surface. Apply Smoothing Attributes to the surface (Figure 11.14).

15. Create a new layer, "Lugnut Cavity Trim Curves," and make it active. Ghost the "Rim" layer, all other layers should be hidden. Create a 20-point circle with 1 1/4" radius, centered on 0,0, 3 1/2". Using world origin (0,0,0) as the base of rotation and 72-degree offset, create four copies of the circle (Figure 11.15).

16. Copy/Paste copies of the circles into the "Rim" layer, and hide the "Lugnut Cavity Trim Curves" layer. Trim the rim surface, and halve the rim surface. Clean up the trim edges. You should retain a copy of the rim surface in a backup layer, just in case. Figure 11.16 shows the before and after cleanup results.

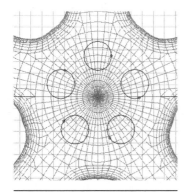

FIGURE
11.15 *4 copies of 20-point circle with 1¹⁄₄" radius.*

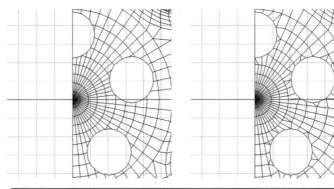

FIGURE
11.16 *"Lugnut Cavity Trim Curves" layer before and after clean-up.*

17. Create a new layer, "Lugnut Cavity Cross-Sections," and make it active. Derive an edge cross-section of the lugnut cavity using the Derivative Surfaces tool set to **Boundary Of Surface Objects**, and **Status Of Objects** set to **Keep**. Then create copies of the edge curve using the Move and Nonuniform Scale tools. Place the cavity cross-sections as shown. If you are unsure what transformation to use, #2, #3, and #4 cross-sections were nonuniformly scaled from the right side view using 1,.9,.9, scale values. Then they were slightly nonuniformly scaled from the front view to make them conformal to the #1 cross-section (the edge curve). After scaling they moved into position with Grid Snap Module set to 1/16″. The #5 cross-section is a projected duplicate of the #4 cross-section. The placement of #2 and #3 cross-sections is critical as it those cross-sections that enable the lofted surface derived from these curves to have tangential (C1) continuity to the rest of the rim surface. Take care when creating cross-sections for 1/2 surface at the reflection axis that the first points lie on the mirror axis. If an error is made, the mirrored and stitched surface will have a fracture in it, resulting in a shading anomaly. A good way to tell if they are correctly placed is by their Y position, which should be 0 (Figure 11.17).

18. Make "Rim" the active layer. Using the C-Mesh tool, create lugnut cavity surfaces using the following settings. DON'T Mirror/Stitch yet, the figure is only for reference (Figure 11.18).

Construct Plain Mesh
Construct Directly
Length OF Net: Use Directly
Depth Of Net: Use Control Line Intervals
Mesh Length: At Control Points
Mesh Depth: # Of Segments: 2, Per Segment: ON, Smooth: ON
Controlled Mesh Smoothing Options:
Length: None

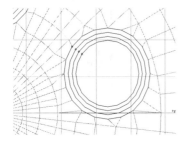 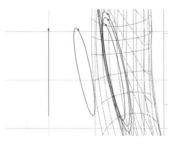 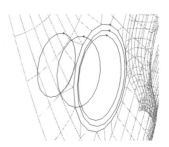

Figure   *"Lugnut Cavity Cross-Sections" layer.*
11.17

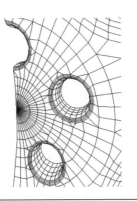

FIGURE *Lugnut cavity surfaces on "Rim" layer.*
11.18

Depth: B-Spline, Degree: 3, **# Of Points:** 64
Type Of Object: Open Ends (Surface)
Status Of Objects: Keep

19. Using the Lasso Pick tool, select the first four rows of polygons, shown as ghosted. Separate those polygons with the Separate tool set to **At Boundary Of Selected Faces**, and **Status Of Objects** set to **Delete**. After the separation, you may delete those polygons as they are no longer needed (Figure 11.19).

20. Create a new layer, "Rim Inner Lip Cross-Sections," and make it active. Using Derivative Surfaces set to **Selected Segments**, derive the edge curve of the lip. Create a paralleled duplicate using the Parallel Objects tool set to 1/16″ and direction IN. Adjust the positions of the first and last point on the duplicate so they lie precisely on the Z-axis. Create the third lip cross-section by moving a copy of the inner curve –1/16″ along the X-axis (Figure 11.20).

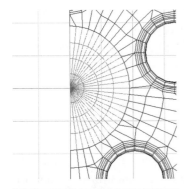
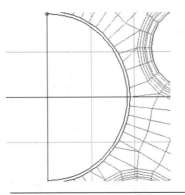
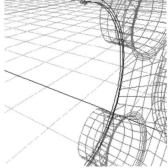

FIGURE *Seperation of first 4 rows of*
11.19 *polygons.*

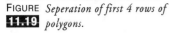

FIGURE *"Rim Inner Lip Cross-Sections."*
11.20

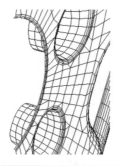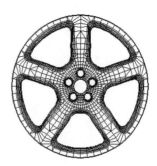

FIGURE *Mirrored and stitched two halves of "Rim" layer.*
11.21

21. Make "Rim" the active layer. Using the C-Mesh tool, create a lip surface using the following settings. Stitch the lip surface with the rest of the rim. At this point you can Mirror and Stitch the two halves (Figure 11.21).

Construct Plain Mesh
Construct Directly
Length Of Net: Use Directly
Depth Of Net: Use Control Line Intervals
Mesh Length: At Control Points
Mesh Depth: # Of Segments: 3, Per Segment: OFF, Smooth: ON
Controlled Mesh Smoothing Options:
Length: None
Depth: B-Spline, Degree: 2, # Of Points: 64
Type Of Object: Open Ends (Surface)
Status Of Objects: Keep

22. Make the "Rim Inner Lip Cross-Sections" the active layer, and create a curve (for revolution) for the wheel mount lug cover surface. Use the figure for guidance but you may exercise your own design initiative as to the shape of the curve. Be sure that the first point lies on the axis of revolution and the last point is point snapped to the three lip cross-section. Revolve the curve 30 steps and transfer the surface to the "Rim" layer. The source curve was derived by converting a 7-point polyline, shown in Figure 11.22, into a 12-point third-degree B-Spline.

23. In the "Rim Cross-Sections" layer, create cross-sections for the inside and the rear surfaces of the rim. Then Revolve the surfaces using around X-axis with 60 steps. Using the Topological Attributes tool, convert the surfaces into one-sided surfaces, and reverse directions so that their normals point inside of the wheel (Figure 11.23).

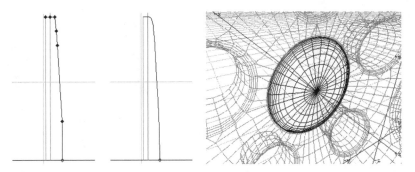

FIGURE **11.22** *7-point polyline in "Rim Cross-Sections" layer.*

We need to add a small hole in the rim for the tire stem. Ghost the "Rim" layer. We will use this layer solely as visual reference for placement of the trim dye. In real-world rims, the stem and the hole are on an angle, so we need to rim the rim surface at an angle of about 15–20 degrees. There are two ways we can approach this problem. The first way involves creating a 3D solid dye object, then rotating and placing it into position. Then trim the rim with the dye. The second way is to move and rotate a planar rectangle so its normal has the same vector as the desired vector of the stem. Define an Arbitrary Plane from the rectangle, and create a circle shape on it. With the custom plane being active, trim the surface with the circle. The trim will occur with respect to the construction plane. In this case, we use the first technique. Create the dye in the "Stem Dye" layer. Don't forget to make a copy of the untrimmed rim prior to trimming.

24. Create a 1/4″ radius 16-point circle and extrude it 3″. From the front view, rotate it 15 degrees and place it as shown (Figure 11.24).
25. Copy/Paste a copy of the dye into the "Rim" layer. Trim the rim surface with the dye. After the trim, clean up the trim edge (Figure 11.25).

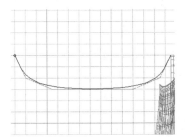
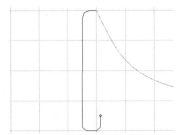

FIGURE **11.23** *"Cross-sections for inside and rear surfaces of "Rim Cross-Sections."*

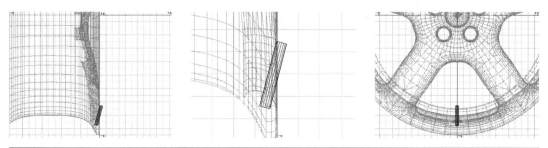

FIGURE 11.24 *3″ extrusion of 16-point curcle with 1/4″ radius.*

To complete the stem trim edge, we need to put a small bevel on it. Since we can't round it we have to manually create the edge bevel. The procedure is very similar to the one we used to derive cross-sections for the lugnut wells, only in this case we only need two cross-sections and C-MESH settings will have no smoothing.

26. Create a new layer, "Stem Edge Bevel Cross-Sections" and make it active. Derive the #1 (edge) cross-section using **the** Derivative Surfaces tool set to **Boundary Of Surface Object**, and **Status Of Objects** set to **Keep**. Be sure to click on one of the trim edge segments. Create the #2 cross-section by nonuniformly scaling a duplicate of the #1 cross-section and move it slightly below the #1 parallel to the trim vector. To achieve maximum accuracy define a custom construction plane based on one of the capping faces of the trim dye. Then move the #2 perpendicular to the plane. However, because the effect is subtle, distance is small, and absolute accuracy is not required, you can eyeball the placement of the #2 cross-section (Figure 11.26).

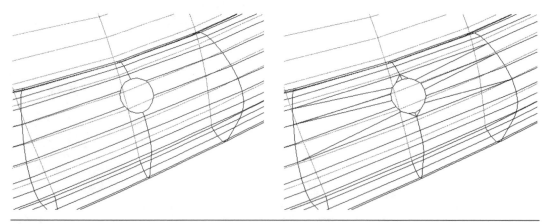

FIGURE 11.25 *"Cleaned Up" trim edge of "Rim" layer.*

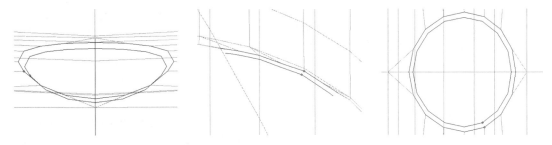

FIGURE
11.26
"Stem Edge Bevel Cross-Sections."

27. Create the bevel surface using the C-Mesh tool. Turn off all smoothing attributes, and set Mesh Length to At Control Points, and Mesh Depth to At Control Lines. Set Status Of Objects to Keep. Afterward, stitch the bevel surface with the rim (Figure 11.27).

28. We now have our complete rim that is composed of four separate objects: front rim, wheelmount cover, inside rim surface, and back rim surface. This breakdown makes the whole wheel easy to texture map, as standard projections can be used. Use Frontal projection for the front rim, mount cover, and back surfaces. Use Cylindrical projection for the inner rim surface. To save time and reduce object count we can join the front rim, mount cover, and back rim surfaces into a single object using the Join tool. This is optional, as you may wish to retain those surfaces as separate objects if each will have a different material. The decision as to the breakdown of the wheel depends on how it is going to be texture mapped and in what application. In form•Z RenderZone, even if the objects are joined, they retain their coordinates through Texture Groups (if mapped prior to joining). However, you may lose the texture groups through the exportation/importation process when you bring the object into your animation environment (Figure 11.28).

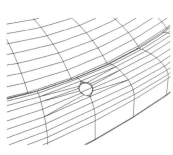

FIGURE
11.27
Stitched bevel surface of the rim.

FIGURE
11.28
Joined rim using the four objects.

Modeling Tires

Creating tires is unique as it can be both very easy and quick or time consuming and difficult. It all depends on the amount of detail that is needed. Specifically, it is how we choose to emulate the tread pattern that has direct bearing on the amount of work involved.

We will discuss two ways to handle tread pattern, textural and geometric. Textural is the easier of the two but is limited in its scope of use as it suffers from all the shortcomings of using texture maps, some of which are texture map resolution, level of realism, and POV proximity and relative motion. Geometric tread pattern construction involves creating actual geometry of grooves. Depending on the pattern, the construction procedures can be tricky, and polygon count will be high. The decision to use either geometric or textural tread is dependent on project considerations. If the wheel is spinning, then the textural approach is the ideal solution as it minimizes polygon count and decreases workload. However, if the model is to be used for static high-resolution shots, lit in a way as to accentuate the tires, and there is a requirement for a high level of realism, then we must consider creating a geometric tread pattern.

If we choose the texturing approach to giving detail to tires, we can use two possible texturing strategies. A tire, which is a surface of revolution, can be created as single NURBZ surface in form•Z v.3, or as meshed surface in v.3 or older. We can create a single NURBZ surface using the NURBZ option in the Revolve tool. Export the model in OBJ, 3DMF format. The parametric UV mapping coordinates will carry with the geometry. Import the tire into a professional 3D paint application such as Metacreations Painter 3D, 4Division 4D Paint, or Amazon 3D Paint, and paint the tire tread pattern and sidewall there. This procedures will work assuming that you can import the tire geometry along with correctly interpreted UV coordinates into your animation package. Sidewall texturing can present a problem depending on the rendering application used, because it uses a different projection method. In form•Z RenderZone, texturing tires is not a problem as RenderZone allows the creation of multiple texture groups, with each group having its own mapping projection. However, the texture may not export/import correctly into your animation environment, as each application has its own way of dealing with multiple materials on a single mesh. For this reason I recommend that initially you use one of the following methods: Model the tire as three curvature continuous surfaces, the tread surface, and two side walls. Export and texture map them as separate objects, within the animation environment, and then group them into a single object. The second method is to model the tire as a single surface, but create three Texture Groups within Texture Map Control. Texture Group 1 would be the tread surface having cylindrical projection. Texture Groups 1 and 2, defining the left and right sidewalls, would have planar projections. Prior to exporting, break the tire surfaces into three objects by selecting the faces of texture groups and using the Separate tool set to **At Boundary Of Selected** faces. The bitmaps themselves are applied as bump maps.

The geometric approach involves creating geometry based on the tread pattern and then placing the tread geometry on a revolved surface. The geometrical approach has the advantages of offering the most realistic output, especially subtle shadows created by the treads.

From experience, road tires (i.e., not off-road 4 by 4 tires) are best handled through the textural approach as it is the quickest and most flexible in terms of implementing changes. For our tire modeling exercise we will model a V-rated performance tire with a tread patterned after one of my favorite tires on the market today, the Toyo Tires Proxes RA-1 competion/road tire. We will use the texture mapping approach to create the tread pattern and sidewall details.

1. Define a new layer, "Tire Cross-Sections." In this layer, create a simple symmetrical 18-point polyline as shown and convert it into a 48-point third-degree B-Spline C-Curve (Figure 11.29).
2. Define the "Tire" layer. Using the Revolve tool, create the tire surface using the X-axis as the axis of revolution. Use 60 in **# Of Steps:** field (Figure 11.30). Even though
3. Set **Topology to Face** and select faces as shown. Then using the Separate tool set to **At Boundary Of Selected Faces**, detach the selected faces. You should end up with three objects, the tread surface and two sidewall surfaces. Leave all three surfaces in the "Tire" layer. Using Texture Map, apply Cylindrical projection to the tread surface and Flat projection to the sidewall surfaces (Figure 11.31).

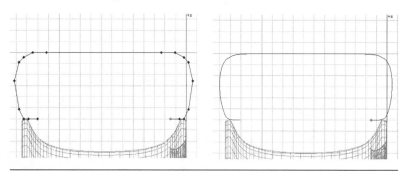

FIGURE *18-point polyline converted into a 48-point third-degree B-spline C-curve.*
11.29

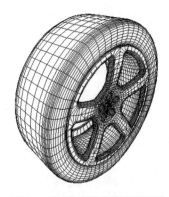

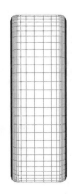

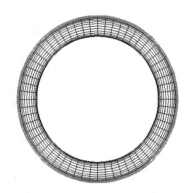

FIGURE *Defined "Tire" layer.*
11.30

FIGURE *Detached "Tire" faces.*
11.31

OK, now that we have delineated the boundaries of the sidewall and tread surfaces we can use this information to paint a bitmap image in an image editing application, such as Adobe Photoshop. To create a tread pattern texture, we need to create an UNFOLDED version of the tread surface. Unfortunately, we do not have a tool within form•Z that will unfold geometry based on its texture mapping. However, we can emulate this process by cleverly using the Projection and Line Creation tools. Our goal is to create a planer rectangle that has its width equal to that of the tread surface and length equal to that of the circumference of the tire. The width is easy as we have the tread surface to snap to. The length we can calculate using a geometric circumference formula. However, we would incur some error depending on the measured radius of the tire. We wish to avoid visible distortion of the texture map as it is applied cylindrically, and for that we need to have an accurate circumference. We can derive an accurate circumference by using the Projection tool set to Unfolded Projection, and unfolding a copy of the tread surface from the top view. The result is a strange mesh that vaguely resembles a peacock tail. Running through the center of this surface is a series of straight segments which represent our circumference.

1. Create a temporary layer, "Temp1," and make it active. Working from the top view, create an unfolded projection of the tread surface using 2D Projection set to **Unfolded Projection**. All other options are not used. Notice the location where you should click to get usable results. The straight line distance from the X-axis line to the tip of the four straight face chains is the circumference of our tire (Figure 11.32).

2. Define a new layer, "Tread Pattern," and make it active. Create a rectangle with the width equal to the tread surface and the length equal to that

of the circumference of the tire. To accurately create the polygon, use appropriate snapping options and then place the polygon so the midpoint of its first widthwise segment is located at world origin. This rectangle represents the area covered by the tire in one revolution (Figure 11.33).

The tread pattern can be painted in any image editing application, such as Adobe Photoshop. All that is needed is to export an EPS (Level 1, RGB, or Gray) file and bring it into Photoshop. Paint the tread pattern map the using EPS as a guide. Then apply the painted tread pattern map cylindrically to the tread surface. Depending on your skill with Photoshop, this can be a time-consuming chore. As we will see, form•Z can be used in conjunction with Photoshop to create tread pattern maps much faster and with more accuracy than with Photoshop alone. Basically we need to create the tread pattern using form•Z Line Creation tools, to duplicate the pattern using the rectangle as a guide. Then export the tread pattern as an EPS Level 1 file, and apply the finishing touches in Photoshop. This procedure allows for the creation of maps in multiple resolutions. Additionally, having a 2D tread pattern gives us a great starting point for the creation of geometric treads should the need arise.

3. Using the wheel/tire sketch and contact patch sketch as guides, create a thread pattern using 2D Line Creation tools and using the rectangle as a surface boundary (Figure 11.34). The groove width is 1/8″. Notice that the pattern is such that when wrapped cylindrically 360 degrees it is seamless. You can test this by radially bending the tread pattern with a 360-degree angle (Figure 11.35).
4. Export the tread pattern, from the orthogonal top view, as an EPS (Level 1, Gray) file. Bring the EPS into Photoshop. Crop the image properly.

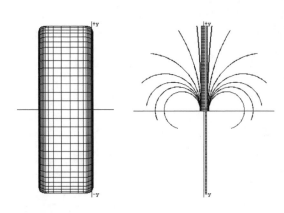

FIGURE **11.32** *Unfolded projection of "Temp1" layer.*

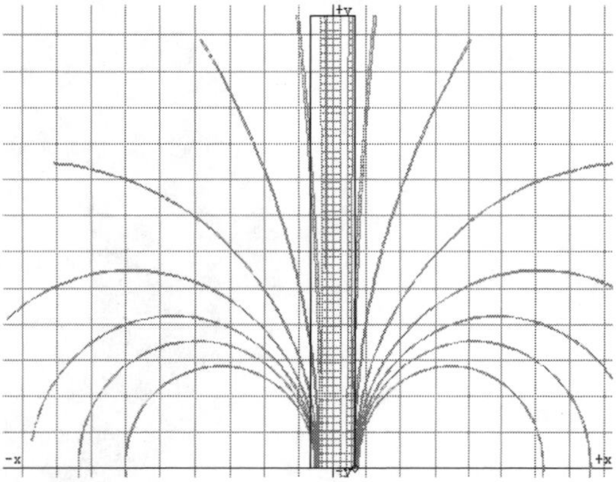

FIGURE **11.33** *This rectangle represents the area covered by the tire in one revolution.*

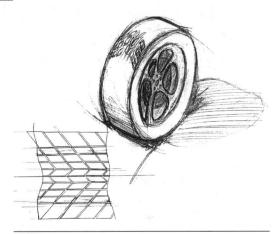

FIGURE *Wheel/tire sketch.*
11.34

FIGURE *Tread pattern constructed using 2D line creation.*
11.35

The map will be used as a bump map, so treads are white and grooves are black. In Photoshop, rotate the canvas 90 degrees and touch up the seam by deleting the black pixels. Because the tread on real performance tires is blended into the sidewall, feather the edges of the tread map with black. This feathering will create the blended tread look. Figures 11.36 and 11.37 show the tread pattern bump map.

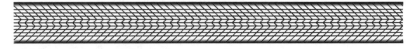

FIGURE *Blended tread look.*
11.36

FIGURE *Tread pattern bump map.*
11.37

12 Automotive Surfaces

In This Chapter

Lead In

For our ongoing automotive modeling project we will model a GT Spyder type sports car. Spyder is a type of sports car characterized by a convertible top, and a short wide wheelbase. They are generally small two-seat two-door sports cars. I must confess that I am a big fan of this type of car. The vehicle that we will model is one of my own design. You car buffs will notice styling elements from many cars, and different eras in my concept. I wish to thank Alberto Scirocco for assisting me in creating the sketches.

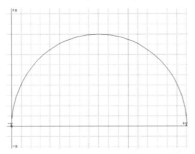 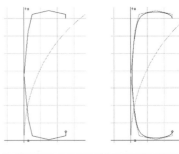

1. Create a new project and rename the default layer "Fender Source Curves." Create a 48-point semicircle with an 18″ diameter and with the first point located at world origin (0,0,0). This is done by creating a 96-point 2-point circle with the first point at 0,0,0 and the second at 0, 1′–6″, 0. Then trim the circle with a line. This semicircle will serve as the path for the wheel-well swept surface. Forty-eight segments will give an optimal mesh density (Figure 12.1).

2. Create the fender cross-sections as shown (Figure 12.2). Start by creating a polyline and then convert it into a plain 36-point 3rd-degree curve using the C-Curve tool. Use the following C-Curve parameters:

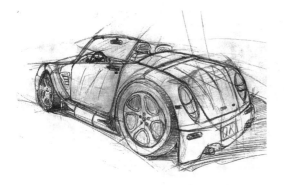 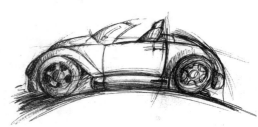

FIGURE *Optimal mesh density.*
12.1

FIGURE *Fender cross-sections.*
12.2

Construct Plain Curve: ON
Construct Directly: ON
Spline: B-Spline
Degree: 3
 # Of Points: 36

3. Create a new layer, "Fender Virgin." Use the Sweep tool to create the wheel-well surface. Use the following Sweep Options (Figure 12.3):

Type: Axial
Cross Section Alignment: Centroid
Status: Keep

Now we create a tangency continuous surface to extend the fender surface and add a rolled lip. In real-world automotive styling, edges of body panels are rarely left sharp; usually they have a slight roll along the edge.

4. With Topology set to Segment, select the bottom segments in the front of the wheel-well surface. Create a new layer, "Fender Extend Cross-Sections," and make it active. Use the Derivative Surfaces tool to extract a cross-section as shown (Figure 12.4). Set Derivative Surface Options as follows:

At boundary of selected segments.
Status objects set to keep

5. Switch to the front view. Create a flattened duplicate of the derived cross-section using the Project tool set to **Orthographic Projection** and **Status** set to **Keep**. The duplicate will be projected onto the XY plane with Z value of 0. After projection, move the flattened duplicate –1″ down the Z-axis as shown (Figure 12.5).

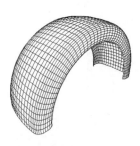

FIGURE *Sweep options.*
12.3

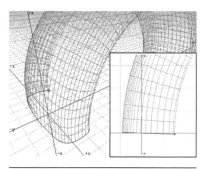

FIGURE *Extracted cross-section.*
12.4

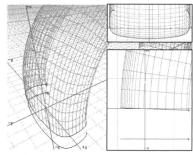

FIGURE *Flattened duplicate*
12.5

6. We want a soft inward curving lip of the fender surface. To achieve this effect we need to create parallel duplicates of the last cross-section. Set the Parallel Objects tool as follows:

Single Parallel (Surface): In
Wall Offset: In: 1/8″
Slab Offset: In: 1/8″
Status: Keep

Create two parallel curves. First click on the last cross-section and then click on the parallel duplicate (Figure 12.6).

7. Create an intermediate cross-section by duplicating the first projected cross-section and moving the duplicate +1/2″ along the Z-axis (Figure 12.7).

8. Create a lofted meshed surface using the C-Mesh tool. Place the resulting surface in the "Fender Virgin" layer (Figure 12.8). Use the following C-Mesh Options:

Construct Plain Mesh
Construct Directly
Length Of Net: Use Existing
Depth Of Net: Use Control Line Intervals
Mesh Length: At Control Points
Mesh Depth: # Of Segments: 2, Per Segment, Smooth
Controlled Mesh Smoothing Options:
Length: None
Depth: B-Spline
Degree: 3, # Of Points: 64
Status Of Objects: Keep

Figure 12.8 shows the lofted surface.

9. We now have the two surfaces. Next we stitch the two surfaces together.

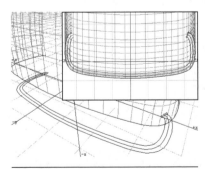

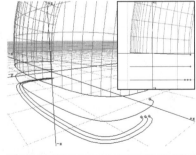

FIGURE *Parallel duplicate.*
12.6

FIGURE *Creating intermediate cross-*
12.7 *section.*

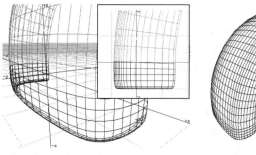

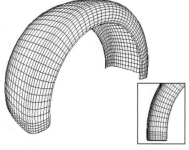

FIGURE *Lofted surface.*
12.8

FIGURE *Stitched surface.*
12.9

However, we always retain the original "virgin" surfaces should the need arise to go back and revise the design. Create a new layer, "Fender Surface," we will perform most of the trimming on the wheel-well surface in this layer, while the original unedited version resides quietly in the "virgin" layer. Copy/Paste the two surfaces into this layer and then hide all other layers. Set Status Of Objects to Delete. Stitch the two surfaces together using the Stitch tool. In V 3.X of form•Z, Stitch is a separate tool. In form•Z 2.9.5 and earlier, Stitch is an option found in the Trim & Stitch tool. Figure 12.9 shows the stitched surface.

Now we will model the rear extension surface of the fender.

10. Working from the right side view, select the faces highlighted (in black) in Figure 12.10. Then separate the faces from the main wheel-well surface using the Separate tool, with Boundary Of Selected Faces options, and Status Of Objects set to Delete. The result should be two separate meshed surfaces. Create a holding layer, "Misc. Objects," and transfer the detached meshed surface into it. Hide the "Misc. Objects" layer after the transfer.

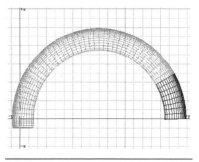

FIGURE *Highlighted faces.*
12.10

We want to combine various design styles so the rear of the fender will have a more classic curvy look. Recall the procedure for creating continuity matched skin surfaces. We will use this procedure to match the rear fender extend surface to the main fender surface. First we begin by deliminating the length of the rearward extension surface.

11. Create a new layer, "Fender Rear Extension Cross-Sections," and make it active. Using the Derivative Surfaces tool, derive an edge curve as shown in Figure 12.11. The procedure is the same as described in Figure 12.4. Be sure to set **Status Of Objects** to **Keep**.

12. We need a frontal flattened duplicate of the edge. Working from the front view, flatten the derivative curve using the 2D Projection tool. Set **Status Of Objects** to **Keep**. After projection, move the duplicate and place it as shown (Figure 12.12).

13. Working from the right side view, create four rotated duplicates of the flattened curve with a rotation offset between each duplicate of 22.5 degrees. The base of rotation is the bottommost point of curve (Figure 12.13).

14. Create two parallel duplicates of the last rotated cross-section. Use the Parallel tool with 1/10″ parallel amount IN. Remember that the second parallel curve is a parallel of the first parallel created (Figure 12.14).

15. Select the cross-sections in sequential order, but do not select the original derived curve (we will use it later). Using the C-Mesh, create a plain mesh 3rd-degree **B-Spline** surface using the same settings as those used to create surfaces in Figure 12.8, except change the following settings:

Mesh Depth:
#Of Segments: 2
Controlled Mesh Smoothing Options:

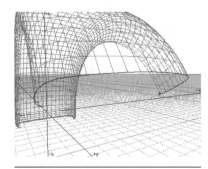

FIGURE *Edge curve.*
12.11

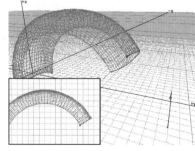

FIGURE *Duplicate placement.*
12.12

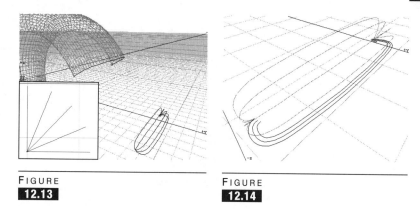

FIGURE
12.13

FIGURE
12.14

 # Of Points: 128
Status Of Objects: Keep

Transfer the surface, shown in Figure 12.15, into the "Fender Surface" layer.

16. Copy/Paste a backup copy of the surface you just created into the "Misc. Objects" layer, or any other backup hidden layer. The surface is going to be deformed. Always have undeformed copies of objects to be deformed in backup layers. Now, working from the top view, apply the Bulge Deformation to the surface with the following settings:

Deform Object:
Bulge
Base Reference Plane: YZ
Initial Limits: Upper: 0; Lower: 100
Perform the Bulge with .05, 0 values.

The deformed surface is shown in Figure 12.16.

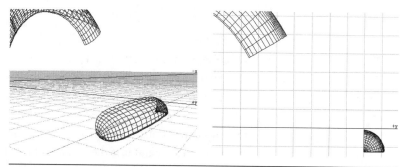

FIGURE   *Transferring the surface.*
12.15

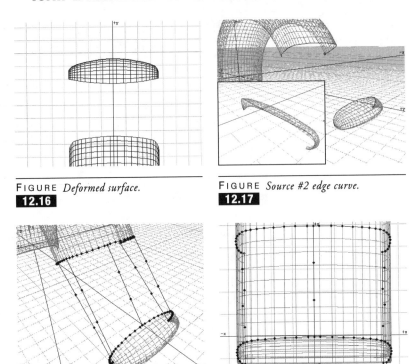

FIGURE *Deformed surface.*
12.16

FIGURE *Source #2 edge curve.*
12.17

FIGURE *Source shapes.*
12.18

Now that we have two surfaces of the fender, we can construct a blend surface between the two. The general procedure for creating a tangency continuous blend surface is the same as the one described in Chapter 9. Prior to continuing with the building of the car, you may want to review the blend surface creation procedure using the Skin tool. Remember that we are building a polygonal model for use in visualization and animation. It is not important for us to achieve precise mathematical surface continuity, our prime criteria is that the surfaces shade cleanly as one continuous surface.

17. Create a new layer, "SKIN Source Curves." Transfer the derived edge curve, shown in Figure 12.11, into this layer. This open surface object will serve as Source #1 for the Skin surface we are going to create. Using the edge curve derivation technique, derive the Source # 2 edge curve as shown in Figure 12.17.

18. Create five straight-line "paths" using point snap. Prior to creating the lines, insert a point into the middle of each of the two "source" shapes, as shown in Figure 12.18. This allows creation of a "path" that perfectly bisects the blend surface. After creating the straight lines, use Insert Point

(v 3) or Insert Segment (v 2.9.5 or earlier) to divide each of the lines into three equal parts. To divide a line into three equal parts, first insert a single point using Segment Part snapping options set to 3 Divisions. Follow by inserting a second point with snapping set to Midpoint.

19. Recall that the next step is to move the points such that the segments of "path" polylines have the same directional vector as the last two "depth" segments of the surfaces to be blended. Working from the right side view, move the points to accomplish this. Use Figure 12.19 as a guide. Recall that this is not a precision operation, as no snapping options are used. Point positions are evaluated visually.

Prior to proceeding to the next step you may wish to retain the copies of the polylines in a backup layer. If an error is made, you will not need to rebuild the polylines.

NOTE

20. Convert the "path" polylines into plain curves using the C-Curve tool with the following settings:

    Construct Plain Curve: ON
    Construct Directly: ON
    Spline: B-Spline, Degree: 3, # Of Points: 24

    Verify that both "source" shapes have matched directions, and all five "path" shapes have matched directions. Verify that all endpoints are snapped to each other, as you may incur minor positional errors when the polylines are converted into C-Curve (Figure 12.20).

21. Now we are ready to create the blend surface. Make "Fender Surface" the active layer. Create the skinned surface using the following Skin Options:

    Skinning Along Paths: # Sources: 2, # Paths: 5, Boundary Based
    Placement Type: By Current Position
    Point Pairing: Must Have Same # Of Points
    Status Of Objects: Keep

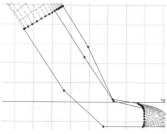

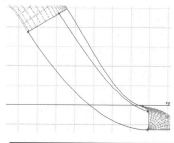
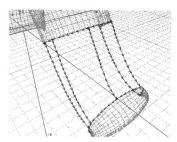

FIGURE *Point positions.*
12.19

FIGURE *Polylines converted to C-curves.*
12.20

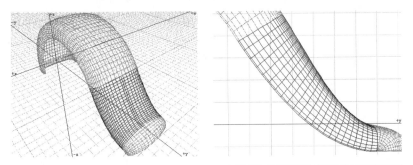

FIGURE *Using reverse direction tool.*
12.21

You may need to adjust the face normals of the skinned surface so that they match the normals of the main fender surface. Face normals can be viewed by turning them on/off in Wireframe Options, and can be reversed using the Reverse Direction tool (Figure 12.21).

22. The next step is to stitch the three surfaces comprising the fender surface into a single smooth surface. Prior to stitching, we recommend that all three are backed up in a backup layer. Stitch the surface using the Stitch tool, (v 3) or Stitch option in the Trim & Stitch tool (V 2.9.5). Set status to delete. After completing the Stitch, assign Smooth Shading to the surface (Figure 12.22).

23. Now we test render the surface in RenderZone. Set up a neutral lighting condition as described in Chapter 4. Notice that our fender surface adheres to many of the guidelines presented in Chapter 4. The material used for the fender surface is a neutral gray; however, it is specular with an environmental reflection. The material used is Neutral Reflective Gray found in the Chapter 12.zmt file (Figure 12.23).

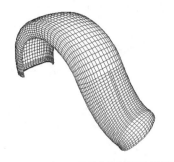

FIGURE *Smooth shading.*
12.22

FIGURE *Neutral reflective gray.*
12.23

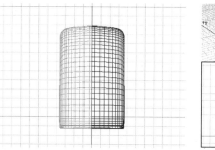

FIGURE **12.24** *Front view.*

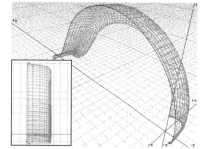

FIGURE **12.25** *Deriving open surface.*

RenderZone rendering was created using Full Raytrace rendering mode. A generic reflection map was used as a Spherical Environment. The map Refmapchrome.TGA can be found on the CD.

24. Working from the front view, create a straight line that bisects the fender surface along the Z-axis. Using the Trim/Split tool, trim the fender. Light gray shows the region of the surface to be trimmed away. Remember to retain an untrimmed copy of the fender surface in an backup layer (Figure 12.24).

Now we need to create the front end of our car.

25. Create a new layer, "Frontend Cross-Sections." Still working from the front view, select the segments that lie on the Z-axis using the Frame Select. Derive an open surface object from the selected segments using the Derivative Surfaces tool. Set **Status Of Objects** to **Keep** (Figure 12.25).

26. Delete the points as shown (Figure 12.26).

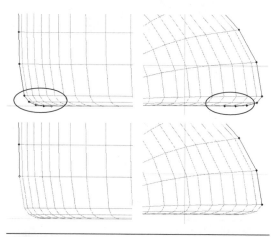

FIGURE **12.26** *Deleting the points.*

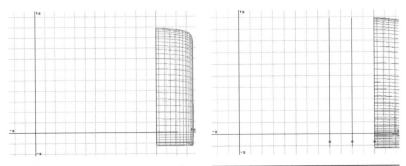

FIGURE *Changing design.*
12.27

FIGURE *Duplicates of derived edge curve.*
12.28

27. Select the derived curve and the trimmed fender surface. Working from the front view, move them +10″ along the X-axis as shown. The +10″ X-axis translation is a design judgment; it is possible that as the design progresses, the width of our vehicle may change (Figure 12.27).

28. Create two duplicates of the derived edge curve and place them as shown, –2″ apart (Figure 12.28).

29. Using the Parallel Surface tool, parallel offset the second duplicate using the following settings (Figure 12.29):

Single Parallel (Surface): Out
Wall Offset: 1″
Slab Offset: 1″
Status Of Objects: Delete

30. Working from the front view, select the paralleled cross-section, create two duplicates of it, and place them as shown along the X-axis. After placement of the two duplicates, select them and switch to the right side view. Nonuniform scale these two cross-sections using 0″, 9″, –5/8″ as

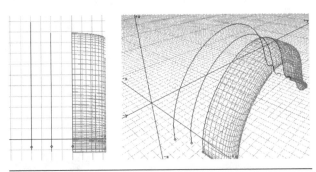

FIGURE *Parallel offset.*
12.29

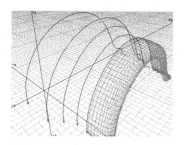 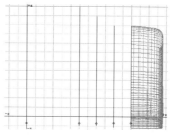 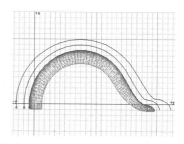

FIGURE *Nonuniform scaling.*
12.30

the base of nonuniform scale, and 1, 1.14, 1.087 as scale values (Figure 12.30).

31. Create a new layer, "Front End Virgin," and make it active. Select the front-end cross-sections, and create a lofted surface using the C-Mesh tool with C-Mesh Options parameters used to create the surface in Figure 4.4 but with the following changes;

Mesh Depth: # Of Segments: 4
Controlled Mesh Smoothing Options:
Depth: B-Spline: Degree: 4, # Of Points: 256

The lofted front-end surface is shown in blue. After creating the lofted surface, create yet another new layer, "Front End Surface," and Copy/Paste copies of the front-end virgin surface and current fender surface into it. Hide all other layers. With Status Of Objects set to Delete, stitch the two surfaces together into a single surface. Figure 12.31 shows the wireframe and the RenderZone Raytracing of the stitched surface. Notice the position of the front-end cross-sections and the shape of the lofted front-end surface, specifically its tangential (C1) continuity to the trimmed fender surface, and that vertices along the stitch edge are matched. Notice that when stitched, the resulting surface shades perfectly without any shading anomalies or seams.

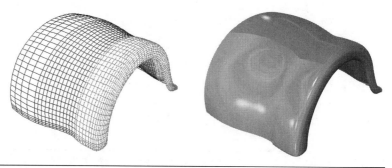

FIGURE *Raytracing of stitched surface.*
12.31

Prior to starting the creation of a bumper, we need to ascertain the height at which our vehicle sits above the ground. For this we create a simple 2D circle primitive that defines the silhouette of the tire, and a straight line that defines the ground level.

32. Create a new layer, "Guides." In this layer, and working from the right side view, create a 64-point circle that is centered at a position of Y: +9", and has a radius of 7". Then create a straight line with a Z-axis position of –7" (Figure 12.32).

33. Now we need to prepare the bottom of the front-end surface so that we can derive cross-sections for the construction of the bumper. Prior to proceeding, Copy/Paste a backup of the front end into a backup layer. We may need it later on when we build the rear end of our vehicle. With "Front End Surface" the active layer, the "Guides" layer ghosted, and Grid Snap Module set to 1/8", create a straight line as shown. Using the Trim & Stitch tool, set to Trim With Line, and trim the front end with the line from the right side view. In this case, we had to trim away the nice edge roll that we created for the fender surface. Such design revisions are quite normal. We will recreate the edge roll for the bottom front of the front end and create cross-sections for the bumper surface (Figure 12.33).

34. Create a new layer, "Front End Edge Roll Cross-Sections," and make it active. Copy/Paste a copy of the front-end surface (Figure 12.33) into this layer. Either hide or ghost the "Front End Surface" layer. Working from the front view, Mirror duplicate the front-end surface about the Z-axis, and Stitch the two halves together, with Status Of Objects set to Delete (Figure 12.34).

35. Select the segments as shown and derive an open surface object using the Derivative Surfaces tool set to Selected Segments, and Status Of

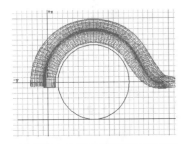

FIGURE *"Guides."*
12.32

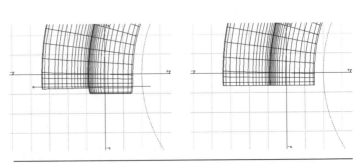

FIGURE *Front end edge rolls.*
12.33

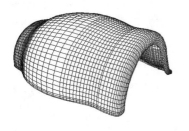

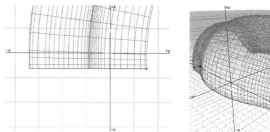

FIGURE **12.32** *Front end mirror duplicate.*

FIGURE **12.34** *Ghosted stitched front-end surface.*

Objects set to Delete. The ghosted stitched front-end surface is shown for clarity, you may delete yours (Figure 12.35).

36. Create two duplicates of this cross-section, spaced 1/8″ apart along the Z-axis. The result should be three cross-sections with the cross-section from Figure 12.35 being the first cross-section. Create a paralleled duplicate of the third cross-section by paralleling it inside 1/8″ using the Parallel Surface tool (Figure 12.36).

37. Using the Topological Segment deletion, delete the segments of the cross-sections that lie on the NEGATIVE X-axis (Figure 12.37).

38. Select the cross-sections in sequential order and make the "Front End Surface" the active layer. Create a lofted surface using the C-Mesh tool with the same settings as used in Figure 12.8 with the following changes:

Mesh Depth: # Of Segments: 4 and UNCHECK Per Segment option.

The lofted surface should have been created in the "Front End Surface" layer. Stitch it with the rest of the front-end surface (Figure 12.38).

39. Create new layer, "Front Bumper Cross-Sections," and make it the active layer. Select the last two cross-sections used to create the edge roll surface

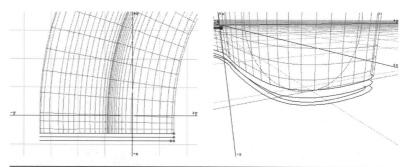

FIGURE **12.** *Paralleled duplicate.*

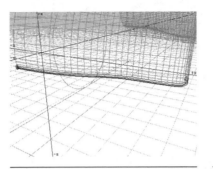

FIGURE *Deleting segments.*
12.37

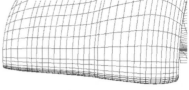

FIGURE *Lofted surface.*
12.38

in the previous step. Copy/Paste copies of them into the "Front Bumper Cross-Sections" layer. Hide the "Front End Edge Roll Cross-Sections" layer and ghost the "Front End Surface" layer. Create a duplicate of the larger cross-section and move it down the Z-axis by 1/8″. Notice the numbering of the cross-sections (Figure 12.39).

Finishing Up the Front End

The curve that we derived has multiple curvatures, and is a compound curve. While we need this curve as the first cross-section, so it conforms to the curvature of the front end, we need the rest of the bumper cross-sections to have a more "uniform" type of curvature. To that end we need to rebuild the third cross-section to have the desired curvature of the bumper.

40. Ghost the #1 and #2 cross-sections. Using Topological Segment and Point Deletion, delete the segments and points as shown (Figure 12.40).
41. Create a 4-point polyline as shown. Then, using Point Snap, place it on the same plane as the #3 cross-section. Finally, point snap the end points

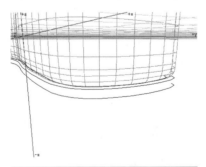

FIGURE *Duplicate cross-section.*
12.39

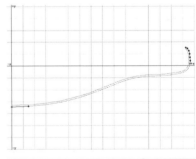

FIGURE *Deleting segments and points.*
12.40

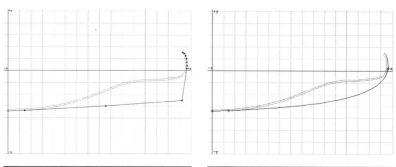

FIGURE *End segments.*
12.41

FIGURE *Joining the 3 lines.*
12.42

of the polyline to the #3 cross-section. Notice that the end segments of the polyline have same vectors as the end segments of the #3 cross-section (Figure 12.41).

42. The #1 and #2 cross-sections each have 35 points, the two lines that are the remainder of the #3 cross-section have a total of 9 points. So the polyline needs to be converted into a 28-point 3rd-degree **B-Spline** C-Curve. The two extra points are needed to compensate for deletion of endpoints when the three lines are joined (Figure 12.42).

43. Verify that all three lines have the same direction and, using the Connect Lines (form•Z 3) or Line Edit (form•Z 2.9.5) tool, join the three lines into one. Set **Status Of Objects** to **Delete**. After joining, delete the duplicate points where the lines were joined. The new #3 cross-section should have 35 points (Figure 12.43).

44. Create four duplicates of the # 3 cross-section and place them along the Z-axis as shown. From the right view nonuniformly scale the middle three cross-sections as shown. Set the Grid Snap Module to 1/8″ and use the rearmost point of the cross-section as the base. Notice how the rearpoints of the cross-sections are lined up (Figure 12.44).

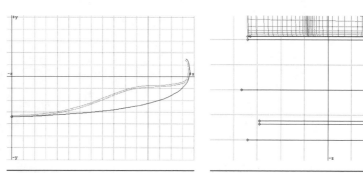

FIGURE *New #3 cross-section.*
12.43

FIGURE *Rearpoints aligned.*
12.44

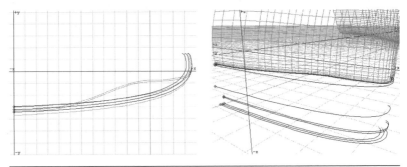

FIGURE *Completed front bumper cross-sections.*
12.45

45. Select the bottommost bumper cross-section, and working from the top view, Nonuniform scale it to create two duplicates as shown. Use 0, 1 1/4", 0 as the base of nonuniform scale and .98, .95, 1 as scale values. Figure 12.45 shows the completed front bumper cross-sections. Take special care to ensure that all first points lie precisely on the Y-axis, and that their X position is 0.

46. Create a new layer, "Front Bumper," and make it active. Select the bumper cross-sections in sequential order, and create a bumper surface using the C-Mesh tool. Use the C-Mesh settings as described for Figure 12.8 with the following changes (Figure 12.46):

    Mesh Depth: # Of Segments: 4, Per Segment
    Controlled Mesh Smoothing Options:
    Depth: B-Spline, Degree: 3, # Of Points: 64

47. We can now test and evaluate proportions of the front end of our vehicle. Create a temporary test layer, "Test 1," and Copy/Paste copies of the front-end and bumper surfaces into it. Hide all other layers. Mirror Copy the surfaces from the front view and then Stitch each two halves together, with **Status Of Objects** set to **Delete**. Figure 12.47 shows the

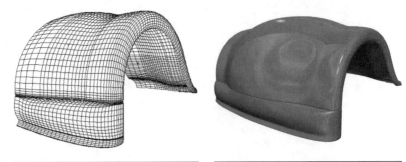

FIGURE *Front bumper surface.*
12.46

FIGURE *Front end rendering.*
12.47

rendering of the front end. Notice that the bumper was textured with a nonreflective low specular material resembling plastic. When evaluating the surface, we look for curvature discontinuities, especially at the stitch edges. They usually manifest as creases. The standard is for stitched surfaces to shade as though they were modeled as a single surface. We also look for polygonal silhouetting, denoting low mesh density. Finally we evaluate the overall proportions of the work in progress.

"Flow" Modeling Philosophy

We now have the basic surface of the front of our vehicle. We will use it as a base to construct other surfaces. You may have noticed that we are creating surfaces using construction elements derived from existing surfaces. This is a style of modeling that I call "Flow," as the design of surfaces flows from the design on existing objects. This approach to modeling works well if you are engaged in exploratory or conceptual modeling where the design of the model is not yet finalized, or if you have received only general guidelines for the look of the model. The "Flow" approach also works very well when you are doing conformal modeling or creating surface meshes that will be stitched into a single mesh. You may also have noticed that as we are modeling, the edges of our surfaces are rolled, and we never have a knife edge surface. Keeping in mind that we are modeling for photorealistic rendering and not manufacture, it is important to achieve realistic specular highlights along the edges and for that we must have geometry there.

Modeling Headlights and Headlight Fairing

In the next phase we will model a blended headlight fairing and the headlights with blinker/parking lights. Since we are going to trim the front-end surface, be sure to create a backup of it in a backup layer.

48. Working in the "Front End Surface" layer, and from the front view, create a 64-point ellipse and extrude it as shown. The shape of the ellipse defines the front profile of the headlight fairing (Figure 12.48).

49. Trim the front-end surface with an extruded ellipse, using the Trim/Split tool set to Trim: First Object. Set Status Of Objects to Delete (Figure 12.49).

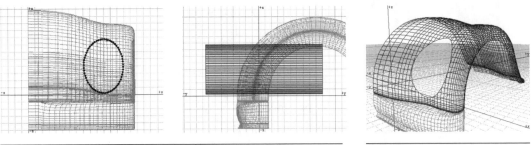

Front profile of headlight fairing.
12.48

Trimming front-end
12.49 *surface.*

Cleaning Up the Trim Edge of Headlight Fairing

In the next step we need to clean up the trim edge of the headlight fairing. We need to ensure that we do not have bunched points, unconnected points, or complex polygons. Any of those may cause shading anomalies. Since we want the ellipse to define the shape of the headlight fairing, the goal is to leave the points on the trim edge that are aligned, from the front view, with the points on the ellipse, and at the same time delete points and segments that would cause shading problems down the road. This can be a challenge to an inexperienced individual; however, there is a rule that can be used to identify points to be deleted. The rule is to delete the points that lie on straight segment chains. That is, if two segments have so little aspect to each other that they look like a straight line, the point at which they meet should be deleted. Often when a curvilinear surface is trimmed with another curvilinear surface or solid, small polygons are created adjacent to the trim edges. Those micro polygons need to be identified and properly deleted; otherwise, you may be inviting a shading anomaly that may be very hard to fix down the road. Since we will have curves derived from the trim edge as construction elements for the headlight fairing, it is vital that they be clean. Otherwise, any problems will be carried over to the fairing surface.

Prior to performing the cleanup, you may wish to review the guidelines of the trim edge cleanup technique discussed in Chapter 9. Of special importance is the sequence in deleting an unwanted segment:

1. Delete the Topological Segment.
2. Delete the Geometric Point.
3. Reconnect points using the Insert Segment tool to form four or point polygons.

When cleaning up the trim edge strive for uniform density of the points on

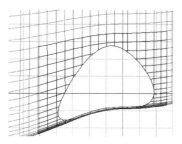

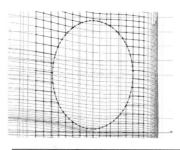

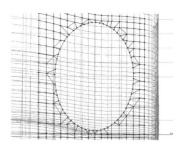

FIGURE *Ghosted front-end surface.*
12.50

FIGURE *Cleaning up trim edge.*
12.51

the trim edge and breakdown complex (5+ point) polygons into quads or tri-angles. Avoid the creation of slivered polygons.

50. In order to simplify and expedite the cleanup process, we should tem-porarily isolate the region of faces that is adjacent to the trim edge of the fairing. Working from the top view, select the faces (shown in black) and separate them from the main front end surface using the Separate tool set to At Boundary Of Selected Faces and Status Of Objects to Delete. After separation, Ghost the main front-end surface (Figure 12.50).

51. Perform the cleanup of the trim edge using Figure 12.51 as a guide. No-tice the uniform disposition of the points along the cleaned up trim edge, and how the points were reconnected. All polygons adjacent to the edge have no more than four points, and none of the polygons are slivered. Trim edge cleanup is an intricate process that requires patience and con-centration on your part.

52. After completing the cleanup, unghost the remainder of the front-end surface and Stitch the two surfaces together to reconstruct the main front-end surface. Set Status Of Objects to Delete (Figure 12.52).

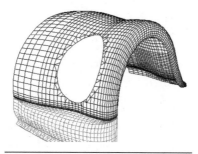

FIGURE *Reconstruct main front-end.*
12.52

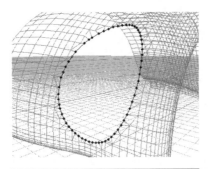

FIGURE *Closed surface.*
12.53

53. Create a new layer, "Headlight Fairing Skin Assembly," and make it active. Derive the edge cross-section from the trim edge using the Derivative Surfaces tool set to **Boundary Of Surface Object**, and **Status Of Objects** set to **Keep**. Click on one of the trim edge segments. The resulting closed surface should have 62 points (Figure 12.53).

54. Create a flattened duplicate of the derived cross-section using the 2D Projection tool. Scale, move, and rotate as shown in Figure 12.54.

55. We are going to use the Skin tool to create the headlight fairing surface and we need to place the "path" curves to have, if not equal, then similar point counts between them. Use the Point Marker tool (V. 3) or **Point Mark** option in Topological Attributes (v. 2.9.5) to mark points as shown. The only reason we are setting marked points is to use them as guides for creating lines that will be converted into "path" curves (Figure 12.55).

56. Create six straight lines with endpoints snapped to the marked points. Then divide the lines into three equal segments using Insert Point (v. 3) or Insert Segment (v 2.9.5) in combination with Segment Part and Midpoint snapping options (Figure 12.56).

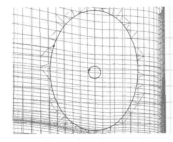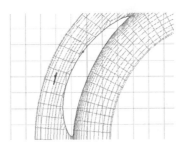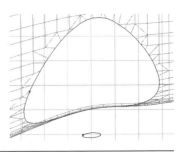

FIGURE *Scale, move, and rotate.*
12.54

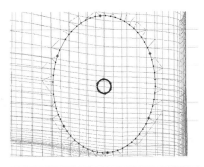

FIGURE "Path" curves.
12.55

FIGURE Dividing the lines.
12.56

57. Using the guidelines outlined in Chapter 9 and using Figure 12.57 as a guide, move the intermediate points on the "path" polylines as shown.

58. Convert the polylines into 3rd-degree 14-point "path" curves using the C-Curve tool. After conversion verify that endpoints are snapped and directions are matched (Figure 12.58).

59. Create a new layer, "Headlight Fairing Surface," and make it the active layer. Using Skin, create the surface. Use the following Skin Options:

Skinning Along Paths;
\# Sources: 2,
\# Paths: 6,
Boundary Based
Placement Type: By Current Position
Point Pairing: Insert New Points As Needed
Status Of Objects: Keep

After creating the surface, Copy/Paste a copy of the small source shape into this layer and Stitch the two surfaces together, with **Status Of Objects** set to **Delete** (Figure 12.59).

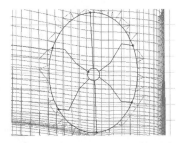
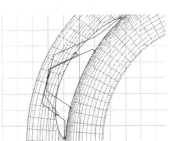
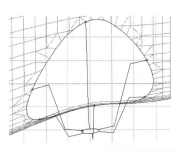

FIGURE Moving the intermediate points.
12.57

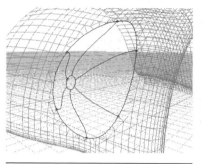

FIGURE **12.58** *Endpoints snapped.*

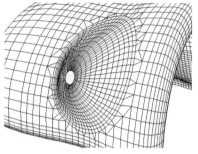

FIGURE **12.59** *Stitch surfaces.*

60. Use Face selection coupled with the Separate tool set to **At Boundary Of Selected Faces** to split the fairing surface into three objects. Object #1 is the Headlight Lens, #2 is the Chrome Strip. Stitch object #3 with the front-end surface. Create new layers for the headlight lens and chrome strip objects and transfer them into their respective layers (Figure 12.60).

61. Now is a good time to create a test rendering to see how our surfaces render. In the later steps we will add more subtle detail to the headlight area, like adding blinker lights and edge bevels. Prior to test rendering the surfaces, assign Smooth Shading to them. Notice that the lens and chrome strip objects have respective materials applied to them (Figure 12.61).

Recall the recommended procedures for geometry management and layer strategies that were outlined in Chapter 3. Recall that the recommended way of organizing geometry is one animation object per layer. At this point you should have four exportable layers: "Front End Surface," "Front Bumper," "Chrome

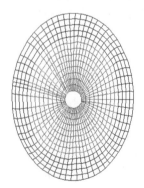

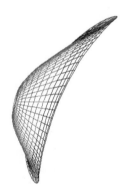

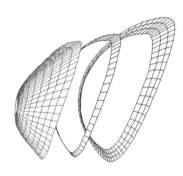

FIGURE **12.60** *New layers.*

FIGURE *Smooth shading.*
12.61

Strip," and "Headlight Lens." The exportable layers should contain only geometry belonging to that layer, and no source or construction elements should be residing in those layers. Take a minute to verify that all is in order, and transfer any objects that are in inappropriate layers.

Modeling the Hood Line and Cabin Surfaces

Now we construct the hood line and build the cabin surfaces of our vehicle.

62. Create a new layer, "Hoodline Trim Curve," and make it active. Working from the top view and with Grid Snap Module set to 1/2″, create a polyline as shown. Convert the polyline into a 3rd-degree 32-point curve using the C-Curve tool. For convenience and double-checking, we have included XYZ position C-Curve control points (Figure 12.62).

63. Copy/Paste a copy of the trim into the "Front End Surface" layer, and hide all other layers. Working from the top view, Trim the front-end surface with the trim curve. Remember to retain a backup copy of this version of the front-end surface in a backup layer (Figure 12.63).

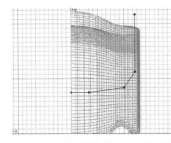

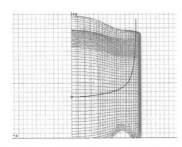

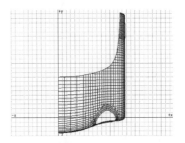

FIGURE *XYZ position C-curve control points.*
12.62

FIGURE *Front-end surface backup.*
12.63

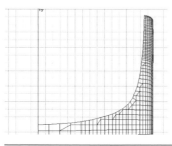

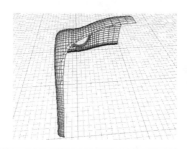

FIGURE *Cleaning the edge.*
12.64

FIGURE *"Body Curves."*
12.65

64. Now we clean up the trim edge. Use Figure 12.64 as your guide for clean up of the edge.

65. Create a new layer, "Body Curves," and make it active. Select the segments as shown and convert to an open surface edge curve using the Derivative Surfaces tool. Alternatively you can use Boundary Of Surface Object to initially get a closed surface running along the border of the surface, and then use Topological Edge delete to isolate shown segments in their own curve (Figure 12.65).

66. Using Nonuniform Scale and the Move tool, scale and position a duplicate of the derived curve as shown. Use Grid Snap Module set to 1/8″ (Figure 12.66).

67. Select the last five points of the duplicate as shown, and working from the top view, rotate the points 90 degrees using the fifth to last point as the base of rotation. Having those points rotated allows us to create a blended transition from the fender to the body panel surfaces (Figure 12.67).

68. Working from the front view, orthographically project the # 2 curve and place it as shown. Using Con-Copy (V 3) or C-Copy (V 2.9.5), place a duplicate of #2 as shown (Figure 12.68).

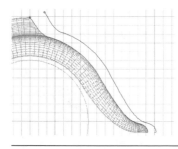

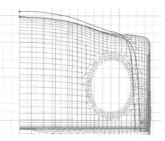

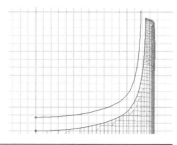

FIGURE *Duplicate of derived curve.*
12.66

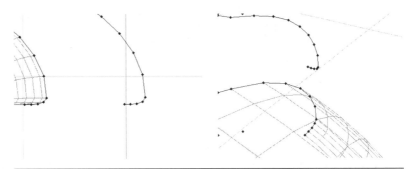

FIGURE *Blended transition.*
12.67

69. Deform the #4 curve using the Deform tool set to **Radial Deform**, and **Base Reference Plane: XY**. Perform the deformation from 30/60 Axonometric view with a deformation angle of 30 degrees. After deformation use Nonuniform scale to scale the # 4 curve so that its bottom point has the same Z-axis value as its counterpart on the #3 curve. You may wish to use temporary guidelines aligned to the #2 and #3 curves for nonuniform scaling of #4. The #4 curve represents the rear edge of the door. Its distance from #2 is a design decision (Figure 12.69).

70. Create a new layer, "Body Panels," and make it active. Create a lofted 2nd-degree B-Spline surface using #2, #3, and #4 curves (Figure 12.70).

71. Ghost the "Body Panels" layer, and in the "Body Curves" layer set a SKIN surface blend assembly as shown (Figure 12.71).

72. Make "Body Panels" the active layer. Create the skin surface. Set the Skin Options as follows (Figure 12.72):

Skinning Along Paths
 # Sources: 2, # Paths: 8
Placement Type: By Current Position

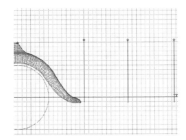

FIGURE *Duplicate #2.*
12.68

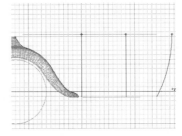

FIGURE *#4 curve.*
12.69

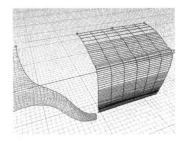

FIGURE *"Body Panels."*
12.70

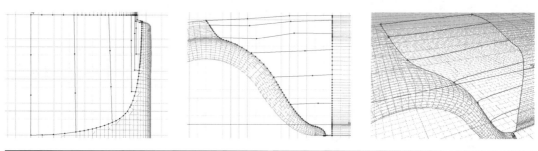

FIGURE *Ghosting and skin surface blend.*
12.71

Point pairing: Insert New Points As Needed
Status Of Objects: Keep

73. Transfer the front-end surface to the "Body Panels" layer. The "Front End Surface" layer should be empty, but do not delete this layer, we'll need it later. Stitch the three surfaces together with **Status Of Objects** set to **Delete**. Prior to stitch, verify that face normals of the three surfaces are aligned. You may also wish to retain a copy of the three surfaces in a backup layer (Figure 12.73).

74. Up until now we have been modeling our vehicle as a symmetrical half with the intent that the surfaces will be reflected and stitched together. Now we need to check how our surfaces shade. What we wish to do is to model our surfaces as symmetrical halves but test render stitched surfaces. Rename the layers that hold 1/2 symmetrical surfaces by adding "1/2" to their names; for example, "Front Bumper" becomes "Front Bumper 1/2". Now create new layers for each "1/2" layer. Name them the same but without "1/2" stuck on the end. So while we create our symmetrical surface in "1/2" layer, we reflect and stitch copies of those

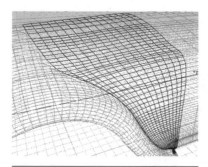

FIGURE *Skin surface.*
12.72

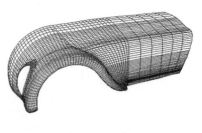

FIGURE *3 surfaces stitched.*
12.73

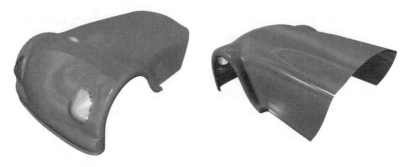

FIGURE *Reflect and stitch surfaces.*
12.74

surfaces in whole layers. Copy/Paste the half surfaces into their respective layers. Reflect and stitch the surfaces (Figure 12.74).

Modeling the Rear End and Bottom Trim

In the next phase we will create the rear-end and the bottom trim surfaces of our vehicle. Notice that the "Flow" modeling approach is not strictly linear. In steps used to create surfaces in Figures 12.70–12.72, we created the cabin surface (which later on we will trim to make the doors) and then created a skinned blend surface to "bridge" the cabin/door surface to the front end. Take note that the front-end surface was trimmed in such a way that the topmost trim point is located at or near the tangent of the hood surface (which will be created later by splitting).

The design of the vehicle calls for the rear end and the rear bumper to have different but complementary curvatures, with rear lights being of wrap-around type. We continue with the "Flow" modeling strategy and use one of the cabin cross-section curves as the base element for constructing the curves of the rear end. This will ensure that the mesh density along the height of the rear-end surface will match, point for point, that of the rest of the body. The basic rear-end surface will a be 3rd-degree B-Spline lofted surface that we will create using the C-Mesh tool. There is, however, a slight difference between the rear-end and other lofted surfaces that we have created up to this point. Up until now all of our lofted surfaces were created with cross-sections arranged in a linear fashion. For the rear-end surface the cross-sections are arranged in a fan-like arrangement that results in a surface that is topologically similar to a hemisphere. I refer to this type of surface as "Radial Loft." Having a single basic surface for the rear end allows us to create other objects, such as the trunk, rear lights, and rear bumper, by trimming/stitching the basic surface. Otherwise, we would have to build the rear fender and trunk as separate surfaces, and be faced with a challenge of manually maintaining continuity between the rear fender, rear bumper, trunk, and existing body surfaces. One distinct disadvantage of radial lofts is the bunching of the polygons around the base of rotation, and the possibility of shading anomalies in that area when the two symmetrical halves are stitched. For this reason, we recommend that radial lofts be used in cases where the area in and around the base of rotation will be trimmed away in later modeling operations. It just so happens that we trim this area later on when we build the cabin and the doors.

75. Make "Body Curves" the active layer, if it's not already. Create a duplicate of the #3 curve and move it into position, with Grid Snap Module set to 1/2", as shown. Set the Grid Snap Module to 1/16", and create four additional rear-end cross-sections by using the Move, Nonuniform Scale, and Rotate tools. Notice that, no matter the attitude of the rear-end cross-sections, their first points lie along the Y-axis. Also the rear wheel placeholder has been positioned as a 3D guide (Figure 12.75).

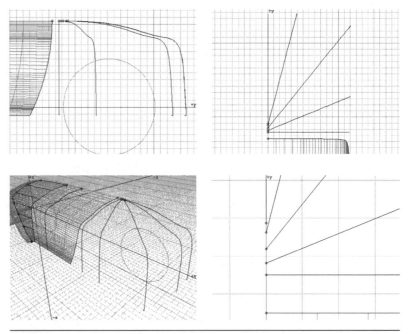

FIGURE *Rear-end cross-sections.*
12.75

Deforming Single and Multiple Open Surfaces

One of form•Z's strengths is its ability to seamlessly apply modeling operations to curves and open surfaces in the same manner as to regular solids and meshed surfaces. This includes the ability to deform an open surface. Within limited scope the Deform tool, when set to **Deform Object**, can be used to sculpt curves (open surfaces) that have no C-Curve controls. This is very useful as many curves we deal with are derivative, and cannot be changed into C-Curves. Even more useful is the ability to deform multiple curves simultaneously. In situations as this one, where we wish to sculpt a surface but at the same time keep it continuous to existing surfaces, it becomes necessary to deform curves instead of the lofted surface.

76. Select the last three rear-end cross-sections, and working from the right side view, apply **Bulge, Taper, Shear**, and **Nonuniform Scale**. Use Figure 12.76 and the sketch as guides. Although not commonly mentioned, Nonuniform Scale is a type of deformation. In some applications, Nonuniform Scale is referred to as a "Stretch." Since this is a tutorial it is not imperative to be precise, just get the curves as close to what is shown as possible. If you wish, you may consult the form•Z project file on the CD as a reference. Notice that one of the deformations was a taper along the ZX plane. the resulting shape of the rear-end surface will allow us to create that unique upwardly curving rear bumper surface.

77. Make "Body Panels" the active layer. Select the rear-end cross-sections and create a lofted surface using the following C-Mesh parameters:

Construct Plain Mesh
Construct Directly

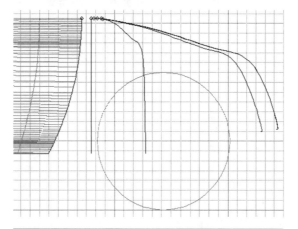

FIGURE *Bulge, Taper, Shear, and Nonuniform Scale.*
12.76

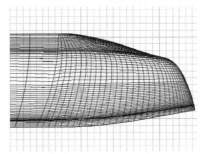
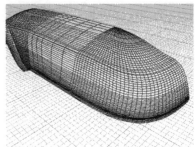

FIGURE *Stitching rear-end surface.*
12.77

Length Of Net: Use Existing
Depth Of Net: Use Control Line Intervals
Mesh Length: At Control Points
Mesh Depth: # Of Segments: 36, Per Segment: OFF, Smooth: ON
Controlled Mesh Smoothing Options
Length: None
Depth: B-Spline, Degree: 3, # Of Points: 128
Type Of Object: Open ends (Surface)
Status Of Objects: Keep

Stitch the rear-end surface to the rest of the body (Figure 12.77).

78. Create a new layer, "Body Trim Curves," and make it active. Create a symmetrical closed polyline, centered around the Y-axis. Convert the polyline into a 128-point 4th-degree C-Curve (Figure 12.78).

79. Working from the top, Split the 1/2 body surface with the cabin trim curve. The result should be two surfaces. We used Split instead of Trim in case we need the middle surface for further modeling (Figure 12.79).

80. After the split, perform the cleanup of the trim edge on both surfaces and transfer the middle surface to a hidden backup layer. Take care to delete

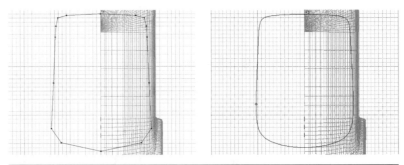

FIGURE *Convert polyline.*
12.78

FIGURE *Splitting surface.*
12.79

FIGURE *Body halves stiched.*
12.80

the same points along the trim edges of both surfaces. After the cleanup you may wish to perform a test render of both body halves stitched (Figure 12.80).

81. In the "Body Trim Curves" layer, create a 96-point ellipse using the Ellipse By Major And Minor Radius as shown. For consistency you may wish to opt to use the following ellipse values. As you may have guessed, we are going to trim the body with this ellipse. The resulting trim edge will serve as an outer boundary of the rear fender flare (Figure 12.81).

82. Copy/Paste a copy of the ellipse into the "Body Panels" layer. With **Status Of Objects** set to **Delete**, Trim the body using the ellipse, from the right side view. Clean up the trim edge afterwards using Figure 12.82 as a guide. As usual, be sure to have a backup of this version of the body prior to trimming.

83. Create a new layer, "Rear Fender Flare Curves," and make it active. Using the Derivative Surfaces tool set to **Boundary Of Surface Object**, derive a boundary line of the body. Then using Topological Delete, isolate the segments of the rear fender flare trim edge as shown. As a slower alternative, you may achieve the same result by carefully selecting the segments, and using the **Selected Segments** option. We will designate this curve as #1 (Figure 12.83).

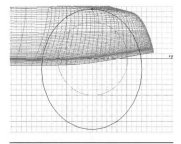

FIGURE *Outer boundary.*
12.81

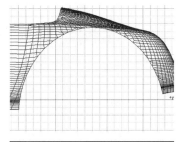

FIGURE *Trim edge cleanup.*
12.82

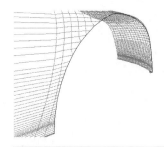

FIGURE *Curve #1.*
12.83

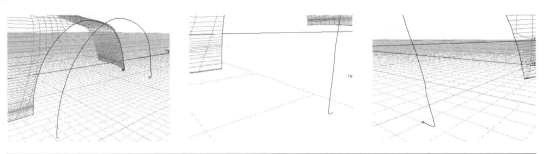

FIGURE *Create curve #2.*
12.84

84. Create the #2 curve by duplicating #1 and move + 6″ along the X-axis only. Take care to limit the movement of #2 to the X-axis. The goal is simply to move #2 away from #1. Select the last 5 points on the end of the #2 curve and rotate 90 degrees so that the last point is inside the curve. Perform a similar procedure on the first 5 points. The reason for this operation is to create a source that will generate an inwardly curving lip (Figure 12.84).

85. Working from the right view, flatten the #2 curve by orthographically projecting it. Then use Scale, Nonuniform Scale, and Deform with **Taper** and **Bend** options to sculpt the #2 curve as shown. It will serve as the second source curve for the Skin assembly. Notice that it is conformal to the wheel guide (Figure 12.85).

86. Select the last 5 points on each end of the #2 curve. Rotate the points 90 degrees inward, using the fifth to last point as the base of rotation for each selection. Create seven lines as shown, taking care to snap their ends to similar points on the source curves. As you may have guessed, we will convert those lines into our path curves; however, in this case we are creating a skinned surface to blend two surfaces. The skinned surface will be the rear fender flare. The surface does need to have at least tangential

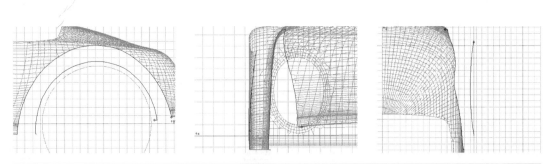

FIGURE *Flatten, Scale, Nonuniform Scale and Deform #2.*
12.85

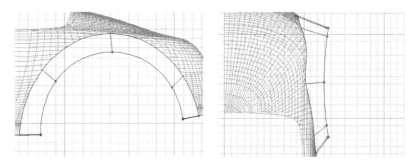

FIGURE *Curving lip.*
12.86

continuity to the body and have a soft curving lip similar to that on the front fender (Figure 12.86).

87. Subdivide each of the lines into three equal segments and arrange points as shown to create the polylines for the creation of path curves (Figure 12.87).

88. Convert the path polylines into 18-point 3rd-degree B-Spline C-Curves, and create the rear fender flare with the Skin tool. Create the fender flare in the "Body Panels 1/2" layer, and stitch the rear fender flare with the body surface (Figure 12.88).

To finish the lip of the rear fender flare, we will create a lofted surface using the C-Mesh tool. The #2 source curve that we used to create the flare surface will serve as the #1 cross-section. Because the inner curving lip is subtle, it does not need to be heavily meshed, it does not even need to be 3rd degree—2nd-degree B-Spline surface using three cross-sections will suffice. We will create the #2 and #3 cross-sections for the lip by nonuniformly scaling the #2 source curve with C-Copy transformation mode. Although we could eyeball the base

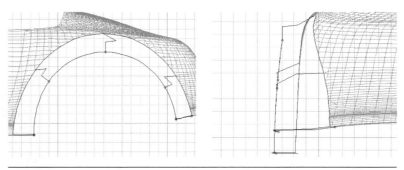

FIGURE *Create polylines/path curves.*
12.87

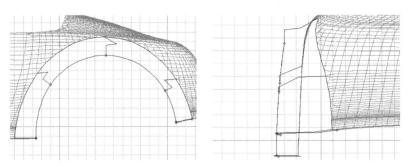

FIGURE
12.87

of scale and get decent results, in this case we will use a locator as the base of scale. Recall that locators are derived from temporary objects.

89. Create a temporary locator line that is snapped to the 5th and the 92 points on the #2 source curve (Figure 12.89).

90. Using the midpoint of the locator line as the base of Nonuniform Scale, nonuniformly scale the #2 source curve, with Cont-Copy (v 3) or C-Copy (v 2.9.5) mode to create two additional cross-sections for the inner lip of the fender flare. Approximate scale values are 1, .985, .985. The #2 source curve is also the #1 cross-section for the lip surface. After scaling, move the #3 cross-section –1/8″ along the X-axis (Figure 12.90).

91. Make "Body Panels 1/2" the active layer, and create the inner lip using the C-MESH tool with the following settings:

Construct Plain Mesh
Construct Directly
Length Of Net: Use Existing
Depth Of Net: Use Control Line Intervals
Mesh Length: At Control Points

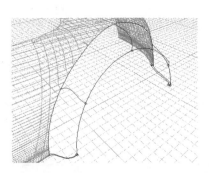
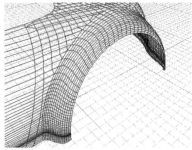

FIGURE *Stitch rear fender flare and body surface.*
12.88

FIGURE *Locator line.*
12.89

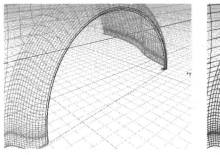

FIGURE *Nonuniform scale.*
12.90

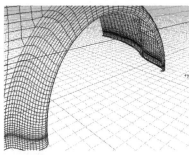

FIGURE *Stitch lip surface.*
12.91

Mesh Depth: # Of Segments: 2, Per Segment: OFF, Smooth: ON
Controlled Mesh Smoothing Options
Length: None
Depth: B-Spline, Degree: 2, # Of Points: 128
Type Of Object: Open ends (Surface)
Status Of Objects: Keep

Stitch the lip surface to the rest of the body (Figure 12.91).

Component Continuity Matched Surfaces

A question that may arise is, "Why would we not create the lip by creating path curves that curve inward?" Well, we could, but not effectively, or as easily, control mesh density on the fender flare and the lip. The mesh density of the lip would have been higher than needed. Creating surfaces by breaking them down into component continuity matched surfaces is the recommended way of modeling when polygon counts need to be watched, or similar mesh density across multiple surfaces is desired.

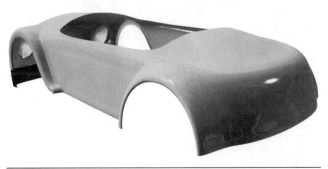

FIGURE *Test rendering.*
12.92

92. With the rear end modeled, now is a good time to do a test rendering. Copy/Paste the half body surface into a test layer, then Mirror and Stitch to form the whole body shell. To have a little fun I decided to play with various color styles, deciding on yellow lacquer color with black bumper surfaces. Doesn't look too shabby, huh? (Figure 12.92)

In this phase we will create the rear bumper and the side skirt surface. Like the front bumper, side skirt and rear bumper are made of impact-resistant resin. They do not need to have continuity to the body surfaces; however, they do need to be conformal to the body surface. Also, like the front bumper, the side skirt and rear bumper have soft rounded edges.

93. Create a new layer, "Side Skirt Cross-Sections," and make it active. Use the Derivative Surfaces tool to derive the #2 cross-section. Create the #3 cross-section by orthographically projecting the #2 cross-section from the top view, and moving it along the Z-axis to be 1/8″ below the #2 cross-section (Figure 12.93).

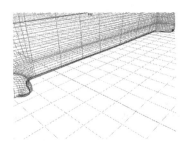
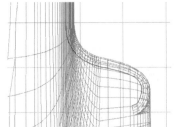
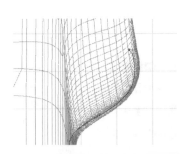

FIGURE *"Side Skirt Cross-Sections."*
12.93

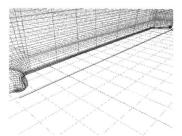
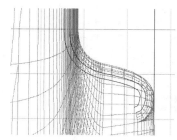
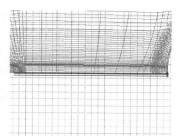

FIGURE *Cross-sections aligned with front and rear flares.*
12.94

94. Create the #1 cross-section by creating a paralleled duplicate of the #3, using the Parallel Objects tool set to 1/8″ IN, and **Status Of Objects** set to **Keep**. After paralleling, move the #1 cross-section +1/8″ along the Z-axis into position. Create the #4 cross-section by first moving a duplicate of the #3 cross-section −1/4″ along the Z-axis, orthographically projecting it from the right side view, then, from the top view with 1/8″ Grid Snap Module, moving into position aligned with the rear and front fender flares (Figure 12.94).

95. Cross-sections #5–#9 are copies of #4. Place them as shown (Figure 12.95).

96. Create a new layer, "Side Skirt 1/2," and make it the active layer. Create an initial side skirt surface using the C-Mesh tool with the following settings (Figure 12.96):

Construct Plain Mesh
Construct Directly
Length Of Net: Use Existing
Depth Of Net: Use Control Line Intervals
Mesh Length: At Control Points
Mesh Depth: # Of Segments :22, Per Segment: OFF, Smooth: ON

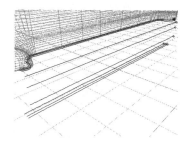
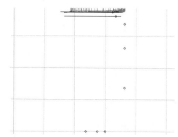
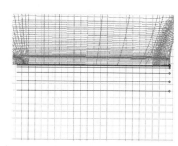

FIGURE *Cross-sections #5–#9.*
12.95

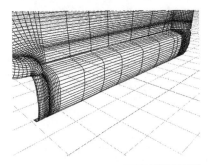

FIGURE *"Side Skirt 1/2."*
12.96

Controlled Mesh Smoothing Options
Length: None
Depth: B-Spline, Degree: 3, # Of Points: 256
Type Of Object: Open ends (Surface)
Status Of Objects: Keep

Although when reflected, there will be two side skirt surfaces, one for each side of the car, we should still adhere to the layering system described earlier. Think of the "Side Skirt" layer as only an exportation and rendering layer. All modeling operations on the side skirt surface should be performed inside the "Side Skirt 1/2" layer.

97. Using the procedures described earlier, derive an edge curve from the front of the side skirt surface and create seven cross-sections from that curve. Place the cross-sections as shown. Cross-sections #7 and #8 are parallel duplicates with offset values of 1/8". Create these cross-sections on the "Side Skirt Cross-Sections" layer (Figure 12.97).

98. Make "Side Skirt 1/2" the active layer. Create the front end of the side skirt surface using the C-Mesh tool. Use the same settings but with the following changes:

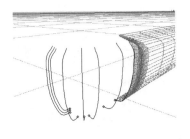
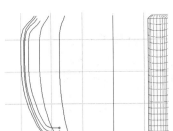
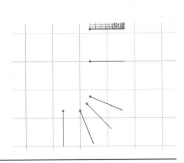

FIGURE *"Side Skirt Cross-Sections" layer.*
12.97

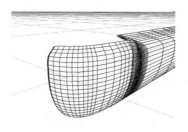

FIGURE *Main side skirt.*
12.98

Mesh Depth: # Of Segments: 3, Per Segment: ON, Smooth: ON
Depth: Bezier, # Of Points: 256

Stitch the surface to the main side skirt surface (Figure 12.98).

99. Derive the cross-sections for the rear bumper using the same procedure used to create the front bumper cross-sections. Take extra care to ensure that all first points lie on the Y-axis. The #8 and #9 cross-sections were derived by nonuniformly scaling of the #7 cross-section (Figure 12.99).

100. Create a new layer, "Rear Bumper 1/2," and make it active. Create the 1/2 rear bumper surface using the same C-Mesh settings as were used to loft the front bumper surface (Figure 12.100).

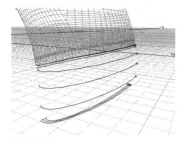 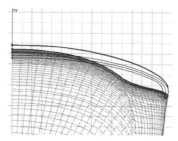 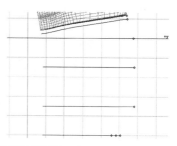

FIGURE *#8 and #9 cross-sections.*
12.99

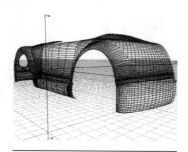

FIGURE *"Rear Bumper 1/2."*
12.100

Note

Prior to proceeding to the next phase, where we will model the trunk, hood, and door surfaces, let's examine the body of the car. One of the parameters that we, as modelers, have to take into account is the flexibility of the geometry that we create. By "flexibility," I mean the ease with which we can adjust or change the geometry without redoing major portions of it. First off, let me say that it is not possible to create a model that is 100% flexible. There will always be some changes that will require excessive and repetitive effort. However, we can reduce the circumstances under which major rebuilds of the model are needed. A model's topological structure, and source curves, largely determine how easy or hard it is to implement geometric changes to the model. In regards to our spyder GT, one of the most prominent changes that we might want to make is the length of the wheel base. The change in length might be needed if the design goal changes, or we wish to create a different version of the car, such as making it a 2+2 instead of a 2-seat car, or even modeling a four-door version. Recall that we modeled the rearmost door cross-section curved, and that curvature translated into curving segment chain, as outlined by the second selection marquee. Because we used the Flow modeling strategy, the segment chains of multiple surfaces line up, which allows fast, easy, and precise selection of either faces or segments. If we wish to lengthen the wheel base and cabin area, all that is needed is selection of segments using the shown rectangle and moving them the desired amount along the Y-axis. Similar action can be performed on the front of the vehicle. The curvature of the mesh at the door extremities is more or less flat. So compensating for an elongated wheelbase by lengthening the doors will create curvature discontinuities and associated shading problems. The mesh topology at the front and rear door limits also allows us to separate the door surfaces without the use of trimming. In the steps to follow we will separate the door surfaces by selecting segments, outlined by red marquees and use the Separate tool (Figure 12.101).

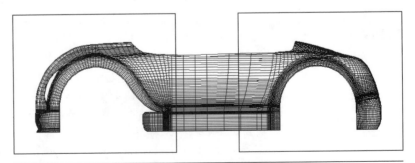

FIGURE *Door surfaces.*
12.101

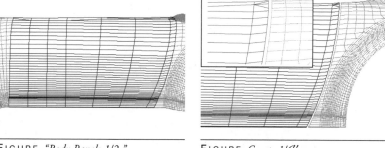

FIGURE *"Body Panels 1/2."*
12.102

FIGURE *Create 1/6" gap.*
12.103

101. Select the faces as shown and separate them from the body using the Separate tool set At **Boundary Of Selected Faces**. The result should be three objects: front end 1/2, door panel, and rear end 1/2. Create new layers for each of the objects: "Left Door," "Front Quarter Panel," "Rear Quarter Panel." Copy/Paste copies of body panel surfaces into their respective layers. The "Body Panels 1/2" now becomes a backup layer holding backups of our body panels (Figure 12.102).

Modeling Edge Roll on Rear of the Door Panel

In the next steps we will create a rolled edge at the rear edge of the door. Ghost the "Rear Quarter Panel" layer, "Left Door" should be the active layer, all other layers should be hidden.

102. The rolled edge radius of the door/rear end seam is 1/16" and we need to allow some gap for placement of the rubber seal. First we need to create a 1/6" gap between the door and rear quarter panel. Select the column of faces adjacent to the seam with rear quarter panel and move them 1/6" along the Y-axis (Figure 12.103).

103. Using the procedures outlined earlier on the construction of edge rolls, construct a lofted 2nd-degree edge roll using three cross-sections. Stitch the edge roll surface to the door panel. Construct the lip cross-sections in the "Door Real Lip Cross-Sections" layer. The translation offset between #1 and #2 cross-sections is 1/16". The C-Mesh had **Depth** settings set to **# Of Segments: 3, Per Segment: OFF, Smooth: ON**. In Smoothing Options, **Depth** was set to **B-Spline, Degree: 2, # Of Points: 64** (Figure 12.104).

104. Construct the edge roll for the rear quarter panel in the same fashion and stitch it with the rear quarter panel. Place the cross-sections into a "Rear Quarter Panel Lip Cross-Sections" layer (Figure 12.105).

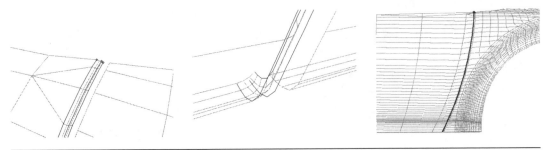

FIGURE *Lofted 2nd-degree edge roll.*
12.104

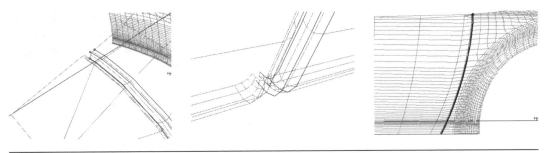

FIGURE *"Rear Quarter Panel Lip Cross-Sections" layer.*
12.105

105. Creation of the edge rolls should have left a small gap between the surfaces. This is intentional and realistic. If the door and rear quarter panel were flush against each other, the door would be impossible to open and the trough formed by the edge rolls would have been too small to look realistic. In real-world cars this space is used to make sure that the panels do not scratch each other and is usually sealed by a rubber or polyurethane seal. Create the door seal by lofting the #3 cross-sections of both the edge rolls (Figure 12.106).

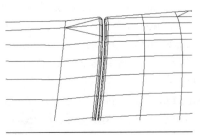

FIGURE *Door seal.*
12.106

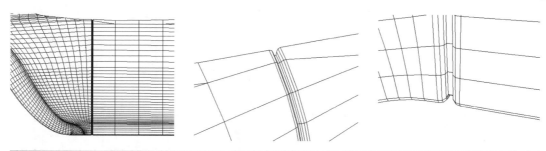

FIGURE *"Door Seals 1/2" layer.*
12.107

106. Perform edge rolls on the rubber seal for the seam where the door panel meets the front quarter panel. Because the edge curve at the front door seam is planar, you can create the # 3 cross-section by paralleling the #2 curve, using the Parallel Objects tool with 1/16" offset. You can also use copies of the cross-sections to create the edge roll for the front quarter panel. Place the front and the rear door seals in their own layer, "Door Seals 1/2" (Figure 12.107).

NOTE

The four rubber seal surfaces (two on each door) can be joined into a single object using the Join Volumes tool. We recommend that the two original seal surfaces be kept as separate objects as backups in the "Door Seals 1/2" layer, which is a backup layer. The single object (from joining four seals) should reside in its own layer, "Door Seals," which is an exportation layer. Because of their small size and inconspicuous nature, they can be textured with solid color black material.

Modeling the Hood

In the next series of steps we will create trim curves for cutting the hood surface from the front quarter panel, and use them to model the hood. The main grill is incorporated into the hood surface with the secondary oil cooler grill cut into the front bumper, along with fog lamps.

107. Create a new layer, "Hood & Grill Polylines," and make it active. With Grid Snap Module set to 1/4", create polylines as shown (Figure 12.108). Notice that the bottom segments of the #2 polyline are precisely aligned with the front bottom segments of the quarter panel surface.

108. Create a new layer, "Hood & Grill Curves." Copy/Paste copies of the polylines into this layer. Convert the polylines into 3rd-degree B-Spline curves using the C-Curve tool and use the following point count schedule:

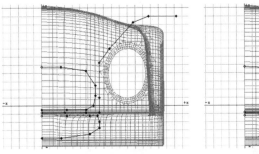

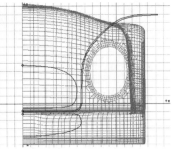

#1 grill trim curve: 38 points.
#2 hood trim curve: 40 points
#3 oil cooler grill trim curve: 38 points

Create a parallel duplicate of the #2 curve using the Parallel Objects tool set to 1/7″. Since IN or OUT is arbitrary in this case, the parallel duplicate is offset away from the center line of the vehicle. After paralleling, connect the two curves using the Connect Lines tool into a single shape (Figure 12.109).

The shape and point count of the trim curves is a design decision. If you wish, you may alter the shape and point of the trim curves. However, we recommend that initially, you use the shown shapes and described parameters.

NOTE

Don't forget to create backups of the current versions of the front quarter panel and 1/2 bumper prior to performing the trims.

NOTE

109. Copy/Paste copies of #1 and #2 trim curves into the "Front Quarter Panel" layer, and #3 curve into the "Bumper 1/2" layer. With Status Of Objects set to Delete, perform the trimming of the surfaces. The result should be three objects: the hood surface, the quarter panel surface, and 1/2 bumper surface. Note the 1/7″ gap between the hood and quarter panel surfaces. As with the door seams, this gap will be filled with edge rolls from both surfaces and a rubber seal. Create a new layer, "Hood 1/2," and transfer the hood surface into it (Figure 12.110).

110. Hide all layers except "Hood 1/2." Using Figure 12.111 as a guide, clean up the trim edges of the hood surface.

111. Clean up the trim edge of the front quarter panel (Figure 12.112).

112. Clean up the trim edge of the 1/2 front bumper surface (Figure 12.113).

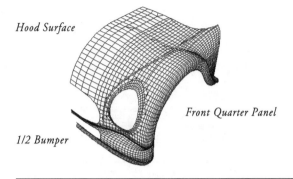

Hood Surface

Front Quarter Panel

1/2 Bumper

FIGURE **12.110**   *"Hood 1/2."*

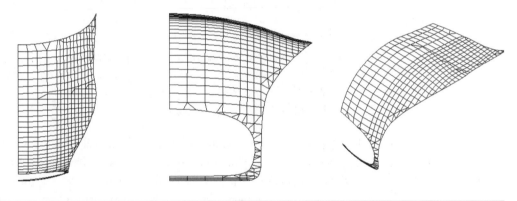

FIGURE **12.111**   *Clean trim edge of hood.*

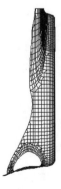
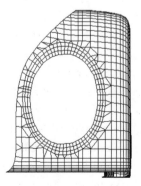

FIGURE **12.112**   *Clean trim edge of quarter panel.*

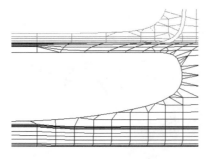

FIGURE *Clean trim edge of 1/2 front*
12.113 *bumper.*

As I mentioned earlier, cleaning up trim edges is a tedious but vital task. Because in "Flow" modeling, we are using curves derived from trim edges, sloppy cleanup work will snowball into inefficient or "dirty" surfaces down the road. Really efficient edge cleanup is a product of experience. After a while, you will develop a feel for which points to delete and which points to connect. If you feel that you are still a novice, use the figures as guides. If you get into a jam, and become really confused, compare your surfaces to the sample project on the CD.

113. Create a new layer, "Hood Grill Curves," and make it active. Construct a Skin assembly. The radius and curvature of the blend is a design decision. If you wish, you may change the shape of the blend. Figure 12.114 shows the recommended shape. Take care to retain at least C1 (tangential) continuity to the hood surface. The "path" curves are 8-point 2nd-degree B-Splines. Create the grill inner surface and stitch it with the main hood. Take care when creating the Skin assembly to make sure that the surface can be mirrored and stitched seamlessly.

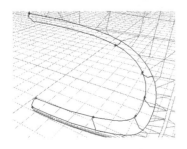
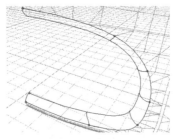
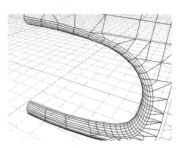

FIGURE *Recommended "Hood Grill Curves" shape.*
12.114

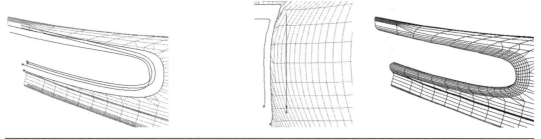

FIGURE *Inner surface.*
12.115

114. Using the C-Mesh technique, create the inner surface matched to the bumper surface. You may use Figure 12.115 as a guide but the final shape is left up to you as modeling procedures are the same regardless of the shape. This where a good sense of design is as important as solid modeling skills. The #3 cross-section is a flattened duplicate of the #2, created with the 2D Projection tool. The #4 cross-section is a paralleled duplicate of #3, paralleled with 1/8″ offset. The lofted C-Mesh surface is a 3rd-degree B-Spline (Depth only) with a total of 12 segments.

115. Optionally add fog lamp recesses and a brake cooler vent. This step is optional and is intended for practice only. The procedures used to create these surfaces are the same as in the previous two steps, so source curves are not shown (Figure 12.116). Use the final result shown as a guide.

116. In modern performance cars, front bumper surfaces have notches in the middle designed to let some air pass. This cuts down air resistance, improves high-speed performance, fuel economy, and just plain looks good. We can use standard geometrical transformations to add subtle detail to our surfaces. When used in moderation, Nonuniform Scale is very effective as a sculpting tool. Set Topology to Segment, and Nonuniform Scale the segments as shown (Figure 12.117).

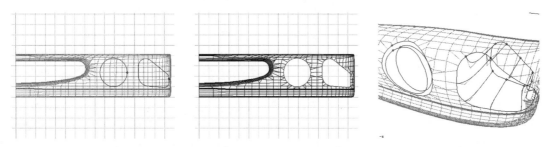

FIGURE *Fog lamp recesses and brake cooler vent.*
12.116

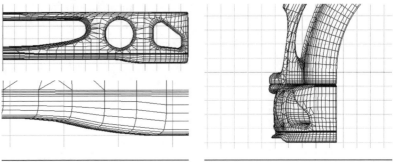

FIGURE *Nonuniform scaling.*
12.117

FIGURE *Deformed.*
12.118

Deform Tool Tips

The Deform tool in form•Z can be very effective as a sculpting tool, under certain conditions. A feature of the Deform tool is that it always applies deformations symmetrically. Because of this, halved surfaces must be Mirrored and Stitched prior to deformation being applied. Even with this limitation, the Deform tool can be used to make subtle and minor changes that would otherwise be time consuming (Figure 12.118). When sculpting with the Deform tool, it is important to be familiar with the following concepts:

- **Deformation Ticks.** A Deform tick is the amount of deformation the surface undergoes when the deform lattice is dragged, with Grid Snap on.
- **Counter-Deform.** Counter deformation is deformation performed on a previously deformed surface using the same or slightly more deformation in the opposite direction. There are certain deformation combinations that when used together sequentially generate subtle curvatures without seriously affecting the geometrical shape of the surface. Examples of such combinations are:
  - **Taper OUT/Taper IN.** This combination of deformations results in onion dome bulging of the mesh. The deformed surface exudes shape that was bulged and tapered simultaneously. It is important to note that Bulge deforming the surface followed by Taper will not produce the same shape. The larger the taper amounts, the more pronounced the resulting curvature.
  - **Taper/Shear.** This combination results in either the bottom or the top (depending on the reference plane of deformation) to be tapered with the opposite remaining more or less flat.

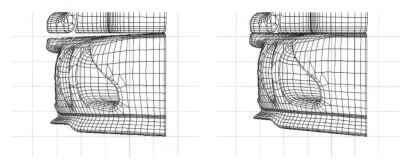

FIGURE   *Taper 1/2 bumper surface.*
12.119

The Deform tool is very useful when experimenting with the variational shapes of the surface without the need to rebuild the surface from scratch.

117. Switch to the right side view, and set Grid Snap Module to 1/6″. Set the Deform tool options to:

Deform Object: Taper, Base Reference Plane: ZX.
Initial Limits: Lower: 0, Upper: 100

Taper the 1/2 bumper surface by one deformation tick. Counter deform with Shear deformation. Notice that deformation and counter deformation were performed with Grid Snap Module ON. At certain times, you may need to reduce the Grid Snap Module by 1/2 for counter deformation to achieve greater accuracy (Figure 12.119).

With the bumper surface complete we turn our attention back to the hood and front quarter panel. First we need to round the sharp corner on the rear left of the hood. However, we cannot use the normal Round tool as the hood is not a solid. Nor can we use Fit Fillet (v 3) or Line Edit /Fit Fillet (v 2.9.5) on the surface. This is where form•Z really shines in its ability to break the surface down, perform the necessary edits, and reconstruct it. What makes form•Z such a powerful modeler is that you almost never run out of options! (Figure 12.120)

118. As noted we cannot use the Round or Line Edit tools to round this point as the hood is a meshed surface. We can, however, use Line Edit if we temporarily separate the face, round the corner using the Line Edit tool, then Stitch it back with the hood surface. Select the face and separate it from the hood surface using Separate tool set to **Boundary Of Selected Faces.** Using Line Edit, set to Fit Fillet round the corner using the values

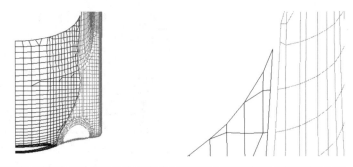

FIGURE *Breaking surface down.*
12.120

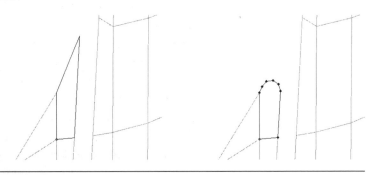

FIGURE *Reconstruct hood.*
12.121

Of Edges: 3, Radius: 1/11″. Reconstruct the hood by stitching the face and the rest of the hood surface together (Figure 12.121).

Creating an edge roll for a complex 3D compound curve such as the hood trim edge is a challenge but by no means impossible. Because of the complex 3D curvature we are unable to use the Nonuniform Scale or Parallel Object tools. To accurately create the #2 and #3 cross-sections, line locators first need to be created. In this case, a locator line is created with the Point Snap option with each endpoint snapped to the corresponding points on the edge of the hood and front quarter panel. The #2 cross-section can then be created by modeling a line with Segment Part snapping options on the locator lines. Locators are covered in Chapter 5.

119. Create a new layer, "Hood Seam Locators." Create locator lines as shown, using Point and Segment snapping options. Notice that locator lines at the seam are point snapped to corresponding points on each of the trim edges. On the rear edge of the hood the locators are 1/7″-long lines that are point snapped to the edge points on the hood. They are also

rotated such that, from the top the lines they are visually perpendicular to the tangent of the rear hood edge, and from the right side view, have matched vectors as segments adjacent to the edge running along the length of the vehicle. It is important to note that locator lines on the rear of the hood were rotated versus having their points moved. When a point on a vector is moved, its length changes. Rotation keeps the length constant. Notice that, for now, we only need the locators for the edge of the hood. Later on we will create additional locators for creation of cross-sections for the quarter panel (Figure 12.122).

120. OK, now we are ready to create cross-sections for the hood edge roll. Create a new layer, "Hood Edge Roll Cross-Sections," and make it active. Derive the #1 cross-section using the Derivative Surfaces tool. The point count on this cross-section should be 68 (Figure 12.123).

121. Create the #2 cross-section using the Segment Part (set to 3 subdivisions) and Midpoint Snap options. The segments of the #2 cross-section at the rear of the hood are snapped to the midpoints of the locator lines. The point of #2 at the seam are snapped to first third distance of the locator lines. This is just about the same thing that we did for door edge rolls. The point count of the #2 cross-section has to match that of #1 (68 points) (Figure 12.124).

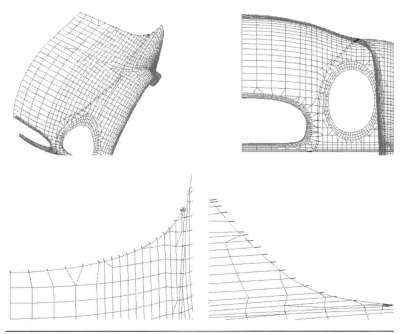

FIGURE   *"Hood Seam Locators."*
12.122

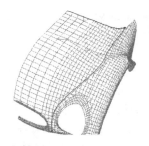
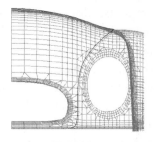
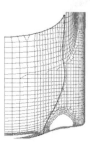

122. Before we can model the #3 cross-section, we need to create locators for this cross-section. Since the desired radius of the edge roll is 1/16″, we need to create the #3 cross-section with its points located 1/16″ from corresponding points on #2. A typical #3 locator line is 1/16″ straight line that is point snapped to the corresponding point on the #2 cross-section. Create a 1/16″ 2-point line. Duplicate it using Cont-Copy (c 3) or C-Copy (v 2.9.5) and point snap them to corresponding points on the #2 cross-section. Rotate the lines to adjust their vectors. The #3 locator lines have visual perpendicularly to the tangents of the hood edge. Create the #3 locator in the "Hood Seam Locators" layer (Figure 12.125).

123. Create the #3 cross-section by point snapping its points to the end-points of locators. Like the #1 and #2 cross-sections, the point count of #3 is 68 points. After creation of #3, verify that all three cross-sections are in the "Hood Edge Roll Cross-Sections" layer and have matched directions (Figure 12.126).

124. Create the edge roll for the hood using the C-Mesh with same settings used to create edge roll surfaces for the doors. Afterwards Stitch the edge roll surface with the rest of the hood surface (Figure 12.127).

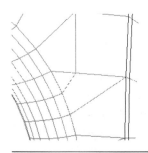
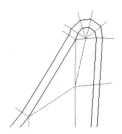
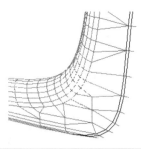

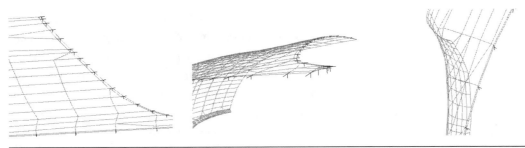

FIGURE *"Hood Seam Locators."*
12.125

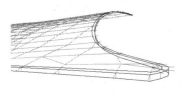

FIGURE *#3 cross-section.*
12.126

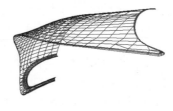

FIGURE *Edge roll surface.*
12.127

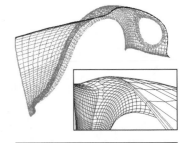

FIGURE *Shared locator lines.*
12.128

125. Using the same procedure, create the edge roll for the front quarter panel. You will need to first create additional locators for the quarter panel. I recommend that locators for the front quarter panel be created in their own separate layer separate from the hood locators. You can Copy/Paste copies of shared locator lines (Figure 12.128).

If you have successfully created the edge rolls for the hood and front quarter panel surfaces, congratulations. Creating edge rolls for complex surfaces is at best a tedious and time-consuming task. Don't be discouraged if you were unable to accomplish the task the first time around. When I developed this technique it took me about 10 attempts to nail down the procedure. If you are of the opinion that this task is easier to perform in a dedicated surface (pure NURBS) modeling system, you are mistaken. It takes almost the same amount of effort to create subtle edge rolls for trimmed surfaces. Where form•Z's polygonal nature surpasses pure NURBS or Solids modeling applications is in the ability it gives you to tightly and precisely control the radius and shape of the edge roll and its meshing. In pure NURBS and Solids modeling, a round will always give you a "Rolling Ball" type round with an constant arc-type cross-section. The manual method that I presented in the previous steps allows you to vary the shape and radius of an edge roll by modifying the shape of the elemental cross-sections. Because we retain all our construction elements and un-stitched surfaces in source and backup layers, we can very quickly regenerate almost any surface in a short amount of time if higher or lower polygonal density is required. By now, you have undoubtedly discovered that it takes a fair amount of time and considerable effort to build edge rolls. Because of the time and effort required, you should exercise judgment as to when to build rolled edges and when to forego the procedure. The decision is dependent on the desired realism level of the model and the proximity of the view point to the model. If you are modeling man-made shiny curvilinear surfaces, such as stamped sheetmetal, and wish to achieve photorealistic rendering, creating edge rolls is almost a requirement. The main advantage of having a rolled edge on a shiny or reflective object is the subtle highlights you get at the roll. Otherwise, when rendered, your surface would terminate abruptly, without any hint of volumetricity of the surface, ruining the illusion. In real life, most sheetmetal products have their edges rolled to prevent injury and reduce the chances of corrosion setting in. We have become accustomed to seeing them without realizing it. However, when the edge rolls are not present, we notice that something is amiss.

| **Modeling Grill** | Let's take a short mental break prior to proceeding to the rear end, and do some simple modeling. In the following three steps we will create simple surfaces to serve as our grill mesh. In the design of this vehicle, the grills are made of black wire screen to prevent debris and insects from entering the engine compartment and possibly damaging the radiator. While it is possible to precisely model the wire mesh, it would not be efficient to do so, as it would generate unnecessary polygons and raise render times. Individual holes in the wire mesh are fairly ubiquitous things, and as such are best simulated through a transparency of a clip map. The map should be grayscale, with a black (0,0,0) background and non-antialiased white lines. Adobe Photoshop or MetaCreations Painter/Painter 3D are excellent tools for the creation of texture maps. The screen pattern is a design decision and we encourage you to exercise your own artistic creativity. The decision whether to use the map as a clip map or as a transparency map is your choice. Be aware, though, that in general, clip maps take longer to render because shadows are computed through them. Transparency maps can be set not to affect shadows in most 3D animation applications, as in RenderZone. The following three steps describe how to create meshed surface grill screens. Specifically, solids are converted into meshed sur |

faces by topological deletion of rear faces. This assumes that the grill screens will be textured with a transparency map. If you plan to use clip maps, leave the grill screens as solids. When they are rendered with clip maps, the screens will look volumetric. This is of course a subtle effect that would only be visible when the camera is very close to the grill screen surface and the output resolution is NTSC or higher.

126. Hide all layers except "Hood 1/2." Create a new layer, "Grill Cross-Sections," and make it active. Create the #1 cross-section for the grill surface by using the Derivative Surfaces tool and clicking on the boundary on the grill recess. Mirror Copy the derived curve and join the two halves into a single closed surface. Be sure to delete the duplicate points at the join points. Create the #2 cross-section by moving a copy of #1 –1/16″ along the Y-axis. Create the #3 grill cross-section by Nonuniformly Scaling the #2 with the center of the curve as the base of Nonuniform Scale, using the following values; 0.99, 1.0, 0.98 (Figure 12.129).

127. Define a new layer, "Radiator Grill," and make it active. Create the radiator grill using the same C-Mesh settings as were used to create previous edge rolls, but with the following changes:

 # Of Segments: 2
Type Of Object: All Closed (Solid)

The resulting object is a solid, make it a surface by removing the rear face. Using the Insert Segment tool, with Point Snap options, insert height segments (Figure 12.130).

128. Using the same procedure, derive an edge curve for the oil cooler grill. The derived curve should be a planar closed surface. Extrude it 1/24″ inside the vehicle. Round the front face using the following settings:

Plain Rounding; Rounding Type: Edge, Bevel
Rounding Method: Use Radius: 1/48″

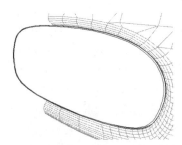

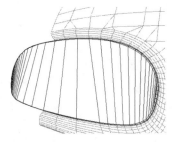

FIGURE *#3 grill cross-section.*
12.129

FIGURE *Height segments.*
12.130

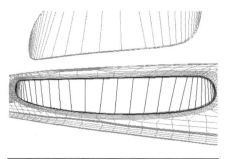

FIGURE *"Oil Cooler Radiator Grill."*
12.131

Remove the rear face and finish the surface by using the Insert Segment tool with Point Snap option to connect the points on the front face. Place the surface in its own layer, "Oil Cooler Radiator Grill" (Figure 12.131).

Modeling the Rear End

We now turn our attention to our Spyder's rear end. We need to model three primary rear features: rear lights, trunk, and spoiler. The procedures are the same surface modeling procedures that we have used up to this point. Because by now you know how to trim, how to clean up edges (practice, practice, practice), and how to create rolled edges, the instruction will not be so descriptive. Instead, study the figures thoroughly. However, if something special needs to be done, or if there is a special consideration, they will be described. The first rear-end feature that we will model is the rear spoiler. Create all construction curves for the spoiler in a "Spoiler Curves" layer. The rear spoiler on our car is conformal laminate. In the real world, the spoiler (made out fiberglass) is finely grafted onto the metal panel surface. When both are painted, the seam disappears That means that although the spoiler and quarter panel surfaces are different surfaces, they shade as a single surface. Because of this we model the spoiler as part of the quarter panel. We will use the Skin tool to create the spoiler surface. Earlier in this project when we used the Skin tool, we were creating a continuity matched surface with the intention that the skinned surface will be stitched. In this case, we are using the Skin tool to create a conformal surface.

129. Create the two *source* curves for the spoiler skin assembly using the Vector Line tool coupled with Point Snap options. Ghost the "Rear Quarter Panel" layer, only "Spoiler Curves" should be the visible layer. Verify that both *source* curves have the same direction (Figure 12.132).

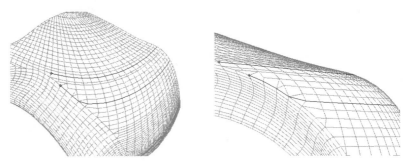

FIGURE *Source curves for spoiler skin.*
12.132

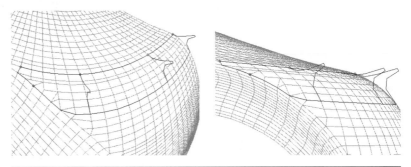

FIGURE *End points of* path *polylines.*
12.133

130. Create *path* polylines. The #1, #2, and #3 polylines have 8 points. As you can see, #2 and #3 are copies of #1. The #4 polyline, on the outside of the car, was initially created by point snapping its points, with 4 points. Add 4 additional points using the Insert Segment (v. 2.9.5.5) or Insert Point (v. 3) tool, coupled with the Midpoint Snap option. Endpoints of *path* polylines are snapped to corresponding points on the *source* curves (Figure 12.133).

131. Convert the #2, #3, and #4 *path* polylines into 16-point 5th-degree B-Spline curves. The #4 is a 1st-degree B-Spline. Using 1st-degree C-Curve causes no geometrical change to the polyline, additional points are automatically inserted. Although in theory, existing polyline points should not displace, in reality some may shift by a small amount. Carefully resnap those points. Verify that all *path* curves have the same direction. Create the 1/2 spoiler surface using the Skin tool, and place it in its own layer, "Spoiler 1/2." Notice that because our *source* curves are point snapped to the points on the rear quarter panel, and the path curve endpoints are point snapped to the *source* curves, the resulting spoiler surface is perfectly conformal to the quarter panel (Figure 12.134).

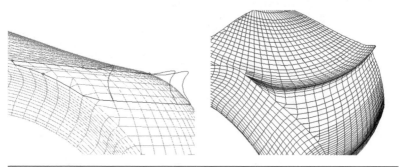

FIGURE *Spoiler surface.*
12.134

FIGURE *Third brake light.*
12.135

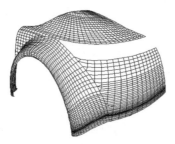

FIGURE *"Spoiler 1/2" layer.*
12.136

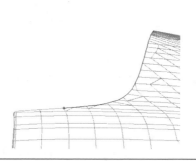

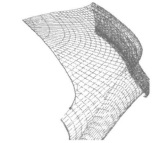

FIGURE *Boot cover curve.*
12.137

132. Use Trim/Split, edge rolling, and trim edge cleanup techniques. Add a third safety brake light to the spoiler. You may either keep the spoiler halved or Mirror & Stitch it prior to creating the third brake light. The choice is yours (Figure 12.135).

133. Separate and Delete the faces on the rear quarter panel surface bounded by the spoiler *source* curves and #4 *path* curve. Copy/Paste a copy of the 1/2 spoiler surface into the "Rear Quarter Panel" layer. Stitch the spoiler

surface with the quarter panel. If you constructed the middle brake light as a whole, you will need to halve the spoiler prior to stitching. "Spoiler 1/2" layer is now a backup layer (Figure 12.136).

Before we create the trunk and the rear lights, we will create the boot for the soft top. For you unfamiliar with automotive terminology, a "boot" is a space that is used to store the folded canvas soft top. Our boot design calls for a fiberglass conformal panel that serves as a boot cover. This design improves the aesthetics and aerodynamics of the vehicle. The procedure for constructing the boot is nearly identical to the one we used to trim out the hood surface. First we will create a trim curve. Split the boot cover surface away from the rear quarter panel, including the gap. To complete the boot cover construction, we will create edge rolls for all sharp surface terminations. Having boot cover surface allows us to model the trunk surface, followed by the rear light housing. Create the boot trim curves in the "Boot Trim Curves" layer, and keep untrimmed backups of the surfaces.

134. First we need to delineate the width of the boot cover panel. Create a curve as shown using the Derivative Surfaces or Vector Line tool with Point Snap option (Figure 12.137).

135. From the top view, orthographically project the derived curve using the 2D Projection tool, with Status Of Objects set to Delete. Select all points except the last one (away from the axis of symmetry) and move them +6″ (1″ Grid Snap Module) along the Y-axis. Delete the third from last point and Fit Fillet the second from last point using the following values (Figure 12.138):

Line Editing Options: Fit Fillet; # Of Edges: 3, Radius: 2 1/2″

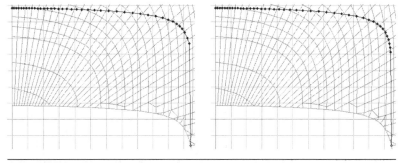

FIGURE *Derived curve.*
12.138

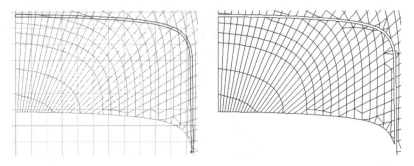

FIGURE *Boot cover panel.*
12.139

136. Create an parallel duplicate of the curve using 1/7″ offset with IN direction. The direction of the curve may need to be adjusted. Reverse the direction of the duplicate. Join the two curves into a single curve using the Edit Line tool set to **Connect Lines & Close Line Sequence. Status Of Objects** is set to **Delete.** Trim the rear quarter panel with the curve. The result is two surfaces: 1/2 boot cover and rear quarter panel with 1/7″ gap between the surfaces. Clean up the trim edges. Create a new layer, "1/2 Boot Cover," and place the boot cover panel into it (Figure 12.139).

137. Review the procedures for rounding a sharp point on a surface. Round the sharp corner on the front/left corner of the 1/2 boot cover panel. Separate the two faces, delete the single segment and points to reduce the corner surface into a 4-point polygon. Fit Fillet the corner point using the following values:

 # Of Edges: 3, Radius: 1/9″.

Stitch the two surfaces back together (Figure 12.140).

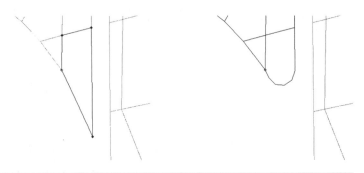

FIGURE *Stitching two surfaces.*
12.140

With the boot cover defined, we can now model the trunk. After the trunk surface is delineated, finish it off by creating the rolled edges. Trimming the trunk surface out of the rear quarter panel is slightly tricky as the shape of the seam cannot be defined as a single orthographic projection, precluding the exclusive use of orthographic trimming. Our procedure will combine trimming the rear quarter panel using both solid dyes and trim curves.

138. Create two trim curves for the trunk as shown. The heightwise section (#2), is an 18-point 3rd-degree B-Spline C-Curve derived from a 4-point polyline. Notice the gentle curvature on it. Its first point is snapped to the first point of the derived curve. The bottom widthwise section (#3) was created using the Vector Line tool coupled with the Point Snap option. The two curves were connected together using the Connect Lines option in the Line Edit tool. The join point was rounded using the Fit Fillet option with the following settings:

Of Edges: 3, Radius: 1/2".

A parallel duplicate of the curve was then created with 1/7" offset and IN direction, and the two curves were joined using the **Connect Lines & Close Line Sequence** option in Line Edit (Figure 12.141).

Because the design of the car calls for a gap between the boot cover panel and the trunk, we cannot simply trim the rear quarter with the trim curve. We need to create a solid dye object that will properly trim the surface. The dye that we need is similar to the dyes that were used to split the door surface away from the main fuselage in Chapter 7. The main difference between this dye and the one used in Chapter 7 is that it does not complete the trimming task. The task is completed using normal orthographic projection trimming using a planar closed surface. Retain the trim curve (cross-section for the dye) and construct the dye in the "Rear End Trim Dyes" layer. When complete, place the trunk surface in its own layer, "Trunk 1/2."

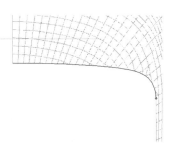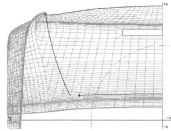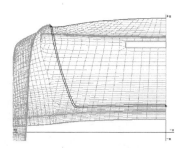

FIGURE *Parallel curve duplicate.*
12.141

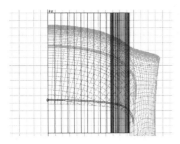

FIGURE *Duplicate parallel.*
12.142

FIGURE *Trim and stitch dye with curve.*
12.143

139. Extrude the trim curve about 18″ using the Perpendicular to Surface option and place it as shown. Parallel offset the derived edge curve with 1/2″ and OUT direction. Create a parallel duplicate of it with 1/7″ offset in the same direction (Figure 12.142).

140. Copy/Paste a copy of the first parallel curve into the "Rear End Trim Dyes" layer. Trim & Stitch the dye with the curve (Figure 12.143).

141. Trim the rear quarter panel with the dye using Trim/Split; Trim: First Object option. Be sure to retain backups of the untrimmed rear panel and the dye. It is helpful to break down the seam between the trunk and panel surface into three sections: top widthwise, heightwise, and bottom widthwise. The solid dye did not trim the top widthwise section (Figure 12.144).

142. Copy/Paste copies of the parallel curves into the "Rear Quarter Panel" layer, and modify them as shown, by deleting unneeded points. Join them together using Connect Lines with the Close Line Sequence option. In form•Z 2.9.5, use Edit Line set to Connect Lines/Close Line Sequence. Notice that one of the points on the corner of the trunk is snapped to a point and another is snapped to a segment. After fine-tuning the point positions, flatten the closed surface using the 2D Projection tool (Figure 12.145).

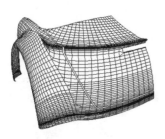

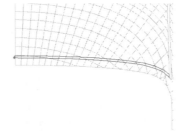

FIGURE *Solid dye.*
12.144

FIGURE *Flatten closed surface.*
12.145

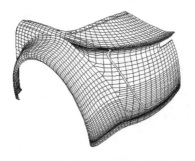

FIGURE *"Trunk Panel 1/2."*
12.146

143. Trim the rear quarter panel surface with this trim shape. The result should be two surfaces, 1/2 trunk and rear quarter panel. Place the trunk surface into its own layer, "Trunk panel 1/2" (Figure 12.146).
144. Round the sharp corners on both surfaces, and clean up the trim edges (Figure 12.147).
145. Complete the modeling of the rear quarter panel, trunk, and boot cover surfaces by creating their edge rolls and rubber seals, using the techniques you learned in creating edge rolls for the doors, hood, and front quarter panels (Figure 12.148). Recall the procedure:

- Create locators.
- Create the #1 edge roll cross-section using Derivative Surfaces followed by segment and point deletion.
- Construct #2 and #3 using Vector Line and Point Snap.
- C-Mesh with a total of 2 or 3 Depth segments, 2nd-degree B-Spline.
- Stitch the edge roll surface to the main surface.

146. Create a 64-point ellipse and taper it with the Deform tool. Extrude 10″ and place it to intersect with the rear quarter panel as shown. When

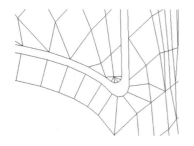
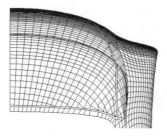
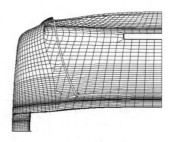

FIGURE *Clean up trim edges.*
12.147

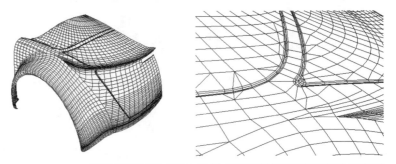

FIGURE *Edge rolls and rubber seals.*
12.148

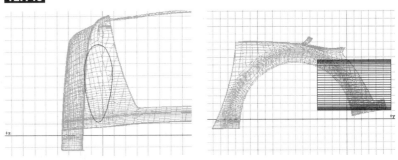

FIGURE *Rear light housing.*
12.149

looking from the back view, the shape of the deformed ellipse is the projected shape of the rear light housing, and is a design decision. If you wish, you may construct your own shape (Figure 12.149).

147. Trim the rear quarter panel with the dye and clean up the trim edge. This is a good time to clean up the polygon clumping on the bottom rear of the surface that might cause some shading anomalies (Figure 12.150).

148. Create a 1/16″ edge roll for the rear light edge (Figure 12.151).

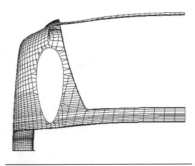

FIGURE *Bottom rear.*
12.150

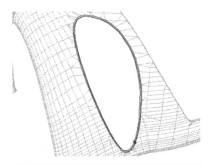

FIGURE *Rear light edge.*
12.151

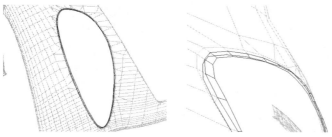

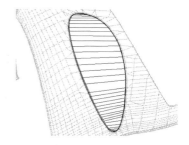

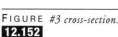

F I G U R E *#3 cross-section.*
12.152

F I G U R E *Rear Light Cover.*
12.153

The design of the rear light calls for rear lights to be covered by a removable panel, ostensibly for easy maintenance. The panel is flush with the rear quarter panel but does not share the fender flare to rear-end transition. It's flatter surface geometry. This is the reason why we trimmed the rear quarter panel instead of splitting it in two. Now that we have the seam where the rear light cover fits, including the obligatory edge roll, we can model the rear light cover itself. Model the source curves in the "Rear Light Cover Cross-Sections" layer, and place the completed surface in "Rear Light Cover."

149. Derive the #1 cross-section using the Derivative Surfaces tool. Derive the #2 cross-section using Vector Line coupled with the Point Snap option, snapping the point to the points in the middle row of the edge roll. To create the #3 cross-section, first model and place 1/16″ locator lines, with their first points snapped to the points on the #2 cross-section. Create the #3 cross-section using Vector Line while snapping to the end-points of the locator lines (Figure 12.152).

150. Model the rear light cover using the same procedure as for creating the grill screens (Figure 12.153).

  • Create a solid using C-Mesh.
  • Delete the rear face.
  • Insert segments into the front face using Insert Segment.

The design calls for three blended recesses for three individual lights: a large ellipsoidal main rear light/parking light, the turn signal, and the reverse warning light.

151. Create a 32-point ellipse and two 24-point circles as shown. Notice that the width of the shapes forms a tapered look when a guideline is passed through their tangents. The three shapes are also centered on the rear light cover (Figure 12.154).

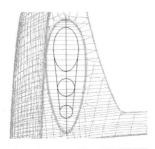

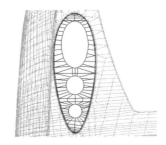

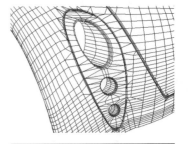

FIGURE *Ellipse and circle.*
12.154

FIGURE *Trim light cover.*
12.155

FIGURE *Tangency continuous*
12.156 *blended recessed light wells.*

152. Trim the light cover with the shapes and clean up the trim edges. Use Figure 12.155 as a guide.
153. Using the Skin or C-Mesh technique, create tangency continuous blended recessed light wells, with an approximate blend radius of 1/8″ for the large ellipsoid well and 1/12″ for the small wells (Figure 12.156).

Modeling Rear Bumper

Now we turn our attention to the rear bumper. The rear bumper in its current state just sort of hangs and presents a linear profile from the back. To give our rear bumper surface a more stylized and sophisticated appearance we will use the Deform tool to give it some additional curvature. Additionally, we need to create blended surfaces where the exhaust pipes and license plate go. Recall that the Deform tool applies deformation symmetrically, so you will need to temporarily Mirror & Stitch the 1/2 bumper surface in the "1/2 Bumper" layer.

154. Working from the right side view, using the Taper/Shear deformation combo, deform the rear bumper. Set Grid Snap Module to 1″. Switch to the front view and follow up with Taper/Taper deformation, six (1″) deformation ticks OUT, followed by eight counter-deformation ticks IN (Figure 12.157).

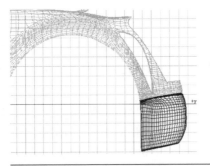

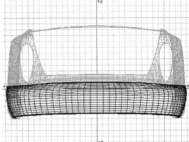

FIGURE *Deform and taper rear bumper.*
12.157

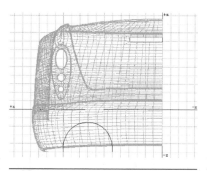

FIGURE *Exhaust ports.*
12.158

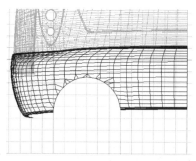

FIGURE *Trim and clean up edges.*
12.159

155. The design of the rear bumper includes dual exhaust ports. Create a 3"-radius 48-point circle and delete half of its points. Place the arc as shown. Create two straight lines that extend below the bumper, and join them to the first and last points of the arc The trim curve should have 27 points. In the real world, the placement of exhaust ports is dictated by the position of the muffler and exhaust pipe. We, however, have no such constraints and can place the exhaust ports almost anywhere on the bumper (Figure 12.158).

156. Trim the rear bumper with this curve and clean up the trim edge (Figure 12.159).

157. Create a Skin assembly for the blended exhaust port surface. The path curves are 3rd-degree B-Spline C-Curves (Figure 12.160).

158. Create the skinned surface and stitch it to the bumper (Figure 12.161).

The license plate recess must be large enough to accommodate the license plate and a single illumination light on each side of the license plate.

159. Create a trim shape for the license plate recess, using Figure 12.162 as guide.

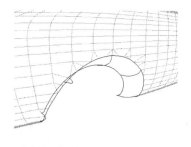

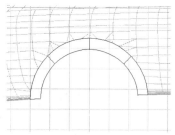

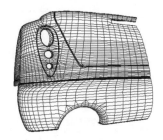

FIGURE *Skin assembly.*
12.160

FIGURE *Stitch skin assembly to*
12.161 *bumper.*

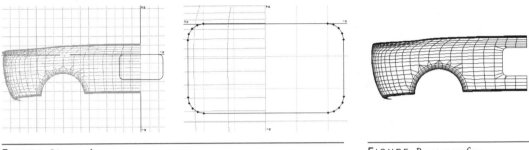

FIGURE *License plate recess.*
12.162

FIGURE *Bumper surface.*
12.163

160. Trim the bumper surface with the trim shape and clean up the trim edge (Figure 12.163).

161. Because the bumper surface is fairly flat in the center, C-Mesh is the faster technique to use in this case. Create four cross-sections using Figure 12.164 as a guide. #1 was created using Derivative Surfaces set to **Selected Segments**. #2 is a nonuniformly scaled duplicate of #1. #3 is a projected duplicate of #2, and #4 is a parallel duplicate of #3.

162. Create the license plate recess using the C-Mesh tool. Set **Mesh Depth; # Of Segments: 6** total. Set **Depth Smoothing** to 3rd-degree **B-Spline**, and **Type Of Object** to **All Closed (Solid)**.

　　Delete the front face, reverse the direction of the surface, and insert segments as shown. Complete the 1/2 rear bumper surface by stitching the license plate recess with the main rear bumper surface (Figure 12.165).

　　My design for the license plate recess is a bit snug. If you wish, you may model the recess larger. Figure 12.166 shows the completed rear end of the car.

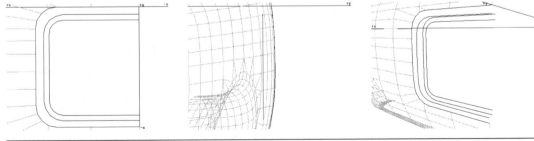

FIGURE *4 cross-sections.*
12.164

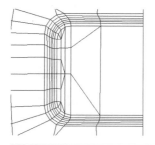

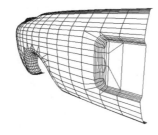

FIGURE *1/2 rear bumper surface.*
12.165

FIGURE *Completed rear end.*
12.166

Modeling Windshield Frame

In real-world convertibles, the windshield frame is a reinforced part of the chassis. In the next exercise we build the chassis of our car. We are building our car from the outside in, and we will only model the parts of the chassis that are visible by the camera. To ease the creation of the windshield frame we will create the windshield glass. The windshield surface will provide us with a base surface around which we will build the frame. This process is similar to sketching with pencils where a general boundary is defined and then refined. We also import the wheel and tire surfaces that we created in the previous exercise. With the windshield and wheels in place, we will have a base of measurement when we construct the interior of our car. We will use the Skin tool to create the windshield surface. Create all windshield curves in the "Windshield Curves" layer, and place the surface in the "Windshield" layer.

163. First we need to delineate the windshield area. The bottom curve was derived using the Derivative Surfaces tool. The other three are normal 4-point Vector Lines. Take care to snap endpoints to each other. After creating the four lines, move them together about 1/6″ along the Z-axis below the hood line (Figure 12.167).

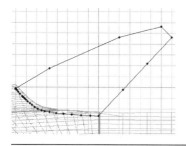

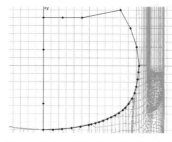

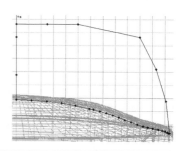

FIGURE *Windshield area.*
12.167

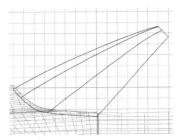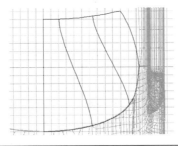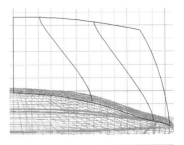

FIGURE *Constructing windshield.*
12.168

164. We will construct the windshield using the Skin tool. The top and bottom curves will serve as our sources. Convert the top polyline into 23-point 3rd-degree B-Spline. Its points must match the bottom derived curve. Convert the two *paths* into 16-point 3rd-degree B-Splines and create two intermediate 16-point *paths* (Figure 12.168).

165. Create the 1/2 windshield using the Skin tool. Mirror & Stitch it to form a complete windshield (Figure 12.169).

166. Import the wheel and tire that we modeled in a previous exercise. Because we modeled the car body and the wheel using "comfortable" scales and grid settings, the wheel/tire will not be properly scaled. Uniformly Scale the wheel/tire (scale value of .29 with 0,0,0 as base of scale) and place it using the Wheel Guides as a placement guide (Figure 12.170).

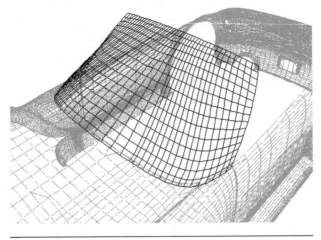

FIGURE *Complete windshield.*
12.169

FIGURE *Completed car.*
12.170

167. Using procedures that you learned in this exercise and from your own experience, create the following details: edge bevels for the front headlight surfaces, rear light lenses, fog lights with lenses, side mirrors, door and trunk handles, fuel cap cover, and key holes.

In the next series of exercises we will construct the chassis and learn how to model the interior of our car using body surfaces as guides.

Congratulations, you have finished one of the most demanding exercises in this book. The final rendering shows a color combination that I find most attractive. Of course, you may choose your own colors.

13 Automotive Interior

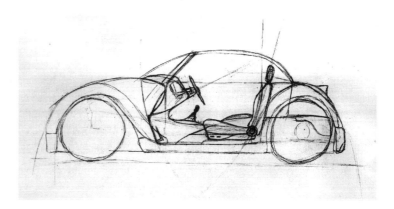

IN THIS CHAPTER

Like styling and body surface modeling, automotive interiors are a challenging task. Interiors actually have more complex surfaces than do body panels. Additionally, true automotive interior design requires an in-depth understanding of ergonomics that we all may not have. Because of that, it is very useful to use sketches and photographic reference for modeling the cabin of the car. As I mentioned earlier, when we are modeling for animation or conceptualizing a design, we work from the outside in. That is why we constructed the body prior to the chassis. Using body surfaces we build the interior to match the body. While it is perfectly acceptable to begin modeling the interior from any point, from experience I have learned that there are two very good places to start. The first is to model the interior surfaces of the door, matched to the door body panel. Because door interiors establish the maximum width of available cabin space, they provide good guides for placement of the seats. The second is to model a seat first, then create the door interior, while continuously adjusting the position of the seat and width of the door interior. In modern cars, like the one we are modeling, door interiors can have significant thickness. Safety equipment, large door speakers, the power window motor, and other equipment all add to a door that can have substantial thickness. Like with all other 3D Modeling, first we need to plan the over all interior, with a fast sketch. The purpose of the sketch is to loosely define proportions and contents of the interior. Figure 13.1 was drawn in about five minutes and shows the side view of the proposed layout of the interior.

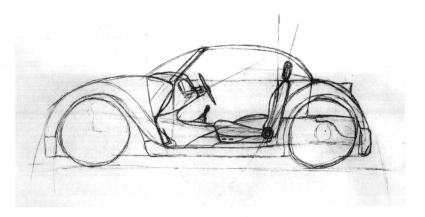

FIGURE *Car sketch.*
13.1

Modeling Padded Seat Surfaces

By far the hardest feature to achieve when modeling auto interiors is the "soft surface" look for the seats and padded areas. Quite often, the seats and other padded surfaces end up looking like they are made out of hard plastic or hard hide instead of soft padded leather. The "soft" look is really a combination of specially curved geometry and careful application of materials. In terms of techniques, most of the techniques that you have learned in body surface modeling fully apply to modeling interiors. However, there is less need to have continuous surfaces, and more of a need for surfaces to come together at a seam that looks like a real-world stitched seam. We are going to start modeling the interior by first modeling a seat. Having a seat will make it easier to decide the precise thickness of the doors and the width of the center console. The lengthwise placement of the seats will assist us in properly modeling the dashboard and the steering column. Study the two sketches of the seat. We will model a seat based on the those used in the 1993–1995 Mazda RX-7, and currently used in the MX-5 Miata sports car. As the interior of our sports car is a bit cramped, the seats have limited reclining ability. The seats are covered in tightly stretched leather with stitched seams. Having visible stitched seams may seem trivial, but from experience I have learned that seats modeled without them or poorly emulated through modeling or bump texturing look like they are made out of hard material.

Take a minute to study the sketches in Figures 13.1 and 13.2. The side sketch shows the approximate proportions and placement of the seat, but it offers very little usable information as to its shape. The two seat sketches show detail as to the shape and seam placement of the seat. Notice that the seams form bulges in the padding. Not using visible stitches or using bump mapping often

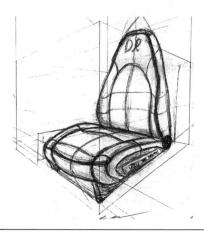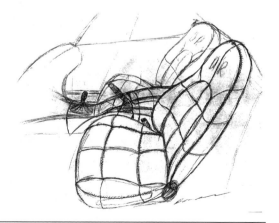

FIGURE *Seat sketches.*
13.2

results in soft padded material that looks like plastic. The second seat sketch also outlines the proposed width and shape of the center console and placement of the stick-shift and parking brake. We will model the seat at a comfortable scale that also happens to be the same scale as for the car body. We will retain the advantage of not having to rescale the seat once imported into the main project.

Now is a good time to consider complex project management. In the previous exercise we constructed the body of our car. We have dozens of exportable layers, dozens of backup and virgin layers, and probably close to a hundred source layers. Very likely, by now, the memory is being taxed on all but the high-end machines. All this and we still have interior and chassis modeling ahead of us. Although we could model everything in a single project, it would be more efficient if we break the project into large assemblies. We already have body surfaces and wheel/tires as separate projects. Although we imported the wheel and tire into the body surfaces project, any changes we need to make to the wheel or tire would be made in their own project and then reimported into body surfaces. Let's leave the body surfaces project alone and create a new master project that will hold only EXPORTABLE surfaces. We will model various assemblies, like the seat in a separate project, and then import the exportable objects only into the master project. Likewise, we will model the seat in its own project.

Our first task is to bring the side sketch from Figure 13.1 into the project and set it up as an underlay. The image, (Interior Side Sketch.TIF), is available on the CD. Set it up as an underlay with the following settings: In Projection Views; Scale: 1 47/100″ = 1′, Horizontal Origin: −4′–5″, Vertical Origin: 2′–1″. This centers the seat on the sketch at world origin, and makes it easier to model it. After the seat is complete, change the Horizontal Origin to −9″. This underlay placement will allow semi-accurate positioning of the seat within the cabin (Figure 13.3).

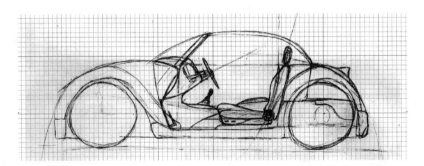

FIGURE *Placing seat in the cabin.*
13.3

**Modeling the
Seat Cage**

To model the padded areas of the seat we will use a combination of Smooth Mesh and other previously discussed modeling procedures. Although it may be possible to model the padded areas of the seat using surface modeling procedures, mesh smoothing offers a more efficient, controllable, and faster way to derive this kind of geometry. Smooth meshing procedures are of prime importance to character modeling using form•Z. The procedures and techniques for modeling with Smooth Mesh are fully detailed in Chapter 14.

When using Smooth Meshing, our goal is to build a "cage" object that will yield the desired shape when processed through the Smooth Mesh tool. We will start the modeling of the seat by constructing the two primary cages for the seat bottom and the seat back.

1. We begin cage construction by creating a volumetric for the seat. The length and height of the box is determined by the underlay, while the width is a best guess based on the perspective sketches. Remember that the width will be adjusted continually. Create the box with the following dimensions, Length (Y-axis): 1'–4", Height (Z-axis): 1'–5", Width (X-axis): 12" (Figure 13.4).

2. Create a general polyline outline of the seat. From the right side view, Trim & Stitch the box with the outline (Figure 13.5).

3. Create a solid with a cross-section as shown. The extrusion distance is any that is wider than the current seat cage. Notice that two corners are perfectly aligned with the corners of the seat cage. Boolean Split (One Way) the seat cage into two solids with the dye (Figure 13.6).

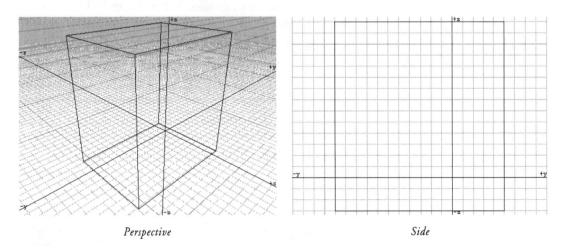

Perspective *Side*

FIGURE *Cage construction.*
13.4

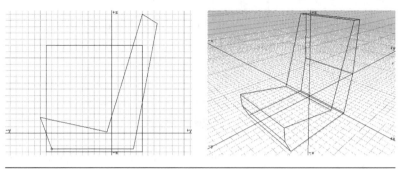

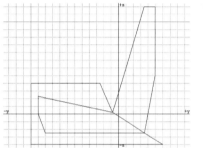

FIGURE *Seat polyline outline.*
13.5

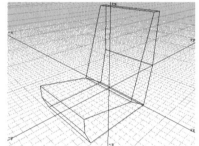

FIGURE *Seat split into solids.*
13.6

Synopsis of Smooth Mesh Technique

While Chapter 14 contains detailed explanations of procedures and concepts for Smooth Meshing, I wish to cover some that are vital to us in this exercise. An important Mesh Smoothing technique is Split & Stitch. The technique involves splitting a surface or a solid in two with a line using Trim & Stitch: Split With Line then stitching the two parts back together. Status Of Objects is set to Delete throughout the process to prevent accumulation of unneeded geometry. In form•Z V3.0 this is available as a one-step tool, replacing the two-part process in v 2.9.5 and earlier. Split & Stitch is often used to quickly insert a vertical row of segments into a symmetrical cage that run along the axis of symmetry. Halving a cage is also a common technique when applying symmetrical changes to the cage. This is identical to the halving that we used when modeling the body surfaces, except that we nearly always need to Mirror & Stitch 1/2-cage prior to Mesh Smooth processing. The majority of cage construction makes use of only three tools: Transformations, Point/Segment Insertion, and Topological Deletion. *Transformations* is a general term referring to movement, rotation, nonuniform and uniform scaling of cage geometry to define the shape of the cage that yields the desired smoothed shape. Geometry transforms do not alter the topology of the cage. While geometry defines the shape of the cage and the smoothed result, topology defines its construction, render quality, and polygonal efficiency. Cage mesh topology is defined by the number of faces, points, and segments in a cage, their distribution density, and relative position to each other. Understanding cage topology is vital to the successful use of Mesh Smoothing, as the derived smooth meshes are more polygonally dense versions of the generating cages, possessing similar mesh topology. Additionally, any problems in the cage will be amplified by the Mesh Smooth tool. Always try to keep as many faces in a cage as 4-point polygons, using triangles only when necessary. Break down all complex faces (more than 4 points) into quads or triangles. Having all faces composed of 3 or 4 points ensures that the cage retains *segment chain continuity*; that is, no segment within a cage terminates at a complex polygon. Cages that contain broken segment chains risk generating a smooth mesh that renders with artifacts. Those artifacts are usually caused by the presence of slivered polygons or triangles in a smoothed mesh, that are the result of broken segment chains in the cage. Cage Mesh topology is largely controlled through Insert Segment and Insert Point (v.3) and Topological Deletion. When inserting a segment, first insert any additional points using Midpoint, Segment Part, or Segment snapping options, then with the Point Snap option insert the segment. In form•Z 2.9.5 or earlier, point insertion is handled through the Insert Segment modifier, and Vector Line tool. To insert a point in form•Z 2.9.5 simply double-click on a segment using the appropriate snap option. In form•Z 3.0, point and segment insertions are handled through two new tools, Insert Point and Insert Segment. These tools were implemented to save time and work the same as Vector Line with Insert Segment modifier. Quite often it will be necessary to delete selected segments. Deletion of segments in cage modeling is a two-step process. First the segment is deleted with Topological Deletion, then any unneeded points are deleted. Never delete a point that is shared by more than two segments. Doing so will cause form•Z to automatically reconnect the remaining points, often resulting in undesirable geometry. If a point needs to be deleted, first delete all segments (topological deletion) until the point is shared by no more than two segments. Then delete the point. Follow the deletion by reconnecting points accordingly. Because Mesh Smoothing procedures use a small amount of tools very often, modeling time can be decreased by defining key shortcuts to following tools:

Pick, Topology Point, Topology Segment, Topology Face, Topology Object, Move, Rotate, Nonuniform Scale, Uniform Scale, Mirror, Insert Segment, Insert Point, and Delete.

Cage modeling should be done in its own layer. The Mesh Smooth tool has no provision for extracting a cage from a smoothed object. It is a certainty that smoothed objects themselves may be subject to deformation or trimming operations. Both will result in a loss of parametric controls for that Smoothed Mesh object and its associated cage. For this reason, perform the actual smoothing on a COPY of the cage in a separate layer. A typical project that uses Smoothed Mesh has a "Cage" layer where the modeling of the cage is accomplished, and a "Smoothed" layer. Prior to processing, a copy of the cage is copied and pasted into the "Smoothed" layer, and Mesh Smoothing is performed in that layer. Always make sure that you have a backup of the cage prior to processing it. Mesh Smoothing as a whole is a very interactive procedure, and is the closest thing to true sculpting that we have in form•Z, alongside parametric NURBZ, and Patch surfaces in form•Z v.3. Think of the points on the cage object as sculpting handles, and the cage itself as a control lattice. Modeling the cage is an artistic process, like real-world sculpting the best that can be done is to explain the general procedures and show the desired result. Success with cage modeling and Mesh Smoothing comes only with experience and a bit of artistic creativity. It would take far more space than this book has to describe every movement, every insertion, and every deletion. Cage modeling is a constant process of deciding where to insert, what to delete, and how to connect. It is not unusual to painstakingly insert points and segments only to delete them later on to create a different mesh topology. Your best bet is to study the figures closely and make the best effort to get cage geometry that is similar. If you get confused, don't hesitate to refer to the project on the CD, and compare your cage to mine. Throughout the cage modeling process, periodically bring the cage into the Mesh Smooth preview window and check on how the cage smoothes using the Preview: Meshed Object options. DO NOT PRESS the OK button, which will process the cage. Cancel out of the Mesh Smooth preview after checking your progress.

When cages become complex, it is beneficial to temporarily Separate a region of cage faces from the main cage and work on them without the overhead. You can also preview smoothing on that region by itself. However, the separated region needs to be stitched back with the main cage prior to final processing. When working with geometrically complex cages, real-time shaded display modes, OpenGL and QD3D are invaluable, with hardware acceleration the workflow is even faster and more intuitive. For maximum utility, tun off Render Using Smooth Shading in OpenGL or QD3D preferences.

4. Use the Split & Stitch technique to insert a vertical row of segments into the seat bottom and seat back cages. Place each of the two cages into sep-

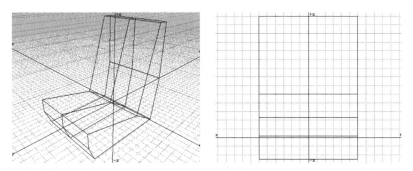

FIGURE *"Seat Bottom Cage" and "Seat Back Cage."*
13.7

arate layers, appropriately named "Seat Bottom Cage" and "Seat Back Cage" (Figure 13.7).

Now we focus our efforts on the back cage of the seat. Many of the changes are symmetrical across the height (Z-axis). If you wish you may work on only half of the cage, then Mirror & Stitch (copies) temporarily to check the smoothing. For clarity most of the figures show a symmetrical cage. Don't worry if your result is not identical; the figure cage building is not a precision exercise. Just get your shape to be as close as you can to the illustration. Use the project on the CD for extra reference if you get confused.

5. Edit the cage using point/segment insertions and sculpting. First insert two vertical rows of segments from the front view using Split & Stitch onto the front and back of the cage. From the right side and 60/30 views, insert a vertical row using point/segment insertions with Midpoint snap options onto the side of the cage. Complete this step by moving the appropriate points (Figure 13.8).

6. Set Grid Snap Module to 1″ and switch to the front view. Use Nonuniform Scale, point, and segment insertion to reshape the cage as shown in Figure 13.9. Note the delineation of the seams. The far right illustration

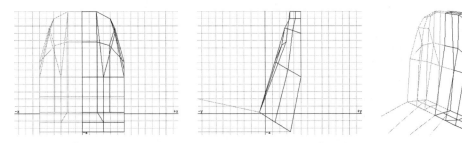

FIGURE *Editing the cage.*
13.8

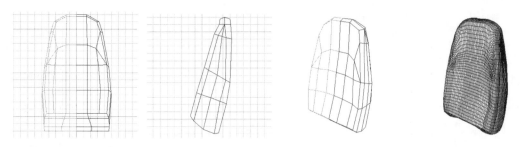

shows a test smoothing performed with the following Smooth Mesh Options:

Maximum # Of Subdivisions: 3
Maximum Segment Length: OFF
Smooth:
Maximum Face Angle: 1
Curvature: 80

7. Figure 13.10 shows further refinement to the cage. At this stage, the general shape of the seat back is developed. Notice the lower back support and seam line development. The cage was test processed with the following Smooth Mesh options:

Maximum # Of Subdivisions: 3
Maximum Segment Length: OFF
Smooth:
Maximum Face Angle: 1
Curvature: 80

8. Figure 13.11 shows further refinement of the seat back cage. To achieve the padded leather look with stitched seams, the seams are outlined by three rows of segments, with the middle row moved to form a trough.

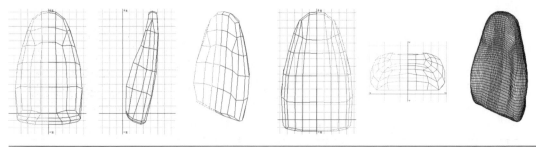

FIGURE *Refining the cage.*
13.10

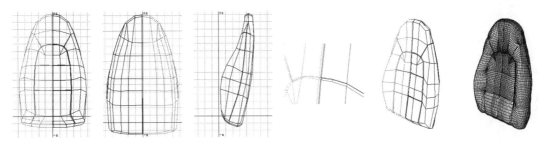

F I G U R E *Refining the seat back cage.*
13.11

When smoothed, the troughs cause bulging of the padded areas, and create depressed seams that emulate hand-stitched leather. The depth of the trough controls the amount of bulging. Overall, the cage also underwent some reshaping. The Smooth Mesh tool still causes some irregularities in the smoothed mesh, so some tweaking is still required to complete this cage. However, this cage is close to its final shape and can be used to determine if the proportions are correct.

NOTE

We need to take care when modeling troughs in a cage. Remember that Smooth Mesh smoothes procedurally created polygons between cage segments. This can create a problem with derived geometry when the segments of the cage are close together, as is the case with the seam. The result is that while the mesh has desired density, the topology of the mesh in and around this area created polygonal silhouetting. Increasing subdivision will not solve the problem. You will simply end up with more polygons that render with polygonal silhouettes. The only way to get around this is to manually increase the density of the cage. Figure 13.12 shows a refinement on the lower back support area. Simply inserting points and connecting them is not enough. They must be positioned in such a way that when processed through Smooth Mesh, the derived mesh has smooth curvature. Figure 13.12 shows close-ups of the cage in Figure 13.11 where such treatment was applied. There is really no set

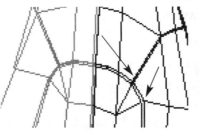

F I G U R E *Close-up views.*
13.12

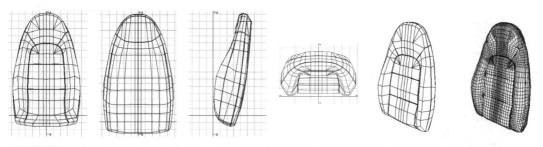

FIGURE *Completed seat back cage.*
13.13

procedure. You must continually test the position of individual points or groups of points with Smooth Mesh. The degree of desired smoothness is dependent on the proximity of that area to the Point Of View (POV) and output resolution.

9. Figure 13.13. shows the seat back cage in its completed form and the derived mesh of the seatback. The following revisions were performed.

— The single side stitch seam was replaced by two seams.
— Additional horizontal and vertical rows of segments were inserted to smooth the curvature of the derived smooth mesh.
— Multiple reshaping of the cage to smooth the derived smooth mesh.

The cage was refined such as desired smooth mesh is derived using two subdivisions. The cage that yields the desired smooth mesh with two subdivisions is optimal as the smooth mesh has an optimized number of polygons. Complex cages that are processed with three or more subdivisions generate overly heavy meshes.

The final seat back mesh was derived with the following Smooth Mesh Options;

Maximum # Of Subdivisions: 2
Maximum Segment Length: OFF
Smooth:
Maximum Face Angle: 1
Curvature: 80

A copy of the cage was processed in the "Seat Back" layer.

Figure 13.14 shows the completed seat back Raytraced in form•Z Render-Zone. Notice how the troughs defining the seams created smoothed geometry that when rendered looks a like a real-world stitch. Smooth meshing a cage can sometimes produce small random imperfections in the smoothed mesh. Quite often those imperfections add small and subtle detail that would otherwise be

hard to model. In this case, the imperfections look like random areas of stretched leather. Subtle effects like that can really sell the reality of the model.

The next phase is to model the bottom of the seat. We will do it using same procedures as the back.

10. As before, begin by inserting segments as shown using the Split & Stitch technique and Insert Point or Insert Segment. Initial point insertions are done with either Midpoint or Segment Part snap options. The "orphan" points (points that make up complex polygons) are connected with Insert Segment using the Point snap option. Vertical and horizontal segment chains are inserted using the Split & Stitch technique (Figure 13.15).

11. Refine the seat bottom cage as shown, using Split & Stitch, point/segment insertions, and geometric transformations. In this state the cage establishes general proportions and rough curvatures of the seat bottom. Notice that the majority of the faces in this cage are quadrilateral, and no face has more than 4 points. There are no faces with more than 4 points. The rectangular topological arrangement of the cage results in an ordered rectangular smooth mesh (Figure 13.16).

FIGURE *Raytraced seat*
13.14 *back.*

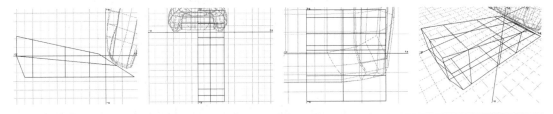

FIGURE *Inserting vertical and horizontal segment chains.*
13.15

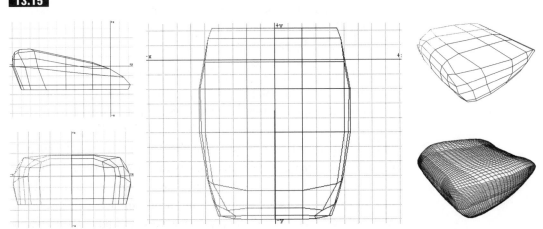

FIGURE *Refining seat bottom cage.*
13.16

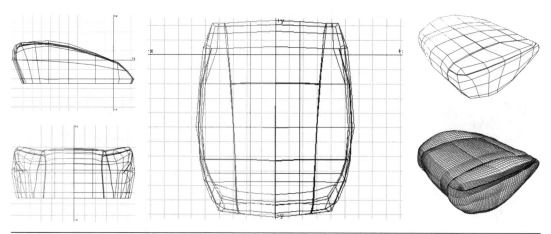

FIGURE *Defining seat troughs.*
13.17

12. The seam troughs are defined, as with the back of the seat. The cage is refined to bring out curvature in the padding. The cage is still rough and needs tweaking, as the smoothed mesh seat bottom has large geometric perturbations in it. However, most of the points that this cage needs are all there, although some deletions, insertions, and reconnections are sure to be made before the cage is complete (Figure 13.17).

13. The cage is completed by tweaking its shape. It is normal, when dealing with complex cages, that tweaking it to get a desired smooth mesh can take more time than it took to get the cage to this point. As with the seat-back cage, our goal is to model a cage that will yield a high-quality smooth mesh with **Maximum # Of Subdivisions:** set to 2. Usually insertions of segment rows using Split & Stitch and some minor reshaping is all that is needed. Basically we are increasing the mesh density and altering the geometry of the cage so it will process into a correct smooth mesh with two subdivisions (Figure 13.18).

Smooth Mesh a copy of the cage in the "Seat Bottom" layer. Use the same Smooth Mesh options as were used to create the seat back. The bottom of the smoothed mesh still has irregular perturbations in it. While we could spend time to fix them, there is no need as we will Trim & Stitch this area. The reason for trimming is that we need a flat area on the bottom of the seat bottom mesh as itself sets on top of slide rails, and seat mount (Figure 13.19).

The completed seat cushions. To complete the seat we need to add slide rails, seat mount, large seat-back angle adjustment knob, and some small detail. We do not need to worry about the seat being perfect as most of it will be cov-

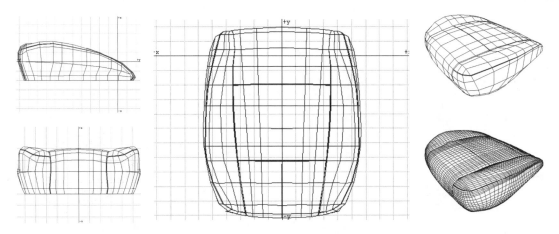

FIGURE *Completing the shape.*
13.18

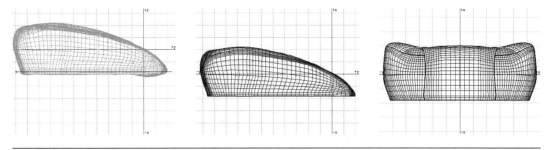

FIGURE *Smooth meshing.*
13.19

ered by the car body. The most visible parts of the seat are the top and front areas of the bottom and back (Figure 13.20).

14. Model the seat slide rails by creating 2D shapes from the right side view and extruding them. Slide rails are wholly optional, they will never even be seen by the camera. Their primary purpose is for vertical positioning of the seat above the floor panel (Figure 13.21).

Now we complete modeling of the seat by creating the back adjustment knob.

15. Create a 30-point 1″ radius circle and extrude it 1/2″ into a cylinder. Create a smaller cylinder with a 3/4″ radius and 1/4″ extrusion depth. Position the smaller cylinder so it intersects the larger with 1/8″ depth. Boolean Difference the smaller from the larger. After subtraction,

FIGURE *Completed seat*
13.20 *cushion.*

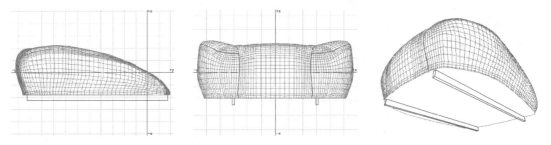

FIGURE *Modeling the seat rails.*
13.21

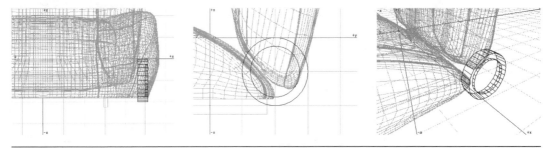

FIGURE *Creating back adjustment knob.*
13.22

and from the front view, move the knob into its X-axis position by moving it 5″ along the X-axis (Figure 13.22).

16. Boolean Union the knob with a 16-segment 1/2″ radius revolved hemisphere. Bevel the faces 1/24″. Notice the inserted segments. The segment insertion is optional but it allows tight control of exported mesh topology, as neither form•Z will break down complex polygons upon importation nor will the animation package have to do it. Mirror duplicate the knob (Figure 13.23).

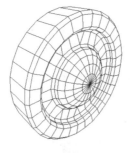

FIGURE *Mirror duplicate of knob.*
13.23

Modeling the Interior

With the seat completed we can start modeling the interior proper. We will construct the interior in phases. In the first phase we will create the floor pan and place the seats on it. Placement of the seats will dictate the precise width of the door interior and center console. Both door interiors and the center console will be modeled in the second phase. Because the center console transitions into the dashboard it will be modeled in the third phase using the center console as a starting base. In the fourth and final phase we will add the stick shift and other details.

Because we will build the interior to match the rest of the car, we need to temporarily import the body surfaces and wheels into this project. Upon completion of the interior, the car body will be deleted. The exportable interior objects will then be imported into a master project along with the rest of the car. Prior to continuing, import the exportable layers of the body surfaces project. Change Horizontal Origin in the Underlay Options to –9″.

The first interior object that we will model is the floor pan. Create a new layer, "Floor Pan Cross-Sections," and ghost the "Side Skirt" layer. Hide all other layers.

17. Using either Vector Line with Point Snap, or the Derivative Surfaces tool, create an edge curve based on the edge of side skirt as shown (Figure 13.24).
18. Working from the right side view, create a projected duplicate of the edge curve using the 2D Projection tool set to Orthographic Projection. Move the projected duplicate 2″ down along the Z-axis. W will use the C-Mesh tool to create the floor pan surface and these two curves will serve as guide curves for the placement of cross-sections (Figure 13.25).
19. Draw a 5-point polyline with endpoints snapped to the endpoints of the derived curves (Figure 13.26).
20. Duplicate the cross-section by placing the first point of each copy on a point of a projected curve and placing the last two segments to be point snapped to the point on the derived curve as shown (Figure 13.27).

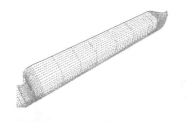
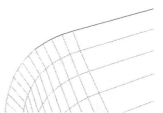
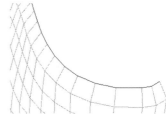

FIGURE *Edge curve.*
13.24

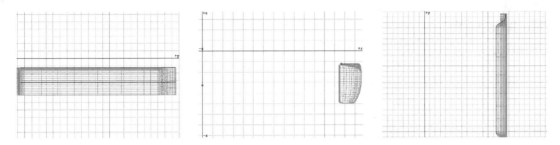

FIGURE *Duplicate the edge curve.*
13.25

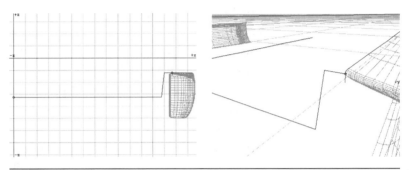

FIGURE *5-point polyline.*
13.26

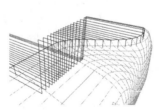

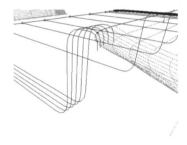

FIGURE *Duplicate the cross-section.*
13.27

FIGURE *Round the 3 points.*
13.28

21. Round the last three points on the cross-section using Fit Fillet (V 3) or Line Edit set to Fit Fillet in form•Z 2.9.5 (Figure 13.28). For the second point, use

    Fit Fillet; # Of Edges: 3, Radius: 1/2″

    For the third point, use

    Fit Fillet; # Of Edges: 3, Radius: 1/3″

    For the fourth point, use

    Fit Fillet; # Of Edges: 2, Radius: 1/8″

You are probably wondering why we are using the C-Mesh tool instead of Skin to create the floor pan. At first glance it looks like we have the required elements for a successful skin, two source shapes and point-snapped path shapes. However, using this Skin assembly would generate the following Skin tool error message:
"For Skin Along Path operation, corresponding points of the paths are colinear, which disallows the proper placement of the source shape."

Here is why this happens and why we cannot use the Skin tool in this case. There is a limitation in Skin that does not allow three or more corresponding *path* shape points to lie in such a way that a straight line can be drawn that passes through all those points. Such a case exists with the projected source shape as it is perfectly straight when viewed from both the right side and top views. In other words, the Skin tool does not allow creation of perfectly flat surfaces or have areas defined by three or more *paths* that are perfectly flat. Versions of form•Z released after this book's publication may have addressed this issue.

22. Using the C-Mesh tool with Length set to At Control Points, Depth set to At Control Lines, all smoothing OFF, and Type Of Object set to Open Ends (Surface), create the floor pan surface. Create the floor pan in its own "Floor Pan" layer. The operation creates a symmetrical half; Mirror & Stitch the surface to finish the floor pan. After stitching, optimize the surface by deleting the segments and points lying on the mirror axis (Figure 13.29).

23. Make a backup of the seat objects so we retain copies of the seat that is positioned where we modeled it. Using the underlay and Figure 13.30 as a general guide, place the seat as shown approximately 1/2″ above the floor pan. Seat mount rails will fill the gap between the rail and the floor pan. Mirror duplicate to create the passenger seat.

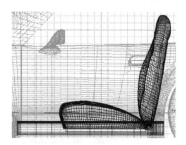

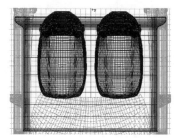

F I G U R E *"Floor Plan" layer.*
13.29

F I G U R E *Backup and placement of seats.*
13.30

We will now proceed to construct the door interior. As I mentioned before, it might be necessary to perform minor positional and scaling adjustment to the seat and to the interior door surfaces to achieve a realistic look, where no surfaces intersect each other.

24. Create a new layer, "Door Interior Cross-Sections," and make it active. Derive the edge boundary of the left door using the Derivative Surfaces tool set to **Boundary Of Surface Objects** (Figure 13.31).

25. Create a projected duplicate of the boundary curve and move it +11″ along the X-axis. Use the 2D Projection tool set to **Orthographic Projection**. Perform the projection from the right side view (Figure 13.32).

26. Complete the cross-section assembly as shown. Create three additional duplicate cross-sections and Nonuniform Scale the #4 and #5 cross-sections as shown. Rotate and Deform the #3, #4, and #5 cross-sections with the **Radial Bend** option and ZX base reference plane to conform to the curvature of the door panel when viewed from the top view. "Left Door" layer is ghosted for visual reference (Figure 13.33).

27. Create the door interior solid using C-Mesh with the following Controlled Mesh Options:

Construct Plain Mesh
Construct Directly
Length Of Net: Use Existing, **Depth Of Net:** Use Control Line Intervals
Mesh Length: At Control Points
Mesh Depth:
 # Of Segments: 2, Per Segment: ON, Smooth: ON
Type Of Object: All Closed Solid
Status Of Objects: Keep
Controlled Mesh Smoothing Options:
Length: None
Depth; Bezier, Degree: NA, # Of Points: 128

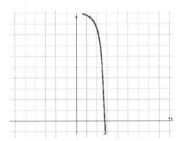

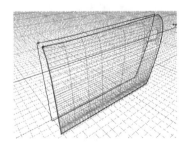

FIGURE **13.31** *"Door Interior Cross-Section" layer.*

FIGURE **13.32** *Duplicate of boundary curve.*

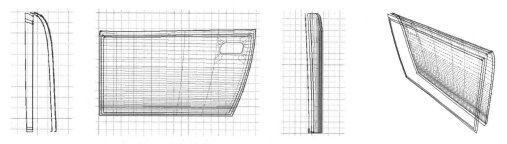

FIGURE
13.33
Cross-section assembly.

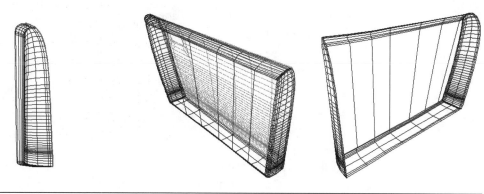

FIGURE
13.34
Basic door interior surface.

Place the door interior solid into a separate layer, "Door Interior." Right after C-Mesh, topologically delete the internal face adjacent to the floor panel. Finish the basic interior door surface by inserting segments with the Point Snap option (Figure 13.34).

We need to split the this surface into two parts. The interior part is the interior door trim itself from which we will build details such as interior handles, speaker grills, and door pockets. The outside part is a metal surface that will be stitched to the door panel. As with the door/body panel seams, we will create edge rolls for realistic rendering, with the edge roll of the internal trim being larger than the metal surface edge rolls. To properly split the interior door surface we need two planar closed shapes. The front shape is a simple rectangle and the rear shape will be derived from segments on the door panel.

28. Create a new layer, "Interior Door Trim Curves," and make it active. Set the "Left Door" layer as visible. Using the Derivative Surfaces tool, derive a curve from selected segments as shown. Delete the segments from the top and bottom of the derived curve as shown (Figure 13.35).

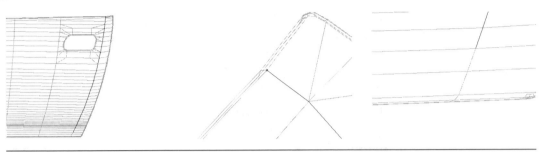

FIGURE *"Interior Door Trim Curves" layer.*
13.35

29. From the right side view, flatten the curve using the 2D Projection tool set to **Orthographic Projection.** Move the top point of the curve to be above the door panel. Create a vertical 2-point line. When creating this polyline use Segment Part Snap set to 4 **Divisions** and Orthogonal Direction snap. The bottom point of the vertical line was snapped to the segment of the door panel with the Segment Part snap option. Flatten the line using the 2D Projection tool before proceeding. Note the direction of the lines (Figure 13.36).

30. Connect the two lines using Connect Lines (V3) or Edit Line (V 2.9.5) set to **Connect Lines.** Create a parallel duplicate using the Parallel Objects tool set to 1/6″ IN. Reverse direction of the duplicate and connect the two lines together with Connect Lines or using Edit Line set to Con-nect Lines & Close Line Sequence if using form•Z 2.9.5 (Figure 13.37).

31. On the bottom right-hand corners of the trim shape, delete nine points on each segment adjacent to the corner point. This deletion is necessary so we can round the corner points successfully, with the desired radius. Round the four corner points using Line Edit set to **Fit Fillet;**

Of Edges: 4, Radius: 1″ (Figure 13.38).

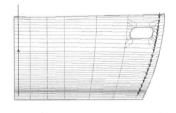

FIGURE *Flattening line.*
13.36

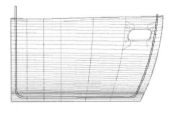

FIGURE *Connecting lines.*
13.37

FIGURE *Rounding the four corner*
13.38 *points.*

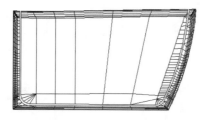

FIGURE   *"Interior Door Trim" layer.*
13.39

FIGURE   *Edge roll creation.*
13.40

32. Trim the interior door surface with the trim shape, and clean up the trim edges. The result is two surfaces. The inner surface is the actual interior door trim, the outer surface is part of the door panel and will be stitched to it. Place the trim panel (inner surface) in its own layer, "Interior Door Trim." Place the outer surface in its own temporary layer (Figure 13.39).

Using techniques learned from the last exercise on edge roll creation, create edge rolls for the two surfaces. First create a 1/16" radius edge roll for the outer surface, then fill the remaining gap, 1/9", with the edge roll of the interior trim surface. It is normal for the interior trim edge to have a larger radius as it is plastic covered by leather. Recall the general procedure for edge roll creation:

- Create the #1 cross-section with the Derivative Surfaces tool.
- Create locators, if necessary.
- Create the #2 and #3 cross-sections.
- Create the edge roll with the C-Mesh tool.

33. Create 1/16" radius edge roll surface for the outer surface and Stitch the two surfaces together (Figure 13.40).

   — First derive the #1 edge cross-section using the Derivative Surfaces tool.

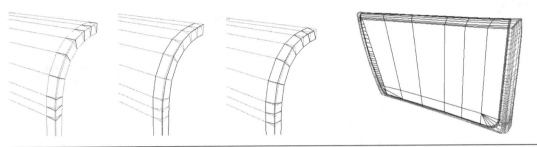

FIGURE *Interior trim panel.*
13.41

— Next create and place locators, a 3-point vector line with two 1/16″ long segments at right angles.
— Create the #2 and #3 cross-sections using Vector Line and point snapped to locator points.
— Create the edge roll surface using C-Mesh.
— Finish by stitching the two surfaces together.

34. For the interior trim panel, create a 1/9″ radius edge roll using the same steps. The only difference is that the locator lines have 1/9″-long segments (Figure 13.41).

We need to create a gap on the top of the interior door surfaces where the window pane slides up and down. We will do it the easy way and just select and separate a single horizontal row of faces on both surfaces. We do not want to delete the separated faces—if we change our mind, all that is needed is to Stitch the faces with a proper surface. Instead of deleting them we place them in a backup layer.

35. Select the shown faces adjacent to the top boundary of both surfaces, and Separate them with **Boundary Of Selected Faces** options and **Status Objects** set to **Delete**. Transfer the separated faces to a backup layer (Figure 13.42).

36. Transfer the outer surface to the "Left Door" layer and Stitch it and the door panel surface together. This step is optional. If you wish you may leave the inner door surface as a separate object, or add any details you wish. Since in this project the doors will remain closed, there is no need to add any more details to the door surfaces. We still have to add details to the interior trim panel, though it goes without saying that you should retain unstitched copies of both exterior and interior door surfaces in a backup layer (Figure 13.43).

FIGURE *Separate the faces.*
13.42

FIGURE *"Left Door" layer.*
13.43

FIGURE *RenderZone Raytraced*
13.44 *door panel.*

Figure 13.44 shows a RenderZone Raytracing of the door and interior door panel. Notice how a combination of a larger edge radius and low specularity material of the interior trim panel makes it look like its made out of softer material than the door surfaces. The interior door surfaces, with tighter edge rolls stitched to the door panel, look like stamped and welded sheet metal. The trough where the interior trim panel and door surfaces meet acts as a shadow pool creating a very realistic delineation between the surfaces. Overall, the door has a realistic appearance despite the lack of details. Its realism is further accented when it is rendered with the rest of the car.

Continuing on with modeling our car's interior, we will now build the boot well. The boot well is a storage area that is divided by a widthwise partition into a large storage area for the soft top, and the smaller area, open to the cabin, that is used for seat reclinement and small article storage. Because of the small proportions of our sports car, this area is very small indeed. The partition wall, which is not padded, is used as a mount for the rear stereo speakers.

37. Create a new layer, "Boot Well Curves," and make it active. Make the "Rear Quarter Panel" layer visible. All other layers should be hidden. Using Derivative Surfaces, derive an edge curve of the boot well. As before you can either prepick the segments and use the **Selected Segments** option, or use **Boundary Of Surface Object** and then delete the extra segments. I recommend the latter as it is much easier and faster to delete the segments than to prepick them. Note that we only need a symmetrical half of the curve as we will Mirror & Stitch the boot well surface. Also note that segments of edge roll faces are not used, as shown in Figure 13.45.

38. Working from the top view, create a projected duplicate using the 2D Projection tool with **Orthographic Projection** option, and **Status Of Objects** set to **Keep**. Move the projected curve –1″ along the Z-axis. Paral-

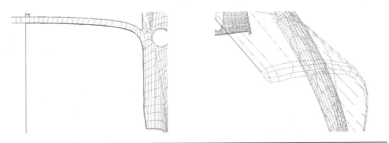

FIGURE "*Boot Well Curves.*"
13.45

lel the offset inside the projected curve by 1.25″ using the Parallel Objects tool. Paralleling this curve will cause its first (or last) point, depending on the direction, to shift of the axis. Adjust its position so that its X-axis position is 0. Move the top curve down along the Z-axis by 1/8″ (Figure 13.46).

39. Create a 7-point polyline as shown, following the shown offset distances between points.

    By now it is apparent that we will use the Skin tool to model the boot well. The first two curves that we created are *source* shapes and now we are building the *paths* for the skin assembly. Copies of the path polyline will be placed on the skin assembly. Prior to skinning the network, we will convert the polylines into 3rd-degree B-Spline C-Curves. The Distance between the points dictates how much curvature the curve will incur in that area. Without a doubt, Skin is one of the most powerful and flexible tools that we have at our disposal (Figure 13.47).

40. Make three copies of the *path* polylines and place them as shown. Verify that the first and last points of the *paths* are point snapped to points on the *source* curves (Figure 13.48).

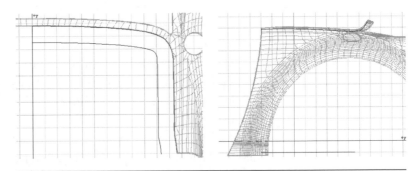

FIGURE *Paralleling the curve.*
13.46

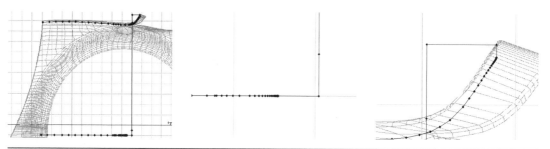

FIGURE *Modeling the boot well.*
13.47

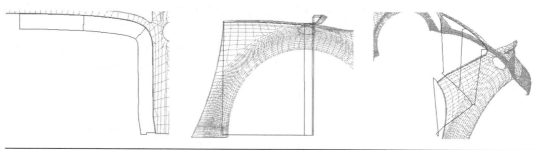

FIGURE *3 copies of* path *polylines.*
13.48

41. Convert the path polylines into 30-point 3rd-degree C-Curves. Using the Skin tool, create the wall of the boot well. Place the surface into the "Boot" layer (Figure 13.49).

42. We need to fill in the gap between the top rim of the boot and the rear quarter panel surface. This is easily accomplished by moving a COPY of the top source curve 1/8″ up along the Z-axis and then creating a C-Mesh ruled surface using the two curves. This is a weather rubber seal so it is a separate object in layer "Boot Weather Seal" (Figure 13.50).

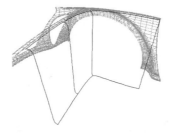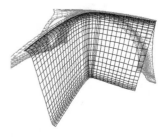

FIGURE *Well of boot.*
13.49

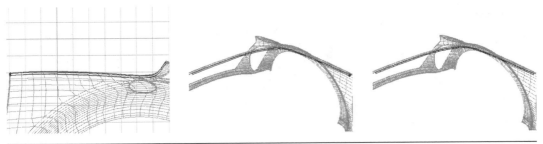

FIGURE *"Boot Weather Seal" layer.*
13.50

43. Create the floor of the boot using following steps;

— Temporarily Ghost the boot surface.
— Copy/Paste a copy of the bottom source curve into the "Boot" layer.
— Draw two locator lines. The first runs along the Y-axis and is snapped to the first point of the curve. The second runs along the X-axis and is snapped to the last point.
— Draw a 3-point Vector Line with its first point snapped to the first point on the curve, the second snapped to intersection of the locators, and the third point snapped to the last point on the curve.
— Reverse direction, if necessary, and connect the curve and the line together into a closed surface using Connect Lines (v 3) or the Edit Line tool (v 2.9.5). Delete the extra points at the corners (Figure 13.51).

44. Manually mesh the boot floor using Vector Line with Insert Segment modifier (v2.9.5) or Insert Segment (v. 3) tools with Point, Segment, and Orthogonal Direction snap options. First insert the X-axis rows, then the Y-axis rows. The result is that the floor has IDENTICAL mesh density as the boot wall and matches it point for point. This step is optional, it is

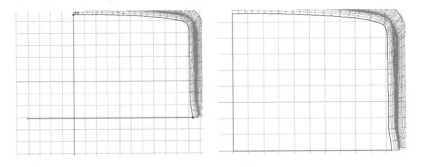

FIGURE *Connect curve and line.*
13.51

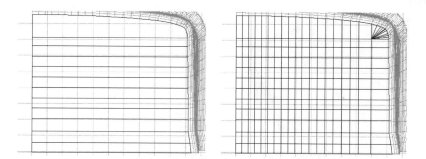

FIGURE *Meshing the boot floor.*
13.52

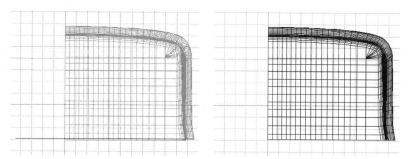

FIGURE *Stitch boot floor and wall surfaces.*
13.53

recommended that if you are planning to export the model to an external animation application, the manual meshing needs to be done. Not doing it will leave the decomposition of this face to either form•Z or to your animation application, which does not guarantee clean rendering (Figure 13.52).

45. Stitch the boot floor and boot wall surfaces. From the top view, create a straight line parallel to the X-axis with its rightmost point snapped to the rightmost point of the boot surface. Trim the boot surface with the line (Figure 13.53).

46. Finish the boot surface by mirroring and stitching the boot surface and boot weather seals. Remember, don't stitch the weather seal with either the boot or the rear quarter panel. Keep it a s separate object. Apply a dark, low-specularity material to it. You may have noticed a gap between the door seam and the edges of the boot. This gap, which we model later, is metal (Figure 13.54).

Next we will build the partition wall. Geometrically, the partition wall is relatively simple. When viewed from the top view, it is flat with the top lip having

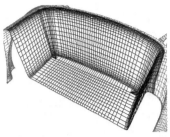

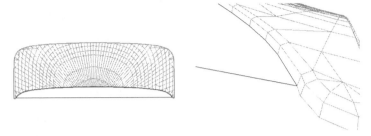

FIGURE 13.54 *Finishing the boot surface.*

FIGURE 13.55 *Top curve of the partition.*

the same curvature as the boot cover surface. It is not blended into the boot well surface. The procedure we will use to build the partition wall is simple. First we will derive a curve based from the boot cover. Then we will create a paralleled duplicate and join the two curves together. This yields a cross-section that has the same curvature as the boot cover. Create the cross-section in the "Boot Partition Cross-Sections" layer, and place the completed partition into the "Boot Partition" layer. The reason for keeping the boot and partition as separate objects is ease of texture mapping, and ease of adding additional details.

47. Using the Derivative Surfaces tool, derive a top curve of the partition from the boot cover surface. Note that we only need a symmetrical half, and we only need the segments shown in Figure 13.55.

    Close the derived curve using Edit Line with the **Close Line: Connect** option.

48. Create a planar rectangle whose width is equal to the width of the shape derived above, and height that extends below the boot well surface. The top corner points of the rectangle are snapped to the bottom corners of the shape. For precision, use the Point Snap option (Figure 13.56).

49. We need a planar closed surface that is conformal to the sides of the boot well and has its two top corners snapped to the corners of the upper surface. Derive a Line Of Intersection between the rectangle and the boot well surface. In form•Z 3.0, Line Of Intersection is a separate tool; in form•Z 2.9.5, it is an option found in the Trim & Stitch tool. Set **Status Of Objects** to **Keep**. After deriving the line of intersection, delete the rectangle. Finish the face using Vector Line with the Point Snap option and Edit Line with **Connect Lines/ Close Line Sequence**. After connecting the two lines together, delete the extra points at join locations (Figure 13.57).

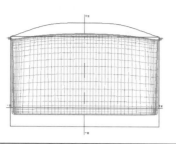

FIGURE *Planar rectangle.*
13.56

FIGURE *Planar closed surface.*
13.57

50. Extrude **Perpendicular To Surface** the lower planar surface 1/8″ with extrusion going in -Y direction, (away from the rear of the car). Bevel the front face of the extruded solid using the Round tool with the **Bevel** option, and **Radius:** 1/16″. After beveling, delete the rear face of the solid, converting it into a meshed surface (Figure 13.58).

51. Stitch the upper and lower surfaces together to complete the partition wall. Finish the partition by connecting points to prevent problematic rendering (Figure 13.59).

Next we will create the interior body surfaces for the rear quarter panel with similar procedures as were used to create the interior door surfaces. This is a more complex case as we need to mate the new interior surfaces to the boot well. Create the following curve in the "Rear Interior Panel" layer. Place the completed surface into the "Rear Quarter Panel" layer and Stitch it with that surface.

52. Using the Derivative Surfaces tool, derive two curves based on the door seams of the rear quarter panel surface (Figure 13.60).

FIGURE *Meshed surface.*
13.58

FIGURE *Completed partition wall.*
13.59

FIGURE *Two curves.*
13.60

53. Reverse direction of one of the curves and create a ruled surface using C-Mesh and the two curves as cross-sections. Remember that a ruled surface has no smoothing in either **Length** or **Depth** direction (Figure 13.61).

54. Create a vertical trim line, the top point of which is point snapped to a shown point on the surface.

    Trim the surface with the line (Figure 13.62).

The surface that we have just created is part of the rear-end sheet metal. In real life it would be either seamlessly welded to the exterior surface metal or stamped together with it. Because it must render as part of the rear end, it must have edge rolls that are matched to the existing edge rolls of the rear-end surface. Now this might seem like a complex problem, but it is actually simple to do. Remember that in "Flow" modeling much of the information to accomplish the task is present; the trick is to sift through your geometry and find the information.

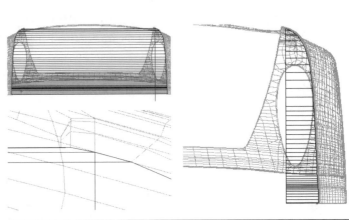

FIGURE *Ruled surface.*
13.61

FIGURE *Vertical trim line.*
13.62

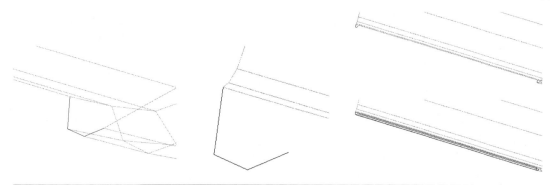

We need to create two edge rolls, bottom and the side. We will do the bottom first, which will make creating the side edge roll easier. With the edge rolls complete we can then create additional surfaces to mate the metal surfaces to the boot well.

55. Create a 4-point polyline using Vector Line and Point Snap option snapping to the points on the bottom right corner of the rear panel. (a) From the right side view, create a projected duplicate of that line using the 2D Projection tool with **Orthographic Projection**, and **Status Of Objects** set to **Keep**. Move the projected line so that its first point is point-snapped to the bottom left corner point of the surface (b) Create a ruled surface using C-Mesh and Stitch it and the surface together (Figure 13.63).

To precisely create a side edge roll, we have to create locators.

56. Derive the #1 cross-section using the Derivative Surfaces tool (Figure 13.64).

57. Create locators for a 1/16″ radius edge roll. The points of the topmost locator are snapped to points of the existing edge roll on the rear quarter

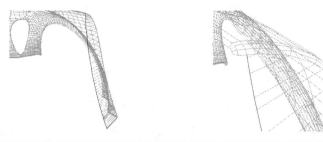

FIGURE *#1 cross-section.*
13.64

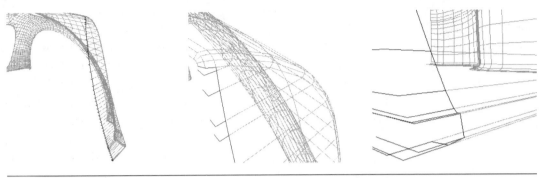

FIGURE *Completing the edge surface.*
13.65

panel surface. Because the open edge of the completed edge roll will itself serve as the base edge for the creation of a mating surface to the boot well, we only want the edge roll to curve inward. To do that, do not rotate the locators on the bottom (Figure 13.65).

58. Create the #2 and #3 cross-sections using Vector Line with Point Snap. The points of the #2 and #3 cross-sections are point-snapped to points on the locators (Figure 13.66).

59. Using C-Mesh, create 2nd-degree B-Spline edge roll surfaces with a total of two Depth segments (Figure 13.67).

Stitch the edge roll with the interior surface (Figure 13.67).

60. Mirror with Cont-Copy (C-Copy in form•Z 2.9.5) the resulting surface. Transfer the two surfaces to the "Rear Quarter Panel" layer and Stitch the three surfaces to form a complete rear end. Remember to keep backups of the unstitched surfaces (Figure 13.68).

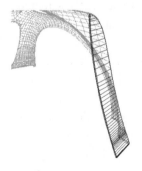

FIGURE
13.66

FIGURE
13.67

FIGURE *Complete rear end.*
13.68

#2 and #3 cross-sections.

Logic Errors in 3D Modeling

Recall that 3D modeling for visual effects and conceptual design is an iterative process. Quite often we need to adjust previously created geometry to better fit the design and "flow" with other surfaces in the model. Because realistic models constructed for effects may contains hundreds of exportable objects arranged in dozens of layers, it is not always possible to create a model that is free of "logic errors" on the first pass. A *logic error* is a term from the movie industry, used by editors and directors. It refers to a condition of temporal inconsistency or lack of connection to reality. An example of a logic error is a scene where a red car, driven by the bad guy, explodes, but the explosion footage shows a yellow car exploding. In 3D modeling, logic errors can be caused by solid (vs. liquid) objects intersecting with each other, or objects that should fit intersect each other. Of course, this is only a problem if the logic error is actually seen. When modeling under the pressure of a deadline, exercise best judgment as to which problems to correct and which ones make no difference. With conceptual design, as with our car, a logic error can exist when objects improperly fit together, or are modeled in away that is unrealistic. The following is a short list of possible logic errors in 3D modeling:

- **Intersecting geometry.** This is the most common logic error. Usually it is a result of careless modeling.
- **Lack of visible seams or subtle gaps between separate but adjacent objects.** This is why we build rolled edges for our surfaces. Without the rolled edges, the seams between surfaces would either not be visible or would be only visible as hairlines, resulting in a synthetic-looking image.
- **Improper fit of geometry.** Such a case exists where gaps are too large or seams of adjacent surfaces are not parallel to each other in all three axes.
- **Unrealistic or illogical range of movement or rotation of an object within an assembly.** An example of this is a car door that when open intersects with other geometry.
- **Unrealistic relative scales between objects.** In visual effects modeling it is the relative scale of objects that denotes their size. Quite often for an object to appear to be correctly scaled, multiple objects must have correct proportions to each other. In the case of our car, the relative wheel diameter cannot be too small as it would make the car seem big. The scale of the seats also cannot be too small as it would increase the apparent size of the car, as seats vary little in size from car to car.
- **Inadequate perceived mass of an object.** An example would be a model of an ancient Greek temple with very thin columns that look like they wouldn't be able to support the building in real life.

Fixing an Existing Geometric Logic Error

Our floor pan surface contains a geometric logic error. Its sills are too narrow, resulting in doors and rear-end surfaces to overhang the floor pan sills. This is unrealistic as cars are not built like that. We need to adjust the width of the sills. We will do this easily and quickly by simply moving the points and segments of the floor pan surface. Prior to performing the steps, halve the surface by trimming it with a straight line. Afterward, Mirror & Stitch the halves to reconstruct the surface.

61. Select the highlighted faces, and set Grid Snap Module to 1/16″. Working from the front view, move the selected faces along the X-axis until the top of the sill is flush with the vertical edge of the interior rear-end surface that we just modeled. Afterwards, Mirror & Stitch to reconstruct the floor pan surface. After stitching the halves, delete the segments and points that lie on the mirror axis. Remember that segments are deleted first, topologically, then points (Figure 13.69).

Next we will construct a surface that will partially cover the gap between the boot and the floor pan. Although the floor pan surface is constructed correctly, it has polygons in it that will never be seen and are thus best deleted. This deletion will also create an open edge to which this surface needs to be attached. The transition itself will be created using the Skin tool and the surface-to-surface blending technique that we learned in Chapter 3.4 so often when building the body surfaces. Place the skin assembly in the "Floor/Boot Transition Curves" layer.

62. Select the shown highlighted faces. Detach them from the floor pan surface using the Separate tool, and delete them. Optionally, you may place the detached faces in a backup layer (Figure 13.70).

63. Using the Derivative Surfaces tool with **Selected Segments** option, derive *source* curves for the skin assembly as shown. Using Insert Point (v.3)

FIGURE *Reconstructing the surface.*
13.69

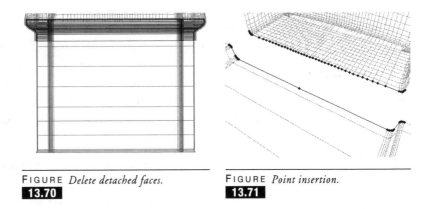

FIGURE *Delete detached faces.*
13.70

FIGURE *Point insertion.*
13.71

or Vector Line with Insert Segment modifier (v.2.9.5), insert a single point in the long segment of the curve derived from the floor pan. Use either tool with the Midpoint Snap option for precise point insertion (Figure 13.71).

64. Create five *path* polylines as shown, each with four points. The blend surface that we will create will have C1(tangent) continuity to the boot and floor pan surfaces; hence, the placement of the intermediate points on the *path* polylines. Take care to snap the first and last points of the *path* polylines to similar points on the *source* curves (Figure 13.72).

65. Convert the *path* polylines into 16-point 3rd-degree B-Spline C-Curves. Verify that all paths have similar directions. Verify that both sources have similar directions. Verify first and last point-snapping of *path* curves to *source* curves. Create the transition surface using the Skin tool. Be sure to set **Status Of Objects** to **Keep**. Stitch the transition surface with the floor pan, but do not stitch it with the boot (Figure 13.73).

Now is a good time to check your progress versus my rendering of the partially completed interior. Notice how the body sheet metal surfaces and interior

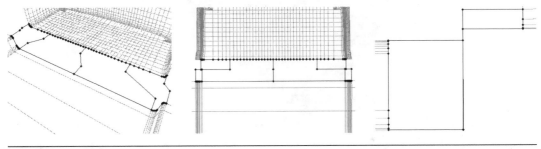

FIGURE Path *polylines.*
13.72

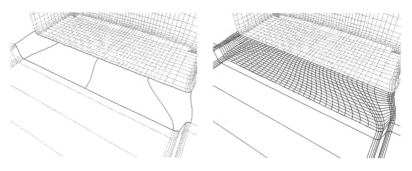

FIGURE *Converting* path *polylines.*
13.73

surface fit together yet look like they are not part of the same surface, and have a "man-made" appearance. The small troughs and gaps between the interior and exterior surfaces create realistic shadowed areas. In general, always strive for this kind of look when modeling for photorealistic output (Figure 13.74).

We now have enough geometric information to begin building the center console. The center console serves a number of purposes. In rear-wheel drive cars, the drive shaft is positioned within the recess of the chassis that the center console covers. In our car, which wheels propel the car is a moot point, as we are creating it for animation, not for manufacture. The primary purpose of the center console is to provide a base of attachment and construction of center storage compartments, and the stick shift. From a design standpoint, the center console provides a "cockpit" feeling in the cabin. The sketch of the interior shows a graceful, gentle arc of the center console sloping away from the aft por-

FIGURE *Photorealistic output.*
13.74

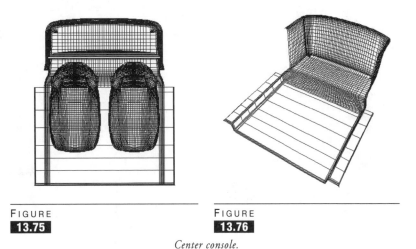

Center console.

tion of the cabin, leveling off around the stickshift area, and finally blending into the dash.

In the next phase of this exercise we will build the center console (Figure 13.75 and Figure 13.76).

66. We need a temporary single surface of the floor pan and boot well that we can trim and derive working shapes from. Create a temporary layer and Copy/Paste copies of the floor pan and boot well surfaces into this layer. Hide all other layers. Stitch the two surfaces together with **Status Of Objects** set to **Delete**.

67. We need a straight line placed along the X-axis that is positioned precisely on the vertical portion of the boot partition wall. We will use this line to trim the temporary surface we just created.

    The line is easily created by drawing a 2-point line using the Vector Line tool, wider than the surface when looking from the top view. Make "Boot Partion" a ghosted and snappable layer. With Midpoint Snap options active, move the line so that its midpoint is snapped to the midpoint of any one of the horizontal segments that are on the vertical portion of the partition (Figure 13.77).

68. Working from the top view, Trim the temporary working surface with the line. This temporary surface precisely terminates at the location of the boot partition wall. In the following steps we will use this surface to create shapes for the creation of the center console (Figure 13.78).

69. Set Grid Snap Module to 1/16″. Create 6-point polyline with Vector Line. Note that the first two segments have the X-axis position flush against the X-axis extremity of the seat bottom (Figure 13.79).

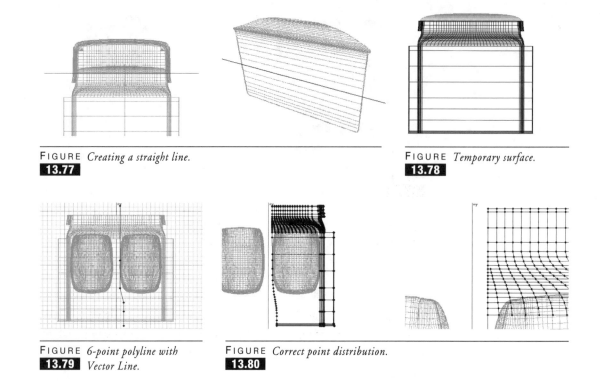

FIGURE **13.77** *Creating a straight line.*

FIGURE **13.78** *Temporary surface.*

FIGURE **13.79** *6-point polyline with Vector Line.*

FIGURE **13.80** *Correct point distribution.*

70. Convert the polyline into a 24-point-3rd degree B-Spline C-Curve. Connect Lines is a separate tool. Working from the top view, Trim the surface with the curve. Clean up the trim edge. Because the purpose of this surface is to provide a clean edge curve, we do not need to reconnect the points. Figure 13.80 shows the desired point distribution of the edge after cleanup.

71. Using the Derivative Surfaces tool with the **Selected Segments** option, derive an edge curve from the trim edge. Working from the top view, Mirror duplicate the curve. After deriving the edge curve you may delete the temporary surface or place it in a hidden backup layer. Rename this temporary layer "Center Console Curves" (Figure 13.81).

NOTE

Using copies of existing surfaces to create temporary "scratch" objects is in a general a good technique as it allows precise creation of derivative shapes.

We will model the basic center console surface using the Skin tool. In the previous step we created two source curves that we will use. To achieve even more control over the curvature of the surface we will use three *source* curves.

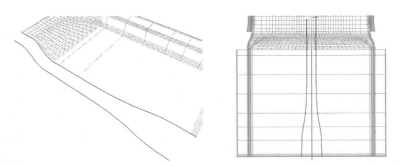

FIGURE *"Center Console Curves."*
13.81

The third *source* curve, running along the Y-axis, will act as top curvature control. Without the third curve on top of the skin assembly, the depth curvature of the skinned surface would be controlled primarily by the bottom source curves.

Before we can create the top source curve, we need to precisely localize the start and endpoints of the curve. To do this we will create two locator lines, the top points of which will be our snap points for the first and last points of the top *source* curve.

72. First create two width locators, with points on the first one snapped to the first points of the bottom *source* curves, and the second width locator points snapped to the last points of bottom *source* curves. Create the first vertical locator line that is 6–11/16″ long and move it such that its bottom point is placed on midpoint of the first width locator. Create the second vertical locator line with the bottom point snapped to the midpoint of the second width locator and the top point snapped to midpoint of the segment on the boot partition wall. Use Figure 13.82 as guide.

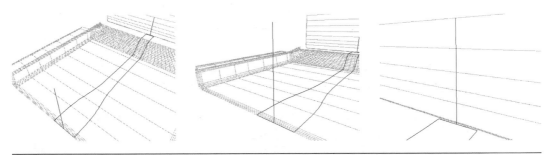

FIGURE *Width locators.*
13.82

73. Make the underlay visible and create a 9-point polyline that is loosely based on the side sketch of the center console. Snap the first and last points of the polyline to the top points of the vertical locator lines. Convert the polyline into a Bezier C-Curve with points equal to that of the bottom *source* curves. Edit the C-Curve to make its curvature follow as closely as possible the curvature in Figure 13.83.

74. Working from the front view, create a symmetrical 9-point polyline, with its topmost center point-snapped to the first point of the top *source* curve and its two bottom points snapped to the first points of the bottom *source* curves (Figure 13.84).

75. Create nine duplicates, sequentially placing them on *source* curves. First a copy of the *path* polyline is moved and snapped to the point on the top *source* curve. Movement is done with point snapping with the top center point being the start of the move. Then the bottom two segments are moved with their bottom points snapped to the points on the bottom *source* curves. The two bottom segments of *path* polylines, one on each side, have equal lengths across all *path* polylines. The topmost four segments are nonuniformly scaled as shown in Figure 13.85.

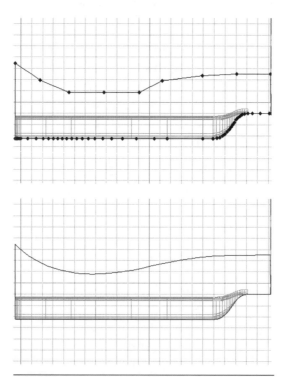

FIGURE *C-curves.*
13.83

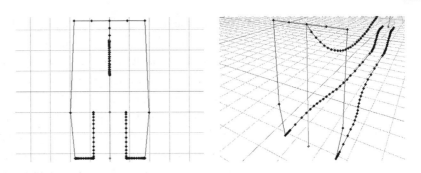

FIGURE *Symmetrical 9-point polyline.*
13.84

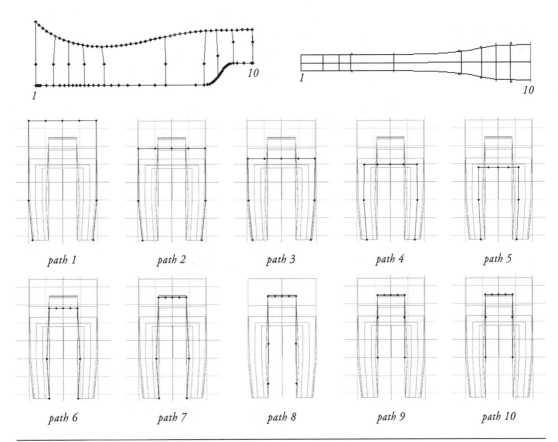

FIGURE *Duplicates.*
13.85

76. Convert the *path* polylines into 33-point 3rd-degree B-Spline C-Curves. C-Curve usually results in the centermost intermediate point to not be snapped to the *source* curve. The error is very small, but may result in an error message generated by the Skin tool. We need to manually zoom in and resnap the centerpoints of the *path* curves to the points on the *source* curve. The points in question all lie on the axis of symmetry. Sometimes even endpoints may be placed out of tolerance by the C-Curve, so they may need to be resnapped. Using the Skin tool on the center console assembly, generate the center console surface and place it in the "Center Console" layer.

Use following Skin tool options (Figure 13.86).

Skinning Along Paths;
Of Sources: 3, # Of Paths: 10, Boundary Based
Placement Type; By Current Position
Point Pairing; Insert New Points As Needed
Status Of Objects; Keep

If you ever receive an error message from the Skin tool, but your skin assembly looks correct, make sure that all path *curve points that are supposed to be snapped to* source *curve points are in fact snapped. In form•Z 3.0, the tolerances of the skin are relaxed, but use caution as the surface that is created may not be as precise as we need it to be. Always make sure that all points are properly snapped before using skin assembly.*

It is important, when converting symmetrical path *polylines with on-axis* source *curves present, that the point count of the C-Curve is an odd number. Having an odd number of points places a point directly on the axis when the C-Curve is derived.*

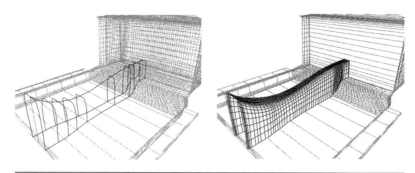

FIGURE *"Center Console" layer.*
13.86

Modeling the Dashboard

Geometrically, the dashboard is the most complex piece of geometry of the car interior. It is conformal to the hood line and to the front panels. Then it transitions into a curved area for the air bag, glove compartment, and instrument cluster bulge. Finally, there is a transition to the center console. Depending on the design, other complex surfaces may be grafted onto the dash. Air bag covers, air vents, steering column, and glove compartment hatch are common surfaces that are part of the dash.

77. Create a new layer, "Dash Curves," and make it active. Ghost "Hood" and "Front Left Quarter Panel" layers, hide other layers. Use the Derivative Surface tool with **Selected Segments** options to derive edge curves from selected segments as shown. Note the hood curve is half of the symmetrical curve (Figure 13.87).

78. Set Grid Snap Module to 1/16″. Create a rough 5-point polyline as shown. Select the LAST point and snap it to the last point of the smaller edge curve. From the front view, flatten the polyline by orthographically projecting it using the 2D Projection tool. Move the polyline with the Point Snap option only, such that its last point is snapped to the last point of the smaller edge curve. Verify that the first point is on the axis of symmetry. The X-axis position of the first point should be 0′–0″ (Figure 13.88).

79. Convert the polyline into a **Bezier** C-Curve with the same point count as the edge curve derived from the hood. In this case, the point count is 18 (Figure 13.89).

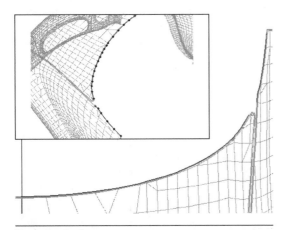

FIGURE   *Dash curves.*
13.87

FIGURE   *Point positions.*
13.88

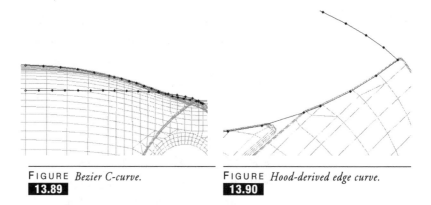

FIGURE *Bezier C-curve.*
13.89

FIGURE *Hood-derived edge curve.*
13.90

80. With the Point Snap option only move the first point of the small edge curve so that it's snapped to the last point on the hood-derived edge curve (Figure 13.90).

81. Create four polylines as shown. Notice the points on the *source* curves where the first and last *path* polyline points are snapped (Figure 13.91).

82. Insert five points into the small derived edge curve, one at each segment midpoint. Convert the polylines into **Bezier path** C-Curves, with the same point count as the small edge curve, which is also a *path* curve. In this case, the point count is 11. Create a new layer, "Dash." Using the Skin tool, create an initial dash top surface, and place it into this layer. Set **Status Of Objects** to **Keep**. Figure 13.92 shows the dash top skin assembly and the skinned dash top surface with its mirrored duplicate.

83. Create a new layer, "Dash front curves." Set Grid Snap Module to 1/16". Create a 6-point polyline in this layer with its first point snapped to the

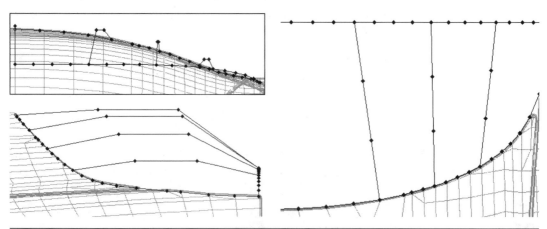

FIGURE *Four polylines.*
13.91

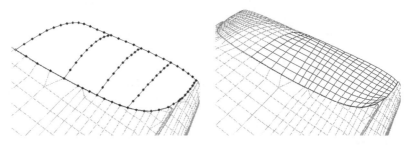

FIGURE *Dash top skin assembly.*
13.92

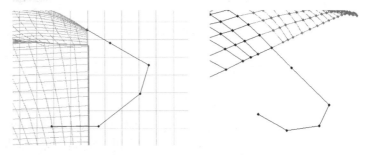

FIGURE *Dash front curves.*
13.93

point on the dash top surface that lies on the axis of symmetry (Figure 13.93).

What we wish to do is to create duplicates of this polyline such that the first two segments are snapped to the points to the edge of the dash top surface, and the last segments of each copy have the same height. To do this we will first create a locator curve, the points of which will provide us with snapping points later on.

84. Using the Derivative Surfaces tool with **Selected Segments** options, derive an edge curve from the dash top surface. This curve will serve as the #1 locator curve. We will not be using the Skin tool in this case. Since our #2 locator curve is a straight line we are unable to skin the surface (Figure 13.94).

85. From the top view orthographically project the locator curve using the 2D Projection tool, with **Orthographic Projection** option, and **Status Of Objects** set to **Keep**. This creates the #2 locator line. Place the #2 locator line by moving it with Point Snap option so its on-axis endpoint is snapped to the last point on the polyline (Figure 13.95).

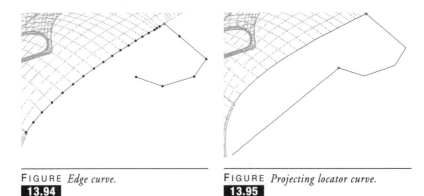

FIGURE *Edge curve.*
13.94

FIGURE *Projecting locator curve.*
13.95

86. With the Point Snap option only, place copies of the polylines on the locator lines such that the first point of the polylines is snapped to a point on the #1 locator line. With the Point Snap option, move the last segment of each polyline so that its last point is snapped to a point on the #2 locator line.

   With only the Ortogonal Direction snap active, move the #2 point of each polyline vertically along the Z-axis so that the first segment of each polyline has the same directional vector as the last segment of the dash to surface (Figure 13.96).

87. Convert the polylines into 24-point Plain Curve 3rd-degree B-Spline C-Curves.

   Using the C-Mesh tool, create the dash front surface. Set Length to At Control Points, and Depth to At Control Lines. Turn off all smoothing.

   Set Status Of Objects to Keep.

   Mirror & Stitch the surface. Unlike the majority of other surfaces, the dash is not a symmetrical object (Figure 13.97).

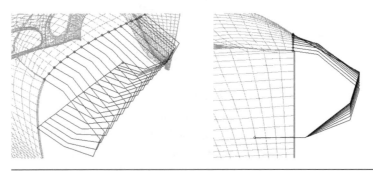

FIGURE *Moving #2 points.*
13.96

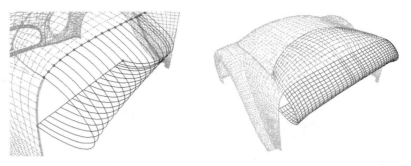

FIGURE *Mirroring and stitching the surface.*
13.97

Right now our dashboard is perfectly flush against the hood and the front panels. This is not realistic. In a real car, the dash is slightly inset with a large gap between it and the hood. This gap is occupied by the windshield trim.

88. Working from the right side view, using the Deform tool with **Radial Bend** setting and **Base Reference Plane:** ZX, bend the dash top surface by 1 degree, using the left bottom corner as a deformation handle. Select both dash surfaces and move them down vertically along the Z-axis by 1/8″. Stitch the two dash surfaces together to form the basic dashboard (Figure 13.98).

Next we will model solid trim dyes for trimming holes in our dash for modeling of the instrument cluster bulge and the passenger-side airbag cover.

89. Create a new layer, "Dash Trim Dyes." Make "Dash," "Left Door," and "Seat Back" layers ghosted, hide all others. Working from the front view, create a 64-point circle—any size will do. Select the lower half of points and nonuniformly scale them using the center of the circle as a base of scale. Nonuniform Scale the whole circle as shown in Figure 13.99. Note that the shape is centered on the driver-side seat.

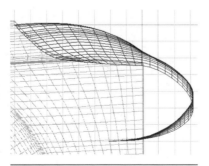

FIGURE *Basic dashboard.*
13.98

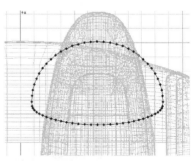

FIGURE *Nonuniform Scale.*
13.99

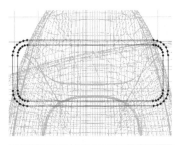

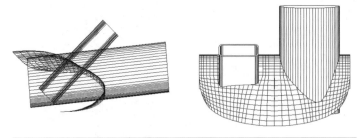

FIGURE *Two rectangles.*
13.100

FIGURE *Solid trim shapes.*
13.101

90. Create two rectangles, and round their corners using Edit Line Fit Fillet. Subtract the small rectangle from the large using Boolean Difference. Note that the resulting shape is centered on the passenger side seat (Figure 13.100).

91. Extrude the two shapes into solid trim shapes. Rotate and place them as shown (Figure 13.101).

92. Trim the dashboard surface with the trim dyes using Trim/Split set to **Trim/Split: First Object**. Be sure to retain backups of the dash and trim solids prior to this operation. The trim results in the formation of two surfaces, the large dashboard and a smaller passenger-side air bag cover. Clean up the trim edges using Figure 13.102 as a guide. The instrument cluster bulge trim edge is one of the more complex trim edges to clean up because of its complex curvature.

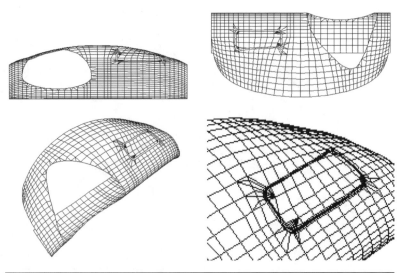

FIGURE *Trimming dashboard surfaces.*
13.102

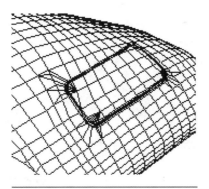

FIGURE *Creating rolled edge.*
13.103

93. Using procedures and techniques learned earlier on the creation of rolled edges, create a rolled edge for the dash and air bag cover to fill the gap between the two (Figure 13.103).

94. Create a new layer, "Instrument Cluster Bulge Curve." Derive an edge curve for the instrument cluster using the Derivative Surfaces tool with **Boundary Of Surface Object** option. Copy/Paste a copy of the shape from Figure 13.99 into this layer. In this case, the destination point count is 67. Insert points into this shape to bring its point count to be the same as the derived edge curve. From the right side view, rotate the shape +5 degrees using its bottom as the base of rotation. From the right side view, bend the shape by +35 degrees, using the Deform tool set to **Radial Bend** and **Base Reference Plane: XY**. From the front view, Nonuniform Scale the shape as shown in Figure 13.104.

NOTE

The cross-sectional shape of the trim dye for the instrument cluster bulge and the resulting shape of the two curves we just constructed is a design decision for the curvature of the instrument cluster. I decided to make it soft. If you wish, you may alter the design to your liking.

 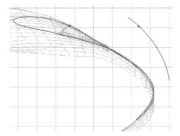 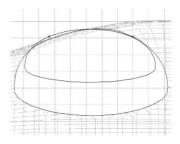

FIGURE *"Instrument Cluster Bulge Curve."*
13.104

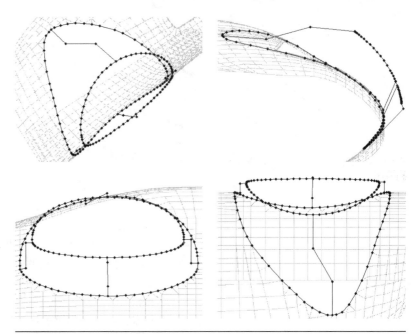

FIGURE *Creating* path *polylines.*
13.105

95. Create *path* polylines as shown, for the instrument cluster bulge (Figure 13.105).

96. Convert the polylines into 18-point 3rd-degree B-Spline *path* C-Curves. Create the instrument cluster bulge surface using the Skin tool. Stitch the instrument bulge surface with the dashboard. Be sure to retain the skin assembly (Figure 13.106).

97. Construct a Skin assembly for the instrument well. Copy/Paste the outer source curve from the bulge Skin assembly into a new layer. Working from the front view, orthographically project it using the 2D Projection

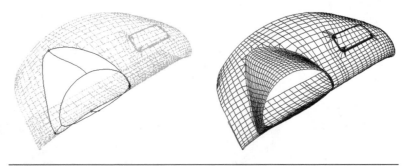

FIGURE *Converting polylines.*
13.106

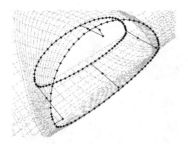
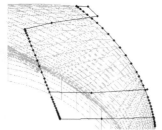
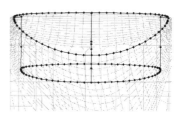

FIGURE *Scaling and creating* path *polylines.*
13.107

tool. Nonuniformly scale the #2 source shape and place it as shown. A copy of this planar surface will be the instrument panel. We will keep it as a separate object for ease of texture mapping. Create four *path* polylines, with the top polyline having five points instead of the usual four (Figure 13.107).

98. Convert the polylines into 18-point 2nd-Degree B-Spline path C-Curves. Using the Skin tool, create the inner surface and Stitch with the dashboard. Copy/Paste a copy of the inner source curve into its own layer, "Instrument Panel" (Figure 13.108).

99. Manually mesh the instrument panel surface using Insert Segment (v3.0) or Vector Line with Insert Segment modifier (v2.9.5). Use the Point Snap option for precision. For texture map you may paint you own color and luminosity map or use maps provided on the CD.

Instrument Panel.TGA
Instrument Panel Luma.TGA

The maps are applied with Flat mapping. The luminosity map may also be used as a bump map (Figure 13.109).

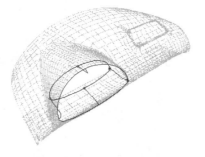
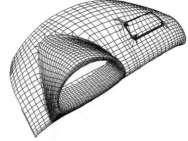

FIGURE *Converting polylines.*
13.108

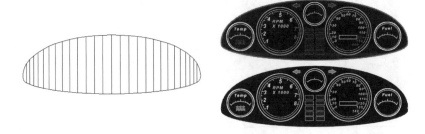

FIGURE *Instrument panel surface.*
13.109

The next interior surface that we will model together is the transition from the center console to the dash. This surface also serves as a panel where accessories like the radio and AC/heating controls are located and we will call this surface "Accessories Panel." Create all curves and lines in the "Accessories Panel Curves" layer. The completed surface will be stitched with the center panel surface.

100. Set Grid Snap Module to 1/16″ and draw a straight vertical vector line. Trim the center console surface with this line (Figure 13.110).

101. With Grid Snap Module set to 1/16″, draw two rectangles, and Join them together into a single object. Derive Line Of Intersection between it and the dash surface (Figure 13.111).

   In the next step we will use the last points of the two Lines Of Intersection as locators.

102. Using Derivative Surfaces set to Selected Segments, derive a vertical edge curve from the front of the center console. Rotate a copy of it 90 degrees, place and nonuniformly scale it as shown. Note that the first and last points of the copy are snapped to the last points of the Lines Of Intersection (Figure 13.112).

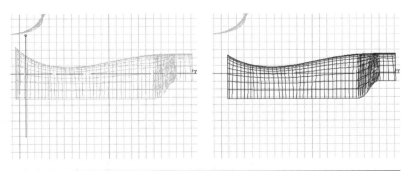

FIGURE *Trimming center console surface.*
13.110

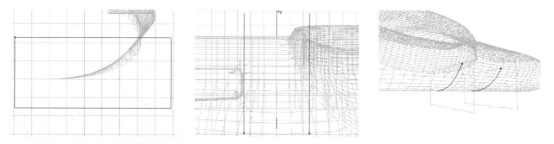

FIGURE *Deriving Line of Intersection.*
13.111

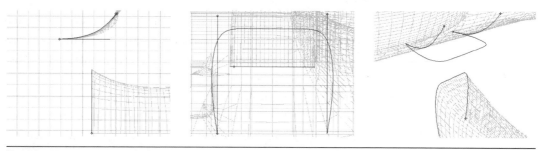

FIGURE *Deriving a vertical edge.*
13.112

103. Move the rotated copy up 2″ along the Z-axis and Extrude it into a temporary surface down the Z-axis by 5″. The extrusion will have generated a *surface solid*, so it needs to be converted into a surface using the Topological Attributes tool. Derive a Line Of Intersection between this surface and the dashboard. Clean up the resulting curve of intersection such that its point count is the same as the derived edge curve from the center console and its point distribution is similar (Figure 13.113).

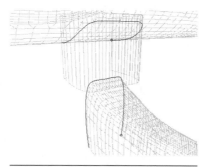

FIGURE *Insertion of surface and*
13.113 *dashboard.*

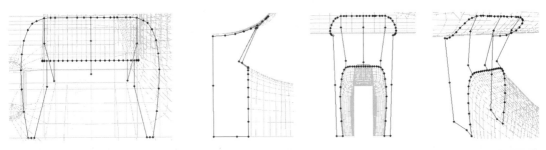

FIGURE *Source shapes and polylines.*
13.114

104. Move the curve of intersection down the Z-axis by 1/6″. The two derived curves will serve as *source* shapes. This will create a gap between the accessory panel surface and dashboard. Later we will fill this gap with an edge roll. Create five *path* polylines as shown, snapping their first and last points to the points on the *source* curves (Figure 13.114).

105. Convert the *path* polylines into 16-point 2nd-degree B-Spline *path* curves. Create the accessory panel using the Skin tool (Figure 13.115).

106. Move a copy of the top source curve 1/6″ up along the Z-axis. Nonuniformly scale a copy of that curve using Grid Snap Module set to 1/6″. Create the edge roll using C-Mesh with **Depth** settings of **# Of Segments: 4**, smoothing set to **B-Spline, Degree: 2, #Of Points: 128**. Stitch the edge roll surface with the accessory panel (Figure 13.116).

107. Working from the front view, create two 64-point planar closed shapes, with the inner closed shape a parallel duplicate of the outer. Boolean Difference the inner from the outer shape. Trim the accessory panel surface with the resulting shape and clean up the trim edges (Figure 13.117).

108. Using techniques and procedures learned, create three segment deep edge rolls for both surfaces. The smaller surface is the accessory panel

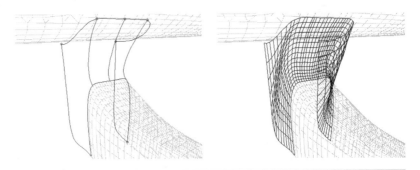

FIGURE *Accessory panel.*
13.115

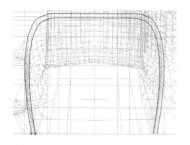
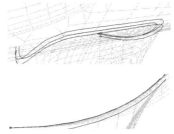
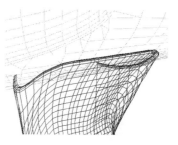

FIGURE *Edge roll surface and accessory panel.*
13.116

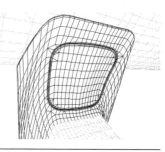

FIGURE *Trimming and clean-up of panel.*
13.117

FIGURE *Stiching the panels.*
13.118

surface and belongs in its own layer, "Accessory Panel." Transfer the larger surface into the "Center Console" layer and Stitch with the center console surface (Figure 13.118).

Modeling Footwells

The next surface that we will model is the footwell. Create the source curves in the "Footwell Curves" layer. The foot well surface will then be mirror duplicated and both footwells stitched together with the floor pan surface.

109. Derive two edge curves as shown in Figure 13.119 using the Derivative Surfaces tool set to Selected Segments from the dashboard and from

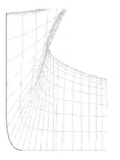

FIGURE *Edge curves.*
13.119

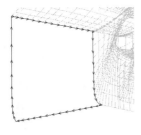 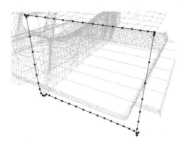 

FIGURE *Completing the shape.*
13.120

FIGURE *Clean up the shape.*
13.121

the center console surfaces. Note the last point of a curve derived from the dash is snapped to the first point on a curve derived from the center console.

110. I shall refer to the edge curve derived from the dash as the *horizontal* curve, and the curve derived from the center console as the *vertical* curve. Working from the right side view, create an orthographically projected duplicate of the vertical curve, using the 2D Projection tool. Place it so that its topmost point is snapped to the last point on the horizontal curve. Working from the top view, create an orthographically projected duplicate of the horizontal curve. Then flatten the duplicate from the front view. Place this curve so that its endpoints are snapped to the endpoints of the two vertical curves. Connect the four curves into a single closed shape using Connect Lines (v 3) Edit Line with **Connect Lines/Close Line Sequence** (2 9.5) options. If necessary, adjust the directions of the curves prior to performing the connection. Complete the shape by deleting a duplicate point at each corner (Figure 13.120).

111. Clean up the shape by deleting the points shown in red. Figure 13.121 shows the shapes before and after wireframes.

112. Set Grid Snap Module to 1/16. From the front view, move the points as shown in Figure 13.122. Use Fit Fillet (V3.0) or Edit Line Fit Fillet (v2.9.5) to fillet the selected points as shown in Figure 13.122. The first number is **# Of Edges**, the second is **Radius:**.

113. Set Grid Snap Module to 1/16″. Create three copies of the shape. Nonuniform scale the #4 shape as shown (Figure 13.123).

114. Create the footwell surface using the C-Mesh tool with the following **Depth** settings, no **Length** settings are used:

    Depth; # Of Segments: 12, Smooth: ON, Per Segment: OFF
    Controlled Mesh Smoothing Options;

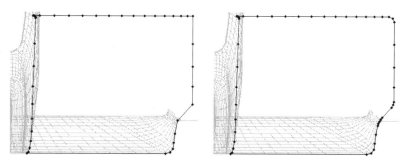

FIGURE *Moving the points.*
13.122

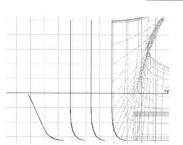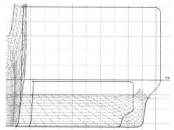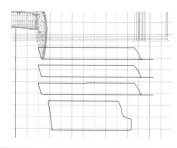

FIGURE *Three copies of shape.*
13.123

Depth: B-Spline, Degree: 3, # Of Points: 128
Type Of Object: All Closed (Solid)
Status OF Objects: Keep.

Transfer the footwell surface into the "Floor Pan" layer. Delete the rear capping face of the solid, the one that faces into the interior. Using the Point Snap option, insert segments to connect the points on the front capping face of the footwell (Figure 13.124).

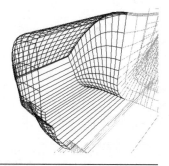

FIGURE *Footwell surface.*
13.124

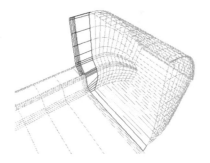
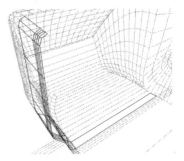

FIGURE *Completing footwell and floor pans.*
13.125

115. Complete the footwell and floor pan surface by filling the gap between the footwell and floor pan surfaces with Vector Line and Point & Segment Snap options. Mirror C-Copy the footwell and filler surface and Stitch them with the floor pan (Figure 13.125).

Figure 13.126 shows the completed floor pan surface stitched with footwells. The center console surface is shown as light gray for reference.

116. Using procedures and techniques learned, add the following details to our car interior (Figure 13.127):

- Steering wheel and steering column
- Air vents for the dash, two in the center and two on the sides
- Stickshift with leather boot placed inside a stickshift recess
- Center Console storage compartment hatch
- Glove Compartment hatch
- Buttons and switches
- Door arm rests
- Any other details which you desire

FIGURE *Completed floor pan.*
13.126

FIGURE *Adding details.*
13.127

Modeling the Chassis

At last we come to the home stretch for the completion of our car. We started with the outside body surfaces and worked our way in to construct the interior. At last we come to the chassis. In real cars, the chassis provides structural rigidity and mounts onto which body panels and drive train are mounted. Look at photographs and videos of real cars and notice that we hardly ever see any part of the chassis. It is usually obscured or poorly lit. When we render our car in its current state we can see through it as we have no chassis. When modeling automobiles for animation purposes, the chassis needs to only provide enough details that give the illusion that the complete chassis is there. The most visible part of the chassis is inside the wheel well and directly behind the wheel rim. In the case of our car, we should be able to clearly see a disk brake and caliper behind each wheel. There is no need to build struts, coil springs, or shock absorbers as they are not visible. In real-life production situations the actual amount of chassis components modeled is dictated by the needs of the project. If the script or storyboards call for a camera to go under the car, or the animation shows the workings of the suspension, engine, and other chassis components, then they need to be constructed. The good news is that the majority of mechanical components have simple geometric forms.

As we model the chassis geometry, place all completed chassis objects into the "Chassis" layer and source shapes into the "Chassis curves" layer.

117. When our car is rendered from the front, we can see through the grill screens. We need to place simple box primitives where radiators would be. Make "Radiator Grill" and "Oil Cooler Grill" ghosted layers. Create two solid boxes and place them as shown. Delete the rear-facing faces. If you wish you may apply a simple grid bump map to them, but for the most part the primary reason for these "radiators" is to prevent us from seeing inside the car (Figure 13.128).

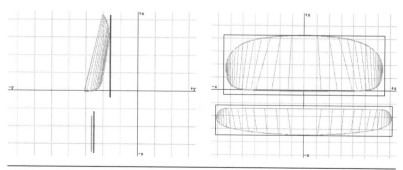

FIGURE *Radiator grill and oil cooler grill.*
13.128

FIGURE *Inserting segments.*
13.129

FIGURE *Rear bumper mud guard.*
13.130

118. Most performance cars with low ground clearance have a mud guard to prevent debris from entering the engine space and possibly damaging the radiator. Create the front bumper mud guard by deriving an open shape using the Derivative Surfaces tool with **Selected Segments** option. Close the shape with Edit Line **Close/Connect**. Insert segments as shown (Figure 13.129).

119. Repeat the process for the rear bumper mud guard. If our car was real, the middle area between the rear bumper exhaust ports would be occupied by the fuel tank (Figure 13.130).

120. Create cross-sections for the rear wheel well. Create the #1 cross-section using Derivative Surfaces. Create others by coping. Place, scale and rotate roughly as shown (Figure 13.131). #1 cross-section was derived from the edges of the side skirt, rear quarter panel, and rear bumper. The three edge curves were then connected together using Connect Lines (V 3) or Edit Line with **Connect Lines** (V 2.9.5) options, to form a single open surface. The composite edge curve was cleaned up to get rid of closely bunched points. The #2 cross-section is a copy of #1. #3 is a projected duplicate of #2. The #4 and #5 cross-sections are copies of #3 that

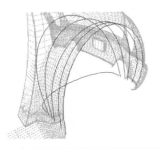

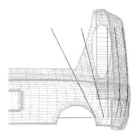

FIGURE *Rear wheel cross-sections.*
13.131

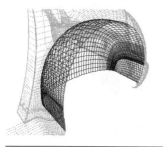
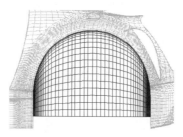
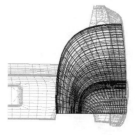

FIGURE *Lofting rear wheel well surface.*
13.132

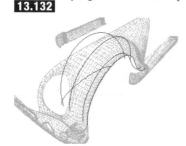
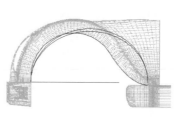
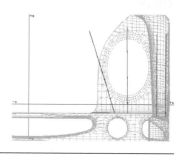

FIGURE *Front wheel well cross-sections.*
13.133

were individually sheared with the Deform tool. #6 is a rotated copy of #5 that was flattened with 2D Projection and nonuniformly scaled.

121. Loft the rear wheel well surface using C-Mesh (Figure 13.132). While the Length mesh density is a product of points on the #1 cross-section as Length settings are not used in the C-Mesh Options, the Depth mesh density is a design decision, subject to output requirements.

122. Construct the front wheel well cross-sections in the same manner. Notice that the last points of the #1 and #2 cross-sections have higher Z-axis position than the first points (Figure 13.133).

123. Loft the first front wheel well section using the C-Mesh tool (Figure 13.134).

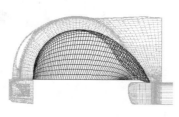
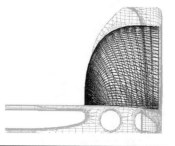

FIGURE *Lofting first front wheel well.*
13.134

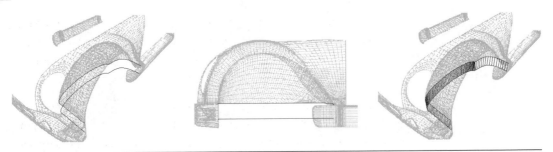

FIGURE *Stitching the extension.*
13.135

The front wheel wells need to be constructed as two surfaces that are stitched together, with the goal of achieving a planar bottom edge. The uneven positions of the last points have created an uneven bottom edge. We need to extend the current bottom edge. That is, we need to create an extension surface that is perfectly mated with the curving bottom edge of the wheel well at its top and has a planar bottom edge.

124. Working from the top view, create an orthographically projected copy of the last front wheel well cross-sections using the 2D Projection tool. Place the resulting planar curve as shown. Create a ruled C-Mesh extension surface using the two curves as cross-sections. Stitch the extension with the first front wheel well to complete it (Figure 13.135).

125. Using any tools that you deem necessary, create a filler surface between the front and rear wheel wells as shown. In this case, simply use Vector Line with the Point Snap option (Figure 13.136).

126. Mirror One-Copy (v3) or C-Copy (v2.9.5) the symmetrical objects. Figure 13.137 shows the completed chassis objects. For exportation pur-

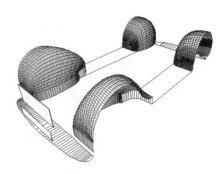

FIGURE *Filler surface.*
13.136

FIGURE *Completed chasis objects.*
13.137

poses, the simplest way is to export all these objects is as a single object. However, if intricate texture mapping is required, like the bump for the radiator, or an air vent transparency map for bumper mud guards is required, the chassis will have to be exported as multiple objects.

A surprisingly difficult object to model, are the front pillars of the windshield frame. In a convertible automobile, such as the one we are building, the windshield frame acts as a structural support. In real-life cars, the primary purpose of those pillars is to prevent the car from crushing its occupants in case of a rollover. Recall that in the Body Surfaces exercise, the last surface that we constructed, prior to starting on the interior, was a windshield surface. We will use this windshield surface as base for construction of the windshield frame.

127. Create a temporary layer and Copy/Paste a copy of the windshield surface. Select the shown faces and detach them from the windshield using the Separate tool, with the **Boundary Of Selected Faces** option. The single boundary row of detached faces that we separated from the general shape of the frame. As the windshield and frame are symmetrical, we will perform all work on a symmetrical half (Figure 13.138).

128. We need to round the two corners of the frame. Recall the procedure for rounding sharp corners on a meshed surface.

- Separate the faces sharing the corner.
- Topologically delete the inner segments to form a single closed surface.
- Fit Fillet or Bevel the corner points using the Edit Line tool.
- Stitch the filleted face with the main surface.
- Reconnect points as necessary.

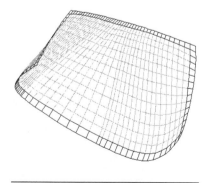

FIGURE *Symmetrical half.*
13.138

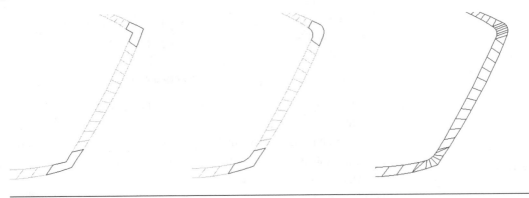

FIGURE *Rounding points.*
13.139

Round the two corner points on the top part of the frame and only the inner point on the bottom. Use the following Fit Fillet/Bevel (V 3) or Edit Line (V 2.9.5) options; Fit Fillet; # Of Edges: 5, Radius: 1″ (Figure 13.139).

We need to create a 1/8″ radius edge roll that serves as a lip, on the inside of the windshield frame. Because of the complex curvature, we will need to create locators for the creation of the #2 and #3 cross-sections. Derive the #1 cross-section using the Derivative Surfaces tool.

129. Create locators and cross-sections for the creation of a 1/8″ edge roll. Derive #1 edge cross-section. Create 1/8″ by 1/8″ 3-point locator lines with segments at a right angle and place them on the edge curve. Create the #2 and #3 cross-sections. Create the lip (edge roll) surface as described using C-Mesh. Use Depth; # Of Segments: 3. Stitch the lip surface with the windshield frame (Figure 13.140).

FIGURE *Stitching lip surface with windshield frame.*
13.140

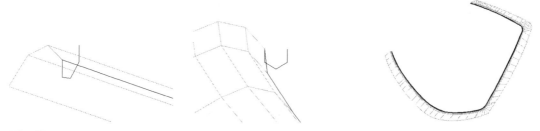

F I G U R E *Windshield weather seal.*
13.141

130. Create a new layer, "Windshield Weather Seal Source." Copy/Paste a copy of the #3 cross-section into it. Create a small 5-point vector line as shown, and note its direction in relation to the #3 cross-section. Create a swept surface using the vector line as a cross-section and #3 as a sweep path. Place the swept surface in its own layer, "Windshield Weather Seal." Use the following Sweep Along Path Options:

Axial Sweep, Cross-Section Alignment: First Point (Figure 13.141).

131. Create a new layer, "Windshield Curves." Copy/Paste a copy of the #3 cross-section into this layer. Split the curve into three curves as shown. The new windshield surface will be constructed using the Skin tool. The blue curve is a *path* curve. The two black curves are *source* shapes (Figure 13.142).

132. Create eight 2-point vector lines snapped to the points on source curves as shown. Insert a single point onto each line with the Midpoint Snap option. Adjust the position of each middle point as shown (Figure 13.142).

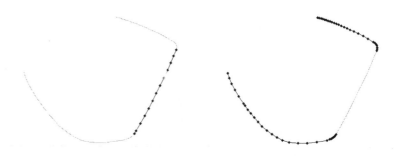

F I G U R E *Windshield curves.*
13.142

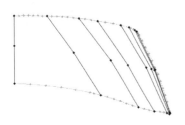
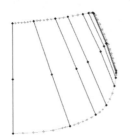
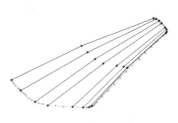

FIGURE *B-spline C-curve paths.*
13.143

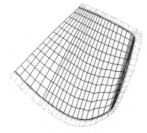

FIGURE *Creating the windshield.*
13.144

133. Convert the polylines into 2nd-degree B-Spline C-Curve *paths*. Match their point to that of the first *path* created as shown in Figure 13.143. In this case, the point count is 13. Create the windshield using the Skin tool (Figure 13.144).

Next, create a 1/8″ lip edge roll on the outside edge of the windshield frame.

134. Create the #1 cross-section using Derivative Surfaces. Create locators. Create the #2 and #3 cross-sections (Figure 13.145).

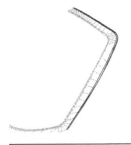
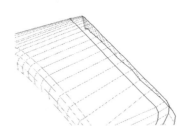
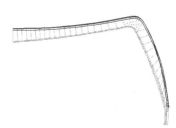

FIGURE *Locators and cross-sections.*
13.145

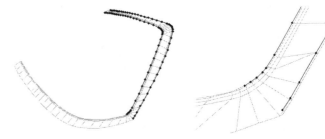

FIGURE *Edge roll.*
13.146

FIGURE *Source curves.*
13.147

135. Loft the lip edge roll using C-Mesh Stitch the edge roll with the windshield frame. Use the same C-Mesh settings as for the edge roll created in Figure 13.140. Notice that the edge roll was constructed only for the visible area of the windshield frame (Figure 13.146).

We have completed the exterior metal portions of the windshield frame. When texturing, apply the same material as for the body panels. Next we will build the interior trim portion of the frame that will give the frame a sense of thickness and strength. In real convertibles this space is occupied by very strong steel roll bars.

136. Copy/Paste copies of the #3 cross-sections created in Figures 13.140 and 13.145 into a new layer, "Windshield Frame Interior Curves." Delete the points from the curve from Figure 13.140 to make its point count identical to the curve from Figure 13.145. These two curves will serve as *source* curves (Figure 13.147).

137. Create *path* polylines, and place them on source curves as shown. First create a planar polyline as shown, then duplicate it and place it on the *source* curves (Figure 13.148).

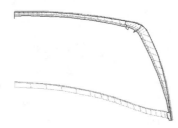

FIGURE Path *polylines.*
13.148

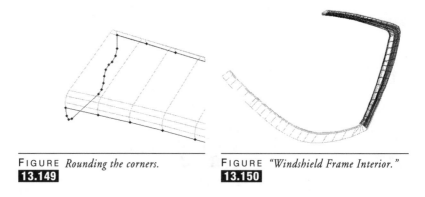

FIGURE *Rounding the corners.*
13.149

FIGURE *"Windshield Frame Interior."*
13.150

138. Round the corners of the *path* lines using Fit Fillet (v 3) or Edit Line Fit Fillet (V 2.9.5) with the following settings: (Figure 13.149)

    # Of Edges: 2, Radius: 1/10″

139. Create the windshield frame interior surface using the Skin tool. Place the surface in its own layer, "Windshield Frame Interior." This surface receives the same material as the dashboard (Figure 13.150).

Figure 13.151 shows the exploded view of the windshield and frame assembly. Verify that in your project each separate object is its own layer named as shown.

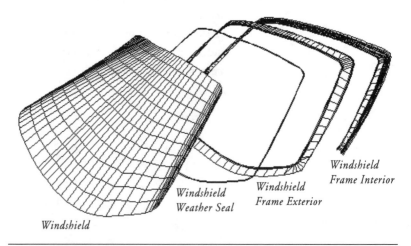

Windshield Weather Seal

Windshield Frame Exterior

Windshield Frame Interior

Windshield

FIGURE *Exploded view.*
13.151

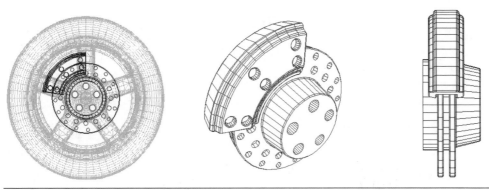

FIGURE *Disk brake rotor and brake caliper.*
13.152

140. Model the disk brake rotor and brake caliper. As those objects will only be partially seen through the wheel during static renderings, and be blurred out with motion blur during animation, their detail level should be kept low (Figure 13.152).

Using reference material and design creativity, add the following details to the car: Rear view mirror, sun visor, chrome hood plaque, roof latches, power window knobs, internal door handles, detailed radio, speaker grills, exhaust pipes with chrome tips, and any other detail that you wish. Additionally, attempt to modify the geometry to change the car from a convertible to a coupe with the addition of a roof panel that blends into the rest of the body. Most convertible cars have an optional removable fiberglass hard top.

14

Character Modeling: Smooth Meshing in form•Z

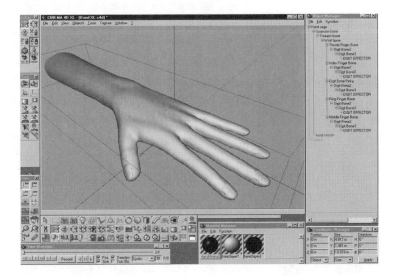

IN THIS CHAPTER

- Introduction
- Smooth Mesh
- Advantages of Smooth Mesh
- Review of Modeling Process
- Character Models and Inverse Kinematics, Bone Deformation
- Smooth Mesh Technical Abstract
- Flex Area
- Lines of Force
- Exercise: Modeling Human Arm
- Nightflyer Modeling Cycle

Introduction

In the field of 3D modeling for animation in the entertainment industry, character and creature modeling stands as being one of the hardest, if not *the* hardest, skills to master. This is because to successfully create a complex realistic-looking creature geometry, the modeler has to be competent in many aspects of 3D-character animation. For animation, unless the character will be a stone statue, the underlying mesh of the model has to be constructed in such an intricate way as to easily and effectively facilitate the application of multiple texture maps and material attributes, and successful interaction of the model geometry with IK/bones/deformation capabilities and procedures of the animation package. The shape itself, regardless of geometric complexity, is only part of the solution. The mesh must have correctly created underlying topology, arrangement of polygons in the mesh, in order to be effective in an animation environment. This creates a demand on the model maker, he or she must be intricately aware of the capabilities of the target animation package. In this tutorial we will be using a model of a human forearm that we will construct as a guide and an example. One further note, some concepts in this tutorial will seem confusing and hard at first. Don't give up, my five years of 3D modeling experience have taught me to practice, practice, and experiment. There are many ways to build complex objects in form•Z, and many form•Z professionals, including myself, have developed proven techniques. I will concentrate on the Smooth Meshing technique in this tutorial combined with other more conventional tools found in form•Z.

OK, let's begin.

Smooth Mesh

There are a number of ways to approach character modeling in form•Z. One of the easiest and the fastest is through the use of Smooth Mesh. When using Smooth Mesh, you begin by modeling a very simple, coarse version of your character. This simplistic model, called a "cage," has all the proportions of your character and has a general shape, but it is very low in polygon count and tends to look very bad when rendered. Upon completion, the cage is processed using the Smooth Mesh tool to produce a detailed highly meshed model ready for further modeling or importation into your animation environment.

Advantages of Smooth Mesh

There are certain advantages that Smooth Mesh gives you in the construction of your character. The most important advantage is the detailed control that you have over the shape, detail, density, and topology of the mesh. The polygonal construction of the cage controls the shape and variability of the mesh density in the smooth mesh. The ability to control not only the shape, but also the variance of the mesh density at selected regions, allows you to build intricate and efficient meshes for bone deformations. When modeling a limb of your character you can make the joint areas of the smooth mesh very dense, while keeping the nondeforming areas relatively light. But the Smooth Meshing doesn't just give the shape and density control of your character. By correctly modeling the cage object you control the topology of your character mesh. By this I mean you control the flowlines along which the polygons of your mesh are arranged. By optimizing the topological arrangement of the mesh, you will ensure clean and flawless rendering of the object in addition to making it easy to texture map. Speed and flexibility are other advantages of this technique. With a little experience, you will be able to build your cages very quickly. One additional benefit of Smooth Meshing is that when complete, you have two models, the Smooth Mesh version and the cage version. You can use the low-resolution cage as a stand-in for the high resolution. Using the cage as a stand-in you can work very fast with the low-resolution version of your model within the animation environment. Because the cage is topologically and geometrically similar to the smooth mesh, you can apply complex animation procedures, such as bones/IK and lattice deformation, to it and be able to accurately predict how the final mesh will behave. When it is time to render, just attach the smooth version as a child to the cage, and set the cage object not ro render.

Review of Modeling Process

Prior to beginning, let's review the modeling process. As a professional 3D modeler you are supporting a complex art and image-driven process. Therefore, let's discuss the considerations that you must be aware of to create a successful model.

The first consideration is the art direction. Art direction is a set of guidelines from art directors or clients describing what they want to see. One of the most common forms of art direction is a character sketch made by conventional artists. Depending on the way the sketch is drawn, its utility may only be limited to visual reference. A more useful sketch can be used as an underlay. For a sketch to be used as an underlay it must be drawn as an orthographic view, such as side or front. The more orthographic views you have, the easier it will be for the model maker to create the correct proportions of the character. Furthermore, the orthographic sketch should be drawn in a neutral pose, standing up right, arms spread out, legs in rest pose slightly spread out. Another form is a storyboard. The information that you receive from sketches should tell the form and look of the character/creature. The storyboard or animated story-boards will tell how the character will move. All this information will drive the *technical direction*, which is a fancy term for you figuring out how to create the creature, which is what this chapter is about.

The next consideration that you as a modeler have to deal with is texture mapping and material definitions. This is driven in part by art directions from the art director or the client, and in part by the texturing material capability of your animation package. How the application textures will depends in part on how the model is arranged topologically; that is, how it is "cut up" to facilitate the texturing process. Each application has its own way of accomplishing this, but many of them have similar features. Applications that have strong polygonal character animation features, such as 3D Studio MAX, Lightwave, and Cinema 4D XL, have equally strong material definition capabilities allowing layering of multiple textures and shaders to create a rich, diverse, and realistic look.

Character Models and Inverse Kinematics, Bone Deformation

The most important and complex consideration is the animation question: Quite simply, how is the model going to be animated, or is it going to be a static statuesque object? Or is the object only going to be transform animated; that is, the object is only going to undergo simple move, rotate, scale animation. If the above is true for a particular project, consider yourself lucky. Then you will only have to concern yourself with form and texture mapping of the object. Most of the time, however, the character will be animated through a series of complex procedures such as layered deformations, or even more high-end systems such as BONES coupled with Inverse Kinematics (IK). With the mesh of the character undergoing complex bone-based deformations, special attention has to be given to the mesh and especially to those areas of the mesh where there are bone joints. The meshing and topology in those areas must be built correctly to prevent shading anomalies. This is because when the deforming region of polygons stretches in such a way as to cause polygons to intersect with each other, or to cause certain polygons to stretch to such an amount that their texture maps start to blur and bleed, the rendered image looks wrong to the eye.

The areas of mesh most heavily affected by bone/IK joints are called "flex areas." It is important to note that in high-end professional applications such as 3D Studio MAX Character Studio, Lightwave, and Cinema 4D XL, the flex areas have fall-offs; that is, bones and their joints have regions that they affect and those affected regions have user-defined fall-offs. If you will not be the one animating the character, close communication between the animator and you (the modeler) is required. You need to understand how the model is going to be deformed. In all the previously mentioned animation packages the bones/IK animation process starts with building a "skeleton" out of bones and defining links. You need to work with the animator and understand the joint limits and amount of possible stretching that the flex areas of the mesh will undergo. The general rule of thumb is that the wider the range of movement at a given joint, the heavier (higher polygonal density) the flex area should be. From direct experience and experimentation, the areas that are the heaviest are the shoulder joints, elbows, and kneecaps. The next heaviest flex areas are finger and toe joints and the neck. Areas that do flex but do not require heavy polyganization are wrists and ankle joints.

Keep in mind that the amount of deformation the flex areas will undergo varies from project to project. This might seem a bit of a challenge to deal with and it is, but lucky for us the folks at auto•des•sys implemented Smooth Mesh to make the job of dealing with flex areas a lot easier. As we progress through this chapter, you will see that with mesh smoothing you can generate meshes with correctly polygonized flex areas.

Smooth Mesh Technical Abstract

Now let's discuss some technical issues regarding the use of smooth meshing. Basically, the Smooth Mesh tool takes a low-count polygonal mesh and, based on user-defined variables, generates a smooth mesh, a more complex and much more polygonally heavy mesh. The resulting shape of the smooth mesh can have subtle detail that would be very hard or even impossible to achieve with more conventional tools. Using smooth meshing you can create a limb of a character complete with muscle ripples and having an appearance of an underling bone structure. Furthermore, depending on the variables set in the Smooth Mesh dialog, the same cage can be used to generate models of variable mesh density. So you have to model a cage once and then generate one model for the Web animation, a moderately meshed model for NTSC/PAL animation, and finally output a very high-resolution model for Film or IMAX.

The cage itself can be used as a real-time preview model within your animation package allowing you or the animator to work out motion without the overhead of a heavy model. When time comes to render, just substitute a high-resolution model in place of the cage.

In the next paragraphs I will discuss, in detail, concepts behind Smooth Mesh and cage modeling that I touched on in the introductory paragraphs. The overall goal of smooth meshing is to model a coarse version of your char-

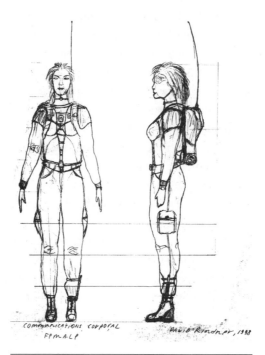

COMMUNICATIONS CORPORAL
FPMALP

DAVID Rindner, 1998

FIGURE
14.1

acter. This coarse version is called a "cage." The Smooth Mesh tool in form•Z uses the vertices and segments of that cage and generates a smooth character that has the same proportions as the cage. It helps to look at a cage as a control hull that you use to make C-Curves. In a C-Curve hull, each vertex is connected to a maximum of two other points; in a cage, a vertex can be connected to any number of vertices. In fact, it is the way that the vertices are connected to each other that will affect the final smoothed shape and will allow you to generate complex effects like musculature or blended organic ridges. It might take some time, practice, and experimentation on your part but its definitely possible and can yield results similar, same as, or at time, even better than those found in dedicated NURBS surface modeling systems. The Smooth Mesh can also generate geometry that is very similar and most of the time better than if that geometry is acquired via a 3D digitizer. As a matter of fact, you can use a 3D-digitizer support for the Immersion 3D digitizer to create the cage.

Now let's discuss some technical issues regarding the use of smooth meshing. Basically, the Smooth Mesh tool takes a low-count polygonal mesh and, based on user-defined variables, generates a smooth mesh, a more complex and much more polygonally heavy mesh. The resulting shape of the smooth mesh can have subtle detail that would be very hard or even impossible to achieve with more conventional tools. Using mesh smoothing you can create a limb of a character complete with muscle ripples and having an appearance of an underlying bone structure. Furthermore, depending on the variables set in the Smooth Mesh dialog, the same cage can be used to generate models of variable mesh density. So you have to model a cage once and then generate one model for the Web animation, a moderately meshed model for NTSC/PAL animation, and finally a very high-resolution model for output such as Film or IMAX.

The cage itself can be used as a real-time preview model within your animation package allowing you or the animator to work out motion without the overhead of a heavy model. When the time comes to render, just substitute a high-resolution model in place of the cage. If the cage is built properly (that is, its points and segments are arranged properly), you can use that cage to create poses and to create morph targets by simply adjusting the position and orientation of selected vertices, edges, and faces. Using a correctly constructed cage the Smooth Mesh tool can generate very geometrically complex and intricate meshes. There are, however, a few weaknesses and limitations that you should be aware in order to properly use the tool. The biggest drawback of Smooth Mesh is also its biggest advantage. If the cage is not built correctly, the smooth mesh will have holes, slivered polygons, and polygons that intersect with each other, causing shading anomalies and other problems. The other weakness is that even if the cage is correctly built, but not properly planned, the resulting smooth mesh will have a lot more polygons than are necessary, increasing memory requirements, smooth mesh generation, and rendering times.

Flex Area

Earlier I touched upon a concept of "flex area." A flex area is a region of that will undergo the largest amount of deformation in an IK/bones system. For example, let's take an arm of the character. If the mesh of the arm is animated in a realistic way through the use of IK/BONES deformation, the polygons in the elbow region will twist and bend, while the polygons in the middle of the forearm will probably undergo very little or no deformation. The area of polygons compromising the elbow is a flex area. During the modeling process, the modeler needs to pay extra attention to this region of the model and to all other flex areas to ensure problem-free animation. The mesh in and around flex areas needs to be much more highly meshed. Now it is perfectly correct to have an entire mesh highly meshed, and the model will animate and deform correctly. However, it will not be an efficient mesh and will result in longer than

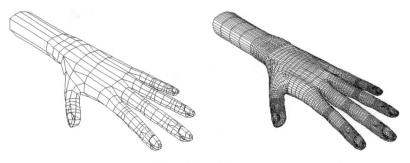

FIGURE *Smooth mesh.*
14.2

necessary rendering times, and use up hardware resources that could have been used to load in more geometry or to have a more intricate animation setup. As professional modelers we must build meshes that render perfectly and, at the same time, must be polygonally efficient. As I mentioned before, the degree of meshing depends on the range of joint movement. Additionally, you need to compensate for stretching of the polygons at the flex area so as to minimize the polygon intersection on the inside of the bend and to minimize the polygonal silhouette caused by stretching of polygons on the outside of the bend. The flex compensation can be adjusted by tapering the cage polygons compromising the flex so as to have the wide base on the "inside" of the bend and the narrow base on the "outside" of the bend. In Smooth Mesh the degree of meshing that a cage gets is dependent on two main variables, the first being the options defined by the user in the Smooth Mesh dialog box, and second, the relative density of polygons in the cage object. Assuming that the Smooth Mesh options remain constant, you can control the mesh density on flex areas by varying the polygon density of the cage. Figure 14.2 illustrates the concept. Various modeling tools and features can be used in order to increase cage density. Some of the more useful ones are Trim & Split and Insert Modifier (v2.9.5) and Insert Point/Insert Segment (v3.0). Examine the wireframe of a forearm in Figure 14.2 and compare the meshing at the wrist and knuckle areas of the smooth mesh with the wrist and knuckle area of the cage. Notice how the higher cage polygon density at a flex area translates to higher polygon density in the smoothed mesh.

Lines of Force

An important concept that you must understand in smooth meshing is *lines of force*. When the Smooth Mesh tool processes a cage, the faces of the smooth mesh flow along the segments of the cage. In other words, the segments of the cage define the lines of force along which the smoothed mesh polygons will flow. Figure 14.2 illustrates how polygons of the derived smooth mesh flow along similar directions as the edges of the cage polygons. By carefully arranging the vectors of the cage polygon edges you can control not only the shape of the smooth mesh but the flowlines of its polygons. This ability is very powerful as it allows you to create meshes that flow along when deforming, and consequently, they will render much cleaner and deform better than meshes whose polygons are arranged along a single force vector. The rightmost illustration is the recommended way to build cages. In this cage, the cage edges are arranged perpendicular and parallel to the lines of force of the intended mesh. Consequently, the smooth mesh derived from the cage on the right is cleaner and more deformation friendly than the mesh on the left. In construction of characters, it is advised that you keep the edges as perpendicular or parallel as possible to each other and to the line of force of your intended model. Take a look at the forearm cage in Figure 14.3. One set of cage edges is nearly parallel to the length axis of the arm, while the other is nearly perpendicular to the length axis. As a result, the smooth arm mesh has a very nicely ordered mesh, without long slivered polygons or excessively small microfacets. This mesh will render and animate very nicely using IK/BONES. Additionally, having nicely ordered meshes like the arm mesh shown makes it easier to see the placement of bones within the animation application, and allows much better visualization of the instanced deformed shape when working out the motion of your character.

Another concept that works in concert with lines of force is the *cage segment continuity*. It is a simple concept, but can be hard to adhere to once your cage gets more and more complex. Basically, if you start at a given edge of a cage, you should be able to trace the connections without any breaks in that given chain of edges. Figure 14.4 shows similar cages but the one on the right has dis-

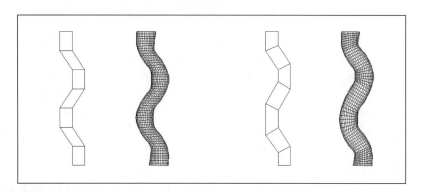

FIGURE *Forearm cages.*
14.3

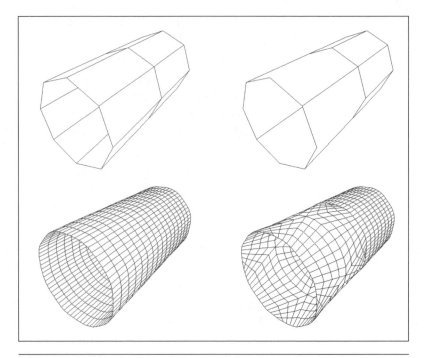

FIGURE *Forearm cages.*
14.4

continuous cage construction. Notice that you can't trace a clean edge chain of the middle edges.

As far as the Smooth Mesh tool works, it is the correct result given this cage construction, but as you can see, the Mesh Smooth has made small slivered polygons in the discontinuous area of the cage. This happens because the Smooth Mesh tool is trying to subdivide a polygon that has more than four points. When deforming, that area of the smooth mesh stands a high chance of developing shading anomalies. Lines of force and edge continuity work hand in hand to ensure a clean smooth result. The cage on the left is built correctly, its cage edges form nice edge chains in both U and V directions if the cage. Consequently, the smooth mesh also has a nicely ordered quad grid mesh. The quad grid mesh is what you should always strive for, regardless of the shape you are working on. This type of meshing will always render, texture, and deform very cleanly, ensuring professional results. A good rule of thumb is to keep all faces on the cage to have no more than four vertices. You can deviate from this concept, but not too much. As a matter of fact, once you get experience working with Smooth Mesh, you can use it to your advantage, build edge chain discontinuities to get effects such surface imperfections, or achieve a look of a small fold or a crinkle, but most of the time, it is recommended that the cages be built clean.

As you build the cage, it is recommended that you build into it flexibility and adaptability. What does that mean? In digital effects production, time and efficiency are priceless. If you can reuse the cage of one character in building another, then so much the better. Also, with a properly constructed cage, you will be able to easily adjust its shape for modeling of multiple morph targets.

Fortunately, cages that are constructed while adhering to the principles of flex areas, lines of force, and edge continuity chains are easy to manage. The easiest and best way to construct complex cages is through individual construction of subcages. For example, build the cage for ankle/foot as a separate object from the leg proper cage. Then, using the Point Snap option and Stitch tools, stitch the copies of both cages together into one complete leg/foot cage. I recommend that each subcage be built in its own layer that is named for it. For example, the Foot cage is build in a layer "Foot Cage" and so on. Copy/ Paste a copy of the foot cage and the leg cage into a separate layer and stitch them together. Then mirror the stitched cage. When you are finished with the torso cage, Copy/Paste the complete leg and torso cage into yet another layer, then mirror the leg cage and joint the torso and leg cages together into a main cage. Then join copies of the arm and head/neck cages to the main cage and run a COPY of a main cage through the Smooth Mesh tool. What is the result, well you still have the original cages that you can modify or reuse. Once you get this system down, you will find yourself spending a lot of time tweaking the small areas of the cage to achieve the desired effects. You will also find that it is much easier to identify and fix cage problems by previewing individual cages in Smooth Mesh without processing them. Catching smoothing problems early on will save you time and headaches and "smooth" your production modeling process.

The following example is a creature that I created as a personal project to test the integration of form•Z with Cinema 4D XL and 3D Studio MAX, involving very heavy meshes. The first thing that I created was a conceptual sketch of the character, although not without doing some explorative modeling. Personally, I find "sketching" in 3D helps me to develop the character in my mind, so I can then sketch it. During explorative modeling I develop rough shapes and proportions of the creature. I want to see what the creature will look like, in terms of proportions, when viewed from various camera angles and different camera settings. Once the proportions are roughed out I print a wireframe and sketch right on top of it. In the pencil sketch I adjust the proportions, but only slightly, and add small detail. I find that having a rough volumetric is superior to the classical approach of first drawing a perspective box and then drawing inside of it. This is a case where form•Z flawlessly melds with traditional art.

To animate the model, two versions of the creature were exported: The cage mesh and the smooth mesh version. In Cinema 4D XL, the smooth mesh body and wing membrane surfaces were made children of the cage object. A skeleton bone skeleton was constructed and attached to the cage. The bone deformation was applied to the cage object, but the cage was given a Display Property/Hide In Raytracer. The children were given Display Property/Hide In Editor. This allowed me to work in real time with a low-polygon representation of my character when creating the animation.

Exercise: Modeling Human Arm

In the following exercise we will model a human forearm, starting with the finger, using the concepts described earlier. Modeling with Smooth Mesh is as close to pure artistry it gets in form•Z, and is very close to sculpting as each point on the cage serves as a sculpting handle. Because so much of smooth meshing, as a technique, is closely related to real-world art, it is useful to acquaint yourself with basic concepts behind human form and sculpting basics. This kind of information is beyond the scope of this book, but there are countless books available on basic art principles and techniques.

Nightflyer Modeling Cycle

- A conceptual sketch of the creature that I did after some experimental modeling sessions. I envisioned a hawk-sized combination of a bat and a lizard with a lamprey-type mouth filled rows of razor sharp teeth.
- A completed cage of the night flyer, modeled with procedures described later in the chapter.
- Wing and foot membranes modeled with the Skin tool.
- Single mesh of the creature after the cage was processed through Smooth Mesh. The body is a single mesh and each membrane is a separate object. Although it may be difficulty to discern, over 97% of faces in this model are quadrilateral.
- Creature exported out of form•Z via 3DMF file format. Imported into Cinema 4D XL, textured and rendered. Texture maps painted in Photoshop 4.01. All geometry was mapped with Flat mapping (Figure 14.5).

1. Generate a rectangular extrusion, roughly as shown in Figure 14.6. Next,

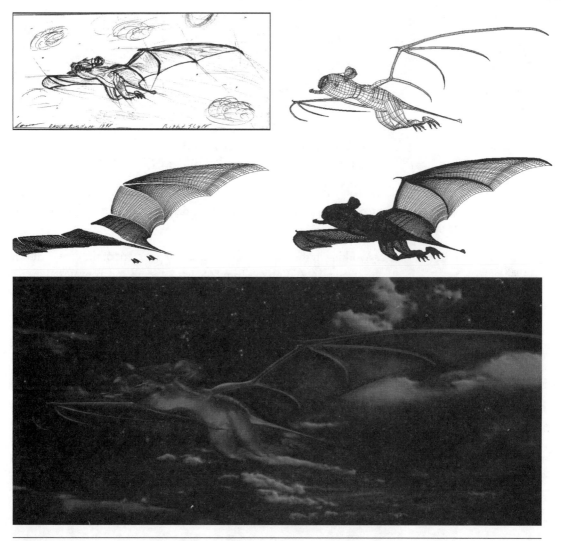

FIGURE *Nightflyer modeling cycle.*
14.5

FIGURE *Rectangular extrusion.*
14.6

FIGURE *Converging points.*
14.7

FIGURE *Working with a finger cage.*
14.8

working first in front and then in top view, move the points at one end to slightly converge it, as shown in Figure 14.7.

We shall refer to this object as a finger cage and will split it in half. Being symmetric we only need to construct one side. At the end we shall mirror it and stitch the two pieces.

2. Working in the top view, draw a line along the axis of the cage as shown in Figure 14.8. With the Trim & Split tool active and Trim With Line selected in its dialog, click on the lower part of the cage and on the line. The cage is split in half, as shown in Figure 14.8.

We shall next insert segments to the cage to articulate its topology so that smooth meshing works better. The new segments are inserted using Trim and Stitch operations.

3. Working in the front view, draw nine vertical lines, as in Figure 14.9.
4. With the Trim & Split tool and Split With Line option selected in its dialog, click on the cage and on the first line. This splits the cage into two pieces. Repeat this operation once for each line. At the end, the cage is split into 10 pieces, as shown in Figure 14.10.

FIGURE *Drawing lines.*
14.9

FIGURE *Cage split into 10 pieces.*
14.10

FIGURE **14.11** *Stitching.*

FIGURE **14.12** *Horizontal line.*

FIGURE **14.13** *Single piece after stitching.*

5. With the Stitch option selected in its dialog of the Trim & Split tool active, click on the first two pieces to stitch them into one. Before executing the operation you may want to select Delete in the Status Of Objects dialog to avoid accumulating extra objects.

6. Repeat the operation eight more times. At the end, all pieces have been stitched back together into a single cage (Figure 14.11).

7. Next draw a horizontal line, as in Figure 14.12.

8. Use the line to split the cage horizontally. Then stitch it back together. The result is a single piece, shown in Figure 14.13. This has the same shape with the original cage, but its faces have been subdivided to a number of tiles.

Next we will apply geometric transformations; that is, we will move points to better approximate the shape of our finger.

9. Working in the right view, which is looking from the tip of the finger cage, we will slightly move the points in the circles, as shown in Figure 14.14. Use the Pick tool and frame picking to select these groups of points. Recall that you will need to press the Shift key to select the second and the third groups. With the Independent Scale tool, click on a, then b and c. The result is as shown.

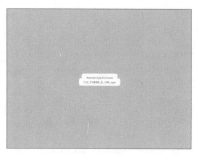

FIGURE **14.14** *Using Pick tool and frame picking.*

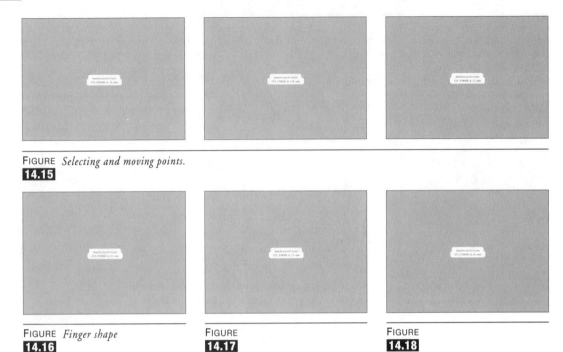

FIGURE *Selecting and moving points.*
14.15

FIGURE *Finger shape*
14.16

FIGURE
14.17

FIGURE
14.18

Inserting segments.

10. Next, preselect the four points at the tip of the finger cage, as shown in Figure 14.15, and after switching to a front view move them the distance e-f, as shown in Figure 14.15.

11. Next, working in the front view, slightly move points up and down to better simulate the shape of the finger (Figure 14.16).

We will now insert some additional segments to delineate and sculpt the area of the nail.

12. Insert segment a-b, as in Figure 14.17. Note that we inserted from point to point, using point snap, which allows more accuracy. We shall continue this practice.

13. To prepare for the next segment insertions, we first insert the points where the next segments will be inserted, as shown in Figure 14.18. Two new points are inserted above and close to existing points, in the areas shown with a circle.

14. We next insert six new segments between the previously inserted points as shown in Figure 14.19.

15. More points are inserted where the circle is as shown in Figure 14.20,

FIGURE *Six new segments.*
14.19

FIGURE *More points inserted.*
14.20

FIGURE *Segments inserted.*
14.21

which is in the middle of segments. Segments are inserted between them as shown in Figure 14.21.

16. Next we move points to improve the curvature of the nail area, as shown in Figure 14.22. We will do quite a bit more of such point moving a bit later.

17. We insert a few more points (by snapping at mid-segment) and segments on the side, as shown in Figure 14.23.

At this point, it is time to put the complete finger cage together by deriving a symmetric opposite and stitching the two pieces together.

18. Working on the top view, draw line b to use as the axis of reflection, as shown in Figure 14.24.

19. With the Mirror tool active, About A Segment and Relative To Reference Plane selected in its dialog, with mode set to One-Copy (v 3) or C-Copy (v 2.9.5), click on c and then d. The result is as shown in Figure 14.25.

20. Next, stitch the two pieces together, which should produce the one-piece cage shown in Figure 14.26.

FIGURE *Moving points.*
14.22

FIGURE *Inserting points.*
14.23

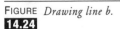

FIGURE **14.24**   *Drawing line b.*

FIGURE **14.25**   *Select c and d.*

FIGURE **14.26**   *One piece cage.*

The final stage for completing the cage of the finger is "art" more than it is a specific instruction we can offer. Look at your own finger and our example in Figure 14.27 and shape the nail area by moving and/or scaling points to improve its curvature.

Note the three "rings" of segments that delineate the area of the nail, the way they are close together will already have an affect on breaking the smoothness of the model. To make the break more distinct, move the segments of the middle ring inward to produce a little groove around the nail area.

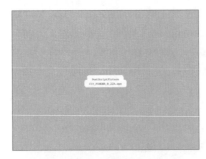

FIGURE **14.27**   *Shaping the nail.*

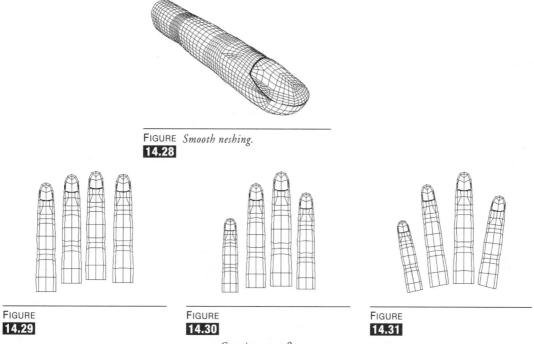

FIGURE *Smooth neshing.*
14.28

FIGURE
14.29

FIGURE
14.30

FIGURE
14.31

Creating more fingers.

For all these manipulations the ultimate test is seeing how smooth meshing works with your cage. If the resulting smooth model does not yet correspond to the shape you would like to produce, make a few adjustments and try again (Figure 14.28).

Now we'll make four more fingers. Three will be copies of the one we just completed, properly sized. The fifth will be the thumb, which will also be based on a copy, but will require additional manipulation. We will be constructing the fingers corresponding to a left hand and you can use your own hand as a model when you need to determine the relative sizes.

21. Copy-move three more fingers and position them roughly as shown in Figure 14.29.
22. Using Non-Uniform Scale, size the new fingers roughly as shown in Figure 14.30. In each case you place the base (first click) of the scale at the bottom end of the finger (a), the second click at the top end of the finger (b), and moving the cursor along the axis of the finger you scale it up or down as appropriate for the respective finger.
23. Using the Rotate tool and placing the centers of rotation where the bullets are, we rotate each finger as appropriate for the position it has on our hand, as shown in Figure 14.31.

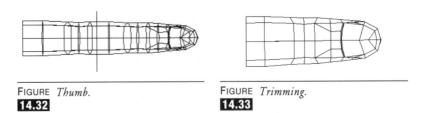

FIGURE *Thumb.*
14.32

FIGURE *Trimming.*
14.33

Next is the thumb. Note that the thumb is different in that it only has one knuckle.

24. Make a copy of the largest of the four fingers just constructed. We shall next cut this finger to shorten it and also eliminate the lower knuckle. Draw a line where we need to cut it, as in Figure 14.32.

25. With the Trim & Split tool active and Trim With Line selected in its dialog, click on the upper part of the finger and then on the line. The finger is trimmed as shown in Figure 14.33.

Next we put the thumb into position, relative to the other fingers. However, prior to moving and rotating it we create a four-sided polygon around it, roughly as shown in Figure 14.34. We shall always transform the polygon with the thumb cage. We may even want to group it with the thumb cage to make sure they move together. This polygon will later be used to create a reference plane that will facilitate the manipulation of the thumb.

Next we'll construct a cage for the palm.

26. Working at the top view, draw a polygon by placing points between the fingers, as shown in Figure 14.35.

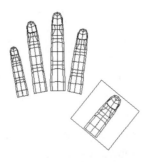

FIGURE *Four-sided polygon.*
14.34

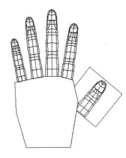

FIGURE *Placing points.*
14.35

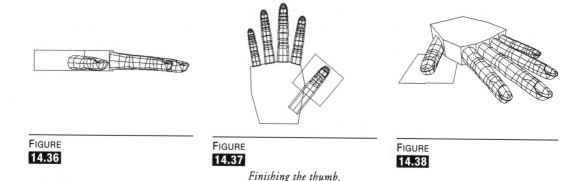

FIGURE
14.36

FIGURE
14.37

Finishing the thumb.

FIGURE
14.38

27. Extrude the polygon to a height slightly bigger than the diameter of the largest finger, as shown in Figure 14.36.

Next we extend the thumb to intersect the palm.

28. With the Pick tool and topological level set to Point, preselect the points at the base of the thumb. With the Move tool move them along its axis far enough to cross the palm cage. Repeat for all finger cages (Figure 14.37).

Next, the five fingers will have to be attached to the palm, using Trim and Stitch operations.

29. With the Trim & Split tool active and **Trim & Stitch First Object** selected in its dialog, click on c and d. Repeat the operation for all the other fingers. This trims and stitches all the fingers to the palm, which are now a single piece (Figure 14.38).

Next, we will be meshing the palm cage by inserting new segments. We will be using the Vector Line tool with the Insert Segment modifier on.

30. Where the segments are inserted is shown in Figure 14.39. Follow these drawings and insert the segments. When a segment is not inserted on ex-

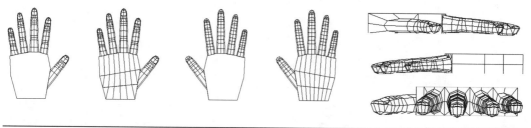

FIGURE   *Meshing palm cage.*
14.39

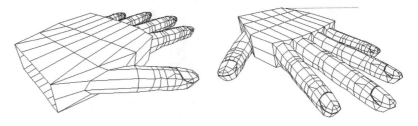

FIGURE *Cage after completion.*
14.40

isting points, we recommend that the points at the ends of the segments be inserted first. Then the segments are always inserted from point to point. This allows for better control of the positions of the insertions. Also, note that all the point insertions are at the middle of segments and are executed using mid-segment snaps. This makes the job a lot easier. Finally, recall that smooth meshing works best with continuous segment sequences, which you should be doing.

Figure 14.40 shows the cage after completion of insertion.

Next we need to move some parts of the hand to shape it better. We shall adjust the positions of the fingers, which is done in two steps: the four fingers are moved first and then the thumb.

31. Using whatever pick options are appropriate (lasso or single point pick) and the Pick tool, preselect all the points of the four fingers. This includes the points at their bases but not the points of the palm that surround the bases of the fingers (Figure 14.41).
32. With the Move tool move the points a bit up, as shown in Figure 14.42.
33. Preselect the points of the thumb (as for the other fingers) and move them a bit to the right, as shown in Figure 14.43.

FIGURE
14.41

FIGURE
14.42

FIGURE
14.43

Adjusting the shape.

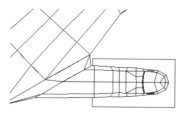

FIGURE *Defining arbitrary plane.*
14.44

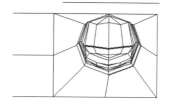

FIGURE *Plane projection: front.*
14.45

Observing your own hand, you notice that the thumb is rotated relative to the palm, which we will also do next. We will use the rectangle we earlier attached to the thumb to generate a reference plane.

34. Set the topological level to Point and with the Define Arbitrary Plane tool active, click on points a, b, and c, in this order (Figure 14.44).

While on the top view, preselect the points of the thumb, as you did earlier.

35. Set view to Plane Projection: Front (Figure 14.45).
36. Select Rotate, place the axis of rotation (first click) at the center of the thumb (d), and rotate counterclockwise about 55 degrees. The thumb should now look like Figure 14.46. Note that we also slightly adjusted the points right after the base and rotated them a bit (about 30 degrees clockwise).

Next we'll move some more points to improve the curvature of our shape.

37. Preselect points e, f, g, and h, marked with bullets in Figure 14.47, and move them up.
38. Preselect the corresponding points at the lower part of the hand and move them down. The result should be as in Figure 14.48.
39. Preselect points i, j, and k in the vertical middle between the four fingers (47) and move them outward. The result should be as in Figure 14.49.

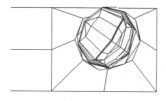

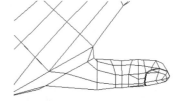

FIGURE *Thumb view.*
14.46

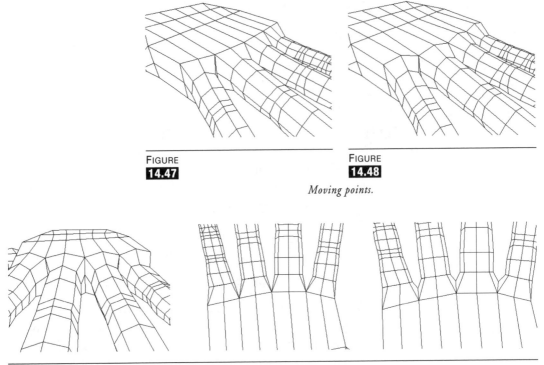

FIGURE
14.47

FIGURE
14.48

Moving points.

FIGURE   *Moving points outward.*
14.49

40. Next, continue to move points to improve the roundness of the cage. This is really "art" and we shall not describe the process in exact terms. Use your own hand and the shapes we display in Figure 14.50 as examples. If your model of the hand is a bit different than ours, it does not really matter.

Building a forearm and joint is the last step for completing this exercise. The forearm is essentially constructed using the open end of the hand as an initial profile.

41. In the Derivative Surfaces dialog select Boundary Of Surface Object.

With the 2D Derivative Surfaces Object tool, click on a segment of the open end of the hand cage.

This produces a closed profile, which is a copy of the end of the hand, as shown in Figure 14.51. We shall next extrude this.

42. In the Extrusion/Convergence Options dialog, select Perpendicular To Surface and from the Heights menu select Graphic/Keyed. With the Derivative Extrude tool active, click on the profile you created a bit ago and

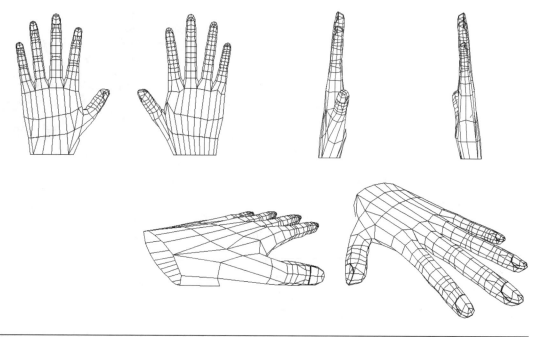

FIGURE   *Example shapes.*
14.50

dynamically rubberband it to the desired position. Its size should be roughly as in Figure 14.52. After selecting Topology for Faces in the Delete Options dialog, use the Delete tool to delete the two faces at the ends of the extruded object you just created.

43. Next insert three lines at the upper end of the forearm, using the Trim and Stitch methods we used at the beginning of this exercise. Their position is roughly as shown in Figure 14.53.

44. At the end also stitch the forearm to the hand and move some points of the recently inserted lines to shape this part like a joint (Figure 14.54).

The very last step is the smooth meshing of the cage. If throughout this model building process you have been testing your results by smooth meshing

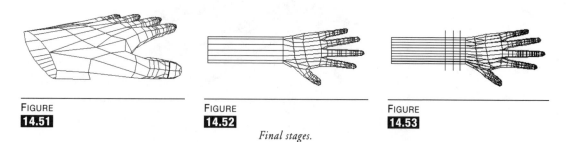

FIGURE
14.51

FIGURE
14.52

FIGURE
14.53

Final stages.

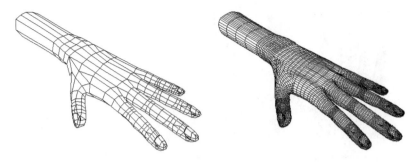

FIGURE *Stitching the forearm to the hand.*
14.54

the partially built cages, you are ready to do it again. If you need some help with the parameters to apply, here is what we used:

> Maximum # Of Subdivisions = 2;
> Maximum Segment Length = off;
> Maximum Face Angle = 1°;
> Curvature = 80%.

Figure 14.55 shows the smooth meshed hand mapped and ready for animation.

I wish to briefly touch upon animation integration, using Cinema 4D XL 5.1 from MAXON as an example. The smooth mesh and cage version of your hand should each reside in its own layers and be the only object within those layers. Do Object Query on both objects, and change their object names accordingly ("Hand Cage," "Hand Smooth"). Hide all layers except the "Hand Cage" and "Hand Smooth" layers. As a note, I recommend that when modeling in form•Z, always model in layers. An object in your animation package

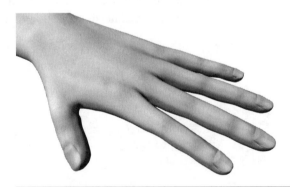

FIGURE *Smooth meshed hand.*
14.55

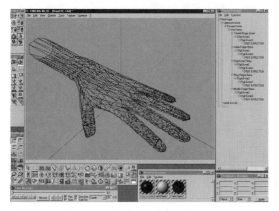

FIGURE
14.56

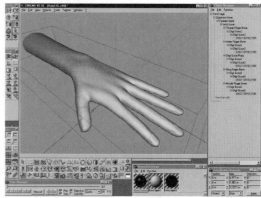

FIGURE
14.57

Bones applied to cage model.

should be a layer in form•Z. Using layers makes managing complex geometry a lot easier in form•Z with large projects having hundreds of objects.

Export the model using the 3D Studio (3DS) format with following settings:

The latest version of Cinema 4D XL has FACT import/export, so as an alternative file format you may export out of form•Z using FACT. For FACT export use the following settings:

Import the model into Cinema 4D XL. In Cinema, the Hand Cage and Hand Smooth should be separate objects. In the Object Manager drag the Hand Smooth into the Hand Cage to make it a child. Add Display Property to both objects. Set Hand Cage Display Property to HIDE IN RAYTRACER, and set Hand Smooth Display property to HIDE IN EDITOR. Remove the Smooth property from the Hand Cage. Now you can perform all animation on a low-resolution animatic model with only the final smoothed one rendering. You will, of course, need to unhide the smooth model for material application and projection map alignment. The particulars of creating a bone skeleton in Cinema 4D XL is beyond the scope of this book. Create the skeleton, define IK limits and bone ranges. Link the skeleton to the cage and animate. The cage model will not render but will pass on all animation parameters to the smooth model, which will render.

Figures 14.56 and 14.57 show the bones applied to the cage model, and Garaud shaded smooth mesh of the hand.

CHAPTER
15
Patch Grafting

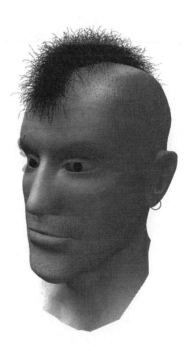

IN THIS CHAPTER

- Introduction to Patches
- Patch Grafting
- Two Methods of Grafting Patches Onto Framework
- Growing Patches
- Creating Digital Hair Inside Cinema 4D XL

Introduction to Patches

With the release of form•Z 3.0, Patch surfaces have been introduced to complement the already rich modeling capability of the application. Patches are parametric surfaces that are controlled by a lattice of corner points and intermediate vectors twist handles. Patches are very useful where parametric surfaces are desired, but the desired geometry cannot be easily or efficiently described by NURBZ-type geometry. Specifically, patches are most suitable for construction of irregular organic forms such as characters. The purpose of this chapter is not to present you with basics of patch modeling within form•Z 3.0, the manuals contain detailed discussion on the use of patches. In this chapter I wish to present a modeling approach that maximizes the strengths of patches while circumventing the weaknesses inherent in patch modeling.

The form•Z 3.0 manual contains a detailed description of patches, and is a very good reference for patch modeling basics. Before proceeding to my main discussion, I wish to cover the basic elements of a patch surface. Figure 15.1 shows the basic elements of a single rectangular patch surface. An important concept is that patches are selected like normal mesh entities with only a few minor differences. Patch edges are selected with the Topology Filter set to Edge. A single patch within a patch surface is selected with filter set to face. Patch objects are selected like any other form•Z object with filter set to object.

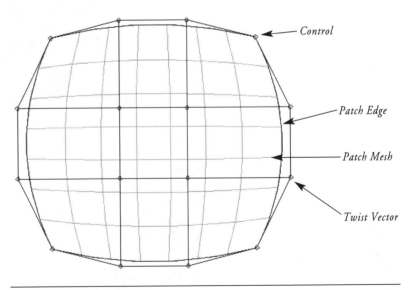

Control

Patch Edge

Patch Mesh

Twist Vector

FIGURE *Basic patch surface.*
15.1

Patch Grafting

From my experience of working with form•Z 3.0 patches I have determined that while straightforward patch modeling is feasible, it can be time consuming and can get confusing when dealing with patch surfaces containing a large number of patches. In this chapter I wish to present to you a technique for working efficiently with patches. The technique is called "Patch Grafting." Basically, in Patch Grafting, you start with an existing low-resolution mesh, properly prepared, called a "framework," and construct an unsmoothed patch lattice based on polygons of the framework object. The framework object can be a mesh constructed manually, digitized via Microscribe 3D, or a legacy data. It is in conversion of low-resolution legacy data that form•Z 3.0 patches have their greatest utility, and I will concentrate on this aspect in the exercise.

Patch Grafting has three basic phases.

- Acquisition and preparation of a framework mesh
- Construction of an unsmoothed patch surface
- Smoothing of the patch surface

Acquisition and preparation of a framework involves traditional polygonal modeling of a low-resolution mesh object or importation and preparation of legacy data. Proper preparation of a framework object is vital to achieving a successful result, when using this technique. In this fashion it is similar to the Smooth Mesh technique discussed in Chapter 14, where the quality of the smoothed mesh was directly affected by the correct modeling of the cage object. When modeling or preparing a framework object, adhere to the following guidelines:

- **Keep polygon count low.** As there will be a patch face in a patch model for every polygon in a framework, keeping the polygon count low in the framework mesh will make construction of the patch graft easier and faster.

- **Keep polygons as 4-point rectangles or equilateral triangles.** When modeling or preparing the framework object, keep as many polygons, all if possible, as 4-point rectangles. Try to keep the aspect ratio of individual polygons as close to 1:1 as possible; specifically, avoid polygons with aspect ratio greater than 6:1. In practice it is not always possible to have framework meshes as 100% rectangular meshes. There will be cases where triangles simply cannot be avoided. In those cases, try to keep the triangles as close to equilateral as possible. The primary reason for keeping polygons as either rectangular or triangular is due to the fact that form•Z 3.0 patches are of two types, rectangular or triangular. Patch surfaces in form•Z 3.0 are not primitives like a Spheric or a Torus. They are derivative objects that work off existing geometry. When the Derive Patch tool encounters a complex polygon (more than four points), it will automatically decompose it into a rectangle and the necessary number of triangles, and then construct a stitched patch surface based on each of the polygons formed by decomposition. While this produces a valid patch surface, it is not predictable as to how decomposition will take place. Often, slivered patches are formed that produce shading artifacts when rendered. When preparing the framework object, manually decompose complex polygons. Figure 15.2 shows an example of a complex polygon that was automatically patched and one that was manually decomposed and then patched. Note that the automatically decomposed patch surface has slivered triangular patches with slivered triangular polygons. The manually decomposed patch surface has rectangles and triangles adhering to the aspect ratio guide lines. When both patches are deformed, the one on the right will render cleaner.

- **For symmetrical objects, halve the mesh.** When grafting meshes that are bilaterally symmetrical, halve the framework across the axis of symmetry. This will greatly reduce the effort it takes to graft a patch surface onto a framework. This is especially vital when modeling characters.

After the framework mesh is prepared it is placed in its own layer, and we then move on to the grafting of the unsmoothed patch surface onto the framework.

The unsmoothed patch surface is created in its own separate layer. The framework layer is ghosted and the Layer Snap option is turned on. The un-

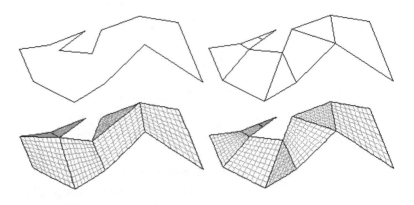

FIGURE *Complex polygons.*
15.2

smoothed patch layer has its snappability turned off, the reason being that we want to limit snapping to the points on the framework and preclude accidental snapping of patch points to points on the patch. The grafting is accomplished by creating a closed rectangle with the Point Snap option enabled. Each point of the rectangle is snapped to the corresponding point of the framework polygon. The rectangle is then converted into an unsmoothed Patch surface using the Derive Patch tool. Subsequent patch faces are stitched together to form a single unsmoothed patch surface. The process of creating a polygon, converting it to a patch, and stitching the patch edges together goes on until the unsmoothed symmetrical half of the model is completed.

The completed unsmoothed symmetrical half is then copied into a new layer. A copy of it is mirrored across the axis of symmetry and two halves are stitched together by selecting two coedges on the axis of symmetry and using the Patch Attach tool. The whole patch surface is then smoothed using Parametric Edit using the appropriate smoothing option.

An exportable mesh is derived by using the Drop tool on a copy of a smoothed patch surface placed in an export layer.

In the following exercise we will graft a patch surface onto a low-resolution legacy mesh.

1. The legacy data is imported into a new project. In this case, the legacy data is a low-resolution mesh of a human head that is an old free model from Avalon. The model can be found on the CD-ROM. Figure 15.3 shows the mesh.

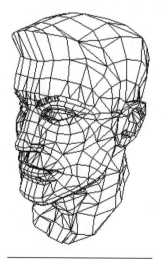

FIGURE *Mesh.*
15.3

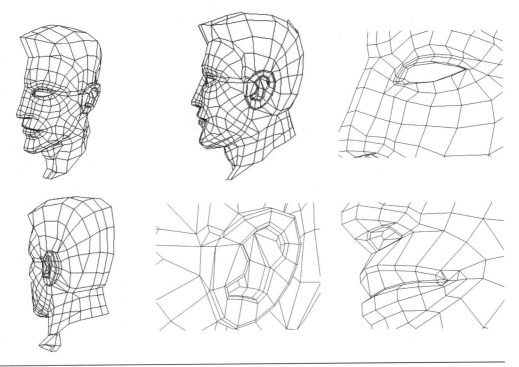

Cleaned framework.
15.4

2. The mesh is halved and cleaned up such that it is composed primarily of quadrangle polygons. Note that many triangles on the legacy mesh have been joined into rectangles. Place the framework mesh into its own layer, "Framework," and ghost the layer. Be sure to have snappability ON for this layer. Figure 15.4 shows the cleaned framework.

3. The resulting mesh can be used as a framework object; however, the source model has hair as part of the mesh. If we grafted the patch surface onto this mesh we would be unable to create realistic proportions once procedural hair is "grown" from the head surface. The resulting patch surface would look something akin to a Frankenstein head. Recall that when we model, we must keep in mind the animation and effects that the model will undergo. To complete the framework object we must adjust the polygons of the portion of the mesh, defining the hair, such that it looks like a bald head. Additionally, we want to keep the hair mesh as a separate object from the rest of the head. Doing so will allow us to create an *emission surface* later for growth of procedural hair. The adjustment of the mesh is accomplished through standard point-level

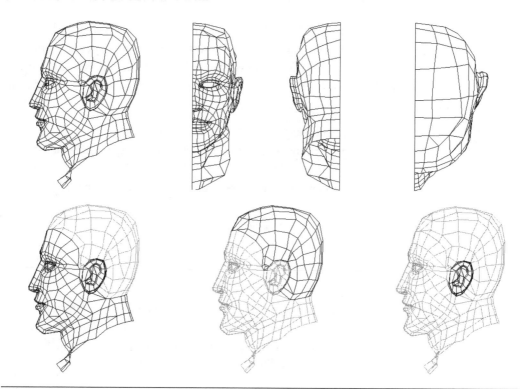

FIGURE   *Completed framework mesh.*
15.5

transformations and separations. Note that the hair, face/neck, and ear meshes are kept as separate objects, but the objects have coresident points and edges at the shred border. Figure 15.5 shows the completed framework mesh ready for grafting.

Two Methods of Grafting Patches Onto Framework

With the framework object completed we can begin grafting a patch surface onto the framework geometry. There are basically two ways to graft a patch surface onto the framework. We will explore both of them. The first way is manually create the patch surface one patch at a time by first creating a polygon by snapping it to a point on the framework polygon, converting the polygon into a patch, and then stitching the adjoining patches until the surface is complete. The second and easier way is to directly convert a copy of the framework mesh into an unsmoothed patch surface. The second way is very similar to the Smooth Mesh procedure described in Chapter 14. On the surface it certainly does appear that the second method should be used, and it should be whenever possible because it is faster. However, in my experience, direct conversion of a framework into a patch surface does not always yield correct results. In general, I have noticed the following conditions that may create a problem in direct conversion. I must point out that these are only trends, and may or may not cause a problem.

- Large number of polygons in a framework
- Large differential in relative size between the largest and smallest polygons with regard to surface area
- Heavy mix of rectangular polygons that share edges with triangular polygons
- Slivered polygons (aspect ratio of 6:1 or greater)
- Unstitched edges or coresident points

Versions of form•Z released after completion of this book may have addressed these deficiencies.

In those cases we must revert to the more tedious method of manually grafting a patch surface onto a framework. For our project we will first manually graft a patch surface into the face and neck of the head framework. The ear and hair framework will be directly converted.

4. Create a new layer, "Head Patch Half," and make it active. Turn the snappability OFF of this layer. When grafting patches onto the framework, we only want to snap to the framework, and not to the patch surface itself.

5. Turn off all **Grid** and **Directional** snapping and enable **Point Snap** only. Working from the right side view, and on the "Head Patch Half" layer, create a closed rectangle that is snapped to points on one of the cheek polygons of the framework mesh (Figure 15.6).

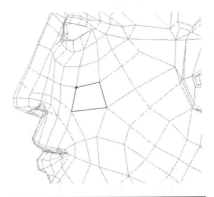

FIGURE **15.6**   *"Head Patch Half" with closed rectangle.*

6. Convert the polygon into a Bezier patch using the Patch Derive tool (Figure 15.6). Set its options as follows:

Bezier
Maintain Four Sided Patches: OFF
Smooth: OFF
Wires And Facets:
Wires Density: Medium
Facets:
Max # Of Facets: Length: 4, Depth: 4
Max Facet Segment Length: OFF
Max Normal Deviation: OFF
Max Surface Deviation: OFF
Triangulate: OFF
Optimize: OFF
Status Of Objects: Delete

When constructing the unsmoothed patch surface it is best to turn off all the patch smoothing and facet optimization options. They will be turned on and correctly set once the patch surface is complete (Figure 15.7).

7. Using the same procedure, create a new rectangular Bezier patch adjacent to the previous patch. Using Lasso Pick, select the coedges and stitch the two patches together using the Patch Attach & Stitch tool (Figure 15.8). Set Patch Attach & Stitch options as follows:

Attach; Move Edge, Scale: ON, Stitch: ON
Status Of Objects: Delete

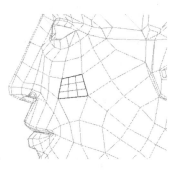

FIGURE *Patch surface.*
15.7

FIGURE *Stitching patches.*
15.8

Growing Patches

Creating patches by patching closed 3- or 4-point polygons is a valid method that will always work; however, it is not the only way to graft a patch surface. Another way is to grow patches between the edges of existing patches, thus simplifying the workflow. Growing patches is most suitable when there is a hole in the patch surface bounded by at least two patches, for a triangular patch, or by three existing patches for growing a rectangular patch. Figure 15.9 shows a partially completed graft with a gap where a rectangular patch can be grown. In the next step we will fill the gap by growing a rectangular patch using the border edges of the existing patch surface.

8. Sequentially select the three patch edges bounded by lasso, as shown in Figure 15.10. Recall that to select patch edges, Topology Filter must be set to Segment.
9. Grow the patch using preselected patch edges, using the Patch Grow tool with the following settings (Figure 15.11):

Between Edges
Triangular Patches: OFF
Stitch: ON
Smooth: OFF
Wires and Facets: As before
Status Of Objects: Delete

For triangular patches, turn Triangular Patches: ON. *This option will only work when there are two preselected patch edges.*

NOTE

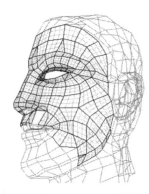

FIGURE
15.9

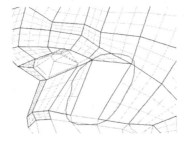

FIGURE
15.10

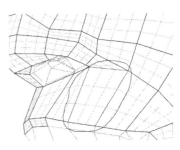

FIGURE
15.11

Growing patches.

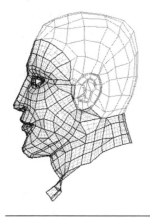

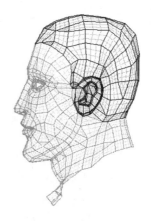

Figure
15.12
Grafting the patch.

Figure
15.13
Patch surfaces.

10. Using the manual patch grafting procedure described, graft the patch surface onto the neck and face of the framework. Keep in mind that we need to create an unsmoothed patch surface, so when stitching patch edges with the Patch Attach tool, do not use any of the Smooth options (Figure 15.12).

11. Copy/Paste copies of the ear and hair framework meshes into the "Head Patch Half" layer. We will use these framework objects as cages and directly convert them into unsmoothed Bezier patch surfaces. After conversion, place a backup copy of the hair patch surface into a backup layer. Using the Patch Derive options listed here, convert the cages into patch surfaces (Figure 15.13):

Bezier
Maintain Four Sided Patches: OFF
Smooth: OFF
Wires And Facets:
Wires Density: Medium
Facets:
Max # Of Facets: Length: 4, Depth: 4
Max Facet Segment Length: OFF
Max Normal Deviation: OFF
Max Surface Deviation: OFF
Triangulate: OFF
Optimize: OFF
Status Of Objects: Delete

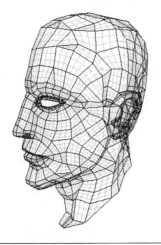

FIGURE   *Unsmoothed patch surface.*
15.14

12. Using the Patch Attach tool, stitch the three patch surfaces together into a single unsmoothed patch surface (Figure 15.14). Set the Patch Attach & Stitch options as follows:

    Attach; Move Edge, Scale: ON, Stitch: ON
    Status Of Objects: Delete

NOTE

When stitching two patch surfaces each containing multiple patches, select only a single pair or copositional patch edges using the Pick tool set to **Lasso Pick**. *Then perform the patch stitch with the Patch Attach tool. The Patch Attach has intelligence build into it, and will automatically scan the border edges of the two patch surfaces and automatically stitch all the edges. This feature is implemented to save the user time when he or she needs to stitch complex patch surfaces.*

13. Create a new layer, "Head Patch Smoothed," and make it active. Copy/Paste a copy of the unsmoothed symmetrical half of the head into this layer. Create a mirrored copy of the surface using the Mirror tool in conjunction with One-Copy mode, and stitch the two halves together using the Patch Attach tool (Figure 15.15).

14. Now we need to smooth the patch surface using the smooth options found in the Parametric Edit tool. With the Parametric Edit tool, click on the unsmoothed head. Select all the control points by dragging a selection lasso around the surface. Set smoothing of the surface to **Smooth In Equal**. This option will adjust the curvature of individual patch faces

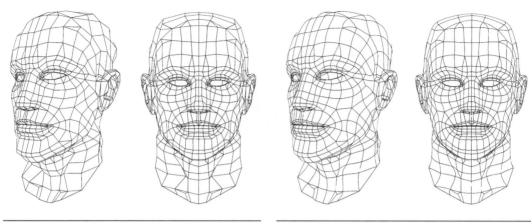

FIGURE *Stitching patches.*
15.15

FIGURE *Smooth patches.*
15.16

to achieve C2 continuity between them across the entire surface (Figure 15.16).

15. Create two parametric patch spheres to be eyeballs. Use Figure 15.17 for proportions and placement of the eyeballs. To create a parametric patch sphere, first create a parametric sphere.

16. Create a new layer, "Eyelash Patch," and make it active. Make the "Framework" layer visible and hide all other layers. On the face framework object, select the segments as shown and convert them into an open surface (polyline) using the Derivative Surfaces tool set to **Selected Segments**, and **Status Of Objects: Keep**. Move a copy of the polyline and place it as shown (Figure 15.18).

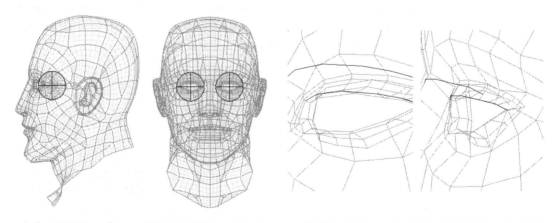

FIGURE *Eyeball patch spheres.*
15.17

FIGURE *"Eyelash Patch."*
15.18

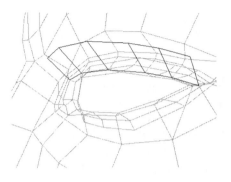

Figure
15.19 *Ruled surface.*

17. Using the two polylines as cross-sections, create a ruled surface using the C-Mesh tool. Recall from earlier chapters that a ruled surface is a plain C-Mesh without any kind of smoothing (Figure 15.19).

18. Derive a **Bezier** patch from the surface using the Patch Derive tool, and apply **Smooth In Equal** as the smoothing option. Then, to the best of your ability, using Parametric Edit, sculpt the eyelash patch surface as shown. Afterwards, create a symmetrical duplicate of the eyelash for the other side of the face (Figure 15.20).

With the geometry of the head complete, we can now create texture maps. I will use Adobe Photoshop to paint the textures and 3DS Studio MAX with Unwrap Object Texture and Texporter MAX plug-ins to create an unfolded projection of the geometry. Unwrap Object Texture is written by Peter Watje of Spectral Imaging, and Texporter is available from Compugraf A.S. Both the head and the eyeballs are best textured using the spherical projection method. Figures 15.21 and 15.22 show the spherical unfolded projections and painted texture maps. Figure 15.23 shows our head, mapped and textured.

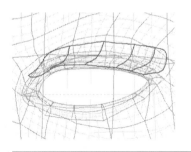

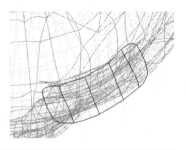

**Figure
15.20** *Symmetrical eyelash duplicate.*

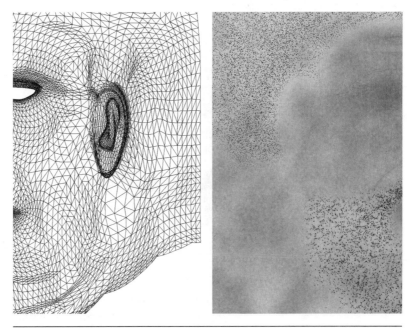

FIGURE *Spherical unfolded projection.*
15.21

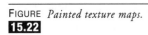

FIGURE *Painted texture maps.*
15.22

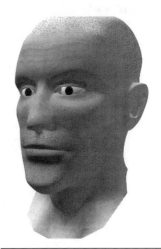

FIGURE *Mapped and textured head.*
15.23

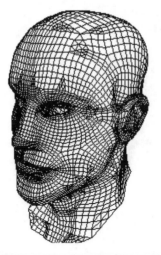

FIGURE   *"Hair Emission Surfaces."*
15.24

Creating Digital Hair Inside Cinema 4D XL

I want to dedicate the last part of this chapter to a discussion on the application of hair to the model that we just created. To create digital hair, we will first model emission surfaces in form•Z and then export the model into Cinema 4D XL and use the CineHair plug-in to generate the hair. The hair style that we will be modeling is a mohawk.

19. Create a new layer, "Hair Emission Surfaces," and place a copy of the head surface into it. Convert it into polygons using the Drop Control tool with the following options (Figure 15.24):

   Parametric Primitives: Faceted Objects
   Derivative NURBZ: Faceted Objects

20. Using the Separate tool, create the hair and eyebrow emission surfaces as shown (Figure 15.25). Use the following Separate Options:

   At Boundary Of Selected Faces
   Status Of Objects: Ghost.

   After separation of the emission surfaces you may clear the ghosted copy of the head as it is no longer needed. However, if you wish to create other hair emission surfaces, you may wish to retain it.

   Using the Attributes tool or Object palette, change the names of the emission surfaces to represent their functions. I recommend that the following naming convention be used, "name-emis." Also change the names of the patch objects, but keep names less than eight characters as

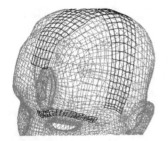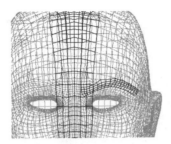

FIGURE *Creating hair and eyebrow emission surfaces.*
15.25

we will use 3DS format to transfer the geometry from form•Z to Cinema 4D XL.

21. Export the patch head, eyes, and emission surfaces via 3DS file format. Use the **Single Group** export method. Import the model into Cinema 4D XL.

22. Cinema 4D XL automatically places the axis of all imported geometry at world origin. You will need to manually center the axis of each object as to be centered in the object's bounding volume. The reason for that is that 3DS files exported from form•Z have no local axis assigned to them, so Cinema 4D XL has to place them at world origin.

23. Apply **Display** property to all objects. Display property for head and eyes should be set to **Hide In Editor: OFF**, and **Hide In Raytracer: OFF**. In this fashion, emission surfaces will neither render nor show up in the editor window, but you will still be able to select them for hair growth.

24. **Display** property for hair and eyebrow emission surfaces should be set to **Hide In Editor: ON**, and **Hide In Raytracer: ON**.

25. Apply texture maps to the head and eyeballs. Figure 15.26 shows the geometry imported and mapped within Cinema 4D XL.

26. Select the mohawk hair emission surface and select CineHair SE from the Plug-Ins menu.

    Set the following values in CineHair SE setup:

Distance:	0.05″	Gravity:	.75
Length:	1.5″	Diff. at length:	15%
Radius:	0.005″	Diff. at trend:	25%
Sections:	20	Diff. at align:	15%
Sidefaces:	3	Force On Vertical:	25%

    Figure 15.27 shows the mohawk hair generated with CineHair SE using emission surface.

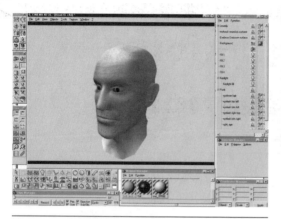

FIGURE
15.26
Cinema 4D XL imported and mapped geometry.

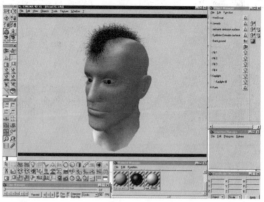

FIGURE
15.27
Mohawk hair generated with ConeHair SE.

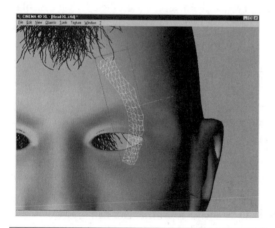

FIGURE
15.28

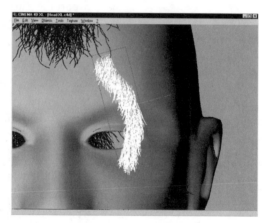

FIGURE
15.29

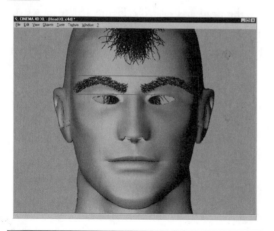

FIGURE
15.30

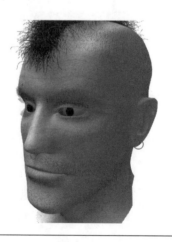

FIGURE
15.31

APPENDIX A

Companion Applications

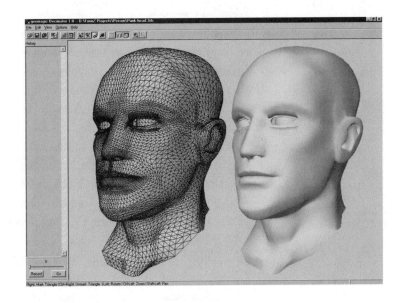

IN THIS APPENDIX

- Companion Applications
- Raindrop GEOMAGIC Decimator
- MAXON Computer Cinema 4D XL

Companion Applications

Although form•Z offers a very extensive set of tools, no application can be considered a master of everything. The prime reason for form•Z's highly regarded ability to create complex geometric forms is that it is a dedicated modeling environment. Its features and interface are geared toward one end: the creation of complex geometric forms within a self-contained digital environment. As complete and powerful as form•Z is, there are applications available which, when used as companions to form•Z, greatly extend the capability of the form•Z user. I wish to do a quick overview of some of those applications.

Raindrop GEOMAGIC Decimator

The first companion application I wish to cover is Decimator from Raindrop GEOMAGIC Inc. Its demo can be found on the accompany CD-ROM. Like form•Z, Decimator is best at what it does. Where form•Z is a dedicated modeling application, Decimator is a dedicated polygon reduction application. Its primary purpose is to convert high-polygon meshes with low-resolution ones. Decimator's utility lies in its amazing ability to retain the smoothness and clean rendering of the original mesh and apply it to the decimated version. In many cases, it is often next to impossible to tell the rendered difference between the original and the decimated mesh, where the latter has one-half the polygons. Additionally, Decimator adds other tools that form•Z lacks. One of the new tools introduced with form•Z 3.0 is a polygon reduction tool that is effective when used given a set of constraints. However, the Reduce tool inside form•Z 3.0 has the following weaknesses: lack of target polygon count, inability to retain smooth triangular topology of the reduced mesh, and lack of relax function to eliminate shading problems inherent in polygon reduction. Decimator fills the gap left by form•Z 3.0 by possessing the functionality for polygon reduction that the Reduce tool lacks. First and foremost, Decimator has the ability to decimate the source mesh to an explicit number of polygons, or to a percentage of polygons. Second, it has a feature that allows relaxation of the decimated surface. Relaxation of points is a smoothing procedure performed on the decimated mash that smoothes out the surface without changing the polygon count. Relaxation is accomplished by a slight movement of points toward the center of the mesh and with respect to other points. This does change the geometric form very slightly, and with many iterations, has the effect of melting the mesh. To control the effect, Decimator has explicit control over the number of relax iterations. Like form•Z 3.0, Decimator has the ability to reduce only the selected regions of polygons. As an additional bonus, Decimator has the ability to export geometry in Silicon Graphics Inventor format, thereby giving form•Z users an additional format.

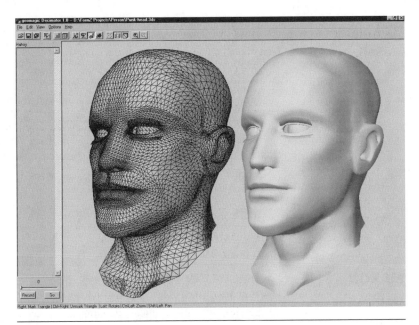

FIGURE
A.1

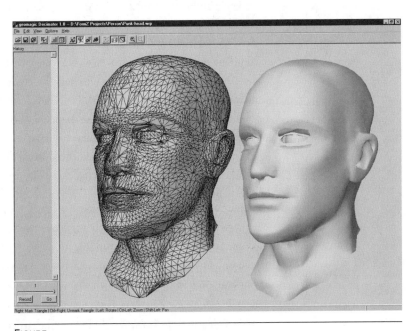

FIGURE
A.2

Decimator is best used with form•Z as a post processor for completed models. The models work best when exported out of form•Z as 3D Studio 3DS files by Object or By Layer, with the Separate Files option. This causes form•Z to write out each object or layer as a separate file, with each file containing a single object. Decimator does not retain individual objects when exporting decimated 3DS files, which is the primary reason for decimating each object individually. Figures A.01 and A.02 show composite screenshots of wireframe and shaded views of original and decimated versions of the head modeled in Chapter 15.

A demo of Decimator is available on the CD-ROM.

NOTE

MAXON Computer Cinema 4D XL

Cinema 4D XL is an animation application to which I have made numerous references within this book. It is an excellent animation package, and its tools and interface are geared toward efficient animation workflow. The combination of form•Z and Cinema 4D Xl is an extremely effective package, with modeling done in form•Z and animation accomplished in Cinema 4D XL. Nevertheless, modeling tools in Cinema 4D XL can be used to supplement modeling ability in form•Z. From experience the most useful support that Cinema 4D XL gives form•Z is in the area of deformations and freeform sculpting of polygonal meshes. form•Z has a rich set of deformation tools, such as bend, shear, bulge, and so forth. However, it lacks lattice deformation tool, a tool that is implemented very well within Cinema 4D XL. Lattice deformation deforms the mesh by surrounding the mesh by a user-defined 3D lattice of connected points. The lattice is initially in the shape of a box with user-defined control points for X, Y, and Z, the directions of the lattice. Additionally, the size of the lattice is defined. In Cinema 4D XL, the lattice is attached as a child of the object to be deformed, and will deform other polygonal child objects of the mesh. Prior to linking the lattice, it is first scaled and centered around the object to be deformed. When deforming the mesh, the points of the lattice act as magnets, pushing and pulling the points of geometry based on their proximity to geometric points and to other lattice control points. In Cinema 4D XL, lattices are parametric in nature, since they were intended to be used in animation as well as in modeling. At any time, the lattice object can be detached from the mesh, thereby removing its effect from it. The parameters of the lattice can be changed at any time; however, this causes the lattice to reset the position of the control points. Very broad or local deformations can be applied to the mesh by

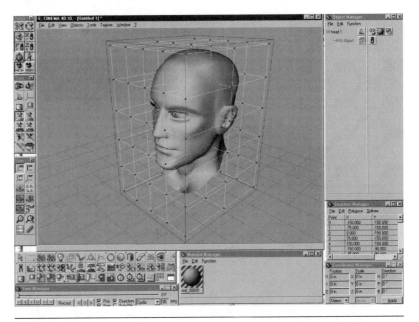

FIGURE
A.3

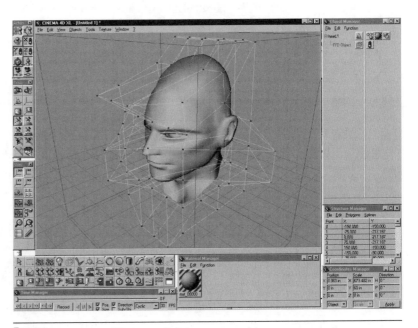

FIGURE
A.4

simply controlling the density of the lattice control points and altering the relative size of the lattice to the mesh. The procedure for integrating the modeling of Cinema 4D XL with form•Z is simple.

- Export the object to be deformed using OBJ or FACT files formats. Refrain from using 3DS or DXF formats as they triangulate the exported geometry.
- Import the object and center a lattice around it.
- Deform the mesh as desired.
- Convert the deformed mesh into polygons using the <u>Convert To Polygons</u> tool with subdivision set to 0.
- Cut and Paste the deformed mesh into a new Cinema 4D project and export as either OBJ or FACT. This is necessary as Cinema 4D XL 5.27 has no provision for exporting only the selected geometry. It exports the entire project.
- Import the deformed object into form•Z and continue modeling.

Animated lattice deformation within Cinema 4D XL is accomplished by morphing the lattice using the differently shaped lattices with the same number of points. Figures A.03 and A.04 show the head from Chapter 15 with 5 by 6 by 3 lattice applied and deformed by the lattice.

My personal favorite and an extremely useful modeling tool inside Cinema 4D XL is the Magnet tool. This tool allows freeform deformation of geometry

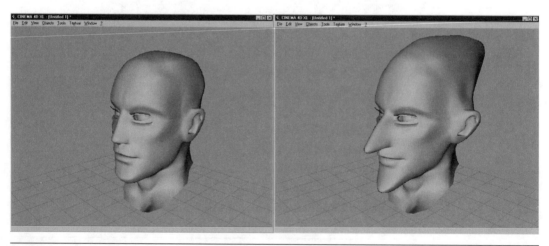

FIGURE
A.5

by pulling and pushing the magnet center. With a bit of practice you can sculpt complex geometry in real time in order to add subtle detail or to change the shape. The Magnet tool is invaluable in the creation of morph targets, for any application as Cinema 4D XL retains polygon count, and vertex/edge order list of magnetized models. Magnet tool's power lies in the nonmodal access to its strength and fall-off settings, accessible by tapping the F key within Cinema's world window and its dependence on the magnet center determined by click location. So for a given strength/fall off setting, the effect of the Magnet tool on the mesh depends on the distance of the mouse click away from the geometry. Figure A.05 shows an example of the now familiar head before and after sculpting with the Magnet tool. Cinema 4D XL is an amazing application, and it has a multitude of other modeling tools that can complement form•Z. I strongly encourage you to experiment with various tools. A demo of Cinema 4D XL is provided on the accompanying CD-ROM.

About the CD-ROM

The companion CD-ROM is intended to help you further understand the topics discussed in the book. It includes figures and projects from the book, as well as demos of other auto · des · sys programs and related products.

The projects covered in the book are organized on the CD by chapter number. Some chapters, such as Chapter 10, "Terrain Modeling, have the project files broken into parts to reduce loading times and memory consumption for the large, polygonal-heavy projects. Within each file, the project is organized in layers. Each layer contains the geometry shown in a particular figure. Figures that contain more then one image may have multiple layers, which are designated by a vowel extension. These layers are named to match the figures. For example, Figure 10.12 in Chapter 10 has a layer named "tm12." Every layer has a Saved View named in the same fashion. The Saved Views are found in the Views window." This layer and view structure allows you to isolate and view the geometry easily. You can also start from the View parameter used to create the images in the figures, and by directly observing the reference geometry you can better understand subtleties associated with 3D modeling. Many figures are included to show the progress of a particular project; however, a figure can only show the geometry in question from a few discreet View settings. By providing the actual geometry of what is shown in the figure, the learning process should be easier.

For Example:

If you are confused by the results in Figure 12.45 of Chapter 12, or you want to compare your results with those shown in the figure, you would first hide all the layers in the project except the layer auto45. Then make the matching auto45 Saved View active and compare your results with those in the project, or reorient the view as needed. This type of comparison will be very useful when learning about the trim edge cleanup. Just follow these steps anytime you wish to make a comparison:

1. Find the layer that matches the figure in question, and make it the active layer.
2. Hide all other layers in the project.
3. Make a matching Saved View and Active View.
4. Compare your results.

Please do not rely too heavily on the project files, however, because they can become a crutch and impede the learning process. Use the files when you are stuck, but exercise self-discipline. If all else fails you may send me an e-mail, and I will do my best to assist you. Many of the concepts and procedures described are challenging, but this is the nature of 3D modeling. Practice and perseverance will take you a long way. I recommend that you do the exercises in the book many times, relying less on the project files for assistance each time. I am certain that many of you will adjust and improve upon the procedures to fit your needs, so please share your ideas with me and your colleagues.

DEMOS INCLUDED ON THE CD-ROM

The CD-ROM contains demos of form · Z RadioZity for Windows and Mac OS, Cinema 4D XL for Windows (Intel and Alpha) and Mac OS, and the Decimator Polygon reduction utility for Windows only.

To install either form · Z or Cinema 4D XL, simply drag the folders onto your local hard drive. form · Z and Cinema 4D XL can also run from the CD-ROM, but this practice is not recommended

To install Decimator, double-click on the installer and follow the directions on the screen.

I highly recommend paying a visit to the respective Websites of the developers to get up-to-date information on features, pricing, system requirements, and technical issues prior to installation. The versions included on the CD-ROM were the latest available at the time the CD-ROM was pressed, but developers may have newer versions available on their Websites. All technical support issues regarding usage, installation, and compatibility of these demos are handled by the respective developers.

SYSTEM REQUIREMENTS

This book deals with complex 3D modeling for effects and animation, and this type of work requires computers with plenty of horsepower and, more importantly, RAM. Windows 98 and Windows NT users generally need not concern themselves with memory issues, but I recommend a minimum of 96MB RAM, 128 preferred for Windows machines. All the projects in this book were modeled on a Gateway 2000 PII-300 machine with 128MB of RAM and a 6GB hard disk drive.

Mac OS users may need to turn on Virtual Memory to load some of the projects. form · Z will issue an error message if it cannot load a project because of memory limitations. In general, users with less than 156MB of available RAM should turn on their Virtual Memory.

WINDOWS 95/98/NT 4.0 (SERVICE PACK 3)

- Pentium class machine, 200MHZ or faster. Pentium Pro, Pentium II, and Pentium III are highly recommended.
- 96MB of RAM, 128 or higher recommended.
- Fast 2D card capable of 1024 × 768 resolution with 24-bit color.
- OpenGL1.1-compliant 3D accelerator is highly recommended if you wish to view models in hardware accelerated OpenGL mode.
- Sufficient available hard disk space. 256MB available is recommended.

Note on Windows 95/98 memory: Virtual Memory can be handled automatically or manually within Windows 95/98. On some systems automatic Virtual Memory may not provide enough memory for form · Z to run or load and render projects. Consult your computer's manufacturer manuals if you need to change Virtual Memory settings.

MAC OS

- PowerPC 601 as a minimum.
- 128MB RAM or higher.
- Mac OS 7.5.1.
- Fast video card capable of displaying 1024 × 768 at millions of colors.
- Quickdraw 3D accelerator is recommended.

IMPORTANT: LICENSING AND USAGE NOTICE

The models and geometry contained on this CD-ROM are for tutorial and educational use only. The buyer of the book does not acquire any legal rights to the models geometry or design. The geometry is intended to facilitate the learning process by providing users with cross-reference material to judge their own progress. The reader may not resell or use the geometry, or any part of it, in a commercial project, in a production, or as part of a model library.

Readers may use the geometry that they themselves have modeled, following instructions in the book, for personal use or to promote their skills.

Index